Seven Paths to Understanding

Seven Paths to Understanding

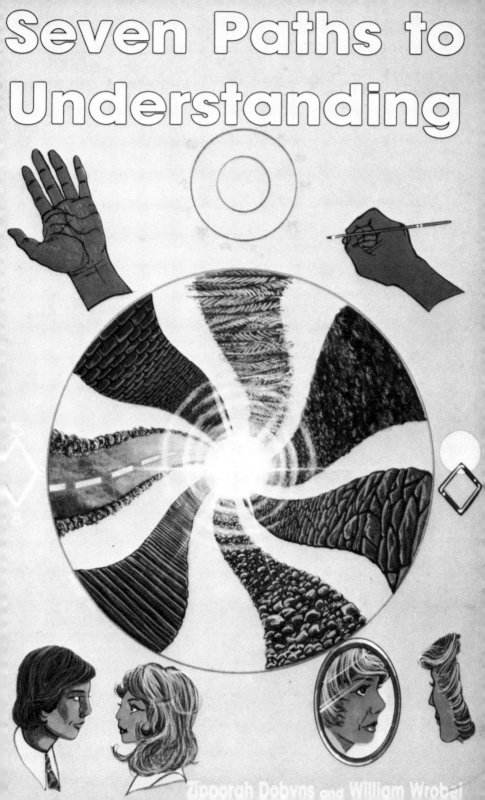

Zipporah Dobyns and William Wrobel

International Standard Book Number 0-917086-46-5

Cover Design by Larry Ortiz

Printed in the United States of America

Published by ACS Publications, Inc.
P.O. Box 16430
San Diego, CA 92116-0430

Contents

SECTION THREE

Introduction

by Zipporah Dobyns

This book was designed as an experiment. I wanted to go a little further afield than I had in my original *Astrologer's Casebook*, written with Nancy Roof and published over ten years ago. I wanted to not only try horoscope interpretations of people I had never met, but also to explore numerology, palmistry, handwriting analysis and psychological interpretations. For years, I have wanted to explore these other "occult" studies in greater depth, to try out some of my own theories by testing them on individuals about whom I had no advance information. One can, of course, be more detailed and more helpful in a personal interview which includes a discussion with the subject, but "blind" analysis is a greater test of theories than a personal consultation, as it is hard to sort out what clues you are picking up from an individual face-to-face versus relying on your tools (astrology, palmistry, etc.) alone.

As I'm sure my regular readers know, I have a mutable dilemma: too many interests and never enough time. I had seen books which compared astrology with palmistry, handwriting and numbers, but had never been satisfied with the proposed correspondences. This book has no final answers, but perhaps it will encourage other mutable dilemma people to take the theories with a grain of salt and to investigate the subjects for themselves.

My primary intent was to include all the raw materials, to let the readers make their own diagnostic judgments before reading the background material about the subjects. My coauthor, Bill Wrobel, gathered our seven subjects, and sometimes it took persuasion. I wonder how many of our readers would be willing to bare their souls along with their horoscopes, numbers, palms, writing, and personal lives? Bill sent me the birth data for the seven in 1983, and I did rather quick interpretations of their horoscopes and even briefer evaluations of the highlights of their numbers (Birthdate and Names). Then I got involved in lecture tours and the book stayed on the shelf for months. Eventually, I came back to do fairly brief analyses of the palm photos and the handwriting samples. I was torn while doing the palmistry between wanting to test it independently of the horoscope (which is my only field of extensive experience) and feeling so curious about possible correspondences that I did peek at the charts now and then. However, I did most of the handwriting analyses without any reference to the horoscopes or other models, and the different stages of writing the book were separated by sizable time intervals so I had really consciously forgotten what had been said earlier by the time I got to the handwriting section.

While I was working on the palmistry and handwriting parts of the book, Helen Ewald, a Los Angeles psychotherapist and a personal friend, worked with the psychological questionnaires which Bill had gotten from the subjects. As with all of my original analyses of the horoscopes, numbers, palms and writing, Helen's evaluations were done without any knowledge of the subjects other than what was presented in the material from the psychological questionnaires.

Bill Wrobel, along with numerologists Stephanie Joseph and Sylvia Abraham, are the stars in Section Two. Sylvia and Stephanie do more complete numerology analyses of the subjects. Bill writes about his interviews with the subjects, and he presents their own words concerning their lives and self-evaluations. Then I get to put in the "last word," the advantage of being the senior author.

What does it take to attempt such a project? A curious mind and willingness to stick one's neck out. I would like to propose that readers do the same; that anyone with a basic knowledge of any or all of our different models of human nature try to analyze the raw material presented here before reading the actual facts of the lives of our seven heroes and heroines.

Introductions come first in a book, but are actually often written last, after the rest of the work is finished. Such is the case here. Looking back, I think the experiment was worth doing. I learned a lot. The results supported many theories already held as tentative hypotheses, but threw doubt on other theories. Of course, we will never stop learning. I think that **Final Truth** is a goal but we are always on the journey. Spiritual Pride, thinking we have already arrived, can be highly destructive. We hope you will join us on the journey and enjoy it with us.

March, 1985

Introduction

by William Wrobel

What is being offered in this book is a unique presentation of viewing and understanding character. Seven individuals are perceived holistically or eclectically, as it were, on several levels, utilizing various systems of character analysis. We are presenting seven case studies and also basically, seven approaches to each case:

(1) Astrology
(2) Numerology
(3) Palmistry
(4) Graphology
(5) Psychological Testing
(6) Humanistic/Psychological Interpretation of Interviews
(7) Self-disclosure

After the initial analyses and overview presented in Section One, I will step in to present four sections of each case study: (1) a brief introduction of the subject; (2) background information given in the subject's own words; (3) a numerological analysis; (4) the subject's interview response to Zipporah Dobyns' initial ''blind'' astrological analysis. That material appears in Section Two.

This book is actually a workbook for serious students of human nature whose intent is to perceive character on deeper levels. The analyses will focus more on astrology and numerology but will include briefer interpretations based on the other approaches. It will be up to you, the serious student, to examine the hard data for your own insight and purposes. This is an exploratory venture, so we are offering, for example, various astrological and numerological correspondences for testing. It is a process of discovery in ascertaining parallels between each of the major systems presented. However, the main purpose is to utilize different yet complementary systems in understanding character, rather than to try to determine exact correspondences between, say, the astrological model and the numerological model.

There **are** correspondences between all systems since (I believe) existence is One, and each part reflects the whole, however differently symbolized. My basic assumptions are that existence is meaningful, that there are universal laws in operation, and that these laws can be symbolized in many forms. For instance, in terms of astrological symbolism, progressions and transits simply represent the operation of the Law of Cycles (e.g., orderly fluctuations of day and night, the ebb and flow of tides, seasonal changes, etc.). Astrology, numerology, palmistry, etc., are interrelated according to the Law of Correspondences (Resonance of the **apparently** separate parts of the Whole), but like a jigsaw puzzle, the pattern is not easily seen at first. There is too much conditioned complexity, too many adopted theories and not enough scientific testing. But then again, it is much easier to test tangible, material realities than intangible, subjective realities such as qualities of character represented by systems of, say, numerical and astrological symbolism.

March 27, 1985

Raw Data

Horoscopes, numbers, palm prints and handwriting samples of the seven subjects. The horoscope progressed information (outer wheel) is for a significant date in the subject's life — or simply a current progression.

Ms. One

INNER WHEEL Tropical Placidus
ACD: 0^h = DEC 23, 12^h = JUN 23
Eastpoint 25♏17 ● South Node 28♌31 ● Anti-Vertex 2♑34

Koch			**Campanus**		
14♏10	18♓21	12♑5	14♏10	18♓54	19♑1
11♐50	16♈27	20♌33	15♐39	15♈51	20♌33
12♑5	14♉10	18♍21	19♑1	14♉10	18♍54
20♒33	11♊50	16♎27	20♒33	15♊39	15♎51

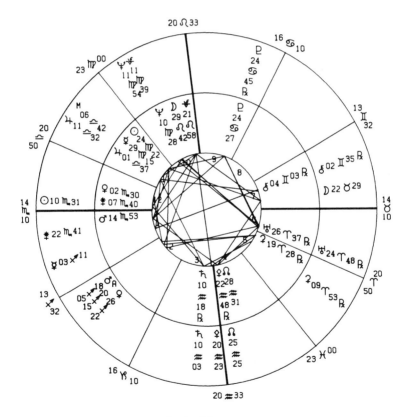

OUTER WHEEL Tropical Placidus
Progressed date is May 12, 1980 — Major Surgery
Eastpoint 5♑38 ● South Node 25♌25 ● Anti-Vertex 4♒38

Ms. One

v 3
c 4 (22)   **7**   v 1
TOTAL   c 5 (14)   **6**   v 3 (12)
TOTAL   c 2 (11)   **5**   TOTAL   **9**   TOTAL
NAME
NUMBER

SOUL URGE	7
PERSONALITY	2
NAME	9
LIFE PATH	6

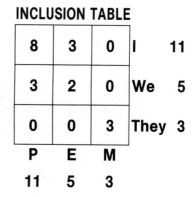

INCLUSION TABLE

8	3	0	I	11
3	2	0	We	5
0	0	3	They	3

P   E   M
11   5   3

Natal Imprint

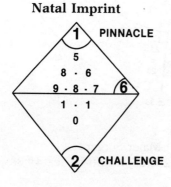

1   PINNACLE
5
8 · 6
9 · 8 · 7   6
1 · 1
0
2   CHALLENGE

Year Imprint

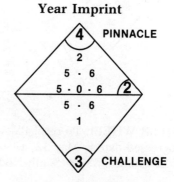

4   PINNACLE
2
5 · 6
5 · 0 · 6   2
5 · 6
1
3   CHALLENGE

Ms. One

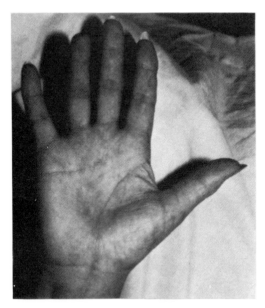

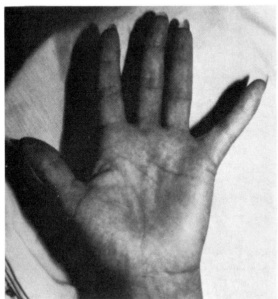

xiv   Seven Paths to Understanding

Ms. One

> Now is the time for me to
> gather my strength ~~to~~ to deal
> myself and to look forward
> to nothing but good days
> and years, lots of them.

Mr. Two

INNER WHEEL Tropical Placidus
ACD: 0^h = APR 4, 12^h = OCT 4
   Eastpoint 20♉40 ● South Node 9♎47 ● Anti-Vertex 5♉7

	Koch			Campanus	
10♊53	26♍41	26♑9	10♊53	6♍39	0♒5
5♑18	8♏44	15♒47	12♋4	16♎28	15♒47
26♑9	10♐53	26♓41	0♌5	10♐53	6♓39
15♌47	5♑18	8♉44	15♌47	12♑4	16♈28

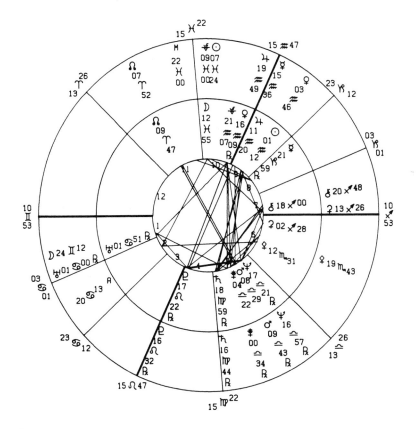

OUTER WHEEL Tropical Placidus
Progressed date is November 1, 1985
   Eastpoint 23♊14 ● South Node 7♎52 ● Anti-Vertex 0♊15

Mr. Two

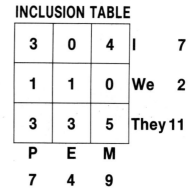

v 8		v 9 (18)		v 6 (15)		
c 8 (26)	**7**	c 1 (28)	**1**	c 1 (19)	**7**	**6**
	TOTAL		TOTAL		TOTAL	TOTAL NAME NUMBER

SOUL URGE	5
PERSONALITY	1
NAME	6
LIFE PATH	1

INCLUSION TABLE

3	0	4	I	7
1	1	0	We	2
3	3	5	They	11
P	**E**	**M**		
7	**4**	**9**		

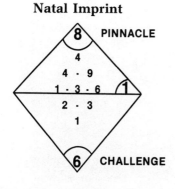

Natal Imprint

8 PINNACLE
4
4 · 9
1 · 3 · 6   1
2 · 3
1
6 CHALLENGE

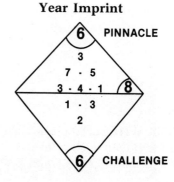

Year Imprint

6 PINNACLE
3
7 · 5
3 · 4 · 1   8
1 · 3
2
6 CHALLENGE

Mr. Two

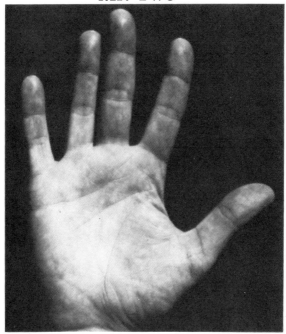

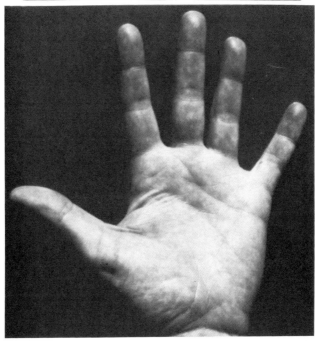

Mr. Two

"From the 28th year to the 35th year one comes into moral responsibility for his actions and appetites. If he develops any negative appetites or selfish habits, such as vulgarity in speech, dishonesty, adultery, or the excessive use of drugs, alcohol, or tobacco — these will produce etheric scars which may remain for life. If these appetites and habits are not resolved before the 35th year, they are carried over into the next life and will appear as certain defects and weaknesses. However, if one becomes discontented and contrite as to these habits and actions, he will have the opportunity to resolve them in this life."

From page 55 of
of *Draughts of
Remembrance*
by Ann Ree Colton

Ms. Three

INNER WHEEL Tropical Placidus
ACD: 0^h = NOV 3, 12^h = MAY 4
Eastpoint 24♊46 ● South Node 4♏47 ● Anti-Vertex 22♉13

	Koch			Campanus	
8♑7	5♏35	28≈22	8♑7	25♎13	28≈50
3♌25	10♐5	23♓48	5♌20	3♐13	23♓48
28♌22	8♑7	5♉35	28♌50	8♑7	25♈13
23♍48	3≈25	10♊5	23♍48	5≈20	3♊13

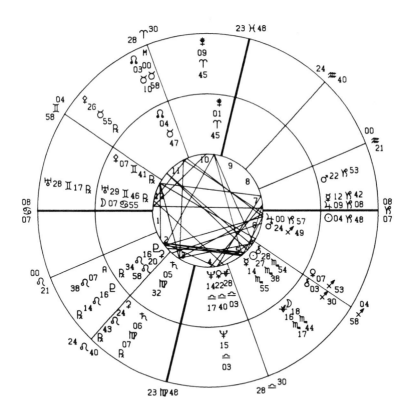

OUTER WHEEL Tropical Placidus
Progressed date is June 25, 1985 — Death
Eastpoint 26♋47 ● South Node 3♏10 ● Anti-Vertex 14♊49

Ms. Three

v 2 (20)
c 8 (17) | 1 | TOTAL   v 3 (12)
c 4 (13) | 7 | TOTAL   v 6
c 9 (27) | 6 | TOTAL | 5 | TOTAL NAME NUMBER

SOUL URGE	2
PERSONALITY	3
NAME	5
LIFE PATH	7

INCLUSION TABLE

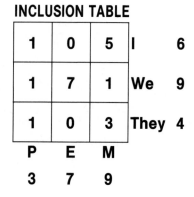

1	0	5	I	6
1	7	1	We	9
1	0	3	They	4
P	E	M		
3	7	9		

Natal Imprint

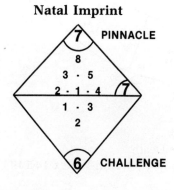

7   PINNACLE
8
3 · 5
2 · 1 · 4   7
1 · 3
2
6   CHALLENGE

Year Imprint

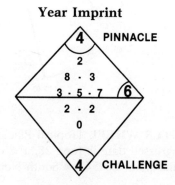

4   PINNACLE
2
8 · 3
3 · 5 · 7   6
2 · 2
0
4   CHALLENGE

Ms. Three

Ms. Three

Dear Bill,

Without benefit of a desk or my usual trusty fountain pen I will answer your request by writing part of our wedding ceremony which was composed almost entirely of Scripture.

"Thou shalt love the Lord thy God with all thine heart, and with all thy soul, and with all thy might."

"Trust in the Lord with all thine heart; and lean not unto thine own understanding. In all thy ways acknowledge him and He shall direct Thy paths."

"Have ye love one for another even as I have loved you."

"In quietness and confidence shall be your strength."

With this ring I Thee wed... to pledge my love and loyalty... to walk with Thee in the ways of Christ. This is my covenant.

Much peace and love to you and Stephanie.

Mr. Four

INNER WHEEL Tropical Placidus
ACD: 0^h = AUG 30, 12^h = FEB 28
    Eastpoint 24♍40 ● South Node 0♐10 ● Anti-Vertex 15♍19

	Koch			Campanus	
25♍53	26♑40	25♉15	25♍53	25♑11	26♉1
25♎49	26♒4	25♊31	26♎12	25♒22	25♊31
25♏15	25♓53	26♑40	26♏1	25♓53	25♋11
25♐31	25♈49	26♌4	25♐31	26♈12	25♌22

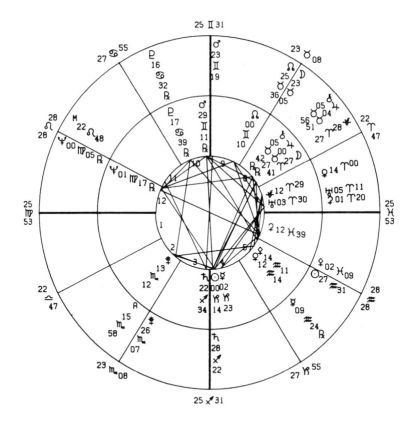

OUTER WHEEL Tropical Placidus
Progressed date is May 1, 1985 — Trip to Europe
    Eastpoint 27♏25 ● South Node 25♏36 ● Anti-Vertex 4♑28

Mr. Four

v 1 (10)
c 6 (24) **7** TOTAL   v 6 (24)
c 9 (27) **6** TOTAL   v 9 ____
c 6 (15) **6** TOTAL   v 0 ____
c 1 (10) **1** TOTAL   **2** TOTAL NAME NUMBER

SOUL URGE	7
PERSONALITY	4
NAME	2
LIFE PATH	8

INCLUSION TABLE

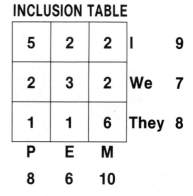

5	2	2	I	9
2	3	2	We	7
1	1	6	They	8
P	**E**	**M**		
8	**6**	**10**		

Natal Imprint

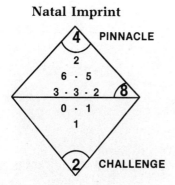

PINNACLE
4
2
6 · 5
3 · 3 · 2   8
0 · 1
1
2   CHALLENGE

Year Imprint

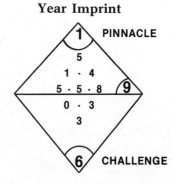

PINNACLE
1
5
1 · 4
5 · 5 · 8   9
0 · 3
3
6   CHALLENGE

Mr. Four

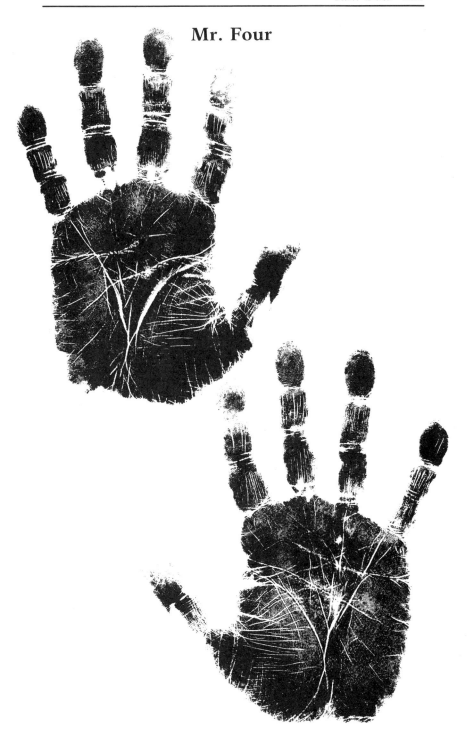

Mr. Four

Bill —

I guess that writing in my lap while lying in bed does not produce the best example of handwriting. Perhaps this is better.

I am afraid that my impression of the "reading" was not strongly positive. It is like someone who has almost learned a new discipline, and has to resort to technical blitzing to show off their knowledge.

I hope this is an adequate quantity of handwriting. If it's not, I'll just have to copy a page of a book. I'm not very wordy all by myself.

Ms. Five

INNER WHEEL Tropical Placidus
ACD: 0^h = JAN 22, 12^h = JUL 24
Eastpoint 22♑12 ● South Node 21♏20 ● Anti-Vertex 22♋12

Koch			Campanus		
6♑40	18♉50	13♍57	6♑40	17♉2	27♍57
6♒14	11♊53	25♎52	17♒30	8♊19	25♎52
13♓57	6♋40	18♏50	27♓57	6♋40	17♏2
25♈52	6♌14	11♐53	25♈52	17♌30	8♐19

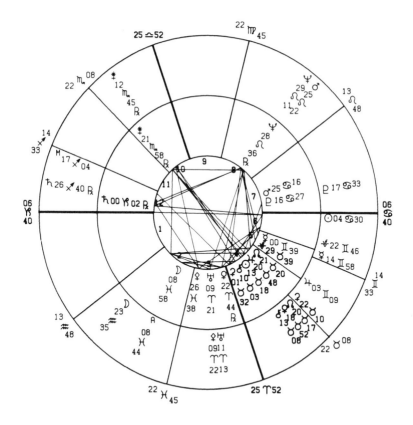

OUTER WHEEL Tropical Placidus
Progressed date is September 12, 1982 — Father's Death
Eastpoint 14♓44 ● South Node 20♏17 ● Anti-Vertex 14♍44

Ms. Five

v 2 (11)
c 2 (11) **4**   v 2 (20)   **1**   v 6   **9**   **5**
         TOTAL   c   8   TOTAL   c 3 (12)   TOTAL   TOTAL
                                                      NAME
                                                      NUMBER

SOUL URGE	1
PERSONALITY	4
NAME	5
LIFE PATH	2

INCLUSION TABLE

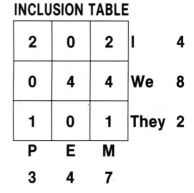

2	0	2	I	4
0	4	4	We	8
1	0	1	They	2

P   E   M
3   4   7

Natal Imprint

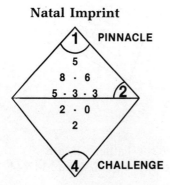

1 PINNACLE

5
8 · 6
5 · 3 · 3   2
2 · 0
2

4 CHALLENGE

Year Imprint

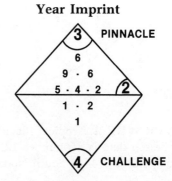

3 PINNACLE

6
9 · 6
5 · 4 · 2   2
1 · 2
1

4 CHALLENGE

Ms. Five

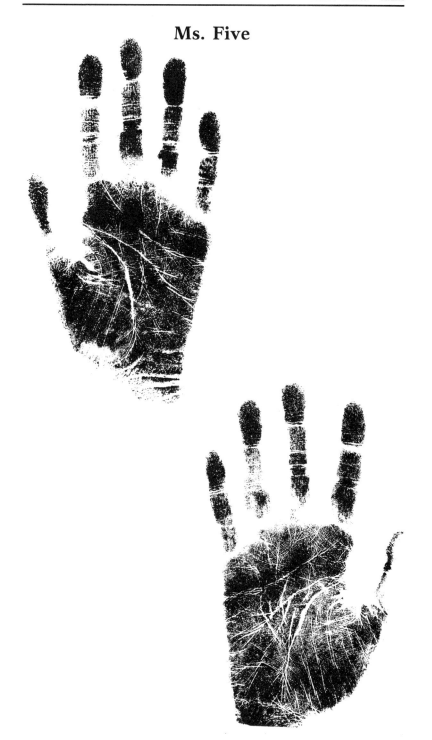

Ms. Five

This is my letter to the World
That never wrote to Me —
The simple News that Nature told —
With tender Majesty

Her Message is committed
To Hands I cannot see —
For love of Her — Sweet — countrymen —
Judge tenderly — of Me.   Emily Dickinson

A long life is favored by aspects to
the Sun and Mars, as these indicate an
active life in which the individual is always
trying to accomplish his objectives and
extend his ambitions. For added longevity
insurance, good aspects between the Sun and
Jupiter help to smooth out the rough spots
and make life easier and more comfortable
over the long run. Capricorn is one of
the best Sun-Signs for male longevity;
the Sun in Cancer promotes female longevity.

Ms. Six

INNER WHEEL Tropical Placidus
ACD: 0^h = JAN 1, 12^h = JUL 1
   Eastpoint 10♋41 ● South Node 9♎34 ● Anti-Vertex 12♊31

Koch			Campanus		
27♋19	28♏0	17♓22	27♋19	13♏43	18♓2
22♌18	0♑42	12♈39	24♌42	21♐55	12♈39
17♍22	27♑19	28♉0	18♍2	27♑19	13♉43
12♎39	22♒18	0♋42	12♎39	24♒42	21♊55

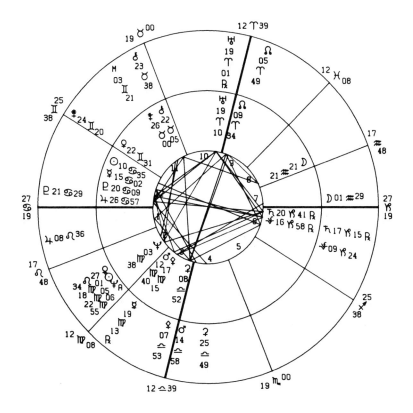

OUTER WHEEL Tropical Placidus
Progressed date is June 23, 1984 — Second Marriage
   Eastpoint 29♌12 ● South Node 5♎49 ● Anti-Vertex 2♌59

Ms. Six

v 7 (16) | v 6 | v 6
c 1 (19) **8** | c 6 **3** | c 3 (21) **9**   **2**
TOTAL | TOTAL | TOTAL   TOTAL
NAME
NUMBER

SOUL URGE	1
PERSONALITY	1
NAME	2
LIFE PATH	6

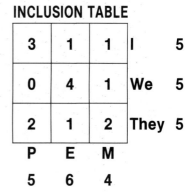

INCLUSION TABLE

3	1	1	I	5
0	4	1	We	5
2	1	2	They	5

P E M
5 6 4

Natal Imprint

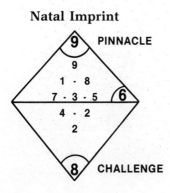

9 PINNACLE
9
1 · 8
7 · 3 · 5 6
4 · 2
2
8 CHALLENGE

Year Imprint

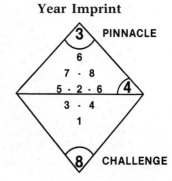

3 PINNACLE
6
7 · 8
5 · 2 · 6 4
3 · 4
1
8 CHALLENGE

Ms. Six

Ms. Six

Bill,

You have asked for a sample of my handwriting. It will be interesting to know if the race against time to accomplish a multitude of things shows in my handwriting. At times like this it is difficult to slow my hand when my mind is racing so.

When I write more slowly, of course, I have better penmanship

Mr. Seven

INNER WHEEL Tropical Placidus
ACD: 0^h = FEB 12, 12^h = AUG 13
  Eastpoint 16♋4 ● South Node 24♉33 ● Anti-Vertex 28Ⅱ43

	Koch			**Campanus**	
10♌19	16♐10	25♓58	10♌19	16♏31	28♓33
3♍5	16♑24	18♈54	8♍8	28♐18	18♈54
25♍58	10♒19	16Ⅱ10	28♍33	10♒19	16♉31
18♎54	3♓5	16♑24	18♎54	8♓8	28Ⅱ18

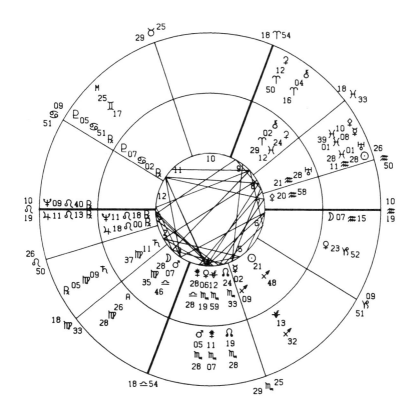

OUTER WHEEL Tropical Placidus
Progressed date is April 1, 1985
  Eastpoint 24♍24 ● South Node 19♉28 ● Anti-Vertex 21♍45

Mr. Seven

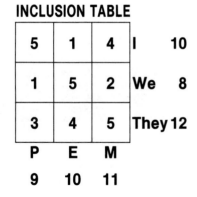

v 2 (20)
c 2 (47) **4** TOTAL

v 2 (11)
c 8 (17) **1** TOTAL

v 1 (19)
c 6 (15) **7** TOTAL

v 6
c 5 (23) **2** TOTAL

5 TOTAL NAME NUMBER

SOUL URGE	2
PERSONALITY	3
NAME	5
LIFE PATH	1

INCLUSION TABLE

5	1	4	I	10
1	5	2	We	8
3	4	5	They	12
P	E	M		
9	10	11		

Natal Imprint

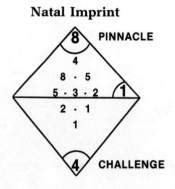

Year Imprint

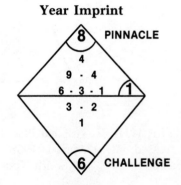

Mr. Seven

Mr. Seven

The true art of living joyously is to live in the ongoing and content now. We must never concern ourselves with what has been or what may be the fact of tomorrow. Being present in the present is to be still in the moment of eternity, and this is immortality.

There is no place where joy does not exist and there who know this have the added exhilaration of that knowledge itself. There is no time wherein this can not be achieved by any who seek their own development, on whatever level they function.

SECTION ONE

ASTROLOGY OVERVIEW
by Zipporah Dobyns

Most of us want to understand ourselves, our fellow-humans and our world. We use road maps, simplified pictures of networks of roads, as guides to new places. Blueprints represent in simplified form the inner structure of machines and buildings. Theories are models created with words or numbers, models that represent or describe bits of the world. Making models is a human pastime (obsession?). Eventually, we usually discover that the world is more complicated than we thought and we revise our models. But even though our models are not "Final Truth," they are useful. They help us to understand and to cope more effectively with our world.

We may sometimes be "just curious," wanting knowledge "for its own sake," without any ulterior motive. But mostly we want useful knowledge. We want to make the machine do what it should, to fix it when it stops working properly. We want to learn how to reach a desired goal such as money, health, love, or we want information to help us choose among possible goals. There are both immediate and long-range goals to consider. Our models may be visual lines on a two-dimensional sheet of paper, or mathematical formulas, or sets of interlocking ideas, concepts, constructs. Science, religion, philosophy and a variety of occult traditions offer us a choice of many models which claim to describe or represent (imitate, correspond to) life and the world. This book will look at several of these systems which attempt to describe and to understand human beings.

Astrology may be our earliest and most widely used model. Scratches on reindeer bones may represent the phases of the moon when neolithic hunters 20,000 years ago noted the correspondence between the moon and the menstrual cycles of women and associated the moon with fertility. Wherever we have written records we find astrology. In many areas, we find circles of stones used to mark the solstices and equinoxes and possibly to predict eclipses. We find buildings oriented toward these important turning points of the year when the relative length of day and night change, or toward bright stars. Apparently, early humans discovered the correspondences between the sky and the earth almost everywhere on Earth. The sky became their clock and compass; their way to orient themselves in time, space and meaning. The Egyptians might not have understood "why" the waters of the Nile overflowed their banks when the star Sirius rose just ahead of the Sun, but it was life-giving information to know that it happened.

Over the centuries, humans have continued to observe the patterns in the sky and the events on Earth. Theories have evolved and new techniques have been invented or discovered. We have added minor planets (asteroids), nodes of all the planets (not just the moon), midpoints, new aspects, etc. There is enormous controversy within astrology over almost every tool and theory in the field. We do not know "why" the sky and the Earth correspond to each other, though we each have our own theories. But those who have investigated astrology in any depth do know that the patterns in the sky offer a useful model to understand human nature and our world. We continue to watch the parallels between the panorama in the heavens and the dramas played out on Earth. Astrology is highly pragmatic. Experience leads to revised theories, followed by new experiences and newly revised theories. I hope that this series of case studies will encourage fellow-students to continue their quest for the best possible fit between experience and the theories (models) we create to try to understand the experience. Hopefully, our expanded knowledge will also help us to better predict and control future experiences and to produce more satisfying experiences for ourselves and our world.

Exploring Models: Astrology

My previous book, *Expanding Astrology's Universe*, offers a more complete explanation of my theories and techniques than can be presented in the current work. Readers looking for in-depth coverage of astrology are referred to that book. In this work, we offer brief summaries of several of the occult models, and much of the material is highly theoretical, needing much more testing. Though I have worked with astrology for almost 30 years, my experience with the other models included here is relatively limited. I have done enough to be convinced that the popular theories are often superficial and inadequate. My own theories may or may not prove more effective. Much additional work is needed to test the ideas. It is the hope of my coauthor, Bill Wrobel, and myself that the format used in this book will help readers to test our theories and the ideas of others. By presenting the "original data," the actual raw materials we experienced (horoscopes, palm prints and photographs, numbers, samples of handwriting, interpretations, interview discussions and self-evaluations), we offer the reader seven ways to seek understanding of seven individuals. I believe that each of these approaches is potentially useful; that no one of them offers "final truth." Hopefully, they should be complementary. By taking photographs of a tree from several different perspectives, with different types of cameras and films, we might expect to gain a better understanding of the tree. But no matter how many photos we take, we know that the photo is not the tree. Our representations (models) of reality are tools. The world we experience is always more complex than our mental pictures.

The Alphabet Model

The astrological model I find most useful is rather like an **alphabet with twelve letters**. We recognize an "a" whether it is a capital letter, lower case, italicized, etc. In astrology, we have **planets** (bodies in the sky), **signs** of the zodiac (divisions of the ecliptic, the Earth's path around the Sun), **houses** of the horoscope (divisions of the space around Earth using lines which radiate out from Earth and cut the horoscope into segments much like pieces of a pie), and **aspects** (angular distances between the planets and/or the house dividing lines). There are also many other forms of the basic twelve-letter alphabet, including the **nodes** of the planets (where their orbits intersect the plane of the Earth's orbit), the **dwads** of the signs (2½° divisions of each sign), **midpoints** and **Arabic parts** (derived from combinations of two or three of the basic planets and house lines), **bright stars**, etc. **Minor planets** (asteroids) have come into increasing use in recent years, and many aspects are being considered in addition to the five used by the ancient world. Especially since the advent of computers, astrology's tools and techniques are expanding at a breathtaking rate, to the discomfiture of some astrologers.

Some of the new ideas may die with their promoters. Some will prove valuable. Astrology is in a profound state of flux at this moment in its venerable history.

Most of the factors listed above seem to me to be variant forms of the basic twelve sides of life symbolized by the planets, signs, and houses. In this approach to astrology, I am not saying that planets are the same as signs and houses, but that all three basic tools symbolize the same twelve "ways of being in the world." We can think of this model as twelve psychological drives, twelve basic principles which may manifest in many different details in the life. I believe that the horoscope shows the **psychological principles that lie behind the visible action**, that each of these drives or desires can be satisfied in many different ways, and that we choose (consciously or unconsciously) our own detailed forms of manifestation.

Lifetimes of Learning

My philosophical premises include a belief in reincarnation. I think that we have created our own character (habitual attitudes and actions) in a series of past lives; that we come back to each new birth where we fit (parents, heredity, horoscope); and we go on growing, with each new life like another year of school. When we realize that our own conscious and unconscious desires and conflicts are creating our own destiny, and that our horoscope (map of the sky at the moment of birth) offers us a mirror view of our urges, we can change the way we express our desires. We can integrate our conflicts, balance our imbalances, and further develop our talents. There are positive and painful ways to manifest each of the twelve sides of life. The choice is up to us.

Astrology's Twelve Sides of Life

Letter one in astrology is symbolized by the planet, **Mars**, by the sign **Aries** and by all rulers of the **first house** of the horoscope. House rulers include **all planets** (or other factors such as nodes, asteroids, etc.) **in the house and all planets that rule the signs in the house.**

Some astrologers limit their attention to the planet ruling the sign on the initial line of the house (called the house "cusp") but I have found that all signs in the house are part of the picture of our handling of that part of our nature. If a sign is intercepted in a house, which happens if another sign is on the cusp of two successive houses, the house with the intercept will have part of three signs in it, hence at least three planetary rulers. Where there are double rulerships due to a planet discovered in modern times being assigned as ruler of a sign while the original ruling planet is retained as a co-ruler, there may be several planetary rulers of a house even when there are no planets actually placed in it.

It is not uncommon for half the chart to be connected to a single one of the twelve sides of life, even without considering the interlinking of these basic drives through the aspects (angular distances) between the planets. Some students have given up in the face of the complexity, preferring to work with a simpler model such as numerology. But astrology is comprehensible if we remember that we are basically dealing with twelve principles, all present in everyone, with each chart a unique combination of the twelve. Plus, since there are many ways to symbolize the same principle, it is the **repeated message that is important.** To be a whole person, we have to handle all twelve sides of our nature, but for most people, a few of the twelve will be far more important, as indicated by the emphasis on those basic principles.

Let's take a hypothetical example to clarify the way such an emphasis can show in a chart. Suppose we have a horoscope with several planets in the first house, several planets in Aries, and Mars in a very prominent position in the chart, perhaps on the MC (the house cusp that points straight up in the horoscope and marks the beginning of the tenth house). Such a person would have a high need to deal with the issues of letter one. In contrast, a person with no planets in the first house or in Aries, and with few aspects to Mars and the first house ruler(s), would be more likely to concentrate on other areas of life.

We could not assume that either person would or would not have problems handling letter one until we examined the placements and aspects of Mars, the planets in Aries, and the first-house ruler(s). We would look to see the sign and house and aspects of all such rulers, to see if they are repeating a similar message to each other and/or to other factors in the chart. No matter how many new factors are added to the chart, the **primary goal is always to discover the repeated themes.**

As previously indicated, letter one in astrology includes Mars, Aries, and the first-house rulers along with other minor forms of the alphabet. The basic drive of letter one can be summarized as "**self-will in action**." We may want to do anything in the world. Letter one just says we want to do what we want, and we want to do it now. Unless tempered by other parts of the nature, an emphasis on letter "one" can represent impulsivity, rashness, aggression, impatience, self-centeredness, reluctance to compromise. A high value is placed on independence, self-reliance, courage, openness, and a decisive and firm will which is carried into immediate action. The action can be almost instinctive, unthinking, out of one's own center, often with a flavor of youth and naivete.

This is not a key to leadership, as is often claimed in traditional books. (I am speaking of the basic nature of letter one, not Sun in Aries. The Sun is one form of letter five, so Sun in Aries is a one-five mixture). Letter one hates to be behind anyone, wants to be in front, but doesn't care if anyone is following. As a capsule summary for letter one, I have suggested the motto "**I do my thing**."

Letter two is symbolized by Venus, planets or other factors in Taurus and in or ruling the second house. The primary focus of letter two is on **physical pleasure**. Details, depending on our choices, may involve money, material possessions, sensuality and appetites, and creating or enjoying beauty in any form. Though the scope may not be as wide-ranging as with letter one, a letter-two emphasis in a horoscope might mark a person obsessed with making or spending or saving money; a collector (with or without good taste); a sensualist (centered on food, drink, tobacco, sex, etc.); or an artist (poet, painter, musician, dancer, gardener, cook, designer, etc.). The keynote of Venus is our search for pleasure: physical with letter two which is earth; intellectual or sociable (involving people and ideas) with letter seven which is air. Letter two is focused on personal pleasure. Letter seven needs shared pleasure for full satisfaction. My motto for letter two is "**I enjoy the physical sense world**."

Letter three in our astrological alphabet includes the planet Mercury, any factors in the sign Gemini, and any factors in or ruling the third house of the horoscope. Our first two sides of life are concerned with personal desires and pleasures. Although our third side of life is still primarily "personal," it does mark the beginning of socialization. For the first time, we realize that other people exist, and we begin to modify our own actions in response to the actions of others. We have moved from impulsive, individualistic action (fire) to energy applied to the physical world (earth), and now with "air" we step back to try to understand the fire-earth action we have experienced. "Air" symbolizes the conscious, reasoning mind; our capacity to learn, think, and communicate. The human obsession with model-building which was mentioned earlier is an air procedure for the most part, though science follows the theorizing with earth action, testing the theory against tangible results.

"Air" also symbolizes peer relationships: people as equals. Letter three indicates the **people around us**, relatives (other than parents and grandparents who hold authority positions so are not equal) and neighbors. In our early years, these peer relationships, especially brothers and sisters, help us to learn to live with our fellow humans. With air — space — literally between ourselves and the world, we learn to see the broad perspective, to take things lightly, to avoid getting hung up in unimportant details, to escape temporarily from the intensity of the other elements. Fire and water both represent intense feelings, with fire tending to express the feelings while water often holds them in. Earth (though Taurus is less so) tends to to be serious and practical. Air is our potential for being casual, superficial, flippant; for saying "mañana," or "it's someone else's turn." The capacity to take things lightly is a lifesaver at times, though we do need to know when such an attitude is appropriate. **We need all twelve sides of our nature, each in its own proper place and time**.

An emphasis on letter three in a chart may express as an insatiable curiosity about everything. A person with a strong Mercury, or many planets in Gemini or in the third house, may have important, continuing ties to people near-at-hand. He or she may read, or watch life, or talk, or travel, or write, or teach, or do some of all of these alternatives. Such people can often do more than one thing at a time, since the attention span is broad, such as talk on the phone and watch a TV show or write a letter. **Flexibility and versatility** are letter three talents, sometimes including bodily as well as mental flexibility, e.g., double joints on the fingers. Remember, my philosophical premises include the power of character to create destiny. A flexible character is likely to be born into a family in which a flexible body can be inherited. Remember also, that the Sun sign is only one small part of the picture, so a person with Sun in Gemini may have greater emphases in other signs and may be trying to **learn** to be flexible or versatile or how to take things lightly. **Astrology shows issues, not details**. The details depend on our choices. If we are clear about the principles of each of the twelve sides of life, combining them is a matter of logic and there are always many possible details associated with each of the twelve principles.

A summary phrase for letter three is: "**I see, conceptualize, talk and take life lightly**."

Letter four includes the Moon, factors in the sign, Cancer and rulers of the fourth house of the horoscope. Though I am listing primarily the major forms of the astrological alphabet, advanced students will naturally want to add some of the minor forms. In the case of letter four, the nodes of the Moon are important enough to be included with the major forms of the alphabet. This fourth side of life symbolizes our **need for emotional security**, whether we seek a mother-figure to provide this need, or are deeply attached to our home, or eat a lot to feel comforted, or have pets, or center our life around a family or try many other variations. Letter four is the **nesting urge**, the baby-mother relationship, domesticity. It introduces us to our fourth element, "water," which symbolizes the unconscious side of the mind. After we have poured our energy out into new action with fire, have dealt with the material world with earth, have detached and tried to understand our experience with air, the last step in the element sequence is to digest, absorb or assimilate our experience; to take it into the unconscious so what we have learned becomes automatic and no longer requires attention. If we had to think about every action, we would have no time to learn anything new. Fortunately, our subconscious or unconscious minds handle most of our body functions automatically, and also take on many activities which originally required attention: e.g., walking, driving a car, fingers hitting the right key on a typewriter,etc.

The basic water instinct is to hold on or to hold in, for the sake of security, whether for ourselves or for others. Individuals with a strong water emphasis in a chart may feel very insecure and may clutch for their own security. Or, if they have faith in themselves and/or in a Higher Power, they may be highly nurturing and generous, caring for others. As with all twelve sides of life, we need to maintain a healthy balance so no part of our nature is totally neglected or so excessively sought that it creates problems.

Since water symbolizes the unconscious mind (with all its buried memories and habit patterns retained from the past), and since it is through the unconscious that we are in contact directly with others, water is the psychic element. At the unconscious level, there is no separation. We can feel with others, receive impressions, have "hunches," whether we use fancy names such as telepathy, clairvoyance, precognition, etc., or just talk about intuition and empathy. Water symbolizes the capacity to be sensitive and therefore vulnerable. Too much sensitivity can be painful and invite a retreat from life, or a tendency to build walls. Water can be dependent or nurturant. Letter four can be baby or mother. Positively expressed, we alternate and can experience both comfortably. Letter four can be encapsulated as: "**I save, protect, nourish and assimilate.**"

Letter five is our second fire side of life, symbolized in astrology by the Sun, factors in Leo, and rulers of the fifth house. Water is the element of closure, finishing chapters. Fire marks the new beginnings: enthusiastic, eager, creative, confident. Letter four, and to a lesser extent letter three, are partly personal (focused on personal needs) and partly interpersonal (dealing with other people and their needs). Letter five is decisively interpersonal. **Letter five needs an audience.** The primary desire of fire, pouring out creative energy, is shared with letters one and nine, but five deeply desires a response back from the world. Whether we give love and receive love, procreate children as extensions of ourselves in the world, teach in front of a class, act onstage, or occupy a throne, letter five is the instinctive drive to be a leader, to be in front and to have a follower. We may be a salesperson and promoter, persuading others to do what we want. We may invest, speculate, or gamble, hoping for a larger return for our efforts. With letter five, we need to be proud of ourselves, we want to have an impact on the world and to get a response back from the world. **We want to do more than we have done before.** The house and sign of the Sun and other keys to letter five tend to increase in importance as we mature, especially after puberty.

One of the problems with popular astrology is the overemphasis on Sun signs. When the Sun is present in a zodiacal sign, we have a mixture of the letter five urges with the nature of the sign involved. In general, the result will be an exaggeration of the qualities of the sign, with the added fire confidence, sense of drama and emotional intensity. For example, the Sun in a water sign is likely to express more of the emotions than would occur with a "pure" water mixture (a water planet in a water sign in a water house). Where Taurus and Venus and the second house are basically laid back and easygoing, the Sun (or other fire planet) in Taurus or the second house will be more of a "steamroller," with some danger of excesses in the handling of physical pleasures.

Though we have not yet discussed the polar partner of letter two, a comment by a professional astrologer is a good illustration of the principle under discussion. Pluto, Scorpio and the eighth house represent the sharing of physical possessions and pleasures. With letter eight, we are learning to give, receive and share. However, the Sun's instinct is to rule, so the Sun in Scorpio is pulled between the urge to be in control and the need to share power. Since the planets (including Sun and Moon for convenience under the term) are more important than the signs, it is common for the Sun in Scorpio to try to keep the power, and to have power struggles as the person tries to learn how to share. The comment by the astrologer was that he had never seen a Scorpio willing to share. The comment is a typical one from people with an inadequate understanding of the principles of astrology. It assumes the person **is** the Sun sign by naming them as "a Scorpio." It overrates the power of the sign and fails to realize that the desire symbolized by the Sun (or planet) is more important than the desire represented by the sign. It shows ignorance of the fact that the Sun and other forms of letter five indicate a part of life we are growing into; one we are increasing as we grow; one that may actually be little in evidence at the start of life when the Moon (automatic habit patterns) and Mars (instinctive action) are more visible in the nature.

I associate letter five with the word "ego", in its popular connotation of a need for self-esteem, a need to feel confidence in our power to have an effect on the world and to get a positive response back from the world. A healthy self-respect is a vital necessity. Individuals who try to put others down are still trying to prove their own worth to themselves or to others. Our goal should not be to "kill the ego," to use a phrase common in religious teachings, but to keep it balanced against the needs and rights of others. But in this first thrust into adulthood, into the fully interpersonal side of life, we are still mostly concerned with establishing our own confidence in our own power.

Wherever we have the Sun, Leo or the fifth-house rulers, we need to be proud of ourselves, to use creative power, to gain attention. Up to this point, we have been children, relatively irresponsible, seeking our own needs, and even letter five still has some of that youth and naivete of the earlier signs unless (with letter four) the person has already switched from the baby role to being parent. In some ways, letter five relates to puberty, the first stage of becoming an adult. The capacity for procreation (sexual maturity) is part of letter five. The orgasm is an intense expression of the power-thrust of letter five. But the need for a positive response from others can also be a hazard. One of the common lessons associated with letter five involves learning not to make one's own self-esteem depend on the responses from others. Somewhere in the middle is a happy medium between a total focus on the ability to meet personal ego needs and a feeling that self-worth totally depends on attention from others.

A possible motto for letter five would be, "**I rejoice in expansion, expressing more and more creatively in the world.**" With **letter six** we can no longer postpone adult responsibility. Mercury continues to be a key to letter six, along with Virgo and all rulers of the sixth house of a chart. We also have two asteroids which seem to symbolize the two sides of Virgo: Vesta and Ceres. The essential principle of letter six can be described as "**efficient functioning.**" In this part of life, we learn to handle a job. We are back with an earth letter, concerned with coping with the material world, but in contrast to the pleasure-seeking of letter two, here we need to be serious. We are learning to analyze, to discriminate, to take things apart, figure how to make them better, and then to do it.

Though there are major differences between them, both letter six and letter ten are associated with work and with all the so-called Puritan virtues: being conscientious, careful, thorough, competent, practical, productive, handling details, well-organized, finishing what we start, etc. The primary focus of letter six is on the details of the job: **doing a good job.**

Another area of "efficient functioning" involves our bodies, and **letter six is associated with health.** If letter six is positively expressed, we do a good job somewhere in our lives (it may or may not be the way we earn a living) and our bodies remain healthy. If we hate our work, illness is one of the ways our unconscious can help us to escape the job. It is possible to combine the two areas of letter six and to turn our health into our job, either successfully as the "health freak" who tells everyone how to stay healthy, or as the hypochondriac whose life centers around an ailing body.

Of course, there are many reasons for illness. Job frustrations are only a small part of the picture. But feeling good about our accomplishments is highly important if a chart has an emphasis on letter six. It is common for such people to have health problems when young; to become healthy once they are adult and fulfilled in their work; and to again have physical problems after retirement when they no longer feel they are able to do something useful in the world. It is no kindness to overprotect children with a strong letter six. The sooner they can gain a sense of competence and accomplishment in life, the sooner they will feel good about themselves and their lives.

Traditional astrology has often seemed contradictory in its descriptions of letter six. One text discusses Virgo as a fertile earth sign, associated with the harvest, grain, domestic animals, with a strong nurturing side that enjoys taking care of people. Another text talks about Virgo as the barren virgin, unable to relate to people, too picky and critical to tolerate ordinary human weaknesses. The asteroids, Ceres and Vesta, seem to symbolize the two sides of Virgo. **Ceres marks the earth-mother** potential — fertile, protective, nurturing. **Vesta marks the potential for placing the job above anything else in life**, including human relationships. With Ceres, the job is for the sake of helping people. With Vesta, the job is for its own sake. The job is to be done well, no matter who gets in the way. It is possible to have either one, or both, or neither, strongly placed in the chart.

In general, early signs and Pisces would tend to mellow Vesta unless the perfectionistic side of Pisces took over. An emphasis on letter ten (Saturn, Capricorn, tenth-house rulers), along with letter eight with its need for control, and letter nine (Jupiter, Sagittarius, ninth-house rulers) if it expressed its perfectionistic side, would tend to support Vesta. Remember, everyone has all twelve sides of life as part of their nature. We have to understand the basic principles represented by each of the twelve; see how they support or reinforce each other and where they conflict; and look for the repeated themes. Letters six, eight and ten all support each other's need for order, organization, care with details, etc., so when they are all emphasized in a chart, there may be some obsessive-compulsive tendencies. Aspects between the planets are the most important form of such an emphasis, so aspects between Vesta, Pluto, and Saturn show a high focus on precision with details. Such a focus does not guarantee that the person will be competent. It is possible to be so anxious to avoid mistakes that the individual does very little rather than risk falling short of impossible expectations.

To repeat again the general premises being offered in this work: the astrological factors show issues, not details. **They do not tell us what will happen. They tell us why it happened**. When we know ''why'' — the psychological drives of the person — we can manifest the drives in different details. We can change the ''what'' and produce different details.

Letter six is included with the interpersonal section of our twelve sides of life, but it also carries a bit of the transpersonal quality. Part of learning to handle a job involves learning to relate to fellow-workers, or those who work for us, so with letter six, we deal with the ''immediate, face-to-face with other people'' issues characteristic of the interpersonal parts of life. But, since the primary focus of letter six is on the job rather than the relationships, letter six also has some of the impersonal quality of the transpersonal sides of life. A capsule description of letter six is, "**I work competently.**"

Letters seven and eight represent the essence of the interpersonal area. Both involve partnership; the capacity to sustain a lasting relationship with a peer or equal. With letter seven (Venus as a ruler, factors in Libra, or factors in or ruling the seventh house), we have the air principle. As mentioned in the discussion of letter three, air represents the conscious, reasoning mind, including some space (air) between ourselves and the world. The talents of air include detachment, objectivity, a sense of perspective and proportion due to the ability to see the overview and to be less personally and emotionally involved. Having said this about air in general, we have to add that letter seven, with its desire for a lasting, peer relationship, is less detached and objective and more emotional than the other two air letters of our astrological alphabet. But some of that air nature is still present. Individuals with a strong emphasis on letter seven in their horoscopes tend to see both sides of an issue, and to have a strong sense of justice and fair play. In fact, they may enjoy the role of devil's advocate, arguing for a position to make sure that side of the issue is represented even when the individual does not personally endorse the position. My motto for letter seven is, "**I seek balance.**"

The primary theme of letter seven is a **need for togetherness**, whether the interactions are cooperative or competitive. Mars and Sun, two of the strongly self-willed factors of astrology, when placed in Libra or in the seventh house tend to be competitive, commonly found in military leaders, sports contenders, lawyers and politicians, etc. But such placements simply raise the issue of personal power versus the power of others, and individuals who are not confident of their own worth and strength may project their power. Alternative results might lead to submission, feeling that we have to please others in order to feel good about ourselves. Or the person might retreat from close relationships: "If I don't get close, I won't get hurt." A common reaction is the "give in, fight, run" syndrome. Remember, the essential principle of letter seven involves learning to be with others in a way that is mutually comfortable. We need a place for cooperation and a place for healthy competition. To be healthy, competition requires the "game-playing" attitude. We have to win some and lose some, and both winning and losing actually help develop our abilities and our confidence. They also help us develop the "air" attitude, the ability to take things more lightly. We discover we can lose and not be wiped out, or win and not destroy the opponent. Life can be a game.

Two of the asteroids, Juno and Pallas, seem to be associated with the concerns of letter seven. **Juno is clearly the marriage asteroid**, wanting a deep, lasting commitment, sometimes feeling more Scorpio than Libra. Remember, both Libra and Scorpio involve partnership. Individuals with a strongly aspected Juno have a deep need for ongoing, close relationships. When their horoscopes also have an emphasis on independence, such people are usually very aware of their ambivalence over freedom versus closeness. An emphasis on Pallas in a chart is more often found in people attracted to fields like counseling, law, politics, etc., though both Juno and Pallas can become involved in causes fighting for social justice. In general, **Venus as a ruler of Libra seems more concerned with peace and harmony while Juno and Pallas represent the more competitive side of Libra**, but as always, sign, house and aspects are all part of the picture. Remember that we are always looking for the repeated themes in the chart.

Letter eight of our astrological alphabet continues the focus on partnership. But, where the air of letter seven emphasizes a natural sense of equality, openness, acceptance and communication, the water nature of letter eight introduces greater emotional depth and intensity, with a tendency to hold in or to hold on. Most astrologers accept Pluto, discovered in 1930, as a ruler of Scorpio, but the traditional ruler, Mars, is still considered a co-ruler of the sign. The eighth house, of course, completes our three major forms of the letter. We have a house, a sign and at least one planet for each of the twelve sides of life.

Letter two (Venus, Taurus and the second house) is the polar partner of letter eight and represents personal money, possessions and pleasures. **Letter eight represents shared money, possessions and pleasures**. All joint resources are part of the picture, whether involving debts (what we owe others), partnership funds, inheritance etc. (what is given to us by others), or the sharing of the material world and really deep emotions. Most astrology texts emphasize the sexual potential of Scorpio, but letter eight includes all shared pleasures and sensuality. With its fixed nature, it also indicates an enduring will' while the water urge includes a drive toward closure, to "persist to the end," so there is considerable potential for excesses with letter eight.

When letter eight is properly handled, the water urge to absorb or assimilate, to turn inward, along with the fixed need to control, combine to mark a capacity for self-knowledge and self-mastery. Since a primary part of letter eight is the need to share the world with a mate (whether marriage, business, consultant, or whatever), we can characterize the positive side of letter eight as **learning to see our own inner depths in the mirror of the mate**, and learning to master our own desires and passions out of respect for the rights of the mate.

I found it fascinating when astronomers discovered that Pluto had a Moon almost as big as the planet, and Pluto is now known to be much smaller than was originally thought. Despite Pluto's position, which is mostly outside the orbit of Neptune, it is clearly one of the keys to the interpersonal sides of life: our capacity to deal with the humans with whom we live, whom we meet regularly face-to-face.

As mentioned earlier, placement of the Sun in Scorpio (or in the eighth house or conjunct Pluto) symbolizes a dilemma: conflict between the Sun's natural desire to be king, in control, and the Pluto need to learn to master the self but not others. Similarly, Venus in Scorpio (or in the eighth house or conjunct Pluto) or Pluto in Taurus (or in the second house) denotes another side of the fixed dilemma. Letter two says that the material world is here for personal pleasure. Letter eight is a burr under the saddle, reminding us of the need to share the world's pleasures, possessions and power, and to master our appetites. A possible motto for letter eight is: **"I seek self-knowledge and self-mastery."**

Each of these twelve sides of life is good and necessary when balanced and harmonized with the rest. Any can also lead to suffering if repressed, if done excessively or in the wrong time or place, or if projected so that others do it for us. Repression involves a complete denial of part of our nature. The blocked desire is buried in the unconscious and eventually will often produce illness. Desires which are manifested in inappropriate ways or times can be described as "displaced." With projection, we attract others who act out our unacceptable desires. The problem with projection is that the others will almost always overdo whatever we are blocking in ourselves and giving away.

We might say that a goal of letter eight is to **learn "when is enough"** and **"how to let go."** Pluto came into its own sign, Scorpio, as this book was started, emphasizing the relevance of letter eight for the world from 1983 to 1995. As we look at the staggering debts of many countries, including our own USA; at the arms race; at the rich getting richer and the poor getting poorer; at pollution (humanity shares the air and water of our planet); at divorce; at crime (violence or theft denies the rights of the victims); we have to conclude that humanity is a long way from learning to handle letter eight of our twelve sides of life. While Pluto is in its own sign, we will learn to handle it or suffer the consequences.

Once we have learned to share pleasures, possessions and power with the human beings immediately around us, with whom we are in face-to-face contact, we are ready for the four transpersonal sides of life. The transpersonal sides of life, in contrast to the interpersonal, symbolize our search for the Absolute (God, Truth, etc.), the impersonal Law and society as a whole. Our last four sides of life are more abstract, distant, inclusive, remote.

Letter nine includes Jupiter, Sagittarius and the ninth house — with the addition of one of our new asteroids, Chiron, as another possible key to our search for **"Truth with a capital T."** We may look to an orthodox religion, to philosophy, to science, to nature, or we may formulate our own faith; but with letter nine, we try to set up a value hierarchy based on what we consider true, desirable and morally right. Underlying our faith are our conscious or unconscious beliefs about the nature of truth, reality, morality, etc. — metaphysical issues which can never be determined with certainty but which are accepted on faith and which guide our choices. My motto for letter nine is, **"I trust, value and direct my life according to my understanding."**

By extension, letter nine symbolizes the **tools or methods used to seek the Absolute**: writing, publishing, books, libraries, colleges, churches, law courts, foreign countries, long trips, etc. It is one of the parts of life strongly committed to freedom, since being too tied down would interfere with our capacity to pursue the quest for the Absolute. In many religions, a family is seen as an impediment to a complete commitment to God. But if we want to be whole persons, we compromise and make room for all twelve sides of life. Another concomitant of letter nine is the capacity for faith, hope, optimism. Those with a positive faith in a Higher Power, whether we use the title "God" or "Universal Mind" or "Spirit," have a natural buoyancy of mind. Of course, excessive faith can lead to gullibility, overoptimism, rashness, impracticality, etc. Or, alternately, we may expect too much of ourselves, others, life in general, and live frustrated for much of our lives. Perfectionism, too high expectations, are the source of an amazing amount of human unhappiness. But such frustrated idealists usually emphasize both the search for the Absolute (letters nine and twelve) and the awareness of flaws (the earth letters of work — six and ten).

Moving on now to **letter ten**, the primary factors are Saturn,

Capricorn and the tenth house. **Letter ten symbolizes the Law**, from natural law (gravity and time, etc.) to cultural regulations (stopping for red lights and going through green ones) to authority figures who carry out the law (boss, police, parent) to the internalized conscience (our internal law). With letter ten we learn **what we can do, what we can't do, and what we have to do** if we want to survive in this world at this time. Letter ten can also be thought of as **karma**, the consequences of how we have handled the law in the past. Since many people associate karma with punishment, though it is simply consequences, an alternate word with more positive overtones is **"feedback."** When we get feedback, we can change our actions to produce different results. But if we do not know that our own attitudes and actions are producing the results in our lives, and that we can change our attitudes and actions, we go on suffering, wondering why such things happen to us. Another metaphor for letter ten is a **report card**. Our grade lets us know whether we are handling things effectively or whether we need to study some more.

As children, we obviously have little power, so we experience letter ten as power in other people or in the world. But as we grow, letter ten becomes our own professional role in the society, including our own power if we work for it. The same Puritan virtues are associated with letter ten as with letter six: hard work, handling details, being practical, productive, well-organized, thorough, realistic, etc. But where letter six is focused on the details of the job, not concerned with power, dealing more with fellow-workers as peers, letter ten must deal with the power of others or power in our own hands. Yet it is quite a different kind of power than letter five which, with the instinct of the king, feels a right to personal power. Letter ten is executive power which carries out the law rather than making the law. Obviously, individuals with mixtures of five and ten (Sun in Capricorn or the tenth house or conjunct Saturn or Saturn in Leo, or the fifth house) may overreach and try to make the personal will into law. Richard Nixon, our disgraced former president, had Sun in Capricorn in the fifth house: one count for executive and two for king. Letter ten shows consequences, and a serious overreach brings a fall from power.

One-ten combinations also warn against overreaching. Personal will is confronting the limits of personal will with such combinations: Mars in Capricorn or in the tenth house or conjunct Saturn; Saturn in Aries or in the first house. The signs in the houses represent the same principles but with less emphasis since the planets are most important and the houses next in weight. But Capricorn rising and Aries in the tenth house are additional ways to combine letters one and ten, while Leo in the tenth house and Capricorn in the fifth house are ten-five combinations.

The opposite of the overdrive is self-blocking, equally possible with the one-ten or five-ten combinations. Instead of the fire self-confidence overrunning the earth practicality, in self-blocking we sit on our courage and confidence and are afraid to do what we want for fear of failure or falling short in some way, whether we fear the power of tne world or our own conscience. Astrology shows us the psychological issues, but we always have a range of possible choices in our manifestation of the basic drives. Too often, astrologers try to guess the details of the person's choice instead of explaining the principles. Frequently, the person will have tried several alternatives and might agree with any of the astrologer's guesses since they all occurred at different times. But it is not only not helpful to guess; it is often harmful. The client feels that the particular form guessed by the astrologer is the only and inevitable consequence of that part of the nature; that there are no other choices possible. **When we understand the principles involved, we can see that there are many different ways we can express those parts of our natures**.

One-ten combinations are an especially good example of the nonsense often offered in astrology. Mars in Capricorn, Mars in the tenth house and Aries in the tenth house are all considered very good combinations. Saturn in Aries or Saturn in the first house or Capricorn rising are all considered bad combinations (by most astrologers). Mars-Saturn conjunctions are considered "outside the pale." Grant Lewi practically suggests you might as well give up and try a new incarnation if you were born with that aspect. Yet all these combinations represent the same principle: self-will meeting the limits of self-will. And any of them can be handled well or badly, depending on our insight. In general, since the planet is the most important, Mars in the tenth house or in Capricorn is a little more likely to do the overdrive potential, while Saturn in Aries or in the first house is a little more likely to do the self-blocking. The value judgment which made Mars exalted in Capricorn was set during the Aries Age when overdrive was desirable (in men only, of course). But I have seen numbers of self-blocking people with Mars in Capricorn and additional numbers of overdrive people with Saturn in Aries. Or, as already mentioned, the same person will do sometimes one and sometimes the other. Since the planets are the most important, the Mars-Saturn conjunction is the most intense form of the one-ten mixture, but I have seen many people who handled it quite successfully — who learned how to live voluntarily within the limits. A shorthand summary for letter ten is: "**I carry out the law.**"

Where knowing and voluntarily accepting the rules of the game is the essence of letter ten, **letter eleven** is focused primarily on **transcending all possible limits.** If we have properly internalized the conscience, we no longer need external limits in the form of authority figures or reminders of the rules. With Uranus, Aquarius and the eleventh house, we can claim **the right to do anything we want provided we are giving that same right to everyone else.** As an air letter, we are again dealing with the conscious mind, ideas and people as peers. With letter eleven the focus is the widest possible range of humans; while letter three is concerned with people in the immediate vicinity; and letter seven with the emotionally closer, more systematic, peer relationships, the adults with whom we interact regularly.

Letter eleven also seeks the **widest range of knowledge,** especially nontraditional or unconventional ideas. Astrology is usually associated with letter eleven, but so is modern technology such as airplanes, space adventures, and computers. My motto for letter eleven is, "**I seek new knowledge, freedom and equality for all humanity.**"

One of the striking facts in astrology is the major differences between adjoining sides of life, and yet each builds on the one before it and we need them all to be a whole person. For example, Sagittarius is one of the most optimistic of all twelve (though all fire letters share that quality) while Capricorn with its heavy concentration on limits and consequences is one of the most pessimistic. Capricorn is the arch conformist while Aquarius is the extreme nonconformist. Aquarius is the most detached, cool intellect while Pisces is the bleeding heart for humanity and an instinctive mystic. Yet each grows out of the preceding part of life and offers a stepping-stone to the one that follows. The faith we formulate with Sagittarius is tested by reality in Capricorn. A proper handling of Aquarius is only possible if we have developed a conscience so the necessary rules are "built-in" and no longer needed outside. When the conscious mind has carried us as far as it can, we must realize that there is still more to life which is only accessible through the unconscious side of the mind.

So we leave the rebel — the air which separates us from the world to permit a view of a wider perspective — to finish our journey by experiencing the oneness which encompasses everything. **Letter**

twelve (Neptune, Pisces and the twelfth house) symbolizes the **mystic searching for infinite love and beauty**. Letter nine sought the rational Absolute which could be described in words. Letter twelve seeks the **emotional Absolute** and takes us beyond words. Letter twelve could say, "**I dream of love and beauty and am absorbed in the Whole**."

Like all water letters, we are dealing with the unconscious or subconscious part of the mind and, therefore, with the potential for psychic ability. There is no separation with water. At the unconscious level, we are connected and open, which can mean vulnerable. Water is also dependent or nurturant, or both if properly handled. With letter four, we cling to home and family. With letter eight, we learn to share the world with a mate. With letter twelve we learn to depend on God, after we have done what we can — or we live anxious. On the human level, letter twelve plays savior or victim. It is a tragedy of astrology that letter twelve is so often presented as necessarily negative. With faith in a Higher Power but willingness to do our share to make a more ideal world, letter twelve is the most beautiful of all our ways of being in the world. Peace.

Aspects

Before leaving this short summary of the basic principles of astrology, a fourth major tool should be mentioned. The twelve sides of life which have just been described can be seen in the horoscope through planets, houses and signs. Aspects are a fourth tool, using the angular distances between the planets or other factors such as the nodes of the planets, the Ascendant, Midheaven, etc. Most of the commonly used aspects involve a division of the circle by a whole number. The **opposition** of 180° is a division by two; the **trine** of 120° is a division by three; the **square** of 90° is a division by four; the **sextile** of 60° is a division by six. These four aspects in addition to the **conjunction** (with the planets very close to each other in the sky), were the ones used in astrology at the time of Ptolemy, about 2,000 years ago. In the intervening years, many more aspects have been added to the collection, including divisions by eight and by twelve which are in common use; by five and ten, which are less commonly used; and by some fractions such as five/twelfths and three/eighths. Within the last decade, exploratory work has been testing divisions of the circle by every number up to 180.

Since one book can only give a taste of the principles of our multiple approaches to understanding human nature, our main goal here is to offer the "raw materials" for readers to explore their own theories about these subjects. The expansion of work with aspects is beyond our scope, but it is important to understand the basic principles of this primary tool in astrology. An aspect, or angular separation between two factors in a horoscope, is a **key to the inner relationship between those parts of the person.** The sextile and trine indicate relative harmony between the two parts of the nature which are symbolized by the planets involved (including their respective signs and houses). The square and opposition show potential tension between the inner drives symbolized by the planets forming the aspects (including, again, their signs and houses). Whether the conjunction will be experienced as harmonious or challenging depends on the nature of the planets involved in the aspect. Planets ruling signs that are naturally square or opposite are more likely to indicate challenges. Planets ruling signs that are naturally sextile or trine are more likely to be experienced as harmonious, as reinforcing or supporting each other.

But it is essential to understand that **harmonious does not mean** that the results in the life will always be **pleasant**, and **tension does not mean** that the results will always be **painful**. Tension indicates an attempt to relate two parts of life which are naturally somewhat in conflict. That simply means that we cannot do both at the same time to their fullest extent. But we can integrate the tension and resolve the problem by taking turns with the two desires, or by doing a little of both in some sort of compromise. Similarly, harmony, which indicates that those two parts of our nature are complementary and tend to reinforce each other, can lead to serious problems through excess in some form. It is not necessarily true that if some is good, more will be better! For example, Mars-Sun, Mars-Jupiter and Sun-Jupiter conjunctions may indicate an excess of self-confidence, a sense that we have a right to everything we want, and that attitude can lead to serious problems.

To repeat what has been said more than once, the horoscope shows the psychological issues. It does not tell us what the person will do with those psychological drives. The person may do many different things at different times. Self-awareness should help to choose effective ways to satisfy the basic needs of the nature.

The Dilemmas

A short summary of the three "dilemmas" of astrology can conclude our brief look at this approach to describing people and life. The **cardinal dilemma** includes letters one, four, seven and ten; so it can be shown in the chart by aspects between the planets which rule those signs (Aries, Cancer, Libra, and Capricorn) or by tension aspects between planets in those signs, or by tension aspects between planets in those houses. As readers can already suspect, you will rarely find a "pure" form of any of the dilemmas. You may have a mixture of cardinal and fixed planets in fixed signs in mutable houses. You have to look for the repeated theme at all times.

But we have to talk about the pure principles before we can begin to analyze the mixtures, so the cardinal dilemma is a **confrontation between the freedom to pursue pure self-will** in action, **the need for a secure nest** (home and family, baby-mother relationship), the **desire for an equal partner** with a little space between, and the **drive to be in control**, accomplishing something bigger in the world. To be a whole person, we should be able to have room for our own interests, for a home and family, for a mate, and for a career. But we can't do them all at the same time to their fullest extent. Something has to give. We can alternate, or we can do a more moderate amount of each of these different sides of life. Compromise is the name of the game.

The **fixed dilemma** involves letters two, five, eight and eleven. Where cardinals tend toward overt changes in the life (in personal action, home, relationships or career), the fixed quality represents an enduring, tenacious self-will. People with a fixed emphasis may change a lot, but it is on their terms. No one else is allowed to make them change if they can help it. So people with charts that emphasize the fixed dilemma may stay in a state of impasse or stalemate with each of the basic drives unwilling to be pushed around. The life may actually be rather stable, in contrast to a cardinal emphasis, but with a sense of the irresistible force and the immovable object in perpetual confrontation. In our society, the freedom-closeness dilemma is common with both cardinal and fixed challenges. Or, an alternate form is the **tension between stability and security versus change and excitement.** Earth and water want the stability and security while fire and air want the variety and stimulation. In general, the fixed dilemma deals with **power, possessions, sensuality and pleasure** — learning to enjoy them, to share them and to master them.

The **mutable dilemma** is centered in the mind, with letters three, six, nine and twelve. Mercury can express as either letter three (interested in everything, casual, superficial) or as letter six applied to the earth world (thorough, wanting to do something well and to get tangible results). The three-six conflict is relatively minor: quantity versus quality, knowledge for its own sake versus knowledge used to accomplish something. Letters nine and twelve are both looking for the Absolute, one more consciously and one more unconsciously. Conflict between them may indicate a conflict between values such as truth versus kindness. Or the person may not be sure what to trust, where to find meaning in life, what is really wanted. Two common forms of the mutable dilemma involve this **uncertainty over ultimate goals and values or a conflict between goals and the limits of what is possible.** In the first form, the person may just scatter the energy, try a little of everything or go in circles. In the second form, there may be considerable success yet the individual is never happy. It is never enough. Or it is possible to do very little, waiting until the really "big" thing comes along, or waiting until the action can be done perfectly.

Other forms of the mutable dilemma include a **lack of faith** with consequent anxiety, depression, etc., or **faith in a part of life** (a kind of idolatry) whether we turn a job or a mate or a child or a home or money or whatever into our source of ultimate trust and meaning. When we make a part of life into God, we usually end up very let down since it fails to give us a perfect life, and often we end up losing it to force us to find a larger God. Solutions to the varied forms of the mutable dilemma include a clarification of our beliefs to permit a clear value hierarchy; acceptance of perfection as a long-range goal plus ability to enjoy the journey toward the goal; and faith in a Higher Power so we can do our best and then release the rest to God.

Summary

The astrological model divides life into twelve parts. Everyone has the potential for all twelve, but some are always more emphasized. The horoscope helps us to see where we are in conflict between different desires and where we need to integrate, or whether there is a danger of imbalance (overdoing some parts of life and lacking skill in others); and it also points to potential talents which can be further developed. The horoscope shows psychological principles, not details. We create the details in our lives by our choices, our attitudes and our actions, and we can change the details by changing our attitudes and actions. The sky is a mirror to help us to change more effectively, to create a better destiny.

CHAPTER TWO
NUMEROLOGY OVERVIEW

Since my coauthor is writing a major section on the theories of numerology in addition to interpretations of our seven subjects, my comments about general principles will be brief. Also, like all of my portions of this book (except for a final summarizing section which I will write on each of our seven subjects in the light of their interviews), this material is being written before reading anything produced by my fellow authors. Readers may well find some contradictions between what I write and what is written by Bill in his numerology section. Remember, everything we write should be considered a theory to be tested by your own experience. The numbers (of the name and birth date) for our seven subjects are provided for you to match against any of the theories.

My primary interest in the subject of numerology has involved the question of the possible overlap between astrology and numerology. I have seen many books which assume an exact correspondence between certain numbers and certain planets, but I have not been at all satisfied with the usual associations. Based on my experience to date, I suspect that the planetary associations are fairly close in some cases, but not exact, and that the order of the numbers is closer to the order of the signs of the zodiac than most authors believe.

Correlations between Numerology and Astrology

To put the matter "in a nutshell," I think that **number 1** is very similar to the first "letter" of our astrological alphabet, to Mars, Aries, and the first house. I see it as independent, self-directed, a pioneer, with immense potential self-will but also a danger of self-centeredness and rash overconfidence when too strongly manifested in the life. It may mark a "loner" or just a very individualistic person. Of course, we may want to express in a Mars way but be blocked by contrary fears or feelings, including our need for other people.

I think that **number 2** may have Venus overtones, but may be more like the Libra form of Venus, including a need for caring relationships as a primary form of pleasure in life.

Number 3 seems very much like the Gemini Mercury, with a sense of lightness, flow, curiosity, ease of expression, talent for words.

Number 4 seems to have a mixture of astrology's four and ten, Moon-Saturn or Cancer-Capricorn: a combination of caution, practicality, a serious approach to life concerned with security and/or accomplishment.

Number 5 feels much like the Sun and Leo: dramatic, creative, expansive, restless, good at "snowing" people but, like number 1, with a danger of too much self-will and overconfidence — though self-blocking is always possible.

If **Number 6** is like Virgo, it is the Ceres side of Virgo, nurturing and helpful in general, at least when properly manifested. Its tradition in numerology is connected to humanitarian service, and some numerologists associate it with marriage and family concerns.

Number 7 is the hardest to match with astrology. Along with number 9, it has traditionally been considered a spiritual number, and I do find that potential some of the time. But I also have seen it associated with difficult interpersonal relationships, almost like a "flight into spirituality to avoid getting close to people." I suspect it may be closer to the issue of respect for others than is usually recognized in numerology texts.

Number 8 fits Scorpio and Pluto rather well, with a potential for power over money, sensuality, and/or knowledge. When handled well, we understand and master ourselves.

Number 9 marks a kind of closure (at least in the numerical system that has come down to us from Pythagoras). It seems to have overtones of Jupiter in both its Sagittarius and Pisces forms. It can show high goals and aspirations but also escapism. It needs to be integrated with the greater realism of numbers 2, 4 and 6.

Number 11 is added as a master number with many similarities to Uranus and Aquarius in astrology. It marks the potential world teacher.

Number 22, strangely enough, seems more focused on mastery of the material level if we can trust the traditions. When not handled on their "higher" levels, 11 and 22 are reduced to their respective single digit sums: 2 and 4. As with all of our occult subjects, I feel that much more research is needed.

An Example

Before beginning the examination of the seven subjects of this book, I would like to mention one of the most striking cases in my experience with numerology. Since most people have much in common, most of us working on the same "dilemmas," the scientific world tends to sluff off our "occult" models as too general and therefore incapable of being really tested. The best "test cases" are people who are really distinct, either possessing unusual talents or extreme problems. Jim Jones certainly qualifies as such a person. His full given name was James Warren Jones, and his birth date was May 13, 1931. He died, with over 800 of his followers, on November 18, 1978, at the age of 47.

His numbers are striking! The birth date numbers of 5 (May), 4 (13 = 1 + 3 = 4) and 5 (1931 = 1 +9 + 3 + 1 = 14 = 1 + 4 = 5) sum to a 5. (5 [month] + 4 [day] + 5 [year] equals 14 or 1 + 4, which is 5.) If number 5 is like Leo, we could certainly see that it fit his need to be a leader and his charismatic power over his followers. The sum of the birth date is generally referred to as the "Birth Path" or "Life Path."

<pre>
      1   5   1   5   6 5
    JAMES WARREN JONES
      1   4   1 5   99 5 1   5 1
</pre>

Looking at his name, we see that his individual letters included six "1's" and six "5's" in addition to one "4," one "6" and two "9's." The vowels, theoretically indicating the inner urge of the person, summed to a 5. (1 + 5 + 1 + 5 +6 + 5 = 23 which reduces to 2 + 3 = 5.) The consonants, supposedly a key to the outer expression, also summed to a 5 (1 + 4 + 1 +5 + 9 + 9 +5 + 1 + 5 +1 = 41 = 5; OR you can drop the 9's because they do not affect the total — then the sum is 23 which reduces to 2 + 3 = 5). The full name summed to another 1 (5 +5 = 10 = 1). I have never seen a case with such an emphasis on numbers 1 and 5, pointing to a person with extreme self-will, the fire principle in astrology but running wild. His two "9's" marked the spiritual aspirations, but they could not match his self-will.

One of the theories in numerology involves **Pinnacles** and **Challenges** as keys to positive potentials and to areas in which we need to be careful. I assume that my fellow author will be explaining cycles and pinnacles in his section, so I will not duplicate a traditional part of numerology. I will just comment that Florence Campbell adds the month and day for the first Pinnacle; the day and year for the second one; the two first Pinnacles for the third; and then adds the month and year for the final one. For Jim Jones, the first three Pinnacles were all "9's," emphasizing a potential spiritual destiny devoted to universal love and brotherhood: just what he preached but failed to practice in his later years. (Month [5] + Day [4] = 9. Day [4] + Year [5] = 9. And, 9 + 9 = 18, which reduces to 1 + 8 = 9. Month [5] + Year [5] = 10 = 1.)

Florence Campbell writes that the Birth Path number (addition of birth month, day, and year) should be subtracted from 36 to give the age at which the first Pinnacle ends. The second and third are said to be nine years each. The last covers the balance of the life. With a number five Birth Path, Jones's first Pinnacle ended at age 31 (36 years - 5 = age 31); the second at age 40 (31 + 9), and his third (40 + 9 = 49) was still in effect when he died in Guyana. His last Pinnacle would have been a "1" flourish with a potential of finally "getting what he wanted in life," if a person with so many "1's" and "5's" could ever reach satisfaction. I have not done enough testing to be confident of this theory. In Europe, the day is written before the month. In their numerology, do they add the month and year for the second, and the day and year for the last one? Or might others just have three periods that are added as there are three periods which are subtracted?

The Challenges are produced by subtracting month from day (whichever is smaller), then day from year, then month from year. Interestingly, Jones's first two Challenges were "1's" (Month [5] - Day [4] = 1; Year [5] - Day [4] = 1), the number that was so prominent in his name. I'm afraid he flunked that one. Number "1," like Mars, can express as self-blocking with a need for more self-confidence and decisiveness, or as too much self-will. If Jones reached his third Challenge, it was a zero (Month [5] - Year [5] = 0), but Campbell is not specific about the timing of the three challenges, just stating that they overlap the cycles.

My questions apply here also, on relative order. Putting the day before the month in Jones's birth date, and calculating the periods in that way, would seem just as appropriate for Jones's life. The three Pinnacles he reached would have been 9, 1, 1, and the three Challenges would be 1, 0, 1. It seems to me that he lived his middle years more like a number "1," was given choice and used it badly.

There are also several systems for "progressing" a name to associate numbers with each year of life. The best known system adds the birth month and day to the current calendar year to get a "Personal Year." The calendar month is added to the Personal Year for a personal month, and the calendar day to the preceding figure for a personal day. This system was appropriate for Jones. On the day he died, along with over 800 of his followers, he was in a "7" Personal Year, challenged to face spiritual issues and relationships with others. His personal month and his personal day were both number "9," the number of ending the chapter.

With this brief introduction to astrology and numerology, let us examine the horoscopes and numbers of our seven subjects.

CHAPTER THREE

CASE ONE

The horoscope of our first case suggests a lady of **passionate depths**, but one who also has a **very good mind. Fire and water are the emotional elements** in astrology, and the combinations of planets, aspects, houses and signs where these elements predominate mark the **warm, feeling people** of the world. Note that in this chart we have Mars, a fire planet, in its own fire house in a water sign. Also, Mars is octile the Jupiter-Mercury conjunction and, though the latter two are in earth or air signs and house, Jupiter is a fire planet. Since planets are the most important factors in astrology, aspects between planets of the same element may be more emphasized than a shared element between the planet and the house or between the planet and the sign. We also note that the Moon, a water planet, is in a fire sign as well as conjunct its own node in the same sign. The Leo-Cancer combinations are the warmest in the zodiac in terms of feeling for close relationships, for home and family. When the Moon is conjunct its own node, it is like a double statement of the same principle. People with this combination are often very magnetic. Others are drawn to them. Another fire and water mixture includes Pluto (water) in a water sign (Cancer) in a fire house (the ninth which is like Sagittarius). Planets in Aries in the Leo (fifth) house and in Scorpio in the Pisces (twelfth) house contribute additional warmth.

The **interpersonal parts of life**, as conceptualized by astrology, include letters four and five symbolizing home and family, and letters seven and eight, which show our desire for a mate. In this chart, all four of these signs are occupied by planets and/or asteroids, while three of the houses are occupied. The **nurturing potential** is also emphasized by the Moon on its own node and by Ceres in the fifth house. The **desire for a mate** is especially strong when we see Venus conjunct Juno in Scorpio. Ceres seems to be a mixture of the need to do a good job with something (Virgo) and the urge to take care of others, so when associated with letters four or five, the individual will normally want children — though I have occasionally seen it expressed as a love of pets. Juno is the marriage asteroid, so its conjunction with Venus, a co-ruler of Libra, and their placement in Scorpio, one of the signs of partnership, strongly reinforces the desire for an intense peer relationship.

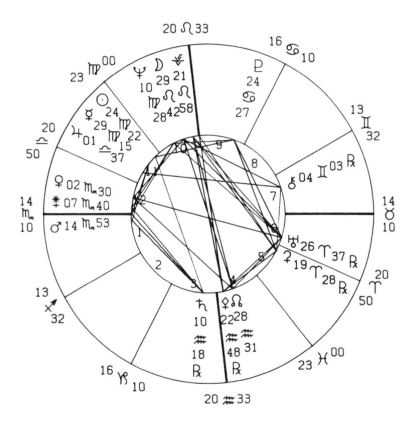

If the theme described so far were the main one in the horoscope, we would assume that the subject rushed into marriage and made it the center of her life. But life (and the chart which symbolizes it) is not that simple. Other themes emphasize the mind (as already mentioned), a **need to work successfully in the world**, and a **strong desire for personal independence**. So we must conclude that our first subject, Ms. One, shares some of the dilemmas that are so common in our culture. One such common dilemma should be discussed before we leave the subject of relationships. The chart strongly suggests a **tendency to idealize love and relationships**. The Venus-Juno conjunction is in the twelfth (Pisces) house. Pisces is on the cusp of the fifth house of love and children. Chiron, which I interpret as similar to Jupiter, is in the seventh house of partnership. Pluto, part of our capacity for sharing the world with others we are close to, is in the ninth (Sagittarius) house. Jupiter is in Libra, the sign of partnership, and Mercury, ruling the seventh and eighth houses, is conjunct Jupiter. The mixtures of letters nine and twelve with seven and eight repeat again and again the search for an ideal in love — and the danger of disappointment since no relationship can ever be a substitute for God.

Of course, there are many different ways we can handle such a mixture of ideals and relationships. Some individuals continue to look for the perfect person and never marry, and/or they are afraid of not being a perfect parent of perfect children, so never have children. Other individuals marry repeatedly, each time finding the feet of clay and separating, but then trying again. Still others project the search for an ideal and are attracted to people who are perfectionistic, so the partner is dissatisfied. It is also possible to stay in a relationship but remain frustrated and critical. If we repress our awareness of the flaws in the other person or in the relationship, we run the risk of becoming ill. We may also choose individuals who need to be rescued; instead of looking to them to be God for us, we play God to them. All of these variations prove uncomfortable in the end. When what should be a peer relationship is turned into a savior-victim one, the victim is being put down and has to get even in some way. The solution to the problem is easy to say but not so easy to do. We have to accept human relationships with human beings, realizing all we can hope for is some mutual pleasure, and to keep our search for the Absolute focused on a Higher Power.

A desire for **personal freedom** was mentioned earlier, and we can see it in the chart with Mars exactly on the Ascendant, with Ceres and Uranus in Aries, with Saturn, Pallas, and north node of the Moon in Aquarius, with activity in the ninth and eleventh houses. All forms of letters one, nine and eleven share the theme of wanting to be free to do what we please, with letters nine and eleven also adding an interest in or concern with the wider world of the transpersonal. Since Pluto, ruler of the Scorpio rising, is in the ninth house, and Jupiter, ruler of the Sagittarius in the first house, is in the eleventh house, the individual is **partly identified with the transpersonal area**. Sun in the eleventh house also connects the ego, our need to be proud of ourselves, to do more in life than just "what comes naturally" (letter one) with the transpersonal area. The Moon in the tenth house in the Sun's sign, Leo, also connects ego to achievement in the world, so Ms. One is likely to have a strong inner drive to reach the top and to be recognized by the world in some way. It is possible for letters four and five (Moon, node, Leo) in the tenth house to choose the role of mother as a way to fit into the society, but where there is any strength in earth in the chart, the individual is likely to want to do more than be a homemaker.

So we need to take a look at the earth in this chart. With the Sun in Virgo and Leo in the Capricorn house, the person is **ego-involved in achieving tangible results** in the world. Aries in the sixth house suggests an identification with doing something well and getting tangible results. In general, fire-earth combinations want to **work in an individualistic way**, with a high degree of independence and variety in what they do. Ms. One certainly fits that picture: with Uranus in the sixth house, Virgo in the eleventh house, and Saturn in Aquarius adding letter eleven to the work picture, reinforcing the **need to have variety and independence in the job**. Letter eleven also adds the desire for an intellectually stimulating job. If the individual is not able to find work which offers independence, variety and intellectual interest, there is a danger of being a **"job-hopper,"** continuing to flit from job to job, even changing the whole area from time to time. This is only a problem if the restlessness conflicts with other parts of the nature, but we can suspect that it will conflict with the water which wants security, and the Virgo emphasis which wants to do something really well! Perhaps the strongest indication of that **drive to excel** in the career is stated by Vesta, the super-Virgo asteroid, placed in Leo on the MC Any planet on an angle is highlighted as a major key to the person, so the **freedom needs are intense** with Mars on the Ascendant and the **achievement needs are also intense** with Vesta on the MC.

In addition to the need to integrate the restlessness and independence with the practical demands of survival in a material (earth) world, the **freedom needs must also make peace with the desire for closeness**. I mentioned that Ceres in the fifth house is usually an indication of a desire to be a mother, but when it is in Aries, we may stop with one child with whom we are *very identified*; that is, the **child is a role model** for us to see part of ourselves reflected back. If we accept and like that part of ourselves, we will like the child. If we are at war with ourselves, we are likely to have conflict with the child. For example, if we have repressed our own freedom in deference to the earth (practical responsibility) and the water (need to nurture others as well as provide our own security), we might have a child who was a truly "free soul." The child might reject security-stability and act out what we would like to do but cannot allow in ourselves. But the danger of projection is that the other person will usually overdo in the area we are blocking. **If we are blocking our ability to fight for our own rights, others may actually attack us**, forcing us to learn to use our own strength in self-defense. Clearly, this chart is a very strong one, but I have seen others with equal will and tenacity who blocked their own power, or alternately blocked it and then exploded when the fire built up enough force. When we have strength, we need to stay in touch with it and channel it in constructive ways before it reaches that eruption threshold. It is **possible for the power to explode out and upset our relationships and our conscience, or to explode in and produce illness, accidents or even surgery.**

Astrology cannot and should not predict illness, but it is highly useful to let us know the psychological roots of illness. It is only when the psychological conflicts (which we all have) are buried in the unconscious and not handled that they manifest outwardly in the body. We can let the M.D. assist the body on the physical level, and we can work on the psychological issues which lie behind the physical problems. Normally, individuals with this much fire have strong energy and recuperative powers so they are rarely ill, but if the fire (our sense of our right and power to do what we want) is blocked, it can turn inward to damage the body.

Since the asteroid, Ceres, is associated with both our capacity to have children or to nurture other people and with our willingness to be nurtured, I find it useful in the horoscope as one key to an individual's early experience of the mother-figure. The Moon and Saturn, along with the fourth and tenth houses, are primary indications in a chart of the person's relationship to parents as well as the capacity to be a parent. Remember that the **chart shows the individual's own experience**. An objective observer might view the parents as they are symbolized in the horoscope, but this will not always be the case. The same parents may be experienced in very different ways by different children in the same family. Any relationship is a two-way street. Even a baby elicits reactions from a parent by its actions and responses. There are cuddly babies, angry babies, depressive babies, fearful babies, etc. Character creates destiny, drawing us where we fit and inviting characteristic reactions from the world.

Though we never know the details of the parents and early home life until we talk to the person involved, the horoscope gives us the general principles or issues in the situation. We can see in the chart of Ms. One that the **mother-figure** (which could be mother, stepmother, grandmother, etc.) **is associated with fire and earth.** We have mentioned Ceres in Aries in the Leo house. The Moon is in Leo in the Capricorn house. The Sun, ruling the tenth where the Moon is placed, is in Virgo while Vesta (like Virgo) is in the tenth house. When a key to mother (Moon or Ceres usually) is in the tenth house, it points to a tenth-house mother and a fourth-house father, and this likelihood is supported by Saturn (usually a key to father) being in the fourth-house sign and being a natural ruler of the fourth-house sign. Although I find the tenth house is the key to father and fourth to mother a little more often, this role reversal of the houses is quite common. I am never sure which house is which parent until I have talked to the individual. Sometimes the roles are so mixed, there is no clear way to assign one house to one parent. But, in this case, the odds point to a tenth-house mother with strong fire-earth qualities in the nature. She might be career-oriented. She might just be strong-willed and independent. She might be very dramatic. We have a double emphasis on Leo with Moon in the sign and Ceres in the house of Leo. She may be intellectually active with Sun in the eleventh house and Mercury conjunct it, or just involved with friends, or working on causes in the transpersonal area. Mercury is also a ruler of the tenth house since we have Virgo in the house and I count all signs as part of the picture, not just the sign on the cusp. Mercury's close conjunction to Jupiter thus becomes a key to the mother as well as to the person's own drive for knowledge and accomplishment. **Idealism is also involved**, since Neptune is in the tenth house, which might mean mother is religious, has high standards, expects too much (of herself or others) or other variations on the search for the Absolute. The combination of Neptune and Jupiter (conjunct a ruler of the tenth) with Vesta and Virgo is a strong mixture of the search for ideals along with the awareness of flaws. Mother might have been critical, though usually fire (except for Sagittarius) and air tone this down a bit. Sun and Mercury are in an air house, with Jupiter also in an air sign to moderate its perfectionism.

Father seems strongly linked to air, with Saturn in double air (sign and house), while Pallas as a Libra asteroid is in Aquarius in the fourth house. But Uranus, another ruler of the fourth house, is in a fire sign in an earth house. Pisces in the fourth is a further complication, since its rulers (Neptune and Jupiter) are connected to mother (one in the tenth and the other conjunct a ruler of the tenth). So we **might have a case of parents who are similar and share roles in some way. Or we might have one parent playing both roles. In our divorce-prone culture, it is common to find that parents have separated.** The nodes across the fourth and tenth houses are one indication of that possibility, especially when they are in air-fire signs which tend to enjoy change. If father was still there, the chart suggests he was rather open, equalitarian, easy to talk to, though the retrograde Saturn and Pallas might mean he listened more than he talked. He would be likely to have a strong sense of individuality or need for personal freedom in his nature, with both Aquarius and Aries connected to the fourth house. Another possibility would be temporary separations between the parents due to travel. Or the family might have moved often, or other people might have come and gone in the home.

The placement of Aquarius in the fourth house is one form of the freedom-closeness dilemma, since the fourth is like the Moon (wanting a secure nest), while the instinct of Aquarius is to resist all limits. It is normal for us to come in to a new life with such ambivalence but to be conscious of one of the contradictory urges while the other urge is unconscious. Since the unconscious always wins, we keep getting the one we didn't know we wanted. **If we consciously want a stable, secure nest, we come to parents who divorce, or move, or travel, or have people coming and going all the time. If we consciously want independence, we come to parents who seem too controlling , and we fight to do our own thing, even to the extent of running away from home.** When we become conscious of our ambivalence, we can resolve the conflict and have some of both: **a stable home but freedom to be ourselves and have variety.**

I see Saturn as a key to our reality lesson. It represents the power of the universe, including natural law (gravity and time), cultural regulations (driving on the proper side of the street), authority figures who enforce the law, and our own conscience as our internal law. Saturn in an air sign and house connects the **lesson to the mind and peer relationships.** The lesson might be in allowing others to do their share, since the chart shows some danger of assuming the "Atlas" position, carrying the world. The lesson might be learning when to accept, to be a spectator rather than a critic. Sometimes the lesson is to realize how capable one really is. It is common for a third-house Saturn to start with doubts about the mental ability, so the person has to prove to himself or herself how good the mind really is. Where earth is weak (it is strong here), the person may need to learn to really apply the mind and not just scatter the ability. Whatever the lesson, we have a chance to learn something about it from early authority figures. If the power people in our early life are handling that part of life well, we get a good example of what to do. If they are not handling things well, we see what not to do. Since the third house also symbolizes other early relationships, there might have been a brother, sister, uncle, etc., who played a power role and was an example. Or Ms. One may have played "parent" to younger siblings. With Saturn square the first-house Mars and Ascendant, there is a **likelihood of some sort of power struggle or stress in the early life involving authorities**. Details can vary enormously. A brother might have been seen as superbright and there might have been a contest for the affection of a parent or for the best grades in school. Responsibility for a sibling might have been seen as an imposition, limiting the personal freedom. The father might have seemed too cool, detached, distant, not offering the warmth desired.

Father is a key to attitudes toward mates, since Pallas (a Libra asteroid) is in the house of father, but that might mean we learn to relate as an equal, to handle a relationship with a mate, through the experience with father. Or we might want a mate like father. Or we might want someone the opposite of father. We might want a mate to be a father to us and protect us, or (with the fire and earth in this chart) we might unconsciously pick a mate who would let us play parent; that "Atlas" danger mentioned above. Since Mercury rules the seventh and eighth houses and a sign in the tenth, and since Moon rules part of the eighth house, **mother is also a key to our capacity to form a partnership**. We may learn from her example and from our experience with her, and may pick mates like or unlike her. It is also possible to turn a parent into a mate; that is, to maintain an adult peer relationship with our parents. When the planets, signs or houses of peer relationships are connected to those of parents (mixtures of letters four and ten with letters seven and eight), we can resolve the challenge easily by taking turns being parent in the relationship with the mate. If both people have something to give that the other values, there can be beautiful, supportive partnerships with interdependence.

Summary

To summarize what has been said, Ms. One has an excellent mind, with the earth ability to handle details and the air capacity for seeing the broad perspective and knowing a little about everything. Her horoscope suggests that she is a very warm and loving person, with a very strong will and streak of independence. She would be likely to want at least one child, but might not have more than two in view of her desire for freedom and her urge to achieve something big in the world. Or, she might choose to work with children, though Leo might also be drawn to the entertainment area, to advertising, selling, promoting, PR work, etc. She has enough fire to be highly creative, enough earth to be practical and productive, enough air for objective detachment, and enough water for sensitivity and empathy. She needs to be out in the world. Intelligent friends may be very important to her. She is likely to be a perpetual student with her Ascendant ruler in the ninth house, or she might travel, write, teach, etc., with the strong mental emphasis in the chart. She came in with a freedom-closeness dilemma, may have resolved some of it with parents, or may have continued to work with it through adult relationships, with mate and/or children. Her south node of the Moon conjunct the Moon suggests that mother was a major lesson, whether in the handling of power, love, career, ideals, or the critical attitude. The chart suggests ample ability to resolve the challenges, though all of us probably go on growing all our lives. I do find some charts with Scorpio rising and a strong tenth house where the person initially held in a lot, and only in the middle years discovered the real strength. Saturn square Mars and Ascendant (as mentioned above) can mark a real danger of self-blocking initially, while its quincunx to Neptune repeats the danger of the ideals remaining in conflict with the limits inherent in this material world. For all who come in to birth identified with letter nine or twelve (in this case, Pluto ruling the Ascendant placed in the ninth house), my favorite motto is "I'll be God tomorrow. Today it's OK to be human, on the way to God. And don't forget to enjoy the journey."

Numerology

Although I consider astrology to be the most complex, complete and sophisticated of our "occult" approaches to understanding and describing human nature and life, I think that other techniques can also be valuable as supplementary tools. One of our goals in this book is to see how these other methods can offer a complementary picture of our cases. Looking first at numerology, we see that Ms. One has a Birth Path of 9 - 8 - 7 to give a 6 total. I would associate these numbers with the transpersonal area, for the most part. I see the 9 as a search for an Absolute, much like a combination of Sagittarius and Pisces. We may be clear and realistic about our beliefs, or we may be confused and escapist, but they are important to us. The 8 may indicate concern with power, whether we seek it over money and the material world, or over knowledge (including self-knowledge). Scorpio rising fits an emphasis on 8. I am still unsure of the nature of 7, sometimes finding it, like 9, associated with spiritual affairs, but also sometimes finding it much involved with relationships, including difficulties in establishing lasting, comfortable peer associations. This issue is certainly suggested in the horoscope of Ms. One. The Birth Path total, 6, fits the Virgo service to humanity, again supporting a strong theme in the horoscope. **Note:** Remember, **individual** assignment of a number to **each** letter value can **not** be used to preserve anonymity, e.g.:

$$\begin{array}{ll} \text{v 3} \\ \text{c 4 (22)} \end{array} \boxed{7} \quad \begin{array}{ll} \text{v 1} \\ \text{c 5 (14)} \end{array} \boxed{6} \quad \begin{array}{ll} \text{v 3 (12)} \\ \text{c 2 (11)} \end{array} \boxed{5} \quad \boxed{9}$$

TOTAL   TOTAL   TOTAL   TOTAL
                                                    NAME
                                                    NUMBER

$$\frac{9}{2 \ \ 3 \ 3}$$ can be deduced as "BILL,"

but giving a **total** of vowels and consonants in each name is OK:

$$\frac{1 \text{ vowels}}{3 \text{ consonants}} \quad \text{[BILL]}$$

Turning to the name, the number present most often in individual letters is number 1. With eight in the name and all but one above the line (present as vowels), the high focus on freedom, individuality, and creativity shown in the horoscope is certainly reiterated. I think that number 1 has a strong fire quality, whether the person seeks to be on top or in front or just unique. The single number 1 below the line might suggest that the inner drives are not easily translated into tangible form in the outer world. Outer appearance may be more conventional or traditional than inner feelings and thoughts. There are three letters each for numbers 2, 4 and

9 plus two 5's. I interpret these as a need for relationships, an ability to handle the practical world, more creativity, and the spiritual quest or some form of idealism. Subtotals (sums of the vowels, of the consonants, of each whole name, and of the three names) give us twelve more numbers which fill in all the gaps except for number 8, so the name suggests the capacity to handle all the areas of life. We even get two of the master numbers in the subtotals. The consonants of the last name and of the whole name sum to 11, which I see as very close to Aquarius in astrology, with an interest in the whole world, an urge to always go farther, to gain knowledge and to share it with others. The consonants for the first name sum to 22, an indication of the drive to master the material world, to achieve something outstanding in it, that seems to be a bit like the Vesta in Capricorn in Ms. One's chart. The whole name is quite powerful and fits a strong chart with its emphasis on fire and earth plus fixed signs in the angular houses. We still have to learn to use the strength properly to avoid either blocking it or applying it in the wrong areas or times, but the potential is here for a life that will count: one that will leave the world different.

CHAPTER FOUR

CASE TWO

In my initial inspection of a horoscope, I look for two different types of patterns. I look for **themes**: combinations of planets, houses, or signs which repeat the same principles. A **stellium** (three or more planets in the same sign and/or house), offers an immediately obvious theme. Planets with close aspects in addition to other planets or angles in their sign(s) or natural house are another example of a theme. Or, the chart may show an emphasis on one or two elements or qualities, an emphasis on a combination of two elements or qualities such as mixtures of fire and water, or a pattern of cardinal signs occupying fixed houses, etc. Or there may be a high focus on one or two sections of the three-way division of our twelve sides of life: personal, interpersonal or transpersonal.

Secondly, I look for **aspect patterns**. Planets closely conjunct any of the angles of the chart are very important. Unless they are very weakly aspected, the MC and Ascendant are as important as anything in the horoscope. I consider the East Point and Antivertex important only when they have close aspects, but they do seem to represent auxiliary Ascendants, suggesting types of natural self-expression. Opposite all of these four angles are their polar partners, also important when closely aspected. For all major aspects, a planet will form aspects to both ends of the axis across the chart. For example, a sextile to one end produces a trine to the other end of the angle axis. I also look for obvious aspect patterns such as a grand cross, grand trine, yod (a third planet quincunx two other planets which are sextile each other), etc. For some years, but rather sporadically, I have been exploring a variety of new aspects such as the quintile (a fifth of the circle — 72°), the septile (a seventh of the circle — 51 + °), the novile (a ninth of the circle — 40°), etc. Other researchers and I are also testing some computer programs which look at many more aspects, and pick out the ones which are most emphasized in the chart.

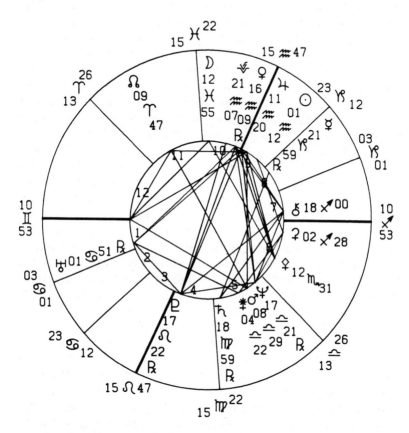

Our first glance at the horoscope of Mr. Two picks up a couple of obvious themes. We note a Libra stellium in the fifth house with Saturn in Virgo also in the same house. When we add a planet in Cancer, Pluto in Leo in the fourth house, Pallas in Scorpio, a planet in the seventh house, and the ruler of the Ascendant in the eighth house, we have a clear emphasis on the interpersonal side of life. But the transpersonal area is also emphasized, with two asteroids in Sagittarius; Mercury, the Ascendant ruler, in Capricorn; a stellium in Aquarius, partly ninth house and partly tenth house; Moon in Pisces in the tenth house; north node of the Moon in the eleventh house; and our two auxiliary Ascendants in the twelfth house. **Mr.**

Two is identified with both the interpersonal (relationships that are face-to-face, close, continuing, deep) **and the transpersonal** (involvement in the larger scene, concern with knowledge, career, more casual contacts).

Obviously, life should be big enough to include both areas. But the mixtures in the chart do call for awareness of the potentially conflicting desires for closeness and space to do bigger things. The nodes across Aries-Libra and the fifth-eleventh houses are both keys to the **freedom-closeness dilemma** that is so common in our culture. Mars in Libra and closely conjunct Juno, the marriage asteroid, is simultaneously an identification with the need for a mate and potential ambivalence over our right to do what we please. Mercury, ruling the Ascendant (so another key to identity), also must work out that **ambivalence over personal power** (letter one) and **shared power** (eighth house). Venus opposing Pluto in Aquarius-Leo reiterates the freedom-closeness issue and repeats the concern with power, possessions, pleasures, etc. Uranus in Cancer and Cancer in the first house give us the message again. Uranus in the first house is a superindividualist: "No one tells me what to do!" But Cancer identifies with a mother-figure and with playing parent to others. Any factor placed in the seventh house counts for Libra, the desire for lasting, shared, peer relationships. But Chiron and its sign, Sagittarius, both want the freedom to pursue the Absolute in some form, while Jupiter, ruling the seventh house, placed in Aquarius in the ninth house, is totally committed to that quest for something higher.

In addition to the mixtures of astrological factors listed, we could assume that **the area of relationships involves lessons** in this lifetime just by noting that both Saturn and the south node of the Moon are in the fifth house, in addition to the node's position in Libra. The lesson might center on the freedom-closeness area. But it also might include the **search for an ideal love** (another common dilemma in our culture) since Neptune is in Libra in the fifth house, and we have already mentioned that Chiron is in Sagittarius in the seventh house with Jupiter in the ninth house — all keys to the hunger for an ideal. The placement of Saturn in Virgo in the fifth house and Venus, natural ruler of the seventh house, in the Capricorn house conjunct Vesta, our Virgo asteroid, shows the other side of the coin of perfectionism. Letters six and ten are **looking for the flaws so they can be corrected to do a good job.** The critical attitude is highly useful and effective when applied in the job. It can be highly hazardous when applied in relationships. If we take Pallas as a key to Libra, its position in the sixth house is another repetition of the combination of factors symbolizing relationships with factors associated with work. The obvious solution, of course, is to work with people, to have work involving some kind of teamwork, and to maintain the "air attitude" toward people. Air is the spectator element. We look at the whole perspective, see both assets and flaws, try to understand it, communicate and accept. Air is not obliged to change anything except knowledge. Certainly there is ample air in this chart, but there is still some danger of the critical attitude in the close relationships whether we express it ourselves or we attract others who do it to us.

In spite of all the planets in air signs, the **possibility of Mr. Two being self-critical and consequently attracting others who would criticize him** is shown several times in the horoscope. Mercury, a primary key to identity as ruler of the Gemini rising, is in Capricorn. Moon, ruling the few degrees of Cancer in the first house, is in the Capricorn house, and also in Pisces. The Capricorn focus on flaws and the Pisces desire for perfection can express as the feeling that we should be perfect but we are not making it. It is also common for Mars (a basic key to identity for everyone) conjunct the south node of the Moon to manifest as self-doubt in the early life. Simultaneously, Mars in Libra and Mercury in the Scorpio house (both letters seven and eight indicating a deep need for other people) ties the sense of personal power (letter one) to others. In the early life, this is often experienced as **"my power is in your hands."** As we develop awareness of our own strength, we usually move toward much more confidence by the middle years. There are six different ways we can deal with the one-seven and one-eight mixtures when our own right and power to do what we please (letter one in all forms) is in the signs or houses of seven or eight. The three painful ways to handle the feeling include giving the power away and remaining emotionally dependent on others for our own sense of self-worth; trying to keep all the power; or retreating from closeness to protect ourselves. The three positive ways to handle the feeling include cooperation (sharing the power); healthy competition in games, sports or business; or helping people. The latter reassures us that we really have the power since the others are obviously weaker than we are.

Of course, **until we have worked out the issue, we can alternate between all six of these possibilities. We give in, fight, run, try compromise, compete and look for victims to rescue.** Where there is a major emphasis on letters seven and/or eight (as in this chart), it is important to do all three of the positive alternatives:

to have a place to cooperate, a place to compete and a place to help. They all assist us in gaining confidence. The competition should include the "game-playing" (not too serious) attitude, and we must win some and lose some for it to be truly competitive. Helping is best done in a professional framework. In peer relationships, it is an invitation to disaster for one person to try to save another who should be an equal. At times, individuals avoid the competitive option in the belief that competition is not "spiritual." But denying a part of the nature only leads to trouble. The buried power-drive can turn inward into illness; can be projected so that others attack us and force us to learn to defend ourselves; or can be displaced so the relationships which should have been cooperative turn into rivalry and power struggles. It really is important to do all three of the positive options.

Since there is so much air in this chart, it would be quite possible for the competition to remain on the mental level. It is a good chart for a debater. Libra suggests a **strong sense of fair play and social justice**, with the ability to see both sides of the picture and to defend whichever is being neglected. As the initial self-doubt and feelings of vulnerability to the opinions of others are worked out, there should be a movement toward immense pleasure through sharing knowledge with other people. The **verbal fluency** should be excellent, once the personal confidence is developed. Mercury retrograde in Capricorn in the Scorpio house shows **depth and thoroughness of mind** to add to the air with its breadth of interests. Often, Mercury in letter eight or ten has a **phenomenal memory**, with fine ability to handle detail. Mercury's trine to Saturn in Virgo is a further support for the practical, productive, organized mind, once the person has accepted his ability, has proved to himself that he does have a good mind. With any form of letter ten, we have to do it first to know we can do it. Until we have done it, letter ten represents the power of the universe. After we have done it, letter ten becomes our power exercised within the universal laws.

My experience suggests that most people move toward developing their capacity to express letters five, nine and eleven as they mature. So Saturn and Mars in the fifth house would tend to become more important from puberty on, while the real freedom of Aquarius in the ninth house and Aries in the eleventh house would gain in strength in adulthood. But as already mentioned, the first house Uranus arrived with a strong sense of individuality and uniqueness. The Sun and Jupiter in Aquarius as well as Aquarius in the ninth house simply emphasize the individual's tendency to develop further in that direction, toward concern for wider issues, the search for new knowledge, the resistance to limits, the equalitarian values, etc. Some of that air was clearly there in the nature from the beginning, but it will be carried much further.

The potential for **artistic talent and appreciation** is also strong with the Libra emphasis. The Pisces Moon, Antivertex and East Point in Taurus in the Pisces house, and the high focus Venus on the MC aspecting Pluto, are additional keys to a feeling for beauty and/or sensual pleasures in some form. With the air emphasis, writing is a possibility, but artistic talent might be manifested in photography, architecture, landscape gardening, music or any number of other ways. The power of the fifth and ninth houses with all three fire planets in them adds to the first-house Uranus capacity for creativity. Fire symbolizes a strong desire to do something unique, out of our own center, while Uranus wants to go beyond tradition or convention. The career might involve the aesthetic in some way, with Libra on the sixth house cusp and Venus in the tenth house along with the Pisces Moon. Certainly, it should involve a response from people in some way, doing something with or for other people. Variety and intellectual stimulation are also desired in the work, while the Sagittarius in the sixth house added to the tenth house Pisces would like something that will make a better world, closer to our ideals. Vesta in the tenth house adds its note of wanting to do something really well, though the air and fire emphasis are likely to be in conflict with the earth. Air and fire want to do something quick and easy and then to move on, to avoid boredom. Vesta added to the Saturn in Virgo and Mercury in Capricorn are in potential conflict with the restlessness. Vesta's sextile to Mercury shows capacity for integration in a practical way, but its quincunx to Saturn could mean a challenge still needing attention, or it could be another key to the need to integrate relationships and career.

As was the case with Ms. One, Mr. Two seems to have had a tenth house mother-figure. The Moon usually symbolizes the mother, though I have had a few cases where the Moon represented the father and Saturn described the mother. Mercury, one of the rulers of the fourth house, is in Capricorn which would support the fourth house being connected to father. But Saturn also is a co-ruler of the tenth house, and Jupiter, one of the co-rulers of the tenth house, is in the same sign and house as the Sun, ruler of the fourth house. A Virgo association is also present for both parents with Vesta in the tenth house and Saturn in Virgo. With this mixture of rulers of four and ten, we have, as with Case One, **either similarities between the**

parents, or one parent playing both roles some of the time.
The fourth house Leo added to Saturn in the Leo house suggests a
father who might be emotionally expressive, dramatic, ambitious,
desirous of power, or some other variation of the Leo potentials. With
both parents associated with Aquarius in the ninth house (unless one
has taken over both roles), they might also be intelligent,
humanitarian, idealistic or independent.

Since projection is a common activity, it would be possible for
the parents to have much in common but to express different parts
of the potentials. One might express the Leo warmth and the other
the Aquarian detachment. One might want power, the other insist
on equality. The symbolism is too blended in this chart to hope to
sort the parents out until we talk to the subject. Both are important
examples in the area of love and sharing, with Pluto (key to our
capacity to share the material world and deep emotions) in the house
of father; Saturn, key to father, in the house of love and children;
Mercury, fourth-house ruler, in the eighth house; and Venus, natural
key to mate, in the tenth house. **Sharing power, learning when
is enough, letting go, seem connected to father. He looks like
a role model in the area of work**, the ability to handle the material
world, whether he was very absorbed and successful in the area or
was a failure and ended up ill or dead. The aspects are more favorable
than otherwise, so we would not assume one of the drastic scenarios,
but we can never be sure until we talk to the person. Both parents
might have worked, or father might have "brought home the bacon"
while mother was active in social causes. But the chart does not suggest a mother who stayed home much. Ceres in Sagittarius in the
sixth house supports the same message we get from Moon in Pisces
in the tenth house, **idealism carried into the physical world in
some form**. We have to consider **mother also a role model for
achievement** in the material world.

If Mr. Two is able to work out his freedom-closeness dilemma
and his search for the ideal love, he is likely to have a **child as an
additional role model**, with his Mars in the fifth house. The Libra
there would want to allow equality, while Saturn in Virgo would
feel highly responsible and guilty if anything went wrong. Neptune
in the fifth adds to the **perfectionism**, which can run the gamut
from no children (holding to other forms of ideal creativity or afraid
to risk failure), to many children, with the added potential of adop-
ting children (the savior side of Neptune). **Some of the major
lessons of the life might be learned through kids or love or
other forms of creativity**. The dramatic potential of the chart is

immense, once the initial self-criticism, self-doubt and tendency to
project the power are worked through. Leo-Pisces mixtures are
among the most dramatic in the zodiac. Somewhere, this showmanship needs to manifest, whether we choose to pour it out in personal
love, to be the teacher in front of the class, the actor onstage, the
promoter, or end up as a guru. Whatever the choice, we wish him
success.

Numerology

Shifting now to a quick summary of Mr. Two's numbers, his Birth
Path is 1 - 3 - 6 with 1 as the total. There is a clear desire to be independent, using communication to offer service to humanity. The
numbers fit the emphasis in the chart on air signs in fire houses with
a strong Virgo-Vesta in the picture.

v 8 c 8 (26)	**7** TOTAL	v 9 (18) c 1 (28)	**1** TOTAL	v 6 (15) c 1 (19)	**7** TOTAL	**6** TOTAL NAME NUMBER

Analyzing the name, we find numbers 2 and 6 missing but the
subtotals bring in two "6's," the capacity for humanitarian service.
It is fascinating to see the potential number of cooperation missing
with a horoscope in which Libra is so strong, appearing as instinctive action with Mars in the sign but also as a lesson with the south
node of the Moon there, and as an ultimate ideal with Neptune joining the others while Chiron is in the Libra house. Mr. Two's name
certainly confirms the importance of relationships as a central issue
for his life. With three "1's" in the individual letters and four more
in the subtotals, the name supports the individuality of the birth date
and fits the freedom theme in the horoscope. Sometimes an emphasis
on number 1 is a warning indication of too much self-will or self-
absorption, but the horoscope reassures us that Mr. Two is well
aware of the needs of others and wants to be approved so is unlikely to abuse his power.

The number most often represented in the individual letters of
the name is number 9 with five letters and one more in the subtotals.
The emphasis on 9 points to a spiritual quest and/or very high ideals.
The prominence of the last three single-digit numbers (7, 8 and 9)
suggests a transpersonal tendency in the life, concern with humanity

or social issues; and the presence of four "3's" with their curiosity and verbal skills can contribute to a mental life as well as possible ambivalence about close relationships. The preceding combination of numbers with the scarcity of 2, 4, and 6 might also point to the need to come out of the head and deal more with the practical world. Since there is one 4 in the name, the qualities of practicality, perseverance, the capacity for hard work, etc., are not missing, but they seem less interesting than the world of ideas. As far as this short survey takes us, the numbers of Mr. Two's name and Birth Path seem to fit each other and also they fit his chart. We hope he has worked out that missing 2 and that he has an outlet for his fine creative potentials.

CHAPTER FIVE

CASE THREE

A first impression of the chart of Ms. Three might note the **interper-sonal emphasis**. The Moon in its own sign is on the Ascendant within twelve minutes signaling an **important mother-figure as a personal role model** and the likelihood of wanting to become a mother in time. Though we have only a fraction of a degree of Leo in the first house, we still might count the Sun as an additional key to personal identity (letter one which marks what we do naturally and instinctively, from the beginning of life). The Sun's placement in its own fifth house is a further identification with loving and being loved. Planets and asteroids in the signs of Libra and Scorpio (symbolizing a desire for a mate) in the houses of Cancer and Leo (representing the urge for home and family) are an additional support for the importance of the interpersonal side of life. Juno, the marriage asteroid, in Aries (another form of letter one in our alphabet), repeats the identification with the interpersonal area.

The need for close relationships with other people is present from the beginning and is likely to increase with the Sun in its own house in Scorpio. Letter five (Sun, Leo and the fifth house) indicates an area in which we want to do more than we have done in the past, to enlarge our expression in some way. Pluto and Ceres in Leo reinforce the theme again. Pluto, like Scorpio, wants a mate. Ceres symbolizes our capacity to nurture others or to accept care from others. In Leo, we may choose a mate to mother us, act as mother to our mate, or permit our children to become equals and continue adult relationships with them.

But, despite the interpersonal emphasis, no chart is totally one-sided. Mars is the natural key to identity and instinctive action, and

Mars is in Sagittarius in the Virgo (sixth) house. The combination of fire and earth seeks **independence and achievement in the material world.** Some **danger of unreasonable expectations and self-criticism** is also present, since Sagittarius is searching for the Absolute while the Virgo house is looking for the flaws in order to

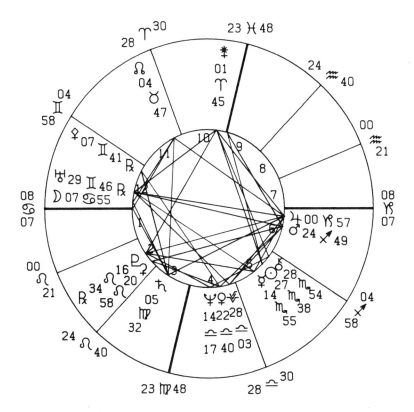

do a better job. Other pointers to idealism include Jupiter widely conjunct Mars and placed in Capricorn, again a combination of desire for the ideal and a very practical awareness of material limits. The Sun closely conjunct Chiron (similar in nature to Jupiter) is another indication of high aspirations whether they are directed to personal growth goals or to children and other loved ones in the fifth house. Two fire factors (Sun and Chiron) closely conjunct in a fire house also add to the **creativity, drama and excitement** in the nature. Their placement in a water sign repeats the likelihood of emotional intensity in the nature. The **idealization of home and/or family** and/or mate, is also shown by Neptune in Libra in the fourth house. Uranus ruling the seventh and eighth houses of partnership and placed in the twelfth house repeats the association again of ideals and relationships. We may simply make relationships the center of our lives, looking to them as the source of our faith, trust and meaning in life. Or we may try to be the perfect wife and mother. We may look for a perfect mate and children. We may pick others who are looking for perfection. If we are self-critical, we are likely to choose others who criticize us, whether parent or mate. Fortunately, there is adequate air in this chart to lessen the danger of mutual criticism in the associations, but it remains a possibility.

Idealism or high expectations are shown for both parents. The MC is in Pisces. Neptune is in the fourth house. Mars, ruling the tenth house Aries, is in Sagittarius. The Moon, a natural key to mother, is just inside the twelfth house. Jupiter in Capricorn may also repeat the theme if we take Capricorn as a key to authority figures. Mutables are connected to father, including Saturn in Virgo in the third house, Mars (ruling the tenth) in Sagittarius, and Pisces on the MC The mixture could indicate an idealistic father, a traveling father, or one so involved in work (with Saturn in Virgo added) that he is gone a lot. He might be intelligent or just value mental ability. He is a role model for the mate with Capricorn on the seventh cusp and with Juno in the tenth house. But mother is also a model for the mate since we have Venus and its sign Libra in the fourth house. **Ms. Three might want a mate like or the opposite of her parents.** She might choose **one to take care of her like a parent**, or she might **play parent to him**. Or she might **delay marriage out of anxiety that it would be similar to what she saw with her parents.** She also might **use the experiences with the parents to learn how to handle a lasting peer relationship.** We have a chance to learn with parents what to do and what not to do, and to practice the skills.

Though both parents are symbolized by Pisces — and there is some danger with this of too high expectations and eventual disappointment and disillusionment — the patterns for **mother** show much **emotional warmth**, suggesting a person even more identified with the interpersonal part of life than Ms. Three herself. **Father** has a strong earth emphasis fitting a role as breadwinner, the one who **copes with the material world**. But earth is also shown for mother with Virgo on the IC and Vesta in the fourth house. If the need to do something well was directed purely into homemaking, mother might have been superconscientious about it. Or, she might have developed the handicraft skills often associated with Virgo. We hope that she did not express the negative side of the Virgo-Pisces polarity: **illness**. A strong **artistic talent seems likely for mother**, so she may have concentrated on maintaining a beautiful home and garden, or on sewing for the family, etc. Sometimes when idealism is associated with parents, the child idealized them or they idealized the child. But the critical potential is strong enough here to require awareness in order to direct the work attitude properly into the job and not into relationships.

Ms. Three, like her mother (or grandmother) who is so important in her self-image, might maintain a beautiful home or might develop other forms of aesthetic satisfactions. The Sun-Chiron conjunction in the Sun's house suggests considerable **dramatic potential**, added to the Ceres on Pluto in Leo. While letter five may simply express as loving and being loved, procreating children, etc., there is showmanship potential in the nature, a natural stage presence. The **emotional warmth of fire-water combinations needs an outlet**: with loved ones, as a teacher, or in some creative activity that can win attention and applause. The fire in all the earth houses will eventually need to do much more than homemaking, and a suitable job would have to include some variety and independence. Fortunately, the grand trine in earth indicates **natural ability to cope with the material world**. The north node of the Moon in Taurus shows artistic talent or capacity to earn a living or to handle possessions, abilities that have been brought in from past lives but that (in the eleventh house) will be developed further in this life. The node trines Jupiter and Saturn, both keys to a lesson in reality (Jupiter because it is in the sign of Saturn), but trines suggest that the person is well able to handle the situation. Such a combination often indicates a person who has the ability to cope with the material world but who **may need to integrate the aspirations with the limits of the possible, including the reality of time limits** when one wants to be the perfect homemaker and also do something bigger in the world.

In addition to letter ten in any form (Saturn, Capricorn and the planets in or ruling the tenth house), I think the south node represents another lesson, or area for growth. We need to integrate the nodal axis, to make peace between them so they function as a partnership. Both the sign polarity and the house polarity are part of the picture. In this chart, the nodes fall in Taurus-Scorpio across the Leo-Aquarius houses, so we have a full fixed dilemma. The fixed parts of life involve **power, pleasure, possessions, sensuality**, etc. We integrate them by learning to enjoy the material world at the same time we share it with others, or, as an inner challenge, to have pleasure but also to master the appetites. The confrontation of Leo-Aquarius is one version of the freedom-closeness dilemma. We need love but also space; self-esteem that permits equality with others; passion and detached intellect. The ability to handle power is usually an important issue in the fixed dilemma. It is important that we neither give it all away nor try to keep it all. The movement of progressed Mars into the seventh house of this chart in the teen years is another flag alerting us to the power issue.

In general, a strong emphasis on the interpersonal area of life points to the possibility of increased emotional vulnerability. The more we need other people to feel good about ourselves, the more we are in **danger of giving up some of our rights to maintain harmonious relationships**. There is too much strength in this chart to give up the power forever, but if the idealism and security needs were too high, it might have taken time (and a job outside the home) to fully realize the personal strength. We really do not know whether the power has been projected until we talk to a person who has an emphasis on the interpersonal side of life. In projection, we credit others with strength (or whatever quality is involved) and we doubt our own capacity. Unfortunately, the more we block our own capacity, the more the other person is likely to overdo the projected activity. When the situation becomes uncomfortable enough, we change. Pain is a warning signal that we need to change our attitudes or our actions. At the same time, it is important not to swing to the opposite end of the polarity. Where power is concerned, the other end would be to try to keep it all, attracting weak people who are willing to be dependent. The same issue could be faced through children or through mates. That is, we might have very strong or very dependent children though strong ones seem more likely. It would be important to compromise and share the power and pleasure along with the responsibilities.

Venus, ruling the fifth house and conjunct Vesta along with Jupiter, ruling the Sagittarius in the fifth house, but placed in Capricorn in the sixth house, could mean taking the family as the primary job; working with children; tension over the desire to do a really good job with both family and work outside the home; need to let the children develop their own work skills by helping share the responsibility; and many other variations.

As already indicated, the Taurus-Scorpio polarity may mean a **need to integrate indulgence with mastery of the appetites**. For some people, the challenge involves dieting versus overeating. Others struggle to cut down on smoking or drinking, debate sex versus celibacy, spending versus saving money or collecting possessions, etc. One primary challenge with Scorpio involves "**knowing when is enough**" or "**when to let go.**" The instinct is to keep on going to the end. The repeated theme shown by Pluto in Leo, Sun in Scorpio, and Scorpio in the Leo house, marks an intensity in the emotional nature that requires awareness and direction. The presence of Mercury in the combination is helpful since Mercury symbolizes the conscious mind. Usually, Mercury in Scorpio indicates introspective people who tend to analyze themselves and everyone else. It also shows psychic ability, though the rising Moon in Cancer is one of the strongest signs of the capacity to be open to the feelings of others. Normally, such a Moon placement would be manifested as a deep mutual psychic openness to a mother-figure in the early life, and later to one's own children. The active fourth and twelfth houses also add to the likelihood of psychic ability. It is through the unconscious, symbolized by water, that we receive information beyond that of the physical senses and logic. That water sensitivity is part of the vulnerability of the interpersonal part of life which includes two water letters, four and eight. I consider letter four to be partly personal (the need of the baby to be cared for) and partly interpersonal (the capacity to care for others).

The Scorpio emphasis in the chart became highlighted in a new way when Ms. Three moved to the Los Angeles area. We carry our natal chart with us, wherever we go, but a new residence provides us with an additional set of houses calculated for the new locality. The Greenwich time is the same, so the planets are not changed, but they may be placed in different houses, and new angles of the chart (MC, etc.) are acquired. Ms. Three's chart for California gives her an Aquarius MC with Pluto almost exactly on the IC. A water planet on an angle in a chart is one of the strongest indications of potential psychic ability, so this location adds further emphasis to Ms. Three's potential development of this talent. Also, while Moon and Neptune tend toward more passive receptive psychic talents, Pluto symbolizes the urge toward self-mastery which may lead an individual with a prominent Pluto into self-hypnosis or other forms of controlled exploration of the unconscious and the world beyond.

We have not mentioned Uranus which is widely conjunct the East Point in Gemini in the twelfth house. I read all water in a chart (planets, signs and houses) as potentials in the nature which have been brought in from from past lives and which are present in the unconscious from the beginning of this life. I also consider the East Point to represent a form of letter one, instinctive self-expression. But Uranus also seems to represent a future-oriented factor. Like the Sun and Jupiter, Uranus seems to mark an area of life that we will pursue increasingly in the future. The Sun (and its sign and house) mark our need to be proud of ourselves, to do more than we have done in the past, and to win attention or approval for it. Jupiter and Uranus (and their signs and houses) seem to be long-range values and goals that may not come fully into manifestation until we are adult, or even into middle-age. In this case, Uranus in Gemini in the twelfth house with the East Point suggests **wide interests in the unconventional or nontraditional**; interests that are present from the past but, since it is Uranus, that will be developed further in this life. The quincunx of Uranus to Sun-Chiron in the fifth house may be experienced as a freedom-closeness issue. How much should we remain conventional wife and mother, and how much time and energy can be spared to pursue the curiosity about the mysteries of the world? Of course, Scorpio wants to probe the depths also, and Chiron is searching for Truth with a capital T, while Uranus rules the houses of the mate. As is common, the combination is not simply a conflict between one planet which represents one side of our nature and another planet which symbolizes a different side. Both sides (or desires) are represented by both (all) the planets involved. We have already mentioned that Mercury in Scorpio is especially likely to dig into the unconscious or the past, yet it is in the house of love. We are all really working on the same dilemmas. How do we put together all twelve sides of ourselves and have room for it all?

Summary

Perhaps we can summarize Ms. Three as a very warm, caring person with well-above-average psychic ability and a strong need to express through the interpersonal side of life. She is likely to have depth and thoroughness of mind, a good memory and good ability to handle detail, though the Saturn in the third house often has to prove the mental ability first before accepting that it is really there. The fixed emphasis shows a very strong will and tenacity, but there was some danger of projecting the power in the early life. Learning to claim her own strength may have come partly through early peer relationships if she had an older sibling who had power over her (with the Saturn in the third house) or by helping take care of younger siblings or other people who were close to her. She might have compared her own mental ability with her father's, or measured it against his demands. Saturn's aspects are mostly harmonious, but there is still some danger of too high expectations (her own or others) and of too much focus on flaws. With her fire in the earth houses, Ms. Three would be likely to find her strength through a job outside the home. Then the challenge is to find the time to do it all well. But the skills seem present to handle the world. Just remember my favorite motto. "It's OK to be human, on the way to perfection, and to enjoy the journey."

Numerology

When we examine the numbers associated with Ms. Three's birth date and name, the Birth Path presents us with a 2 - 1 - 22 (or 4) to give a total of 7. The "2" starts us off with a desire for a mate, which certainly fits the Libra-Scorpio emphasis in the horoscope. The "1" immediately counters with a need to also find independence somewhere in the life. "1" is the pioneer, capable of "going it alone." The "22" for the year of birth is a master number seeking power. I think of it as somewhat like Capricorn but it might also have some Scorpio qualities. When not manifested on the higher level, the "4" may be conscientious and careful, concerned with basic security and the ability to handle needed details. Even numbers, in general, seem to be more like earth and water in astrology while odd numbers are more like fire and air. The total for the Birth Path is a "7," a number I find often ambivalent, seemingly pulled between spiritual aspirations and human relationships, with perhaps extra potential for imagination and psychic openness. These qualities seem very appropriate for Ms. Three.

v 2 (20) c 8 (17)	**1** TOTAL	v 3 (12) c 4 (13)	**7** TOTAL	v 6 c 9 (27)	**6** TOTAL	**5** TOTAL NAME NUMBER

Looking next at the name, we see a striking emphasis on the odd numbers. Ms. Three's individual letters include five "3's," seven "5's," and three "9's," a striking preponderance out of nineteen letters. The subtotals add two more "3's" and two more "6's," with one of every other single digit number plus one "11." The picture emphasizes creativity, dramatic potential, expressiveness and spirituality, with the slight extra emphasis brought by "6" for humanitarian service and the urge to teach shown by the "11." The "5's" are almost evenly divided above and below the line (present in both vowels and consonants) so we can conclude that Ms. Three not only has the inner drive to be creative and warmly expressive and dramatic, but that she is manifesting those qualities in the outer world. Two of the "9's" are below the line, being expressed in the world, but one "9" in the vowels fits what we know from her horoscope, that the spiritual drive is also a deep, inner desire. The "3's" are all below the line, so we would expect her to be outwardly friendly, verbally fluent, expressive, with some potential for writing or teaching and possibly a love of travel. The totals for the three names are "11" for the inner urge, repeating the desire to expand knowledge and share it with others, and "3" below the line suggesting she is actually following through on the sharing of knowledge though its scope may be more limited than she likes, being manifested largely with people in the vicinity. "5" as a final total sums up a warm, loving, dramatic person with a lot of restlessness and need to keep reaching for something more.

CHAPTER SIX

CASE FOUR

Our first impression of Mr. Four notes a **mutable dilemma** in high focus, with the Virgo Ascendant square Mars in Gemini on the MC and Saturn in Sagittarius on the IC. The three mutable planets, Mercury, Jupiter and Neptune, form a grand trine in earth signs in water houses. The Moon and Chiron, which I interpret as much like another Jupiter, are conjunct Jupiter in the eighth house, while Sun is conjunct Mercury and the IC in a very close opposition to Mars. Though the Sun and Moon are in cardinal signs and in cardinal and fixed houses, the strong configuration with all the mutable planets aspecting the two lights and the angles of the chart puts further emphasis on the importance of the mutable dilemma. The earth-water mixtures indicate a **strong need for security**, whether we are more focused on our own security or very concerned for the protection of others. The mutable emphasis suggests the **importance of the mind**.

The mutable dilemma includes the Mercury-Gemini-third-house **interest in everything**; the Vesta-Virgo-sixth-house **need to do something well** and to get tangible results; the Jupiter-Sagittarius-ninth-house **desire for Final Truth**; and the Neptune-Pisces-twelfth-house **potential for mysticism, oneness with the whole**. Among the common forms of the mutable dilemma are **problems in deciding what is true, valuable, most important in the life**, so the person may scatter a lot. Where there is strong earth, as in this chart, a more common form of the dilemma is a **conflict between the high aspirations and the limits of the material world**. Unlike the first type of mutable dilemma, such people know what they want; they want more than is possible! Other common forms of the dilemma include a **lack of faith** and consequent anxiety or depression. Another danger involves **putting one's faith into a small part of life** which becomes an idolatry and lets us down. Fortunately, people with a mutable emphasis are normally highly intelligent and versatile. They can learn vicariously, from reading, from using logic or just from watching life, so they can usually understand the problem and resolve it.

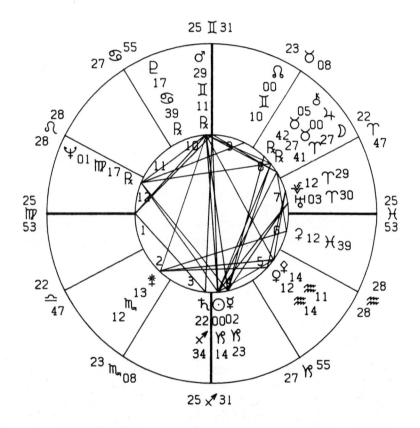

In spite of the probability of a very practical, capable mind shown by the earth in the chart, it is very **possible that Mr. Four had initial doubts about his ability**. Note the theme of letters three and ten combined in three different ways in the chart. Saturn is in the third house. Mercury is in Capricorn. Gemini is in the tenth house. It is also common for the south node of the Moon to be experienced as similar to Saturn, as a part of life which requires effort and attention, where we feel secure only after we have proved to ourselves that we can handle the issues involved. In this chart, the south node in the same sign and house as Saturn is a reinforcement of the **need to develop the mental ability in a systematic way**, to include knowledge and communication as part of the career, to find ways for the faith to manifest in the world immediately around the person.

Lessons in handling the intellect and faith are likely to have come early in life through a father figure or other relationships such as siblings, uncle, etc. With such a strong association between letters three and ten and also between four and ten with Cancer in the tenth house and Capricorn in the fourth house, added to the Virgo rising, Mr. Four **probably learned to work very young**. He might have had other relatives who played the parent role, or he might have been responsible for the care of younger relatives. Sometimes with such patterns, a parent is ill or missing. Saturn in a mutable sign and house often shows a traveling parent. But sometimes the parent is committed to the Puritan work ethic, and may be critical, rigid, domineering, judgmental, narrow or some other variation of the principle.

The chart suggests **strength for both parents**, with Mars and Pluto in the tenth house, Sun in Capricorn in the fourth house, Moon in Aries in the Scorpio house. Both parents may also have been religious or had high standards and expectations, since the Moon is conjunct Jupiter, Ceres is in Pisces, and Saturn is in Sagittarius. Pluto in the tenth house and Moon in the eighth house might suggest that mother died young, but letter eight may simply mean concern with joint resources or shared power. I am tentatively assuming a tenth-house mother since Cancer is placed there, and a fourth-house father with Saturn in the sign on the IC and Capricorn in the fourth house. If this theory is correct, the **father figure is a personal role model** with Mercury, ruler of the Ascendant, in the fourth house. But Mars, the natural ruler of the first house, is in the tenth house, so we have a **mother-figure also as a role model**, reflecting parts of us back to let us learn about ourselves. The oppositions across the fourth and tenth houses suggest some tensions between the parents whether they involved power struggles, concern over security, or illness or death that impacted the family. Often, the third-house Saturn or south node is a key to problems involving another member of the family. Whatever the details, **the first few years look eventful**, as progressed Ascendant squared Mars, MC, Sun, while progressed Mars opposed Sun-Mercury, and solar-arc directed Saturn moved across the IC.

Though our initial attention was given to the mutable emphasis in the chart, there is clearly a cardinal dilemma as well. Mars and Saturn are cardinal planets close to angles (which always carry the cardinal quality regardless of sign). We also note the Sun-Mercury in Capricorn square Uranus in Aries. Since we have a reverse zodiac here, signs mostly in their opposite houses, the Capricorn in the Cancer house and Aries in the Libra house, give us a full cardinal grand cross. The power issue has already been noted as connected to the parents and as an important part of Mr. Four's early life as he strove to find ways to use his own power. The freedom-closeness dilemma is also part of the picture, with Uranus in Aries in the seventh house square the Cancer house Sun. Uranus, Aries, Jupiter, Chiron, as well as Venus and Pallas in Aquarius, all represent **an attraction to independent mates**. Moon, Taurus, Sun and fourth house want **stability and security**. If we are not conscious of our ambivalence concerning such issues, it is **common to project one side of ourselves and to attract someone who will express it for us**. For example, if Mr. Four remained conscious of his need to work, to be responsible, etc., he might attract a "free soul" who would be willing to let him carry most of the load. It is common for the Virgo rising person to attract a Piscean person with faith that God (or the mate) will handle everything. But with Vesta, a Virgo asteroid in the seventh house, Mr. Four also wants a worker, so if he consciously wanted a capable person but unconsciously picked a victim, he would feel let down.

Of course, the Pisces in the seventh house and Jupiter-Chiron in the eighth house are also **looking for an ideal mate or an ideal relationship**. As has been indicated in other cases, we may continue looking for perfection and never feel satisfied. We may pick others who are looking for perfection. We may choose victims. We may stay in a relationship and stay frustrated, or we may repress our dissatisfaction and get sick. The solution to the complicated mixture of freedom, wanting a mother (Moon in the eighth house), looking for an ideal, wanting a worker, wanting sensual pleasure or material assistance (Taurus in the eighth), and so on, can be solved by choosing someone who is practical and independent but who shares similar ideals and goals. Such a choice would require giving up some of the power and being willing to compromise, but it would be worth it. It is highly improbable that Mr. Four would be happy with a weak person, despite his temptation to play "Atlas" at times. As one more important key to choice of mate, Juno in Scorpio in the Taurus house shows an attraction to someone who would be strong and sensual.

The two asteroids, Juno and Ceres, form a grand trine with Pluto in water signs in earth houses. Added to the grand trine already mentioned in earth signs in water houses, the chart shows **ample ability to cope with the material world**. Water can express as either dependence or nurturance. Earth feels uncomfortable if the individual is not achieving tangible results in the world. Virgo and Capricorn especially **need to do something well**. Taurus is willing to relax and enjoy the physical world. If Mr. Four were not sufficiently in touch with his own Taurus, he could project it (as already suggested) and pick a mate who would let him do the work while she enjoyed the fruits of the labor. With the Moon in the eighth house, Mr. Four's **mother-figure was in some way a role model of what he was looking for or avoiding in his choice of mate**. Sometimes we are consciously doing one but unconsciously doing the other. For example, we may think we want someone the opposite of mother, but actually pick someone much like her. The chart shows a conflict within the mother, with Ceres octile Moon, though Moon is sextile Mars in the tenth house. As already suggested, the chart suggests that mother was a strong person, but she might still have blocked her strength and ended up ill. If she remained in too much conflict between her strong need for freedom (Aries Moon and Mars in the tenth house) and her idealism and work ethic (Ceres in the sixth house in Pisces), passing on might have been the only way she could escape. Or, father might have been the one caught between the responsibility of the Capricorn and the Sagittarius yearning for something better, and he might have taken off in one way or another, leaving mother to handle both parental roles. Normally, earth-water trines such as those in this chart indicate a life of material security while cardinal squares (partly formed by cardinal planets and partly by houses and signs) show an eventful early life with major changes periodically. We never know the details of the life from the chart alone. We just see the issues, that Mr. Four is **learning to have space for his need to work and provide security without totally denying or projecting his independence; that he is learning to share the power and the pleasure; that he needs to make peace between his aspirations and his realism**.

The **identification with work** has been mentioned in passing, but it is worth another look since it is a good example of a theme — a repeated message in a chart. Virgo is rising. Mars is in the tenth (Capricorn) house. Mercury, ruling the Virgo, is in Capricorn. Antivertex and East Point are also in Virgo. We do have Venus, ruling the Libra in the first house, in Aquarius in the fifth house, bringing in the capacity for freedom and pleasure, but the rest of the keys to letter one are heavily weighted toward work and the danger of self-criticism. Letters six and ten both want to do a good job, and to accomplish that, our first instinct is to **look for flaws so we can correct them**.

Flaw-seeking is a very useful occupation when done in the occupation. When we do it to ourselves (or relationships), it can be a drag. For all people identified with Virgo or Capricorn, I suggest a sign prominently displayed: **"Is this my job?"** We can't do everything well. Part of the mutable dilemma involves being clear about what is important so we can do one or two things well and keep the rest of our life for fun. The need to have reasonable expectations has been mentioned repeatedly, and the probability is that one or more family members provided an example of either what to do or what not to do in the setting of goals. The same issue seems important in later personal relationships.

In addition to the importance of harmonizing the peer associations, Mr. Four may have had **lessons through children** since Saturn rules the fifth house. With the Capricorn-Aquarius mixture in the fifth house, we have many possible variations with kids. Saturn in Sagittarius wants to be the perfect father of perfect children, but the Aquarius and Saturn's position in an air house may have helped to permit equality, nonjudgmental understanding and acceptance. However, the danger was also there of feeling too responsible and attracting a variety of problems. When we are willing to take on the "Atlas" role, we may have children who are willing to let us. "Let Dad do it." Or, we may have kids who rebel and do the radical things our solid earth-water finds uncomfortable, But usually, Venus in the fifth house really enjoys the family, and Aquarius lets them become friends, so the odds are pretty good that Mr. Four would be able to work out his love life.

After all that has been said about the importance of work, including the likelihood of learning to work very early, we have not commented on the type of career that would be suitable. People with earth-water trines usually are attracted to a **field that provides security**, whether they supply material needs to the public (and that can include almost any business) or whether they choose a service profession that aids or comforts people. Pisces in the sixth house is attracted to **activities that help the world or make it more beautiful**, but the range may be anything from medical fields such as pharmacy to the persuasive arts, from music to oil-based products to shipping, and infinitely more. Mars in the tenth house would like to be an **entrepreneur**: to work as an individual in some way. Pluto in the tenth tends toward a **managerial role** that involves others. Both Mars and Pluto are often attracted into medical fields, but they are equally at home in engineering, or repairing cars or computers. Uranus, ruling the sixth house and placed in Aries, also supports a martial career, which could be literally armed services though the Cancer-Capricorn mixture might want more home stability than is promised by the military life. As usual, there are lots of options, and the chart only points up the issues. There is enough fire and air connected to the work rulers, including the Saturn in Sagittarius in the third house, Mars in Gemini in the tenth house, and Uranus in Aries in the seventh house ruling the sixth house, that Mr. Four **needs variety, independence, intellectual stimulation and communication** in some form in his work. But there is enough earth and water to require a job which offers some security. There is also enough faith and talent (the two grand trines we mentioned earlier) to be **quite successful**, though if the aspirations are set too high, he may never be satisfied. (Remember the mutable dilemma where we started.)

Summary

To summarize some of the highlights of the horoscope, the earth and water trines show someone to whom security is very important, someone likely to learn to work early, and with the capacity for success but a danger of too high expectations. With the Virgo Ascendant square Mars and Saturn, there were probably some self-doubts or self-criticism in the early life which may have been connected to problems with authority figures. Mr. Four may have learned to trust his own ability early by helping others in his family, but then had to learn to play some of the time. If he projected the fun-loving, free side of his nature, he could have attracted mates or kids who overdid it for him. If he kept on looking for the ideal job or mate, he might have waited a while before he found his air potential, the ability to take things lightly and to take turns. But he has a very good practical mind and should have found ways to share the power and the freedom with his relationships. Being clear about his goals might have been a challenge, but it seems more likely that he needed to learn to enjoy the small steps toward the big goals, to enjoy the journey. And if he claimed his own Venus (did not project it), he may have learned that as early as the teenage period. I think that we develop our fifth house more after puberty.

He did go through a long period with progressed Saturn opposite the MC when the ambitions and aspirations may have been in heavy confrontation with the limits of the material world. As this book is written, Saturn has reached the opposition to Mars. Some years ago Mars reached the opposition to Saturn. So Mr. Four may still be working on integrating personal drive with the limits of personal power. From other current patterns, he also seems to be working on the area of relationships with Venus sextile natal Venus but conjunct Vesta and quincunx Juno. Progressed East Point and progressed Juno are also conjunct the south node of the Moon to repeat the current importance of a lesson involving peer relationships. The solution lies in sharing the work and sharing the pleasure. Hang in there, Mr. Four.

Numerology

Turning to the numbers for Mr. Four, he has a Birth Path of 3 - 3 - 2, with a total "8." The three carries a strong mutable flavor for me, showing the importance of learning and communication. The two needs partnership: others to share the life. With "8" as a total, the life goal is associated with some form of power, whether over the material world or people or knowledge or the Self.

v 1 (10) c 6 (24)	7	v 6 (24) c 9 (27)	6	v 9 c 6 (15)	6	v 0 c 1 (10)	1	2
	TOTAL		TOTAL		TOTAL		TOTAL	TOTAL NAME NUMBER

The three names include all nine letters. If we add the letters individually, the total for the whole name is an eleven, supporting the horoscope emphasis on versatility and the strong drive to share knowledge with the world. If we sum each name first and then add the three names, the total for the whole name is a "2." Perhaps the details of the life will offer evidence supporting which system is more accurate. Or perhaps we are just seeing another open-ended issue in which the details of the life depend on the person's choices. Manifesting on the "two" level would imply an interpersonal "face-to-face" focus, while an "eleven" expression would be more transpersonal, dealing with the public.

Individual letters emphasize the odd numbers: one, five, and especially nine. The odd numbers seem more like air and fire in the horoscope, emphasizing creativity and restlessness. Seven, another odd number, is high in the subtotals, appearing in the first name, twice in the last name, and again in the total for the whole name. As indicated with other cases, I suspect that seven is a mixture of the spiritual quest and need to pay attention to relationships; perhaps at times, a key to conflict between these two areas of life. Such an interpretation would fit the horoscope of Mr. Four. With two spiritual planets in the houses of partnership and the third (Neptune) ruling the seventh house and in its own house, it was imperative for Mr. Four to find a mate who shared his values and goals. If relationships were not comfortable, there might easily have been a flight into work or into spirituality. Six, a number associated with service to humanity, is also strong in the subtotals, appearing once in the first name and twice in the middle name. Nine, the essence of the quest for something higher, is present in six individual letters of the name and in two subtotals. The spiritual path is clearly a major issue, shown by both the horoscope and the numerology. Remember to enjoy the journey toward the Absolute.

CHAPTER SEVEN

CASE FIVE

The interpersonal area of life seems highly important to Ms. Five, though Aries and Taurus are strong enough to provide a healthy degree of awareness of personal needs, and the first house brings in the transpersonal with Capricorn rising and Saturn in its own sign in the house of Pisces. A **father figure is suggested as a personal role model** with Capricorn on the Ascendant, and the placement of Saturn in the twelfth house could point to a father who was artistic, idealistic or a victim in some form. Since Saturn is part of a grand trine to Neptune and Ceres (and more widely to Venus), **father is more likely to have been idealized or idealistic** though we can never rule out one of the variations of victim such as ill, alcoholic, missing, etc. We can speculate that the tenth house symbolizes father since Ceres (usually a key to mother) is in the fourth house in Taurus, and the Moon in the Taurus house supports a **mother concerned with letter two** in some form. Mother might focus on money, or material possessions, or appetites, or artistic activity, and, of course, Ms. Five is also likely to be concerned with one or more of these areas. Mother might also be idealistic, whether involved with a conventional church or holding high standards, since the Moon is in Pisces, and Jupiter and Chiron are both in the fourth house. But the Pisces-Taurus mixtures are especially likely to be **concerned with the aesthetic part of life**, whether the feeling for beauty is expressed in a lovely home, in gardening, in poetry, or music, or whatever.

With the tenth house considered a probable key to father, the placement of Juno in Scorpio in the tenth indicates **father as role model for mate**. Juno is the marriage asteroid, and Scorpio is one of the signs of partnership, calling for attention to our capacity to share the material world with a mate. The south node of the Moon conjunct Juno in the tenth house points to a **lesson involving the sharing of power and/or pleasure and possessions**. If the lesson is learned through the relationship with father, we have minimal

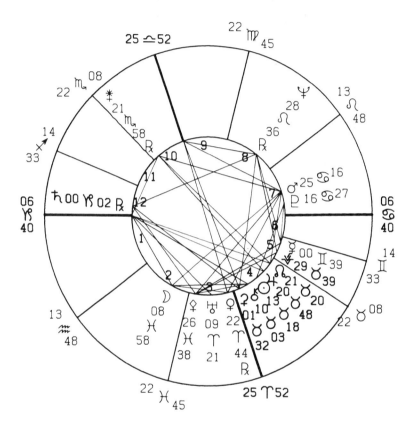

problems in the later relationship with a mate. If we haven't worked things out with father, we go on working on the issues with later peer relationships, either personal or in our career. The Taurus-Scorpio nodes call for an integration of our capacity to handle the material world for our own pleasure with an ability to share it with others. We are successfully integrated when we can earn part of our own needs and handle them wisely but can also give, receive and share for mutual pleasure. There is also an internal form to the Taurus-Scorpio polarity: the need to balance appetite indulgence against mastery of the appetites. Whether the focus is dieting versus overeating, smoking or drinking versus cutting down or stopping, sex versus celibacy, spending money versus saving, the goal is moderation. We should be able to enjoy the material world without being obsessed by it.

Normally, **when we find a key issue in a chart associated with the parental houses, planets or signs, we come to a family where we experience the issue through the parents**. We have a chance to see something in our own nature acted out by the parents. If the latter handle things well, we have a good example. If there are problems with one or both parents, we are provided with a negative example. Venus and Mars rule both the fourth and tenth houses, so are a key to both parents. As has been indicated in other cases, such a combination might mean that the parents are like each other in these areas, or one parent might play both roles some of the time. Both Mars and Pluto (the latter another ruler of the tenth house) are in the seventh house in Cancer, so **both parents are again associated with partnership**. We may learn to handle peers through our experience with the parents. Or we may maintain an adult, peer relationship with one or both parents. We may pick a partner like a parent or the opposite of a parent. We may play parent to a partner or want the other to take care of us. The solution involves taking turns with the parental role, achieving interdependence.

With Venus in Aries square Mars in Cancer and the East Point axis, as well as quincunx Juno in Scorpio, we have our common **freedom-closeness dilemma**. It may have been an issue with parents, or they may have been more concerned to work out the handling of power. The placement of Mars in the seventh house is a warning flag, indicating a **need to deal with personal power in interpersonal relationships**. Our six options (also discussed in other cases) include three painful and three positive potentials. We may give our power to others and look to them to take care of us. In the past, most cultures encouraged that attitude in females. We may try to keep all the power. Or we may retreat from closeness to avoid the danger of being hurt. On the positive side, we may share the power, learning to compromise and have teamwork. We may gain strength and confidence through healthy competition in sports, games or business. Or we may help people. It is important for the assistance to be professional. Personal relationships are poisoned if there is no mutual give-and-take. To handle the Mars in the seventh house, it is wise to have a place in the life for all three of the positive forms of handling power with others.

With Aries in the third house, **some of the personal power**

to do what we please is also connected to siblings or other relatives in the early life. If the person projects that self-confidence and spontaneous action, it is possible to have siblings or others in the early life who are very independent, assertive, strong-willed, etc. With projection, the other person almost always overdoes whatever we are blocking in ourselves. Sometimes with a ruler of the parental houses (Venus in this case) in the third house, we have a sibling who plays parent to us, or we have younger siblings that we take care of. But Aries can also indicate sibling rivalry, perhaps over the attention of a parent, and occasionally it indicates an only child. There is always the "do-it-yourself" potential with Aries so it sometimes marks a sense of "aloneness," whether we choose it consciously or attract it unconsciously. With Venus and Uranus in the third, it is more common to eventually have pleasant relationships with the collateral relatives, though the Uranus square the Ascendant and Venus square the East Point could be rivalry initially. Sometimes with such a mixture, there are several siblings. We may be very affectionate with some and rivals of others. The highly occupied fourth house often marks a large family, whether it is the one we are born into or one we create ourselves.

Water-earth combinations are the fertile ones, so the potential is here for several children. With Jupiter and Chiron both in the fourth house, home and/or family are likely to be highly important. Though both Jupiter and Uranus like to roam, the strong Taurus — including Ceres, Sun, and the north node of the Moon placed in the fourth house, are likely to indicate a sense of deep roots. Travel may be acceptable so long as there is a stable home to come home to. On the whole, **this chart is more attached to home base than any in our sample.** A large extended family is one possibility — that is, lots of cousins, aunts, uncles, etc. But Vesta in the fifth house requires some attention. Vesta tends toward an all-or-none attitude. It symbolizes the need to do something really well and can mark a real tunnel vision. In the fifth house, individuals may decide that unless they can give all the attention to children, they will not have any. In this chart, it would seem more likely that the person would give the lion's share of the attention to the home and family, and might only consider work outside the home after the kids are older. Vesta in the fifth can also indicate very capable children, while Mercury suggests intelligent kids and a good capacity for communication with them. People with Venus ruling the fifth generally can enjoy their kids, or they might share the artistic talent so strongly suggested in the chart.

Neptune in Leo repeats the **association of love and ideals**, and its placement in the eighth house connects ideals to the partner. As with the parents, we have a choice of picking someone artistic, someone with high standards whether or not religious in a conventional way, or someone who is a variety of victim. We have to guard against too high expectations in ourselves or in others, but the emphasis on Taurus and Cancer in this chart make unrealistic expectations less likely. The handling of power and pleasure is a more likely area requiring attention. The fixed letters of our alphabet all relate to sensuality and pleasure in different ways, but the Vesta (symbolizing some danger of inhibition) in the fifth house square Neptune (representing spiritual aspirations in some form) in the eighth house is another statement of the same principle mentioned for the Taurus-Scorpio polarity. There is a **need to integrate personal forms of pleasure with those desired by the mate.**

The other common issue of **conflict patterns between factors representing work** (Vesta) **and relationships** (fifth house, eighth house and Leo) has already been discussed but might be amplified. For the generation of Ms. Five, the proper female role was considered to be wife and homemaker. A major focus in the houses of the interpersonal part of life would support acceptance of that role. Juno and Scorpio in the tenth house can symbolize marriage as the primary role in society. Mercury, ruling the sixth house, placed in the fifth house along with Vesta, the natural Virgo asteroid, can support work with children, whether our own or those of others. Venus, ruling the tenth house, has spent many years progressing through the fourth house, again reinforcing the focus on homemaking. The Moon, ruling the seventh house of the partner, placed in the second house of personal resources, may feel that personal needs are provided by the mate. The Capricorn rising and Saturn, ruling the Ascendant in its own sign, show a need to accomplish something bigger in the world, including a desire for tangible results, but almost immediately after birth Saturn retrograded into Sagittarius, and it remains in the twelfth house, offering the possibility of spiritual work; some sort of service to humanity that might be a gift. But there is a hazard in this possibility of dependence on a mate. We have mentioned that **one of the challenges for Ms. Five is to discover her own strength and to be able to share the power.** The primary element mixture in the chart is earth and water: earth signs in water houses and water signs in earth houses. This combination is very **security conscious** and tends to feel somewhat insecure when totally dependent on others. Both earth and fire need a sense of power in their own hands. So, sooner or later, Ms. Five needed to get out into the world and do more than homemaking. We only know we have abilities when we manifest them. Since the progressed Sun has been moving through the sixth house of the chart for many years, it seems likely that Ms. Five is on her way to discovering her strength. If she took care of younger siblings when growing up, she may have found it much earlier.

The general **emphasis on the interpersonal area of life** would befit a **career working with people in some way.** Teaching is one obvious possibility, but Ms. Five's mind is original enough to represent a danger of boredom in ordinary teaching. Scorpio in the tenth house may also be drawn to healing work, as can Saturn in the twelfth house. But the Taurus-Scorpio emphasis may also work with fields such as banks, accounting, trust funds, insurance, etc. Real estate would be another possibility, with the strong fourth house, or interior design with the artistic potential. She should have a **quick, sharp mind** and (when she lets it express) a **quick, sharp tongue.** But the water emphasis in both signs and houses is likely to **hold back out of reluctance to hurt others.** Taurus also really wants life to be comfortable. Though Mercury in Gemini tends to be **interested in everything** (as does Uranus in the Gemini house), Mercury's conjunction with Vesta adds the potential for **thoroughness and skill with detail.** I also often find close Vesta aspects in charts of people with psychokinetic ability, including a talent for spiritual healing. The Sun conjunct Chiron, and Jupiter more widely, suggests growth toward **increasing involvement with knowledge and/or spiritual interests.** The Sun marks our growth potential, areas where we want to expand our capacity beyond the talents brought in from past lives. Mercury and Vesta in the Sun's natural house also support **growth in mental ability and general competence.** The importance of growth in mental ability, and a search for something higher as a source of self-esteem, are both reinforced by Jupiter moving into Gemini and into the fifth house.

Summary

In summarizing the horoscope of Ms. Five, the central themes point to interpersonal relationships and artistic talents. She had something to learn from father about sharing power and/or pleasures, and about ideals or faith. Mother may have been concerned with material security or pleasure or beauty, but also is much connected to the search for an ideal. Trying to guess the details in the life from the horoscope is rather futile since there are so many possibilities associated with each of the twelve principles. Sometimes letters nine and twelve simply represent far-off goals and places, so the parents might have come from another country. But the family looks very important as a center of the life. A major challenge for Ms. Five involved learning to share power and pleasures with a mate, learning how to be truly an equal rather than alternating between parent and child. Since she has a good mind, the capacity is present to understand the issues and to work them out. The fire in the chart is mostly tied to earth or water, so there is some danger of it expressing largely in the creative mind. But she may need to move the body more. The choice of an artistic career would have been appropriate, though helping people make their life more comfortable and pleasurable may be as mundane as work in a boutique, selling cosmetics, clerking in a record shop or other prosaic jobs. The chart combines a very down-to-earth side of the nature with a hunger for higher things. To integrate the two, it is important to enjoy the journey toward the heights. Usually, Taurus can do that.

Numerology

Shifting to the numerology for Ms. Five, her Birth Path is a 5 - 3 - 3 which give a total of 11. The combination is highly mental, with the potential of creative, artistic talent, good at verbal expression, and with a strong urge to teach. But the preferred choice would be teaching in an unconventional setting, or sharing nontraditional knowledge. "11" is called a "master" number and seems to operate much like Aquarius.

v 2 (11) c 2 (11)	**4** TOTAL	v 2 (20) c 8	**1** TOTAL	v 6 c 3 (12)	**9** TOTAL	**5** TOTAL NAME NUMBER

When we inspect the letters in the birth name of Ms. Five, the first name impresses us with a total of "11" both above and below the line, showing the urge to teach as an inner desire that is likely to be manifested outwardly. Adding the two "11's" gives a total for the first name of another master number, "22." I think "22" is much like Capricorn, symbolizing a drive to reach the top and to be in a power position controlling part of the material world. Since Ms. Five has Capricorn rising, the name seems very appropriate. If we fail to manifest the master numbers on the higher level, they are reduced to the single digits "2" and "4." Instead of doing something unique in the world with "11," we stay in tandem and operate as an equal in association with others. When we reduce the "22" to "4," we focus our attention more on personal and family security than on the world scene.

The second name has a "2" above the line for the inner drive and an "8" below the line for the outer expression, with a "1" total. Ms. Five does want a mate and also is likely to strive for some degree of power in her own hands. We are reminded of the fixed dilemma emphasized in her horoscope. The final "1" repeats the drive toward some form of uniqueness or independence. The last name has "6" above the line, willing to give humanitarian service to those near at hand; "3" below the line for the talent with verbal communication; "9" as a total for the urge to seek something higher in life, the spiritual quest. The total name sums to "1" above the line, again wanting to be in front; "4" below the line, showing the capacity to handle the ordinary world, including the focus on home; and "5" as a total for creative warmth, love and power. The individual letters particularly emphasize "5" and "6," fitting the attention to personal attachments and service to those near at hand, but with this, the urge to have variety and drama. "2," "4" and "8" are not present as individual letters but do appear in the subtotals. The overall picture seems to fit a person much involved with other people, with talent for artistic expression and for the sharing of knowledge with many others.

CHAPTER EIGHT

CASE SIX

My initial impression of Ms. Six includes a house focus on the transpersonal area complicated by a stellium in the sign Cancer. The transpersonal third of our twelve sides of life includes letters nine to twelve, but the remaining two mutables, letters three and six, also have some transpersonal tendencies since they are primarily mental so less emotional and personal. Mercury, Gemini and Virgo, and the third and sixth houses, tend to be aware of the world, though their focus is on the world more immediately around us rather than the long-range view. In this horoscope, the house emphasis is strongly transpersonal, backed by the power in the third and sixth houses, especially since the planets and asteroids there are largely in the work signs and include Saturn and Vesta, both keys to concern with earth matters. Even the Moon, the only planetary factor in an interpersonal house, is in the transpersonal sign, Aquarius.

When the Aquarius Moon is added to the stellium in Cancer in the Pisces house, we have a **strong need to integrate the interpersonal and the transpersonal**. Some women choose to have a family first, and then to enlarge their nurturing role through work in a field such as nursing, teaching, social work, child care, etc. Some choose the helping profession in place of marriage and a family. Some adopt children, which may include marriage to someone with children by an earlier marriage. With Pluto and Jupiter, rulers of the fifth house, both in the twelfth house, there is a strong **tendency to idealize love and children**, but as readers know by now, such an attitude may manifest in many different details. The person who idealizes her own family will want to be the perfect mother of perfect children, and may have a large family. Another with the same high ideals may not have any children for fear of falling short of perfection (and the fear is not always conscious but is all the stronger if unconscious). Some individuals are drawn to work with young people, whether they teach, heal, become housemother in an institution, etc. When we have this idealistic drive, it is also possible to unconsciously attract children of our own who need to be "saved," so we may have children who are ill, emotionally disturbed, very dependent, etc. As has been said before, it is wise to be a professional savior if we want to make a better world. Even though the helping professions have a high rate of burnout, playing savior in one's personal life is much more painful and too often much less effective.

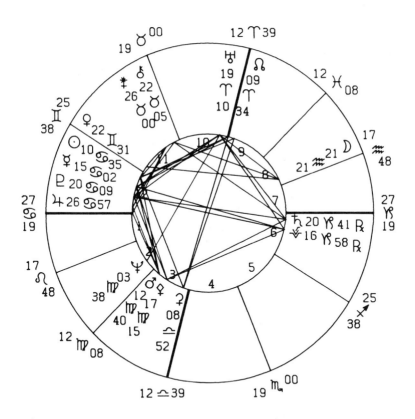

In addition to the transpersonal emphasis with its high idealism and need to be involved in the world, the Cancer side of the nature is also challenged by the need for personal freedom shown by the Aquarian Moon and the Uranus in Aries, dominating the chart from the tenth house. Close aspects, Moon quincunx Pluto and Uranus square Pluto, emphasize the **danger of conflict between the need for space and the need for closeness**. In cases where the conflict is unconscious, drastic events are possible such as loss of babies (miscarriage, stillbirth, etc.). In such cases, the individual is very conscious of the desire for children, but unconscious of the fear of losing freedom or of failure to do a good job. Mars, a co-ruler of the fifth house of love and children, is in Virgo, and a Vesta-Saturn conjunction in Capricorn in the Virgo house is a double-whammy **need to do everything flawlessly**. We note that Saturn-Vesta are also opposite the Cancer stellium (work versus home and family) while Mars, that fifth-house co-ruler, is quincunx the MC, again the **possibility of conflict between career and love**.

It is also possible for the individual to have taken the mother's role early in life by caring for siblings. Mercury, one ruler of the third house of collateral relatives, is in Cancer, the sign of the baby-mother relationship. Ceres, another key to our capacity to mother others or to accept mothering, is also in the third house, along with the south node of the Moon, another form of letter four. The south node indicates a lesson of some sort: something to learn and then something to give. A combination such as this in the third house may be called on to help care for siblings or others who are ill, younger, or just less capable and they may decide they have done enough mothering in the early life. It is **common for an earth-water emphasis such as we find in this chart to attract a situation in which the person plays Atlas and carries the world for a while**. But eventually, the Aquarius Moon and the strong Uranus in Aries will almost certainly shrug.

In a personal counseling session with Ms. Six, we would discuss her **relationship with a mother-figure as an important key to her sense of personal identity**. Both the Cancer rising and the Sun, ruler of the Leo in the first house and placed in Cancer, indicate a mother or grandmother as a personal role model. We may want to emulate them if we have a positive relationship, or we may want to do the opposite. The **mother-figure shared the freedom-closeness dilemma**; Ceres is on the Moon's node in Libra and the Moon is in the eighth house, all connected to the interpersonal area of life. But Ceres is trioctile the Moon, showing conflict within mother, and the Aquarius added to Venus, ruler of the fourth house, being placed in the Aquarian house, shows the freedom side of the mother. If the mother was able to resolve the conflict, Ms. Six had a good role model. If the mother did not resolve this issue, she demonstrated "what not to do." She might have denied her need for a life of her own and remained totally committed to relationships. Or she might have neglected her family to pursue wider interests, friends, knowledge, etc. Or she might have stayed frustrated that she could not do it all. But since the mother is strongly connected to air — Ceres and Venus, ruler of the fourth house, in both an air sign and an air house while the Moon is in an air sign — the mother may have been highly intelligent and versatile and managed to handle it all. Still, Ms. Six had something to learn from or with the mother, with Ceres on the south node of the Moon.

Assuming that the tenth house is father, my tentative theory because Ceres is in the fourth-house sign, the chart also shows **inner conflict in the father figure**. Uranus in the tenth house is square Saturn, natural key to father, and Mars, ruling the tenth house, is quincunx the MC. When planets in a house are in conflict aspect to planets ruling it, including natural rulers, it shows conflict in that part of the life. The combination suggests a very **work-oriented father**. Mars is in Virgo; Saturn is in Capricorn, in the Virgo house, and conjunct Vesta, our super-Virgo asteroid. But Uranus in Aries also wants **freedom and self-will** in action, and Venus (a ruler of both fourth and tenth houses) is in the eleventh house, repeating the Aquarian theme. Father might be so wrapped up in his work he was rarely there for the family. Or he might manifest the critical, work attitude in the wrong place and be impossible to please. Or he might never find a job that satisfied him and become ill to escape the responsibility. Or he might want to be in control and force others to do all the compromising. If Mother was true to the air emphasis suggested for her, Ms. Six might have taken her for a negative role model and refused to give in to father's demands, or decided against marriage since it seemed too one-sided.

Father is a role model for mate, with Capricorn on the seventh cusp, which might mean we want a mate to take care of us, to give us what father did or didn't do. Or we might avoid marriage as a threat to our control over our own life. Or we might (unconsciously) pick a weak person so we could keep the power in our own hands. Sometimes, we try several of these options in succession, looking for a solution. That is, a person might first marry a strong father figure, have power struggles, divorce, then marry a weak person, get tired of being Atlas, stay single a while, etc. The solution, of course, is to take turns being father with the mate, to compromise and share the power. If there is unfinished business with either parent, it is a good idea to explore the unresolved feelings, to see whether they are still influencing actions. We may have to forgive and release the past.

Still another option, with these patterns of keys to both parents involved with signs or houses of mate (letters seven and eight), is a continued, adult relationship with the parents. For example, a family business is one possibility. Or the person might work in the same field as the father, even though they do not work together. Working for the government is common, whether local, state or national, with Saturn or Capricorn ruling either of the work houses, but Uranus in Aries in the tenth and Venus ruling the tenth but placed in the eleventh house both suggest a need for more independence in the career. Unless the work is varied, with some personal freedom of action and intellectual stimulation, the person is likely to change it periodically. The **fire-earth conflict** shown by Uranus in Aries square the Capricorn-Virgo mixture, and by Mars in Virgo quincunx the MC in Aries, is **between the practicality, productivity, thoroughness, precision, need for tangible results, etc., of the earth versus the restlessness, independence, low threshold of boredom, resistance to taking orders, etc., of the fire.** We have to find some kind of compromise in which we have some stability-security but also some variety. The earth wants to do something really well, while the fire wants to keep moving. If father was able to work out his conflict in this area, Ms. Six got a good example of how to do it. If father stayed frustrated, took it out on the family or himself, or ran away, he offered an example of how not to handle things.

The **strong idealism** that is such a basic part of the identity for Ms. Six is shown by Jupiter exactly on the Ascendant as well as by the Sun, ruling the first house, in the twelfth house. As mentioned in earlier cases, my favorite motto for such "I should be perfect" people, is "I'll be God tomorrow." The Gauquelin research has found the rising Jupiter in actors and politicians who tend to take the stance "I am God already and have the right to do what I want" or "the world should give me what I want." This version of the one-nine or one-twelve combinations was most often present in the Nazi leaders. But I think when a study is mounted of spiritual leaders or simply deeply spiritual people, we will see the other side of the coin. Certainly it is the "I ought to be perfect" side that I see in my clients, and they need to keep the high goals but accept the reality of human limitations. It is a long journey to perfection. As long as we are on the way, doing the best we can to move toward our ideals, it is proper to enjoy the journey.

If the cardinal dilemma in this chart were in cardinal or fixed houses, we would concentrate our counseling on the issue of human relationships, handling power and the freedom-closeness struggle, including the need to integrate career and relationships. But since most of the cardinal signs are in mutable houses, the mutable dilemma is centrally involved, hence the emphasis on ideals. It seems likely that one of the most common forms of the mutable dilemma may need to be integrated: **ideals and the limits of what is possible.**

Not only are the mutable houses involved, but Jupiter is a central part of the cardinal T-square, and Neptune in Virgo is octile-trioctile the T-square. Chiron, our idealistic asteroid, is more harmonious in the chart, with trines to the earth and sextiles to much of the Cancer, but it does conjunct Juno and square the Moon, repeating a possible freedom-closeness challenge, or stability-security versus risk-change, as well as bringing the issue of idealism into the attitude toward a possible mate. Since Taurus in the Aquarius house is normally fairly logical and practical, Chiron may simply suggest a high value placed on relationships.

Sometimes, Juno and Venus in the eleventh house, along with Aquarius in the seventh and eighth houses, may substitute friends for marriage. For a successful marriage to be sustained, the **mate should be a competent worker** (Saturn ruling the seventh house in an earth sign and house and conjunct Vesta and Uranus ruling the seventh and eighth houses in the tenth house) and he should be **able to communicate and be intelligent** (Aquarius in the seventh-eighth plus Venus and Juno in the Aquarian house with Venus in Gemini). Pallas in Virgo repeats the need for a practical worker while its position in the Gemini house repeats the desire for intelligence, equality and communication. Neptune ruling part of the eighth house in Virgo in the Taurus house again reiterates the desire for a capable, practical person. But Jupiter, co-ruling the Pisces in the eighth house, and Pluto, natural ruler of the eighth house, are in Cancer in the twelfth house, marking a desire for emotional warmth and idealism in the relationship. That massive Cancer nesting urge must be expressed somewhere, whether in helping work or in an idealistic personal relationship.

The **importance of the mind** has been mentioned several times. The nodes across the third and ninth houses mark the perpetual student, teacher, writer, traveler. Individuals with this pattern are ready to satisfy their curiosity anywhere, any time. Virgo in the third house takes the mind seriously; works at it. Sometimes the person is self-critical, especially with the south node there to suggest some self-doubt at the start of life. Individuals may have a relative such as a brother or sister who is very capable, and they compare themselves to their own detriment. Or the opposite may be true. There may be a relative with a problem, and the subject of the chart may discover personal ability through helping the inadequate family member. Either way, the earth emphasis in this chart suggests a person who started life quite able to cope with the material world despite the conflict between the earth and fire.

Mercury, another primary key to the mental ability, when placed in a water sign and house and conjunct a water planet, indicates considerable psychic ability: openness to the unconscious through which we receive information that does not come through the physical senses or through logic. So Ms. Six seems to have the mental capacity to handle life successfully. She is likely to be interested in new and unconventional areas, but also to be quite capable of keeping one foot solidly on the ground. But the rising Jupiter added to Aries in the ninth house marks a special identification with the search for Truth with a capital T. In the end, she will have to find her own answers to the nature and meaning of life.

We have not mentioned the auxiliary Ascendants as yet. The Antivertex is in Gemini, in the Aquarian house, repeating the **intellectual curiosity** about the world. The East Point is in Cancer in the twelfth house exactly conjunct the Sun. The latter combination is like a rising Sun, supporting the **great emotional warmth** in the nature and also indicating **natural dramatic instincts**. However, the strong earth and water in the chart might have put a thumb on the showmanship. The **creative imagination** is clearly present, but may have been subdued much of the life. We hope that it has found an outlet by now. Remember, the Gauquelins found the rising Jupiter in actors. But it is sadly common for individuals with an earth water emphasis to hold back on the fire. The fire may be expressing in an individualistic career with Uranus in the tenth house and Mars in Virgo, or Jupiter may be manifesting as a personal search for Truth, or the Sun may be seeking to heal and help the world. Somewhere, that capacity for warmth, creativity, spontaneity and enthusiasm should be functioning.

Numerology

Turning to the numerology for Ms. Six, her Birth Path is a 7 - 3 - 5 with a total of 6. "7" is the number I question, with its possible meaning of ambivalence over relationships versus spirituality. Certainly, that issue is present in the horoscope. The "3" has a Gemini quality for me, marking a need and a capacity for learning and communication. The "5" tends to be creative, changeable, warm, expressive. The "6" total for the Birth Path is a statement of the "service to humanity" theme that is so strong in the chart of Ms. Six.

v 7 (16) c 1 (19)	**8** TOTAL	v 6 c 6	**3** TOTAL	v 6 c 3 (21)	**9** TOTAL	**2** TOTAL NAME NUMBER

Shifting to the numbers of the name given at birth, we find individual letters for every number except the "4." This omission seems puzzling, since the horoscope certainly shows the ability to be practical and productive, to cope with the material world and its details. But it is true that there is a conflict shown in the chart between the earth and the fire. Three "1's" and four "5's" in the name strongly support the fire in the nature, some "above the line" for inner talents and desires, and some "below the line" for outer expression or manifestation. It is possible that the emphasis on number "6" in the name might provide some substitute earthy practical accomplishment. Although there is only one individual letter that is a "6," there are three "6's" in the subtotals. Three more "1's" also appear in the subtotals, making that the strongest individual number. (I use the term "subtotal" for the vowel and consonant summaries in each name and for their sum for each individual name, so each word in the name has three subtotals. The "total" name number is the sum of the whole name.) The accent on individuality is certainly emphatic and fits the high-focus Jupiter, Uranus in Aries, and Aquarian strength coming through planet, sign and house in the horoscope. In general, the numbers seem to complement the chart, though the absence of "4" leaves us with a question. Of course, absence of a number does not mean total inability to handle that part of life; it alerts us to an area for attention. And the Saturn placement in its own sign in the Virgo house conjunct the Virgo asteroid is also a statement of a lesson connected to earth. I took Saturn to mark more a danger of staying in conflict between the fire and the earth or the water — the possibility of overdoing the earth at the expense of spontaneity and creativity and freedom. But it could also express as pendulum swings between the extremes until the different areas of life are integrated. If "4" turns out to be closer in meaning to a focus on security through home and family, the lack of a "4" in the name might prove a clue to the choice of a transpersonal life rather than the role of homemaker. We will see what the life has manifested, to clarify these questions.

CHAPTER NINE

CASE SEVEN

In the horoscope of Mr. Seven, our attention is immediately caught by the close Neptune-Ascendant conjunction with Jupiter more widely involved in the combination in Leo in the first house. Pope John Paul II is one of the better-known current leaders who shares this Jupiter-Neptune conjunction in Leo. Since these two planets both symbolize the **search for the Absolute**, a rising conjunction suggests an **intense concern with spiritual issues from the beginning of life**. Neptune remained on the Ascendant by progression for many years of the life, emphasizing the greater importance of the unconscious hunger for ideals. As has been noted repeatedly, letter twelve can manifest as an artist creating beauty in the world, as a savior trying to make a better world, or as a victim who wishes the world were more ideal but who is waiting for God to do it or looking for inner peace in ineffective ways. Jupiter was widely conjunct the close Neptune-Ascendant at birth so it is possible that the conscious search for truth was less important in the early life. But progressed Jupiter retrograded back to reach Neptune some years ago, suggesting an increased conscious focus on the desire to understand life. Jupiter will continue to conjunct Neptune and the Ascendant for many years more, symbolizing the continuing importance of faith in the life of Mr. Seven.

The **identification with the search for ultimates** is also said in the chart by the Sun, ruler of the Ascendant, being placed in Sagittarius. The emphasis so far is intensely on fire, with the water planet, Neptune, adding its element. Strongly fire people are usually **enthusiastic, dramatic, spontaneous, fun-loving and creative**.

The water addition brings in **empathy and sensitivity to**

others, which is often missing in fire. The primary feeling in fire could be stated as "I know what I want and I have the right and power to do it. Now that I've done that, I want to do something new." Both fire and water are emotional, but fire expresses the emotion while water tends to hold it in until sure it is safe to do something. Concern may be for the security of oneself or of others. Since both

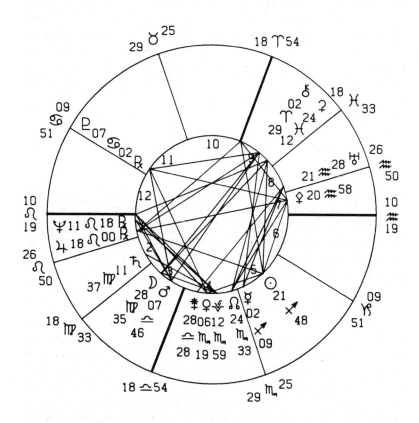

Neptune and Jupiter represent the issue of faith in a Higher Power, individuals who have such faith will face anything, dare anything, try anything, confident that God will take care of them. But prominent planets simply highlight an issue. In some cases, a high focus on Neptune or Jupiter may indicate a need to gain faith in a Higher Power. When rising, the person may be identified with God, trusting only personal power, or feeling that he or she has the right to do anything they desire. The other side of the identification with God is the feeling that one ought to be God (perfect) so no mistakes are allowed. To fall short in any way is unforgivable. It is possible for that feeling to almost paralyze action. "I can't do it unless I can do it perfectly. I will wait until I can do the great, super achievement. Anything less is beneath me."

Normally, a chart with strong fire will not hold back in this way. It is the heavily water charts that tend to hold back. Earth also tends to be cautious until confidence is developed by successful action. With two fire planets (Jupiter and Sun) in fire signs in fire houses, the fire emphasis in this chart is more likely to **invite risk-taking**. But with both parents symbolized by Virgo (Moon and Saturn in the same sign), Mr. Seven was undoubtedly **confronted by the constraints of the material world at an early age**. Vesta in the fourth house repeats the **association of Virgo with the parents**, and Venus, ruling the tenth house, is also in the sign. Virgo parents might be hardworking, whether from necessity or commitment to the Puritan work ethic. They might be too critical of themselves or others. They might be ill. Several planets in the third and fourth houses often indicate a number of siblings as well as the potential of forming one's own family. Saturn in the second house and Taurus-Scorpio in the parental (fourth-tenth) houses suggest **attention to security needs in the early life**. Usually, placement of the rulers of letters one, four and ten in Virgo indicates an **early introduction to work**. Growing up on a farm is one possibility. Everyone has chores and learns to work early.

As in some of our other cases, **siblings or other relatives are likely as role models**. Mars in the third house is occasionally an only child, but this is rare when in a sign of relationships such as Libra, and also rare with the Moon in the third house. With Mars, we may have sibling rivalry or we may project our own power into others, but a Venus-ruled sign and Mercury, ruler of the third house cusp placed in Sagittarius in the fifth house, both suggest the capacity to have fun together. Libra in the third house may mean we have an opportunity to learn how to handle peer relationships with these early family members and neighbors. Or we may remain in contact into our adult lives, in effect, turning siblings into partners. Or we may take the siblings as models for what we want or what we wish to avoid in our later choice of mate.

The Moon, in an air house, suggests a parental quality in the early peer associations. Mother might have been like a peer or remained a partner into the individual's adult life (Libra and Scorpio in the fourth house). Older siblings (or other relatives such as uncles, aunts, etc.) might have acted as parents, or Mr. Seven might have been called on to care for younger relatives. In view of the high focus on personal freedom suggested by the rising Jupiter and Sun ruling the first house in Sagittarius, such duties might have been resisted. But if the search for an ideal was expanded to include the well-being of others, Mr. Seven might have successfully integrated his independence and his capacity for nurturance. The interpersonal part of life was clearly highly important for Mr. Seven in his early years.

If the freedom-closeness dilemma was not resolved with the early family relationships, it would be faced with potential mates. Pallas and Uranus in Aquarius in the seventh and eighth houses want an open accepting relationship, closer to a friendship than most traditional marriages. Yet Venus and Juno in the fourth house want a deep emotional commitment with a spouse like a mother. If the subject is not conscious of the ambivalence over two conflicting desires, it is common to project the unconscious one and to choose a mate who will "do it for us." For example, we may stay conscious of our need for space and pick a mate who clutches and tries to possess us. Or we may be aware of our need for a deep emotional attachment and pick a mate who wants more independence. We resolve the issue when we are both conscious of the ambivalence and can compromise somewhere in the middle. I have seen similar charts of people who maintained an adult relationship with the early family in place of marriage, or who turned their friends into family. And there is always the potential for the Pope's choice: marriage to the Church. Chiron in Aries repeats the identification with God and the need to personally find the final truth about the world, including the need for freedom to pursue the quest. Chiron closely trine Mercury in Sagittarius indicates a quick mind engaged in the quest.

However, in spite of the independence and the idealism, there is enough emphasis on the interpersonal signs and houses to suggest that Mr. Seven would **want to experience the domestic side of life**. The need for close relationships is especially strong when connected to the personal identity (letter one) as it is here with Mars in Libra and Sun (ruling the first house) in the fifth house, as well as with Leo rising. Also, the East Point, another form of letter one, is in Cancer along with Pluto, a ruler of the fourth and fifth houses. The identification with letter five (five-one mixtures) may lead to love being the center of the life. A large family is possible, including the potential of famous children. But it is also common for five-one combinations to have a single child and then (like typical fire) to say, "Now I've done that, I can do something else." We have to talk to the person to find out whether they have made the family an ultimate value (in which case a large family is likely though they might also adopt children), or whether there is a need to save the world in some large way and a reluctance to have children if the individual cannot be a perfect parent.

If a person with a one-five mixture does have one or more children, **one will usually be an important role model**, offering a mirror to reflect back part of the parent. Children might be bright with Mercury and Sagittarius in the fifth house and Jupiter in Leo, or very idealistic (Neptune and Jupiter in Leo and Sagittarius in the fifth house), or very independent, creative, dramatic, fun-loving, expressive, etc. I would recommend charades as a family pastime, so that everyone could have a turn onstage getting the applause. Of course, other elements are also involved in the fifth house. Pluto ruling the cusp is in Cancer showing sensitivity though its house brings in detachment. Mars, ruling Scorpio on the cusp of the fifth house, is in double air (sign of Libra and house of Gemini), supporting intelligence, communication and the importance of relationships. On the whole, I would expect Mr. Seven to have fun with his kids and to be very proud of them. And before we leave the area of offspring, Ceres in the ninth house might mean playing parent to grandchildren. The ninth house is the fifth house from the fifth house so shows the children of children. Since we can never know the details from the horoscope, it would also be possible for Ceres in the ninth house to mean spiritual work that nurtures the world rather than one's own kin. But if Mr. Seven has children, he is likely to also have at least one adored grandchild who might also be a role model. We have Aries in the ninth house.

So far, the major challenges mentioned have been the freedom-closeness struggle and the danger of excessive expectations of the self or loved ones. The first issue can be handled by compromise: a committed relationship that still permits some space. The second issue is resolved by enjoying the journey toward the ideals, not waiting until we reach them to be happy, and by having some small goals along the way to provide a sense of progress. Saturn in double earth (sign and house) is a strong reinforcement of the **lesson involving ideals, calling for realism in handling job, (Virgo), money, pleasures, appetites, possessions, etc.** (second house). Saturn also rules the sixth (Virgo) house while Taurus is in the Capricorn (tenth) house, repeating the lesson of learning to deal realistically with the material world. Such an emphasis does not mean that the individual is not capable of handling the physical world. There may be ample ability with the Virgo Moon, but the lesson may be in living comfortably and happily within the limits.

The nodes of the Moon across Taurus-Scorpio reinforce the lesson of earth, whether the primary challenge is in handling the job or possessions and pleasures. For some people, the challenge is to learn to share the power and pleasures with others. A fire-earth emphasis often indicates an "Atlas" feeling, with difficulty in accepting dependence on others. But the strong air in this chart makes this less likely. Uranus in its own sign, Juno in Libra, and the Antivertex (as an auxiliary Ascendant) in Gemini in the Aquarian house are in a close grand trine in air suggesting the **capacity for teamwork** and letting others do their part. Mars in Libra also normally can take turns unless the person lacks faith and retreats from others or feels safe only when in control. It would be possible to project some of that air into a mate, but an identification with some of it seems likely.

The other common lesson of the Taurus-Scorpio nodes involves an **inner resolution of appetite indulgence versus appetite control**. Whether we struggle with overeating, drinking, smoking, sexing, spending money, collecting possessions, etc., the goal is moderation — the ability to enjoy the appetites without being controlled by them. The combination of fire and fixity emphasized in a chart are especially likely to lead to some sort of excesses. One of the lessons of Taurus and the second house is the ability to enjoy the world as it is, even though it is far from ideal. As has been mentioned in other cases, it is also important for individuals identified with the Absolute to accept their own humanness, their inevitable failings, on the journey to perfection.

With earth signs in the earth houses, Mr. Seven needs a **vocation in which there are tangible results.** Though Aries on the MC and Capricorn on the sixth-house cusp would **prefer a position of power in the job**, Mars in Libra in the third house suggests **working with other people** in some way, while Saturn in Virgo suggests a **service to others**. Mr. Seven should have a good ability to handle details since Pluto-Saturn-Vesta have sextiles or trines to each other. Letters six-eight-ten are the obsessive-compulsives of our twelve sides of life, and the planets are the most important form of the different factors we use. Unfortunately, ability does not necessarily mean we will enjoy details. The fire emphasis in the chart as well as the air trines would **like to skim the surface and move on quickly**. It would be a highly suitable chart for a freelance salesman with the fire enthusiasm and charisma and need for variety, the air verbal fluency, but with the capacity to handle the details needed to discuss the product. Earth is the weakest element in the chart, and the main lesson area, but the Moon trines its south node and Jupiter trines the MC so there is fine ability for success if Mr. Seven can hang on to his patience and remember the need for bite-sized goals.

With the fire and mutable identification, Mr. Seven **might have traveled widely**. Or he might have journeyed in the mind, through reading. Teaching and writing are potential talents and would be the next choice of career after sales. Usually, writing offers less security, and Mr. Seven does need a rooted home with the Scorpio in the fourth house. The ideal solution for that aspect of the freedom-closeness dilemma is a permanent home with a chance to travel. Since Mr. Seven was born in another country, he has obviously expressed his travel potentials to some degree. It is interesting to note that he maintained a fire sign on the MC when he moved to California (his Sun is conjunct the MC in the ninth house in the Los Angeles area), and he replaced his rising Neptune with its sign, Pisces, on the Ascendant in Los Angeles. The same basic themes appear in the local chart: the **personal idealism**, which could expect too much of the self or of life, and the **lesson in earth**. Capricorn is in the tenth house and Saturn is in the sixth house in the Los Angeles chart.

Summary

To summarize the themes we have been discussing, the chart pictures a warm, emotionally expressive person with great potential magnetism, charm and verbal ability. The major challenge may have been the need to integrate the high aims with the limits of living in a material world. There is ample ability to be successful; the question would be whether Mr. Seven was ever satisfied for long. But there is enough fixed emphasis in the chart to enjoy the journey once the 9-12 idealism accepts the fact that it will take time and effort to reach the ultimate. Fire is the "fun" element when the person is able to do what he or she wishes immediately, and then to move on to a new impulse, but no one can do that all the time. We hope that Mr. Seven was able to work out the freedom-closeness dilemma since he could have had a very good time with some outstanding children. He needed to learn moderation in some form, but hopefully without destroying his sense of humor, enthusiasm and creativity. He should be in a leadership role! He was born a ham, and if the earth world has not dampened his fire too heavily, he should be onstage somewhere.

Numerology

It's time to inspect the numbers for Mr. Seven, and looking first at his Birth Path, we see that it is 3 - 5 - 2 which give us "1" for a total. The odd numbers are emphasized, fitting the air-fire emphasis in the horoscope. We have the "3" for verbal facility and an optimistic, easygoing attitude; the "5" for the Leo drama and creativity; a "2" for a desire for a mate to share life; and the "1" total for an insistence on being in front of the pack.

v 2 (20) c 2 (47)	**4** TOTAL	v 2 (11) c 8 (17)	**1** TOTAL	v 1 (19) c 6 (15)	**7** TOTAL	v 6 ___ c 5 (23)	**2** TOTAL	**5** TOTAL NAME NUMBER

Mr. Seven has four names, so we have 30 individual letters and 16 subtotals. Again, the emphasis is clearly on the odd numbers which are like fire and air. "1" and "5" are present five times each, making up a third of the individual letters, fitting a chart dominated by Aries and Leo or their rulers or natural houses. The other odd numbers include four "3's" for versatility and artistic expression, three "7's" for imagination and the pull between people and the spiritual quest, and five "9's" for the hunger for the Absolute with its danger of wanting more than is possible. The strongest even number is "8," present in four letters, fitting the Scorpio emphasis in the horoscope, suggesting the urge toward mastery in some form. Two "6's" support humanitarian feelings, and there is one each for "2" and "4" so all numbers are present. The subtotals are especially impressive because they include four "11's," the master number that seems to be similar to Aquarius in many ways, marking the urge to find knowledge beyond the ordinary and to share it with others. Subtotals also include two more "1's" and two more "5's" to further emphasize the personal will, energy, restlessness and intensity. The overall impression one receives from the numbers certainly seems appropriate in light of our discussion of the horoscope of Mr. Seven. Both the numbers and the chart suggest someone who would want to stand out in the crowd. We hope he is there.

CHAPTER TEN

PALMISTRY OVERVIEW

Palmistry as a Key to Character

My discussions of the other ways to describe life and human nature are far more theoretical than the material on astrology. I have read a good bit but have had only limited experience with these other models. However, even my limited experience has demonstrated clearly that the same problem is present in the other models that has been described in astrology. Most practitioners in palmistry and many in handwriting analysis and in numerology try to be too specific in their interpretations. They try to guess the details instead of dealing with the basic principles. Sometimes their details are right, especially if their psychic ability is working at the moment. Often, they will guess wrong. But even when the guess is correct, it is not helpful. The message to the person is that life is fatalistic, that those things had to happen, that there were no alternative options. I think it is just as true when working with palmistry and the other models as it is with astrology, that **character creates destiny and that we can change our character**.

Examples are usually helpful to bring abstract principles down to earth. One clear example comes from a lecture given by a supposed "expert" on palmistry. The speaker made a flat statement that a line connecting the **Mount of Mars** with the marriage lines under the little finger (the **Mount of Mercury**) was always an indication of divorce. A middle-aged woman in the audience held out her palm to confirm the presence of such a line. The speaker agreed that she had a good example of the line and anticipated her statement that she was divorced. However, the woman said firmly that she and her husband had worked out their difficulties, that they had been married for many years and it was highly unlikely that they would ever consider divorce.

If we interpret the Mount of Mars as similar to the nature of Mars in astrology, and if we accept the horizontal lines under the little finger as keys to marriage, we might theorize that a line connecting Mars and marriage would be a symbol of a potential freedom-closeness dilemma. But to jump to the conclusion that the urge toward freedom to do what we please would inevitably end in divorce is clearly a risky prediction. It is quite possible to resolve the freedom-closeness dilemma. Many people learn to compromise, to maintain a commitment which still allows each individual some space.

Another example was described by one of my clients just a few days before this section is being written. My client's horoscope showed a danger of overvaluing relationships, a tendency to be too loyal and devoted to friends and to expect too much from relationships. Jupiter, Neptune and/or Chiron in signs or houses of relationships can show a danger of putting our faith in people rather than in God, and consequently being let down when the people turn out to be human. I had discussed that danger in an earlier interpretation of the chart for this woman client. Her return a few days ago was to sort out her feelings of being betrayed and hurt when trusted friends had let her down during the intervening months since I had seen her. She understood the problem (too much faith in other people at the expense of faith in herself and in God), but she still experienced the hurt and was not sure how to proceed in dealing with the relationships. Understanding is a first step, but we still have to change the character (the attitudes and actions) before the destiny changes. She was working on making the changes but was finding it difficult, though it was helpful to know why the hurt could occur and what she could do about it.

Palmistry came into the conversation when she commented that she had been told that a certain palmist was "really good!" With her tendency to trust people, including overrating their knowledge, she went to the palmist with great faith that he would be accurate and would help her. But, from what she said, he gave little information that was of any value. His principal statement which fit her life was that she "would be betrayed by friends." She agreed that this had happened, but a statement such as that, specifying a detail, without offering any insight into why such an experience could happen and how to prevent it from occurring again, can hardly be considered helpful. If she had not had the insight from her horoscope, the interview with the palmist would have left her feeling like a helpless victim, destined always to be betrayed by friends.

How Much Do Our Models Overlap?

If my theories are correct, astrology, palmistry, numerology, etc., offer different models of the same subject, different ways to describe life and human nature. The important question is whether each model selects different aspects of the shared subject (life) for emphasis, or whether the models are like different languages using different words for the same aspects of human nature. In other words, does the Mount of Mars on the palm symbolize the same human drive as Mars in a horoscope? Or, are they really quite distinct? Or do they have some qualities in common so there is overlap, but they still have some basic differences? Only much additional work will answer that question.

Correspondences between Astrology and Palmistry

Many individuals working with palmistry and astrology have assumed that there is an exact correspondence between the factors (fingers, mounts, lines, etc.) in palmistry and the factors (planets, signs, houses etc.) in astrology. Fred Gittings, author of *The Hand and the Horoscope*, presents one version of this viewpoint. I feel that the issue is still undecided, and the following pages should be considered highly theoretical, needing much more work to either support or fail to support the ideas.

My limited experience to date suggests that the correspondences between astrology and palmistry and numerology are moderately close, but I disagree with the usual linkages offered in books that compare two models. I think that the mounts and/or fingers with the same names as the planets do have much in common with their namesakes, though I believe there has been a reversal of the finger assigned to Apollo (Sun) and the **Mount of Venus**.

Readers who are already familiar with palmistry will know that the index finger and the slightly raised area at its base are connected to Jupiter. The second (longest) finger and the area on the palm just below the finger are traditionally associated with Saturn. The third or ring finger and its mount or raised area have been assigned to Apollo (a God associated with the Sun in ancient Greek myths), while the little finger and its mount were given to Mercury. The raised area (or mount) at the base of the thumb is assigned to Venus and the raised area opposite the thumb, on the other (distal) side of the base of the palm, is connected to the Moon. I think that the Moon association is probably accurate, but that the mount below the thumb is more like the Sun principle.

The Sun and Moon are the two lights in astrology, seen as almost equal size from Earth's perspective (though we know that the Sun actually dwarfs everything else in the solar system). The Sun and Moon are usually given a little extra weight in an interpretation of a horoscope, and the larger mounts at the base of the palm would fit this view. The two joints of the thumb are sometimes unassigned and sometimes given to Mars. The first joint is considered a key to willpower. Certainly, astrology's letter one (Mars, Aries and the first house) is associated with an emphasis on will. The second joint on the thumb is theoretically a key to the intellect, and might symbolize Mercury, though the little finger is also considered to be of a Mercury nature. At this point in my exploration, I am not sure of these correspondences. It is possible that the joint on the thumb is more like the Gemini Mercury while the little finger is closer to the Virgo Mercury. (Gittings suggests these relationships.) This second thumb segment is traditionally supposed to indicate the capacity for logic, reason, tact, etc., all potentials of the conscious, reasoning mind (Mercury). But Gemini is not noted for tact, tending to be outspoken unless modified by an earth or water emphasis, and the second joint of the thumb is only considered a sign of tact when it is quite narrow.

We could make a logical case for the whole thumb symbolizing the Mars principle if what is described as "tact" is actually inadequate self-confidence and consequent need to avoid open confrontation with others. A thick, bulbous thumb like a "club" has been called a "murderer's thumb," but in company with other modern palmists, I am skeptical of such detailed interpretations in palmistry as in astrology. Of course, in a horoscope, Mars in conflict aspects to other planets may indicate a person who expresses aggression outwardly or inwardly. The former might occasionally be a murderer; the latter has headaches, fevers, accidents, surgeries, etc., when the personal power is turned in against the self. If physical violence can be associated with a certain type of thumb, Mars may fit at least the first joint of the thumb. The traditional **Lower Mount of Mars** lies on the palm just above the thumb. If we decide that the thumb

Traditional Mounts and
Lines and Fingers

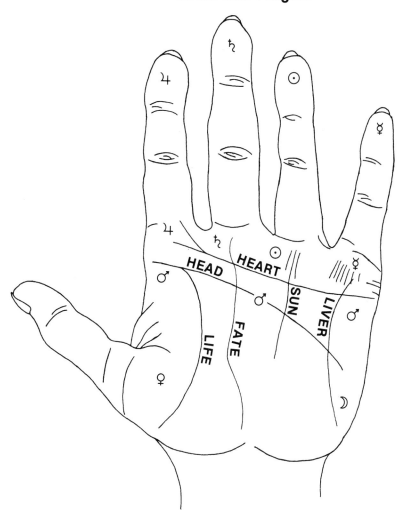

10.1a

Theoretical Mounts and Lines and Fingers

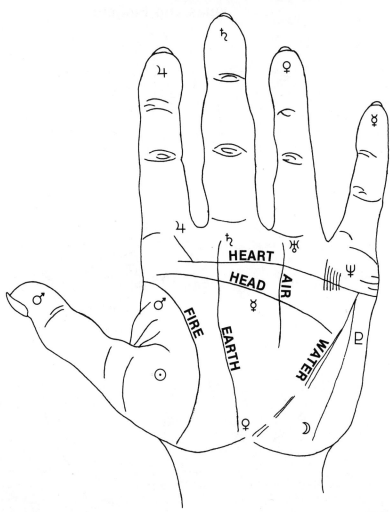

(Alternate Theory Shown in Figure 10.6)

10.1b

meaning is close to Mars in astrology, we would have a "finger" for each of the five planets known to the ancient world and visible without a telescope.

In addition to the logic of the Sun and Moon facing each other at the base of the palm, the shift of Venus to the ring finger gives us the association of the fingers with the five visible planets. The first two fingers are assigned to our two gas giants which are visible without a telescope: Jupiter and Saturn. In ancient astrology, Jupiter and Saturn ruled all four of the transpersonal signs which deal with society, humanity, the **Law**, and our search for Absolutes. Connecting Venus to the ring finger would put together the two inner planets which lie between Earth and the Sun, since the little finger is traditionally given to Mercury. In the sky, Earth and Mars orbit between Venus and Mercury on one side and Jupiter and Saturn on the other side. It is easy to see how confusion could arise between the Venus and Sun areas. In astrology, both are keys to love; both are fixed (ruling Taurus and Leo, marked by enduring self-will); both are often associated with sensual indulgence. But Venus is especially the planet of marriage in its rulership of Libra, its other sign, and the ring on the ring finger has been a significator of marriage for a very long time, in at least the culture areas in which palmistry has been practiced. Venus is also associated with artistic interests, and the ring finger carries that potential. In fact, the "**Line of Apollo**," which rises from the palm to the base of the ring finger, is associated with the possibility of fame through artistic talents.

In addition to the size contrast, the planets differ from the Sun and Moon in their periodic retrograde motion. We could see these shifts in apparent motion metaphorically as a kind of freedom or flexibility of motion as the fingers (including the thumb) can express far more varied motion than can the palm. Yet a hand motion led by the palm may be far more forceful than action with a single finger. Remember, my theory suggests that these models are like related metaphors with shared symbolic meanings.

In general, the Jupiter and Saturn fingers and mounts seem to come close to the meanings I associate with these parts of life in the astrological model. An emphasis on Jupiter in palmistry is said to indicate ambition, pride, leadership, high aspirations and sometimes excesses. The language sounds much like an excess of fire in a horoscope; "I know what I want and I have the right and power to get it." It is particularly fascinating to me that the descriptions of a Jupiter emphasis in both palmistry and astrology are so similar in the old texts, and so lacking in an adequate understanding of the

Theoretical Mounts and
Lines and Fingers

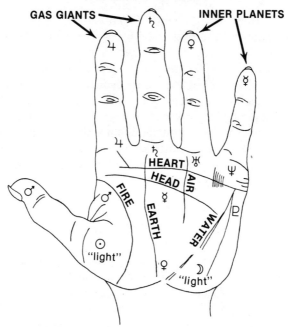

10.2 (Alternate Theory Shown in Figure 10.6)

spiritual potential of the Jupiter principle. All of our models have "grown like Topsy" through human experience, and it would seem that humans have often abused the Jupiter search for the Absolute, turning personal desires, power and ego into Absolutes. When we truly seek to do the will of God, we avoid the destructive potentials of the Jupiter principle. But if we are convinced that what we believe **is** Absolute Truth, and that what we want **is** God's Will, we can produce some very destructive fanatics. In astrology, Jupiter (our faith and value hierarchy based on our beliefs) does "point the way we will go," just as we use the index finger as a pointer.

As with Jupiter, the Saturn finger and mount seem quite close to the Saturn principle in astrology, with the same traditional associations in the older books on both palmistry and astrology. Unfortunately, Saturn is as poorly understood as Jupiter in many texts. Where the overdrive side of Jupiter is mostly emphasized, the limitation side of Saturn is assumed. Both astrology and palmistry books do recognize the practical, Puritan virtue potentials of the earthy Saturn, but too often it is pictured as always denying or blocking human desires. The **Saturn Line**, called the **Fate** or **Destiny Line** in palmistry, which runs up the palm to the base of the second finger, is sometimes given credit for career success, sometimes associated with our handling of the practical earth world. If the line originates on the **Life Line**, the Fate Line is said to symbolize help from or continuing ties to one's family. Other texts suggest that the presence of the Fate Line implies the necessity of hard work while still other authors believe that a good Fate Line indicates few restrictions or limits in the life, the potential power to control one's own fate.

If we acknowledge that character (attitudes and actions) creates fate or destiny (to use biblical language, that we reap what we sow), then the Fate Line is rightly named and does correspond closely with the Saturn principle of karma or consequences. If we know the rules of the game and play by the rules voluntarily, we get good consequences. If we ignore the rules or think we can outwit them, eventually we discover they are bigger than we are. Saturn does symbolize the reality of rules as part of life, including authority figures to enforce them and our own conscience which handles inner enforcement. When we understand the rules and handle them well, we can become "authority" figures: executives, managers, wielders of power who enforce the Law. In the period when astrology and palmistry were presumably being formulated some thousands of years ago in the Middle East, kings and priests were the power figures (Sun and Jupiter), backed up by their warriors (Mars), all fire factors. The earth principle was associated with the hard work of commoners, with limitations, though the merchant class eventually developed and gained power through money. In a democratic society, elected representatives make the rules and elected executives enforce them. Fire now shares power with earth.

If the first three fingers seem reasonably close to the astrological principles of Jupiter, Saturn and Venus, does the little finger fit Mercury? Palmistry does associate the little finger with the conscious mind, including oratorical talent, keen wits and business acumen. As with all the astrological associations in palmistry, the language of the traditional texts is often closer to ancient astrology in its rather negative descriptions of human nature than to the more modern, psychologically oriented astrology books. The ancient Mercury was often portrayed as a conniving trickster, a schemer. The old palmistry books describe the low-set little finger as lacking in ability to communicate, and the crooked little finger as a liar and thief. Throughout even modern palmistry and astrology books, we find the same basic mistake: an assumption that the palmist or astrologer can guess whether the details of the life will be positive or negative. I am convinced that in both palmistry and astrology **the tool shows the psychological issue but the person determines the details of how that principle will manifest in the life**. With self-awareness and self-control, any pattern in a horoscope or in a palm can be expressed in a positive way in the life.

The little finger does seem to be similar in meaning to Mercury in the horoscope as a key to the intellect; perhaps, indeed, to the more practical intellect where the mind is put to work in Virgo. Traditional palmistry associated the little finger with business and trade, fitting artisans and craftspeople and the rise of the merchant class through their success in providing goods and services to the public. The mount at the base of the little finger might offer another Virgo association since it is said to be a key to healing ability when there are many short vertical lines just below the finger.

However, we have a mixed association since the horizontal lines at the edge of the mount, running onto the distal edge of the hand, are said to mark marriages or other emotionally important relationships. There is some question about this association, and some modern palmists have said that they found no relationship between the small horizontal lines and the important peer relationships. I have not found the lines to be a dependable tool, and am holding the issue open subject to more experience. The vertical lines under the little finger, called the **medical stigmata**, seem more useful as a clue to healing potential, but they might simply indicate verbal ability.

My own experience has also failed to confirm the use of very tiny, hair-like vertical lines rising or falling from the so-called relationships' lines as a key to the number of children born to the subject. As has been said repeatedly, I think people try to get more detailed information from these tools than is possible. The models point to psychological issues. We create the details in our lives.

In traditional palmistry, Mars is given a band across the whole central part of the hand. The space between the base of the thumb and the **Mount of Jupiter** is called the **Mount of Lower Mars** and is associated with the aggressive side of Mars, the traditional god of War. The center of the palm is called the **Plain of Mars**, and the area on the distal edge of the palm (opposite the thumb) is generally called the **Upper Mount of Mars**.

Although the ideas expressed here are my own original theories, I have talked to others who have independently come to similar conclusions. For example, Beverly Jaeggers of St. Louis agrees with me that Venus and the Sun have been reversed in traditional palmistry, and I think that she also may agree that what has been called the **Mount of Upper Mars** may actually relate to Pluto. In astrology, Mars is the ruler of Aries, associated with the capacity for open self-assertion and aggression, and it is also a co-ruler of Scorpio (now assigned to Pluto as primary ruler) where Mars tended to manifest more in a tenacious, cautious, less blatant way. The traditional qualities associated with Upper and Lower Mars would fit its two rulerships: Aries for the Lower and Scorpio for the Upper Mount. (Fig. 10.3)

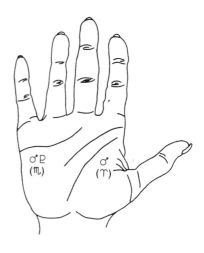

I am less sure of the nature of the plain of Mars in the center of the hand, and would prefer to leave that area open for more study. There does seem to be some truth in the Mars Mounts as a key to a person's readiness to fight (when Lower Mars is high and especially when it is quite red in color) versus an ability for self-defense but reluctance to attack others when Upper Mars is adequately high but Lower Mars is sunken rather than raised above the adjoining areas of the palm.

10.3

During my early years in astrology, I worked for a time with a palmist comparing her reading of a palm with my understanding of the person's horoscope. I still remember one man with a stellium in Scorpio in the sixth house and other signs of power in the chart. While I was suggesting that he might choose a career which required strength, my palmist friend noted a mark like a star on his Lower Mount of Mars and commented that it might signify a military career. The subject confirmed that he had been in the army for 20 years.

If readers have been visualizing the palm as we have discussed these theories, they may have noted that the three fire "planets" (lumping the Sun with the planets for convenience) have been associated with the thumb side of the hand; Jupiter for the index finger and area just below it; Mars for the area between the Jupiter Mount and the thumb; Mars for at least the top part of the thumb;

and the Sun for the area at the base of the thumb, which is actually the third joint of the thumb. In astrology, fire initiates new action and it is followed by earth as we apply the new creative energy to coping with the physical world. The thumb and index finger lead the way when we reach for objects.

On the hand, the **Saturn** finger and **Mount** follow Jupiter. I am proposing that Venus comes next on the hand. In astrology, Venus symbolizes our capacity for pleasure, whether for physical pleasure (Taurus) or more mental enjoyment (Libra). The air side of Venus is concerned with lasting, equalitarian relationships. In astrology, air follows earth as we seek to understand our experience and to learn to deal with peers. But water comes next in astrology, and the little finger as Mercury spoils the neat fit, since, like Venus, Mercury is associated with one earth (Virgo) and one air (Gemini) sign. Perhaps all the fingers which grasp and grapple with the world are primarily fire and earth, the elements I call the "steamroller" potential. Perhaps the addition of air to earth as a blend in the last two fingers is symbolizing our movement toward humanness, the conscious reasoning mind and the capacity to relate to peers modifying the purely practical focus of the earth on material results.

We do have two water planets assigned to the distal side of the hand opposite the thumb: the Moon at the base, next to the wrist, and Pluto tentatively associated with the middle area. If the upper area, the mount below the little finger, were assigned to Neptune, it would fit the healing idea as well as Virgo does. In astrology, healing is associated with the Virgo-Pisces polarity. But the system seems uncertain at this point. (Fig. 10.4)

Even if we decide eventually that the correspondences are pretty close between many of the factors in palmistry and those in astrology, the little finger and its mount pose a problem. I have also known astrologers who associated both the little finger and its mount with sex. If Pluto is related to the middle area of that distal side of the palm, one's sexual potential might be part of the meaning of the area. In contrast to the Pluto concern with shared possessions and sensuality, strong Virgo-Pisces emphasis in a horoscope (especially a strong Vesta) may be associated with an inhibition of sex, with work and spiritual pursuits taking precedence. Some of my palmist friends are convinced that the low-set little finger is a sign of sexual inhibition. Could this mean that Virgo or a Virgo-Pisces mixture is impinging on and partially replacing Scorpio, the space below the little finger's mount?

Gittings makes a flat statement that "a ring on the Mercury finger

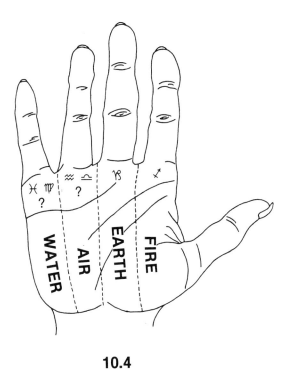

10.4

is always connected to sexual problems." (p. 114). I am appalled when palmists or astrologers make such flat statements of details in the life. In some cultures, it is customary to wear rings on all the fingers. The wearer of a ring on the little finger might prefer the aesthetic side of life to the practical intellect or to ordinary jobs. In general, I found Gittings's book highly male chauvinist with spirituality and creative giving considered "male" while materiality and sensuous enjoyment through receiving were called "female." A low-set little finger is fairly common and might express as reduced verbal fluency, or as a challenge in the work, or as sexual inhibitions, or many other variations. In astrology, Virgo can mark an introverted, workaholic and/or sexual repression if the work ethic or self-criticism leading to self-doubt overshadow other parts of life. At this point, I need more evidence on the **Mercury** finger and **Mount**, and prefer to keep the issue open.

Water is the inner element in astrology, symbolizing the unconscious mind and the process of absorption and assimilation. It is the psychic element. There is no separation at the unconscious level. We are open to the universe. But that very openness implies vulnerability and a need to retreat from or wall off the world at times. Fire and earth are "out there," dealing with the world. Air and water live in the head, analyzing and digesting the fire-earth experiences. It seems logical to have our fingers which manipulate the world assigned to fire (initial outreach) and earth (the practical follow-through) with air increasingly blending with the earth as we evolve toward intellect and respect for our fellow-humans. Also, logically, water would trail behind the other elements, symbolizing the digestive phase of life which follows the experiences symbolized by the other elements. Fire and water are our emotional elements, fire normally pouring out the emotion while water normally holds it in. As already indicated, though water symbolizes our tendency to turn inward, it also connects us to all of life through the unconscious, while fire symbolizes our capacity for expressing our personal uniqueness. Seen in this way, fire is the most personal of the four elements. It is intriguing that the fire (thumb) sides of the hands hang next to the body when the arms are allowed to hang in a relaxed way, while the water side of the hand which unconsciously connects us to life is on the outside. (Fig. 10.5)

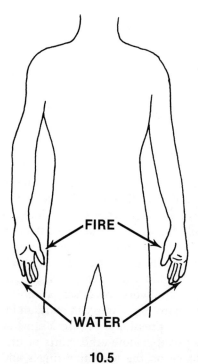

10.5

Evolution is a basic part of my belief system. Paleontology traces the physical evolution of species through millennia of time. Cultures also evolve and disintegrate. Behind the tangible results studied by modern science, I believe spiritual evolution occurs, maybe subject to setbacks but driven by an inner hunger to reach higher. Certainly knowledge evolves. We change our models hoping that the new one will be a better fit for our complicated world. I am sure that the models offered in this book will be superseded in time. Final

Truth is a goal we seek and never reach. As humans and cultures and knowledge evolve, we need to remember that all models are tentative and temporary and incomplete. The world is always bigger than our models.

Some palmists have assigned definite areas of the hands to Uranus and Neptune, but I am still hesitant to make any strong pronouncements. In the first issue of our journal, *The Mutable Dilemma*, published in December 1977, I included an article on palmistry and astrology suggesting that Neptune might be connected to (perhaps sharing the rulership of) the mount below the little finger, and Uranus associated with the mount below the ring finger. The assignment gives a temptingly neat fit between astrology and palmistry with the planets all in the same order that they occupy in the sky if we omit the asteroid belt. Beyond earth, we would have Mars for the mount above the base of the thumb; Jupiter for the mount below the index finger, Saturn, Uranus, and Neptune continuing across the top of the palm, and Pluto just below Neptune on the distal edge of the palm. When we look inward from earth, toward the Sun at the center of our solar system, we come first to the Moon which palmistry assigns to the large mount at the base of the palm. Venus and Mercury might fit in the center of the hand, each ruling both an earth and an air sign to fill in element strips running down the hand. Finally, we end with the Sun at the thumb. The element strips on the palm would occur in the same order as the elements in astrology; fire on the thumb side, earth next, then air, and finally water on the distal side of the palm. The system is temptingly neat, as already indicated, but I'm afraid it is too pat and that the fit of astrology and palmistry is not quite so precise. In the end, we have to keep testing our models against the world and revising them when they prove inadequate. (Fig. 10.6)

The danger of overemphasizing logic at the expense of experience is demonstrated by the astrologers who make Pluto the ruler of Aries rather than of Scorpio. The assignment is justified by the fact that Jupiter, Saturn, Uranus and Neptune orbit at increasing distances from the Sun, and that the signs they are said to rule occur in order from Sagittarius to Pisces. Some astrologers, perhaps beginning with Carl Payne Tobey, reasoned that Pluto follows Neptune in the sky (though it is currently inside the orbit of Neptune for about 20 years) and that it should therefore rule Aries which follows Pisces if we see the zodiac as a continuous circle. Unfortunately, despite the logic, experience with Pluto (by which I mean human experience when Pluto is prominent in relevant horoscopes) clearly fits Scorpio more

**Alternate Theory of Mounts,
Lines and Fingers**

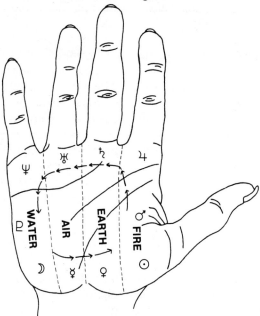

Planetary Orbits

10.6 (See also Figures 10.1b and 10.2)

closely while experience associated with a prominent Mars is a closer
fit to Aries. Naturally, the differences are most visible when the
planet is in its own element (Mars in a fire sign or house and Pluto
in a water sign or house), but even in conflicting elements, experience
testifies to the association of Pluto with Scorpio. Until I have much
more experience with palmistry, my speculative association of Neptune as a possible co-ruler of the traditional Mount of Mercury and
the even more tenuous possible connection of Uranus to the mount
below the ring finger remain truly speculative.

Could humanity be evolving in the direction of the transpersonal?
The discovery of Uranus and Neptune added new understanding to
astrology. Could the meanings they symbolize in astrology be entering palmistry through a shift in the meanings of areas of the palms?
As the women's liberation movement grows, and the divorce rate
in the Western world expands, is the principle of Uranus over-
shadowing Venus? As we evolve and change our beliefs, values and

actions, our ways of describing ourselves and the world evolve with us. Is it possible that the associations of areas of the hand are changing also, to fit our changing attitudes? Or are we just beginning to recognize potentials which were there all the time?

Marriage in the ancient world of palmistry's origins was probably ruled by Cancer rather than Libra. In most areas for which we have written records, women were owned by men. Libra was largely associated with male partnerships or with open competition and warfare. Our relatively recent effort to achieve equality between the sexes in the lasting relationship of marriage is a real challenge. In the Western world where this goal is encouraged, we frequently see Uranus overtaking Venus. It is easy to accept people as they are when we only see them occasionally — the ideal of Uranus which is traditionally associated with friendships or superficial contacts with people in general. It is not easy to practice that "goal of air" with people we live with. When we try and fail, we move from Libra-Venus (marriage in our world) to Aquarius-Uranus (divorce). When the principles are successfully integrated, we achieve marriages in which the couples are also friends. Wouldn't it be fascinating if the air side of Venus is contending with Uranus for rulership over the mount below the ring finger? So far, this is pure speculation.

To summarize the preceding material, the palmistry model I am offering to be tested by anyone interested in the study of the hand, would associate the fingers (including the thumb) with fire and earth, with the last two fingers including an earth-air blend. The palm would incorporate all four elements, starting with fire on the thumb side and ending with water on the distal side. Venus, ruling both an air and an earth sign, might be associated with the central part of the base of the palm, between the **Mounts of Sun and Moon**, while Mercury, also ruling both earth and air, is potentially given the traditional "Plain of Mars" in the center of the hand. If we could assign the four elements of astrology to four strips running down the palm, it would give us some intriguing correlations with the major lines in the palm. The Life Line is clearly a fire line, associated with physical strength and vitality and recuperative power. Modern observations have discarded the old idea that the length of the line is a key to the length of the life. A short but deep line with minimal wavering branches or cuts by other lines can indicate a long and healthy life. A long, faint, interrupted line may indicate illness and early death.

As already suggested, the traditional Fate Line resembles the earth principle, symbolizing our capacity to cope with the material world. In addition to a beginning on the Life Line in the area of the Sun at the base of the thumb, which may indicate help from or attachments to the early family, the Fate Line rising from the Mount of the Moon or with a branch to it, is associated with work which depends on public attention or approval or which uses the creative imagination. Since both Sun and Moon are keys to home and family, procreation and the care of children, I have suspected at times that a branch of the Fate Line to the Moon might also be connected to strong early or continuing links to the family. A Fate Line rising from the center of the base of the palm is said to be a "self-made" person. As with many of the traditions in palmistry, I have read the theories in books but often have not had enough personal experience to really test them, so hold them tentatively, subject to more experience.

The so-called **Apollo Line**, which runs up to the ring finger and which seldom starts below the **Head Line**, might be an air line: a key to our ability to think, reason, communicate, and/or to appreciate beauty and to please people. The presence of several vertical lines on the mount below the ring finger is traditionally associated with versatility and multiple talents. (Fig. 10.7)

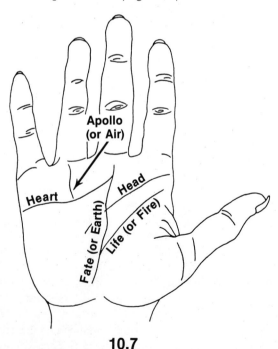

10.7

Theoretically, there are three possible water lines. One runs from the Mount of the Moon, curving a little toward the center of the palm and then returning to end on the mount below the little finger, but mostly remaining in the "water zone" of the hand. Traditionally, this line is associated with intuition, or psychic ability: a water phenomenon according to astrology. Even the slight incursion into the air part of the palm fits astrology since a water-air mixture in a horoscope is associated with the ability to become conscious of the psychic knowledge which is present in the unconscious part of the mind.

Another possible water line is the one traditionally called **Hypatica**, or **Liver**, or **Health**. Palmistry texts suggest that one is better off to lack the line altogether, but if present, it should be relatively firm and deep. A wavering, branched, intersected line running from anywhere in the middle of the palm and ending on the mount below the little finger is associated with poor health, including lung problems, liver disorders, allergies, etc. Note that all the listed illnesses are connected to the mutable planets or signs or houses in astrology. The mount below the little finger could be associated with either Mercury ruling Gemini and Virgo or with Pisces ruled by both Jupiter and Neptune, and it would fit an association with that group of illnesses.

Some texts describe one more line which ends on the water side of the palm in the middle area which I am tentatively associating with Pluto. The line is traditionally called the **Via Lascivia**, a fitting title for some Pluto interests, though the line might simply indicate strength of will with the ability to keep going to the end. The dictionary defines lascivious as "characterized by or expressing lust," while lust is defined as "bodily appetite, especially excessive sexual desires." Benham describes the Via Lascivia as a sister line to the **Mercury Line**, starting near the center of the palm, at the inner boundary of the Mount of the Moon, and running parallel to the Mercury Line, but ending sooner, before reaching the mount under the little finger. Benham states that the line adds to sensual appetites in a sensual hand, as shown by many other details, but that in a "good" hand, the line just strengthens the Mercury potential for health and success in life. (Fig. 10.8)

There are two other major lines in most palms, but they cross the hand horizontally so they usually intersect the element zones being proposed here. The **Heart Line** runs across just below the mounts at the top of the palm, starting anywhere from the Jupiter Mount to the area below the Saturn Mount. Traditionally, an origin

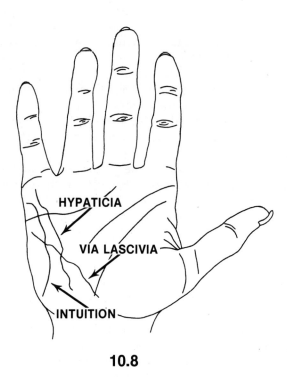

10.8

on Jupiter is associated with romantic idealism, the search for the perfect mate. We may think we have found one, or we may keep on searching. An origin below Saturn suggests caution or practicality, which may lead to an avoidance of commitment if we are afraid of being hurt, or may lead to marriage in which security is a primary goal.

The Heart Line may end below the little finger or it can continue on to the distal edge of the hand. It can also end as a single line, in a fork, or in a tassel with many little lines. Branches at the end may be associated with more than one love. The tassel might be a key to a capacity for universal love, especially if Neptune shares the mount with Mercury.

A second Heart Line (traditionally called the **Girdle of Venus**) is sometimes found above the normal line. Traditional palmistry usually associates the double line with sensual excesses or a nervous nature. In my experience, the extra Heart Line may indicate a capacity to love deeply and/or broadly but there is not always a physical expression of the feelings. Among the keys to physical excesses are fat lower segments on the fingers, high puffy mounts, reddish coloring on the hand, etc. Modern palmists do mention the potential for the Girdle of Venus to be associated with artistic creativity. Since the line forms a ring around the Saturn and Venus fingers, the linkage of career and beauty seems appropriate. As has been said repeatedly, we determine the details in our lives. We can manifest our pleasure in tangible ways by an artistic career or by sensual indulgence. (Fig. 10.9)

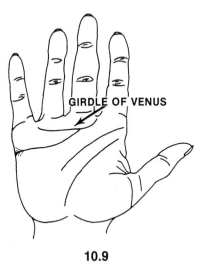

GIRDLE OF VENUS

10.9

Our last major line is the Head Line, usually originating between the Heart and Life Lines and running across the hand under the Heart Line. As with the Life Line, a short Line does not necessarily mean a poor intellect though an end under the Saturn finger in the earth area of the palm might mean excessive practicality. Normally, the Line end under the Venus (ring) finger in the air part of the palm. Depth and firmness, lack of cross lines or branches drooping from the main line, may be more important than simple length. A Head Line which extends into the water part of the palm links the conscious and unconscious aspects of the mind. A straight Line extending into the Pluto area may indicate the capacity for sustained mental effort such as research. A Head Line which

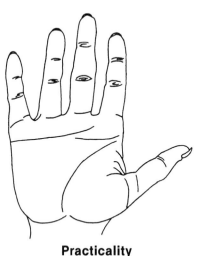

Practicality

10.10

curves down to the mount of the Moon suggests great imagination which might be used in writing, psychic ability, sensitivity, restlessness. Two or three branches forming a fork at the end of the

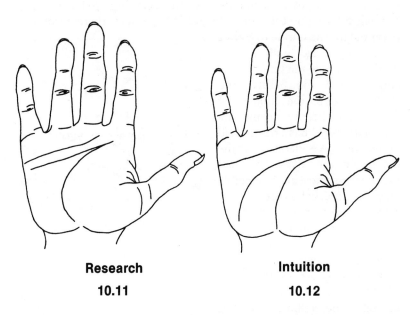

Research

10.11

Intuition

10.12

Head Line may indicate more than one area of special interest and talent. Of course, too many interests may lead to a scattering of the energy and less accomplishment. (Fig. 10.10-12)

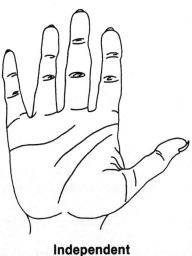

Independent

10.13

One of the ancient traditions which seems to work, at least in my limited experience, involves the origin of the three major lines: Heart, Head, and Life. When they are all connected at their origin approximately at the boundary between the Mounts of Mars and Jupiter, the individual seems to be somewhat dependent and/or sheltered. Wide separations between the three lines seem to mark a more independent person, though one may be independent mentally or emotionally or physically. Not everyone will manifest the potential in all areas of life. (Fig. 10.13-14)

The most common pattern seems to be a connection at the beginning of the Head and Life Lines while the Heart Line rises a little higher on the palm. In some cases, the Heart and Head Lines are joined in a single line stretching straight across the palm. If the intellect dominates the individual, the emotions may be repressed or expressed with difficulty. If the heart dominates, there may be problems involving the conscious mind. The line is said to occur somewhat more often in individuals with Down's syndrome (mongolism), but I have not been able to verify the claim. Gittings presents a series of palm prints which he describes as having the single Heart-Head Line (called traditionally the **Simian Line**), but in almost all cases, two lines are clearly visible though one is less developed than the other.

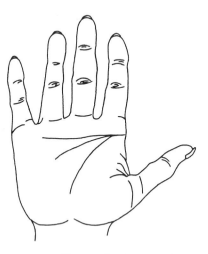

Dependent

10.14

It is important to study both hands, since there can be major differences in the lines and other factors. Traditionally, the less-used hand marks the past and the more subjective side of the person, while the dominant hand marks the direction in which the life is evolving and its more outward, visible manifestations. For example, a right-handed person would look at the left hand to see more about the tendencies in the early life and the inner states, while the right hand would presumably indicate the outer expression, including activities which are increasing in importance as the individual matures.

Since the goal of this book is not to provide another textbook of palmistry (or numerology or any of our techniques) but rather to explore the potentials of these approaches to the shared goal of understanding humans, and to offer readers a chance to try their own skills at interpreting the data, perhaps enough has been said to let us proceed to the actual data: palm prints and photographs of the hands of our seven subjects.

At this point, we have to apologize for the inadequate quality of our palmistry raw data which appears in the introductory section of this book. So far, we have not been able to get proper ink prints of the palms of our subjects. We have Xerox photos and film photos, but the quality of many leaves a lot to be desired. We are reminded that of all the models under consideration in this book, palmistry most needs a personal contact with the subject. We really need to "handle" the hands, to see the degree of flexibility, the texture and resilience of the skin, the height of the mounts, etc. Without special close-ups or ink prints, we also lack the markings on the fingertips (loops, whorls, etc.). It was the hope of Bill Wrobel, my fellow author, and myself that readers of the book could apply their own specialized knowledge and use the raw data offered on each subject in each of the different approaches to understanding, to compare the value of the different approaches. But the full potential of palmistry is obviously not available through these inadequate data samples. We can only promise that if the approach in this book proves helpful and a sequel is planned, next time we will try to have much better raw material for the palmistry part. Meanwhile, this section will include artist's sketches of features which seemed visible in the raw data.

Ms. One

Looking at our subject Ms. One, our first impression is of a fairly square hand with the length of the second (longest) finger close to the same as the width and length of the palm. The two middle fingertips are also fairly square though there is naturally some rounding. The index, little finger and thumb seem to be more conical, though it is hard to be sure from the angles of the fingers in the photos (Fig. 10.15). Square hands and fingertips are associated with a solid, practical nature, normally very down-to-earth and fairly conservative or traditional. They would seem to fit the Virgo grouping in Ms. One's horoscope, and her loaded tenth house, but not the Aquarius (sign and house). The more conical fingertips with the connotation of openness to new ideas and a strong mental side to the nature, provides a possible match to the Aquarius theme in the chart.

Other traditional keys to mental openness include the open spaces between the bases of the fingers and the tendency to carry the little finger well away from the ring finger. The top joint of the little finger is also the longest of its three joints, another traditional clue to a highly active mind. Suggesting a possible conflict between the independence of mind and a desire for human companionship and approval, we note that the top joint of the little finger bends

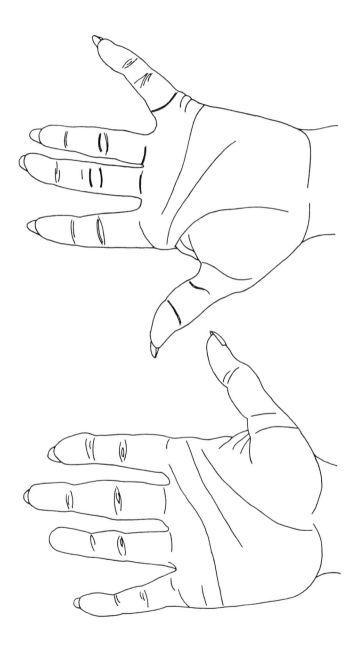

10.15

toward the ring finger on both hands. Unless the effect is an illusion created by the photos, there is a difference between the two hands in the slant of the fingers. The ring finger stands most upright on the left hand, with all the other three fingers bending toward it at least slightly. On the right hand, the long finger seems most upright, with at least the upper joint of the other fingers bending toward it. The implication would be a subjective (and early) tendency to put relationships at the center of her life, while in her later years, Ms. One might move in the direction of making a career and personal independence more central through her ability to support herself.

The strong, clear line running from the Life Line up onto the mount below the Mercury finger would seem to support the potential for both good health and competence in handling a job. The wide space between the Life and Head Lines also supports the likelihood of much greater independence than the average person. Though there are both "hills and valleys" on the Lower Mount of Mars, the raised areas seem strong enough to emphasize a good ability to assert her own needs. The fire strength with its physical vitality is also supported by a strong, deep, clean Life Line and by a long, broad, straight thumb. (Fig. 10.16)

Though it is less clear on the left hand, the Heart Line on the right hand originates on the Mount of Jupiter, testifying to a search for an ideal love. Islands on the Line may be a clue to difficulties in finding the ideal. Theoretically, it is also possible that islands, like a final tassel, might indicate a broadening of one's love to include more than one mate in a lifetime. The deep horizontal lines on the Mount of the Sun at the base of the thumb are said to indicate many important relationships in the life, whether with peers or with our children. The bulging Mount of the Moon also testifies to deep emotions and a need for close relationships. The combination of emphasis on independence and on relationships suggests that Ms. One may be working on a freedom-closeness or independence-dependence dilemma, like so many in our Western world.

With a relatively straight and adequately long Head Line, Ms. One should be able to understand herself and to work out the "juggling act of life."

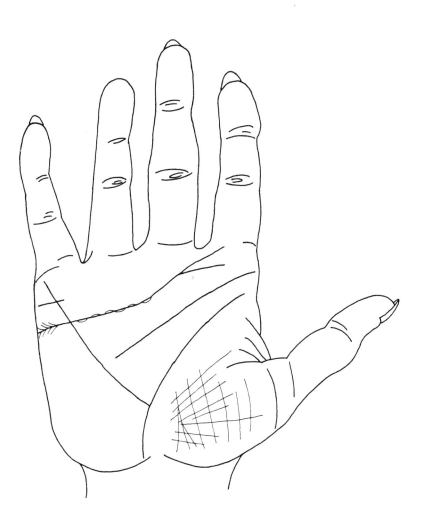

10.16

Mr. Two

Continuing to our second subject, we can see some interesting parallels to Ms. One. Mr. Two also has a wide space between his Life and Head Lines, indicating a highly independent person. Some books claim that individuals with this wide a separation can be rash and impulsive, but the independent mind might be expressed in Mr. Two's willingness to investigate astrology and palmistry and to be

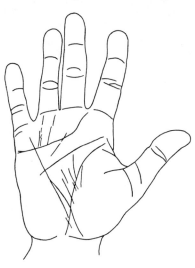

10.17

a subject for a book like this. The separate little finger is theoretically another key to an open mind, along with a somewhat low-set thumb. Mr. Two also has a series of parallel lines, some starting from the Life Line and some more in the center of the hand, which run up the palm together, diverging as they go, with some going to the Saturn, the Venus and the Mercury fingers. (Fig. 10.17) The combination supports the importance of the mind but connects the mind and work to either desire for relationships or to aesthetic interests. If the different parts of life are integrated, Mr. Two might have handicraft talent, the ability to write, or to make things that are both useful and beautiful. Or he might be able to talk persuasively to others, using his ability to relate to others in his job. The line to the Mercury finger seems straighter and deeper on the right hand, suggesting an increasing focus in the life on work, or service, or possibly health. Though the Fate Line does not reach all the way to the Mount of Saturn, its beginning is clearly a fork rooted in the Mount of the Moon suggesting a career dependent in some way on the public or on the creative imagination or on sensitivity and empathy. The fork might indicate two different interests or talents which were eventually combined to create the career. (Fig. 10.18)

Mr. Two also has an interesting combination of contrasting lines at the beginning of his Heart Line. Either a branch or the Line itself originates high on the Mount of Jupiter, a sign of idealism and the search for the perfect mate. But another branch or a fork at the beginning of the Line curves down toward the Head Line, indicating a possible tug-of-war between the critical or analytical intellect and the emotional ideals. The combination so fits Mr. Two's horoscope; it is impressive. His Chiron (like Jupiter) in the Jupiter sign and in the house of partnership, plus his Neptune in Libra, both show the search for the ideal mate, while his Mercury in Capricorn in the other (eighth) house of partnership and his Saturn in Virgo in the fifth house of loving and being loved are signs of acute awareness of the flaws in prospective loves.

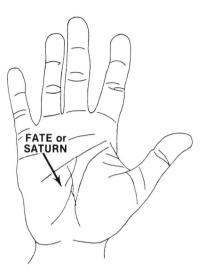

10.18

Further support for challenges in the area of relationships is shown in the hand by many small lines and some islands on the Line of Heart, and what looks like a tassel at the end of the Line. (Fig. 10.19.) We would need to talk to Mr. Two to determine whether he had a heart big enough for many loved ones and has universalized his emotions, or whether he wanted a lasting commitment with one person and had to work to attain that goal and to be satisfied with a human (not perfect) relationship. A fragmentary Girdle of Venus also seems present in both

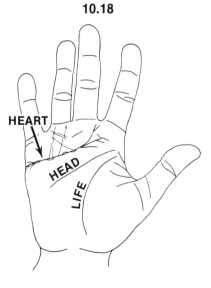

10.19

hands, saying once more that heart issues are important and need an outlet. And, finally, the low-set little finger would fit a possible conflict between the sensual desires and the intellectual and/or spiritual inclinations, with a need to make room for both in the life.

Though there are creases across the Lower Mount of Mars on both hands, there are also raised areas, and there are also distinct bulges on the percussion (distal) side of the hand. The combination looks like enough self-confidence and strength to confront life and to be clear about personal desires and rights. But the many lines on the Sun and Moon Mounts at the base of the palm repeat the need for emotional ties, reiterating our culturally common "freedom-closeness" dilemma as a likely issue in the life. (Fig. 10.20.) The numerous lines on the Mount of the Moon highlight the likelihood of emotional sensitivity, as do the raised pads on the fingertips. The person might express this through a search for security through home and family, or might be sensitive and nurturing of others. The traditional "restlessness" associated with the lines on the lunar mount may lead to wandering if the person is searching for emotional satisfaction which seems unattainable at home.

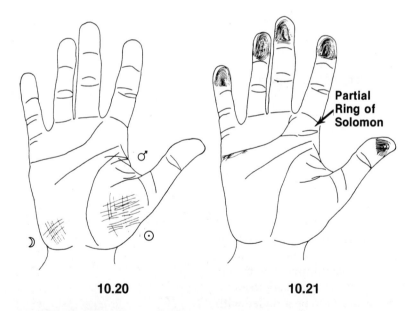

Partial Ring of Solomon

10.20   **10.21**

The strength and depth of the major lines in the hand point to vitality and emotional intensity. A partial but double (adding strength) **Ring of Solomon** around the Mount of the Jupiter (index) finger is traditionally an indication of someone who searches for wisdom and wishes to share it with others. Most of the fingertip markings seem to be loops, an indication of flexibility or adaptability in dealing with others. However, the index finger on the right hand looks like a mixture of a whorl and a composite that has not quite made up its mind. The whorl is associated with individuality while the composite suggests the ability to see both sides of an issue: a talent often found with a Libra emphasis in a horoscope. (Fig. 10.21.) We hope that Mr. Two is enjoying his journey as he searches for his ideal world.

Ms. Three

Continuing to Ms. Three, we see a fairly square, practical palm with moderately long fingers with square tips except for the thumbs and the index finger on the right hand which are clearly more conical. Most of the fingers are also quite straight, though the ring and little finger on the left hand are just slightly bent inward, pointing to some subjective need for other people and to initial conservatism. Our primary impression is of a capable, realistic person who is good at detail, likes order and system, and is able to cope with the world. The major lines are clear and strong, further supporting a life of decision and action.

On closer inspection, we see the open spaces between the fingers denoting the curious intellect. The conical index finger shows movement during the life toward more sociability, more development of the intuition, more appreciation of the aesthetic side of life. Since the thumbs, like Mars in a horoscope, show tendencies present and highly visible from the beginning of life, the need for people in the life is clearly there from birth, but with the right hand showing our outer manifestations and the index finger showing directing goals and values, Ms. Three is likely to broaden her contacts and increase her openness as she grows. The Head Line dipping down toward the Mount of the Moon and the deep lines on the **Lunar Mount** are also an indication of intuition and the creative imagination.

Love and relationships also seem important to Ms. Three. (Fig. 10.22.) Her Heart Line, like both of our first two subjects, branches up to the Mount of Jupiter with its search for an ideal. It also is somewhat chained and feathered with small branches in its later part and it ends in a tassel. We wonder whether Ms. Three started with a conventional committed marriage and then widened her life to include more empathy for others. The Girdle of Venus as a second Heart Line, more developed on the right hand, offers further support for a warm, caring nature. The deep emotions may express through love, sensuality or artistic channels. The Fate Lines on both hands seem to start well inside the Life Line, suggesting strong ties to home and family whether they are to her original "family of orientation" (to use an anthropological phrase) or her later "family of procreation." (Fig. 10.23.) Her role in the world seems firmly connected to family in some way. Midway between her Life and Head Lines, the Fate Line splits, with one line continuing toward the Saturn finger while another rises to the Mercury finger. Both of these lines may imply a concern with the physical world, with Saturn-Capricorn connected to our status or place in the society and dealing with power, while Mercury-Virgo is more a key to the details of the job or sometimes to a concern with health whether of ourselves or others.

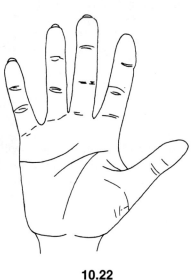

10.22

Ms. Three also has a number of parallel, vertical lines on the mount under the ring finger. Whether we give this mount to Venus or to Uranus or to a blend of the two, the lines seem to indicate versatility with aesthetic appreciation and/or talent. But the strength of the hand including the long thumb suggests ample will and determination to make decisions and to follow through on goals. The Head and Life Lines joined at their beginning and the general feeling of squareness may fit a solid citizen, but the emotional warmth is deep behind the capable front. We hope that Ms. Three has found

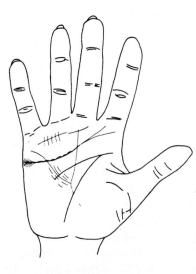

10.23

ways to manifest her warmth without conflict between the emotions
and the practical side of her nature.

Mr. Four

Moving on to Mr. Four, we are beginning to note some similarities
in our subjects. As with the first three, we have the Mercury finger
widely separated from the ring finger and wide spaces at the bases
of all the fingers, both signs suggesting an active and open mind.
A strong line to the Mercury finger has also been present in all subjects though this is considered one of the minor lines and is often
missing. The Mercury Line might indicate business ability or health
interests or it might just repeat the importance of the mind. A single
line starts inside the Life Line, pointing to strong family connections.

It then splits into the Fate and
Mercury Lines and a **Venus**
(Apollo to use its traditional
name) **Line** splits off from the
Fate Line to run up to the ring
finger. The single origin for the
Mercury and Saturn Lines, as
seen clearly in Mr. Two and with
less depth and strength in the
lines in Ms. Three, would seem
to emphasize the practical side of
life. (Fig. 10.24.) We might think
of it as similar to finding Mercury
in Capricorn or in the tenth
house or aspecting Saturn. Or
Saturn might be in Virgo or in the
sixth house. Mr. Four does have
Mercury in Capricorn as well as
Saturn in the third house, the
other house ruled by Mercury.

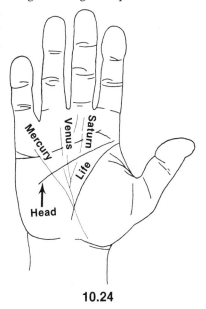

10.24

The mind tends to be serious and practical with such combinations.

The hands are broad but long, with relatively short fingers, giving an impression of strength and a good ability to handle details.
A low-set thumb seems a possible source of conflict, since it is usually
read as impulsive or rash while the rest of the hand looks fairly stable,
solid and realistic. But the wide separation between the Head and

Life Lines confirms a side to the nature that is willing to take chances and potentially very independent. All of our subjects except Ms. Three have had this separation though a majority of humans are supposed to have the Head and Life Lines joined at the start. Besides the potential conflict between caution and risk, the short fingers are traditionally said to indicate impatience with details while the Saturn and Mercury Lines imply skill with details. Of course, one can be capable but still frustrated if life gets too routine and repetitive. The spatulate fingers show a need for action and results!

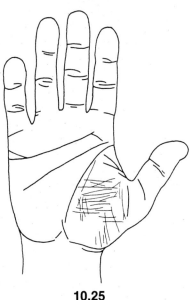

10.25

Another indication that tempers the practicality of the hand can be seen in the differing Head Lines in the two hands. On the left hand, the Head Line takes a sharper slant down toward the Mount of the Moon where it crosses the Mercury Line. The Head Line on the right hand maintains its gradual slant and does not extend so far into the water zone of the hand. (Fig. 10.25.) The patterns suggest sensitivity and/or psychic interests early in life but some caution or reluctance about going too far in outward manifestations, showing a practical mind to the world. A conflict is possible between the inner sensitivity and the outer realism. A strong branch from the Head Line to the Mount of Jupiter is another indication of a high value placed on the mind. We may study or teach or write or travel, but there is a restless search for something higher. The squares on the Mount of Jupiter are often found on students of metaphysics and the occult, and are said to protect the individual, to assist the judgment which is based on the personal belief system.

In addition to the similar Fate-Mercury Line origin, Mr. Four shares a Heart-Head similarity with Mr. Two. The Heart Line on the left hand has a branch up to the Mount of Jupiter, while the Heart Line on the right hand starts with a fork, one prong bending down toward the Head Line. The combination suggests a need to integrate the inner idealism about love with the practical intellect, with growth in the direction of the practical. We can aim high but be satisfied with a human relationship. We might also read the Heart branches toward the Head Line as an effort to integrate the emotions and the intellect.

A number of signs in the hands support a strong will and capacity for self-assertion. Both Mounts of Mars look highly developed, with Upper Mars somewhat more bulging out on the left hand to show the strength present from the early life. The Mars (and fire in general) qualities of courage, self-assertion, vitality, etc., are also supported by a long and deep Life Line, and by a Mars Line running inside and parallel to the Life Line. The strong, broad thumb is further support for the willpower.

The highly developed Mounts of the Sun and Moon at the base of the hand, including the many lines on the Sun's Mount, are further support for a warm nature to whom family and personal relationships are important. With Mars and the Sun and Moon all emphasized, we might wonder about a possible freedom-closeness issue in the life. An interesting line from the Lower Mount of Mars to the Heart Line might also fit such an issue. Life should be big enough for both our personal desires and will and our sharing with loved ones. I'm still questioning the possibility that a low-set little finger might show an issue involving sensuality and/or relationships on one side versus intellect or spiritual involvements on the other side. I'm looking forward to reading the interviews and self-evaluations of our subjects, since my analyses are all being done prior to any background knowledge about the people.

Our **overall impression** of Mr. Four's hands suggests an active achiever who wants success in work and in love and still wants time to pursue individual interests and the curious mind. With his drive and talents, we trust he is achieving his goals.

Ms. Five

Looking next at Ms. Five, we see our most linear hands to date: a long palm and medium length fingers in comparison to the palm. We have an impression of a sensitive person and the likelihood of deep emotions. The Heart Lines on both hands rising high on the Mount of Jupiter add to this impression, showing the search for the ideal love. A partial second Heart Line on the right hand repeats the theme. Traditional palmistry named the line which looped around the second and third fingers the Girdle of Venus. When the line extended to the mount below the little finger or to the edge of the hand, it was theorized that the intellect tempered the emotions and sensuality. The latter might be true, but I think the line is really a second Heart Line and can indicate deep emotions, and/or sensuality, and/or strong artistic interests and possible talent. The much-lined Mount of the Sun would further support the capacity for emotional and/or sensual attachments or creative talents.

The left hand has a fragmentary Fate Line but stronger lines to the Venus and Mercury fingers, again fitting a life more concerned with the mind and the aesthetic or with the details of a job, the Virgo principle of wanting to do something well. The Fate Line is stronger in the right hand, suggesting an increasing concern with Ms. Five's larger role in the society. Since it rises from the Life Line, we have the potential of early ties to the family being important. It is possible that such a pattern might mean delaying a career in order to have a family first. (Fig. 10.26)

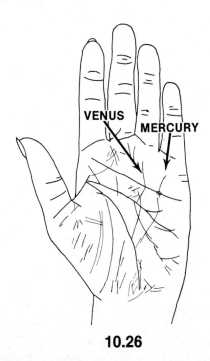

10.26

The fingers held closely together are further support for a cautious or conservative nature, as is what looks like a common origin of the Head and Life Lines on the left hand, while they are slightly separated on the right hand. But the Head Line ending in a fork and extending well into the water zone of the hand shows a potentially fine mind with the ability to be both practical and imaginative. Both hands show a similar pattern with the Head Lines, including a slight upward slant at the ends of the forks which would fit an attempt to move toward practicality. The Head Line reaching the mount of Pluto could support a feeling for pleasure and beauty being channeled into action with the mind, perhaps through an artistic hobby or job. Since the side of the hand appears quite flat in the photos, there does not seem to be a likelihood of sensual excess, and the low-set little finger might indicate some inhibition in that area, perhaps subordinating the sensual to work or to mental or spiritual interests. Although the little finger is set low on the palm, it is actually very long, offering additional support for the importance of the mind.

The Life Line looks stronger in the right hand than in the left, which is an encouraging sign of increasing physical vitality and perhaps courage or self-confidence. On the left hand, the Life Line ends in a spread of little branches somewhat like the common tassel on the end of the Heart Line. Like the multiplicity of little lines below the fingers, the patterns might fit a mutable dilemma with a variety of interests and talents and some danger of scattering the energy. Or, Ms. Five might need to increase her physical activity to build strength and endurance, to avoid a danger of living too much in the mind and the emotions. It is hard to tell from the photos, but the Mount of Mars looks sunken, repeating the need to develop more self-confidence and self-assertion. Anything we do successfully can help in such an effort. (Fig. 10.27)

There are strong markings on the Mount of the Moon and Sun to emphasize the importance of relationships and a warm nature. An unusual line rises from the Lunar Mount, formed by a series of small, overlapping lines, and rises to join the Head Line in the middle of the palm. If we think of it as a branch of the Head Line drooping almost to the bottom of the Lunar Mount, the old books would be very negative about depression or an imagination out of control. But since the hands show a good mind, we might think of this line as a strong indication of psychic ability and the possibility of integrating the conscious and unconscious aspects of the mind in a constructive way. The depression or anxiety might have been present in the early life and later overcome as Ms. Five gained self-confidence.

The variety of small lines on the upper part of the palm might be seen as a number of stars, a marking that is subject to much controversy in palmistry texts. Some authors consider a star as a negative sign, indicating trouble in the area of life represented by the place of the star. Other authors consider it a mark of brilliance and potential success. I am always more inclined to prefer the positive interpretation, but the neutral reading would suggest that the star marks an important part of life for us, and that we can handle it well or badly, depending on our own actions.

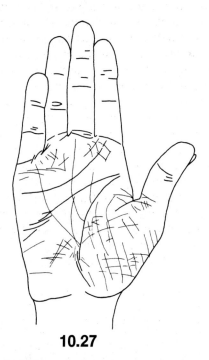

10.27

Perhaps we can **summarize** Ms. Five's hands as pointing to a sensitive person with potential artistic talent who may have needed to build her self-confidence in her early life and to integrate her practical and her spiritual sides. The square on the Mount of Jupiter in the left hand supports an inner wisdom which we hope is seeing her through.

Ms. Six

Looking next at Ms. Six, we have an impression of another long palm and long fingers, but the palm is also fairly broad suggesting strength rather than fragility. The fingers tend to narrow somewhat at their bases where they join the palm, a traditional indication of some restraint placed on sensuality, sometimes tending toward asceticism. At the same time, the space between the fingers at the base suggests open-mindedness while the closeness of the fingers in the photograph when the hand is presumably laid down in a natural position shows some caution in the nature. The fingers seem fairly square, a sign of practicality, while the length theoretically indicates skill in handling details.

The right hand's strong, deep Saturn Line rising from the base of the palm gives us a chance to test the theory that the subject faced the practical earth world early in life, whether needing or choosing to be self-sufficient and make her own way or handling material needs for herself. The line shifts to a series of parallel lines after the Head Line, suggesting a change in Ms. Six's handling of the material world as a result of mental changes. The latter might have included additional, later-in-life schooling, or (perhaps more likely) studies pursued on her own. The mental change seems to have opened up new interests or new talents and broadened her life, since above the Head Line the parallel lines suggest several interests or activities though they might be hobbies taken somewhat seriously or leading to tangible results.

On the left hand, a fragmented Mercury Line rises from the Life Line, forming two branches above the Head Line with one running to the Venus (ring) finger while the other continues on to the Mercury (little) finger. The upper portions of these lines, like the Saturn Line, are formed by shorter, parallel lines suggesting a diversity of interests in the later years. (Fig. 10.28)

An exceptionally strong, clean, deep Life Line points to excellent recuperative capacity, drive and energy. The fire potential in the nature is also implied by a deep crease or line from the base of the thumb across the top part of the Mount of the Sun to the Life Line. Another parallel line above it runs from the bottom part of the Lower Mars Mount in the right hand. Traditionally, lines parallel to the Life Line are considered a sign of strength while horizontal lines on the Sun's Mount (called the Mount of Venus in traditional palmistry) are associated with relationships and possible blocking of personal

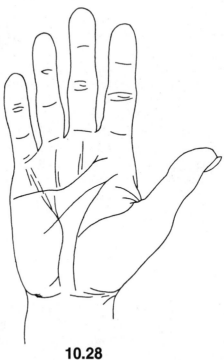

10.28

ability to do what we please. Such lines might represent our common freedom-closeness or independence-dependence dilemmas. The mixture of raised areas and depressions which appear to be present on the Lower Mount of Mars may be another sign of inner conflict or ambivalence over the handling of aggression. The distal edge of the hand that we are tentatively assigning to Pluto is softly rounded, suggesting adequate capacity for self-defense, but Ms. Six may have needed to find a way to comfortably handle her capacity for self-assertion. When we have fire power and inhibit it, we run a real risk of illness or accidents, but the recuperative power shown by the Life Line is highly positive. The low-set and moderately long thumbs also fit the confidence and independence associated with Mars and Jupiter, two of our fire planets in astrology. But we wonder whether the low-set little finger seen in several of our subjects is a sign of possible conflict between enjoying the material world (including relationships with loved ones) and spiritual aspirations. The finger seems slightly lower on the right hand, so the issue might have become more important in the middle years.

A partial Girdle of Venus or second Heart Line and the origin of the Heart Line on the mount of Jupiter in the left hand point to a warm nature from the beginning of life, including some idealization of love. (Fig. 10.29.) A fork at the beginning of the left-hand Heart

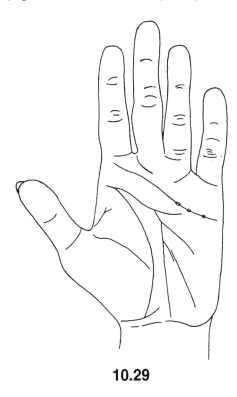

10.29

Line has one prong dipping slightly toward the Head Line, and the right hand offers further support for a trend toward increased caution or practicality. The right-hand Heart Line droops slightly toward the Head Line (the head reigning in the heart) without the fork reaching up toward Jupiter, and it starts closer to the boundary between the Jupiter and Saturn Mounts. Islands on the latter part of the Heart Line on the left hand offer an additional indication of a challenge in the emotional part of life, perhaps an inner emotional sensitivity and vulnerability which Ms. Six avoids showing in her outer expression. Still another indication of intense sensitivity and a potential for psychic openness is seen in the strong, deep line rising from near the base of the Mount of the Moon to end near or on the Head Line in the left hand. The right hand seems to lack this line, so the sensitivity may have lessened with maturity or may be hidden in the subjective side of the nature. The raised pads visible on the fingertips are also associated with sensitivity.

The same message appears in the Head Lines on the two hands. On the left hand, the Head Line droops toward the Mount of the Moon, while the line on the right hand ends in a fork, one pointing down toward the Moon but the other prong heading straight across the hand, a theoretical indication of a very practical mind. The Head Line ending in a fork is said to indicate mental versatility and flexibility. The narrow second joints of the thumbs are said to indicate tact or diplomacy, and the longer second joint is also considered an indication of a good mind.

In summary, Ms. Six seems sensitive but also strong and practical. The joined Head and Life Lines fit a capacity for common sense, action guided by intelligence more than impulse. The direction of the growth seems toward less emotional vulnerability, less heavy focus on material security, and more opportunity to expand the mind. Note how the right hand fingers are spread more widely than the left hand fingers. The knots of order on the finger joints suggest someone well able to organize and handle life in practical ways so long as the emotional hungers are also acknowledged and fed. The differences between the two hands suggest major growth during the life.

Mr. Seven

We wind up our journey with Mr. Seven who offers us a very broad, solid hand and short fingers: a combination of practical competence with the ability to see the overview and perhaps be impatient with the details. Major and some minor lines are strong, clean and deep, an indication of vitality, power and decisiveness. There are wide spaces between the bases of the fingers showing open-mindedness despite the fact that the third joints of the index (Jupiter) and little (Mercury) fingers widen as they join the palm. These wide bases of the fingers are associated with someone who can thoroughly enjoy the physical world.

Perhaps it is fortunate that the Head and Life Lines are joined at their beginning, showing the head guiding the life. (Fig. 10.30.) Or could the personal will of the Fire Line be shaping the thoughts? I am convinced that our minds create our reality, but most of us do it unconsciously. Mr. Seven has exceptionally deep lines on the Mount of Lower Mars, especially on the right hand, which put the

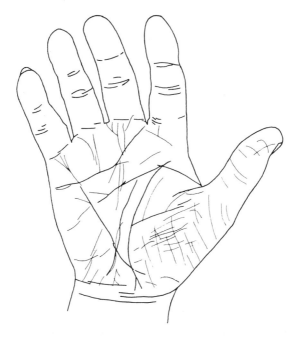

10.30

fire element in high focus, symbolizing self-will in action. The raised Mount of Lower Mars and the enlarged distal edge of Upper Mars, especially on the left hand, suggest a deeply emotional nature with fire and water both strong. There might be conflict at times between expressing the emotions (the fire tendency) and holding them back (the water instinct). (Fig. 10.31.) As with Ms. Six, we wonder whether the deep line near the top of the Sun Mount and nearly at a right angle to the Life Line might mark a strong fire component in the nature but some ambivalence over expressing it too vigorously.

The practical side of the nature seems also well represented with a Saturn Line rising from the base of the palm on both hands and a Mercury Line separating from it. The status in the world and handling of power (Saturn) and the details of the job (Mercury) are linked to a common source. (Fig. 10.32.) Does this indicate someone who realized early what he could and wanted to do and continued to pursue the goal? But the Saturn Line changes and continues on, both below the Head Line and at the Heart Line, with the last segment created by several parallel lines. These patterns suggest repeated

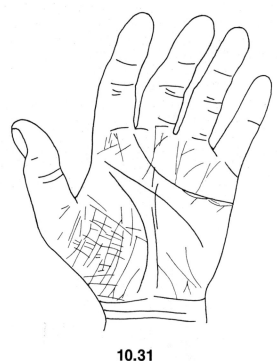

10.31

changes in the handling of the material world, though continuity is

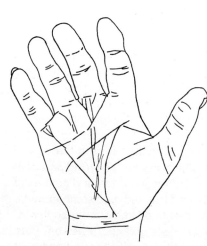

10.32

possible with the new line overlapping the old one. At the time of the big change, the right hand Saturn Line forks with one prong extending up to join the Head Line and the other joining the new Saturn Line. Did studies contribute to the new role? It seems to have started before Mr. Seven fully relinquished the old one.

The Head Line on the right hand also makes a new start which joins the original line where the Saturn Line crosses it. I have not attempted to speculate on timing in these brief discussions of the hands of our subjects, but most texts place the crossing of Head and Saturn Lines around the age of 35. Whether a "mid-life crisis" was involved, or a major change in worldview that influenced Mr. Seven's role in the world, the palm suggests important developments in those middle years. I am not sure how to read the island on the left Head Line. Many books treat the sign as a key to a physical problem with the brain. I suspect it might just mean a new openness of mental views with possibly some discomfort if the individual is giving up the security of a single old worldview and is not yet sure of the new one or is even contemplating the possibility that we have not yet arrived at final Truth. The lines on these hands look like someone with strong opinions and feelings, but the Head Lines extend into the water zones of the palm, and the left Head Line bends deeply down toward the Mount of the Moon.

Psychic guidance or interest is certainly suggested by the sloping Head Line, seen more clearly in the photos, and also by the lines rising from the Lunar Mount, at least one on the right hand and two clearly on the left hand, to join the Mercury Line. (Fig. 10.33.) The contact between conscious and unconscious aspects of the mind (air and water in astrology) is an indication of psychic openness.

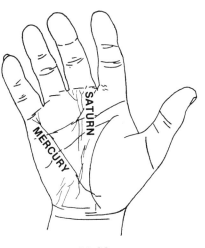

10.33

In addition to the warmth shown by deep lines on the Mounts of Sun and Moon, Mr. Seven's Heart Line runs all the way to the base of the Jupiter finger. It looks like superidealism about love, or perhaps his heart thrown into a spiritual goal. The Ring of Solomon on both hands, a line circling through the mount of Jupiter, is traditionally associated with a sense of spiritual mission and guidance. (Fig. 10.34.) Branches connect the Head and Heart Lines on the left hand, suggesting an inner urge to integrate heart and intellect, perhaps the intellect trying to rein in the emotions. The fingertips suggest a similar mixture, with the Saturn and Venus middle fingers fairly square (there are always rounded tips) while the Jupiter and Mercury fingers and possibly the thumbs look more conical, sloping to a narrower end.

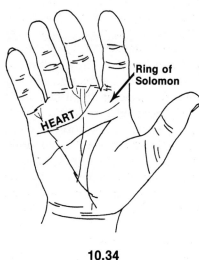

10.34

The square fingers trust the practical intellect while the conical fingers tend to be intuitive, listening to the feelings. The heart is also connected to the aesthetic side of life, with several parallel lines rising from the Heart Line to the Venus finger. And the Mercury Line on the right hand seems to join the Heart Line while new parallel lines rise from the Heart Line to continue up the mount below the little finger. I suspect that the choice is ours whether we use the talents for healing, for artistic creativity or for practical business goals.

In summary, Mr. Seven looks like an emotionally intense and warm person with considerable power to affect people, but also with the ability to cope with the material world. I would expect a lot of fire, which, indeed, we see in his horoscope. Mostly, I have tried to ignore the horoscopes to look at the hands as a separate model in this exploratory effort to see what can be said about a human being prior to actually being given any background information on them. A quick look at the handwriting, and I will be ready to see how our seven subjects have actually handled their potentials.

CHAPTER ELEVEN
HANDWRITING ANALYSIS OVERVIEW

In the various approaches to understanding ourselves and life, handwriting analysis or graphology occupies a unique space. Astrology, numerology and palmistry have been used to describe humans for several thousand years, but they have been almost totally ignored by the modern scientific community. They have therefore remained largely in the hands of uneducated individuals, usually possessed of good intentions but often with inadequate understanding of the complexity of their subjects. In contrast to this total dismissal without examination of astrology, numerology and palmistry, the use of handwriting as a psychological diagnostic tool is fairly common in Europe, especially in Switzerland and Germany. In the United States, most psychologists are unfamiliar with this work by European scientists, much of which has never been translated from German. Many people working with handwriting here have little or no scientific training. They may have taken a correspondence course or a class, but the teachers have often been uneducated and unqualified. Though the field has moved in the direction of improved understanding and acceptance in the U.S., most psychological practitioners probably still lump it with the rest of the "fringe" procedures. It is actually more widely acknowledged and used by businesses making vocational decisions. The study of handwriting is, of course, a fully accepted and technically developed subject in cases dealing with forgery.

I took a course in handwriting analysis in the early 1960s, along with the palmist friend mentioned earlier. My friend, Star, was a competent palmist attending my classes in astrology while I was just beginning to learn some palmistry. We shared our insights in our fields, and explored handwriting at the same time, but were very disappointed in the caliber of the handwriting teacher.

I had further evidence of the teacher's incompetence and of the inadequacy of his "school" of handwriting analysis somewhat later when I served as a psychological intern on the mental ward of a local hospital. The chief psychologist on the ward was a skeptical but not hostile scientist who had conducted an experiment involving my erstwhile teacher. The self-proclaimed handwriting "expert" had approached the psychologist with the claim that he could diagnose the type and degree of severity of mental illness of patients on the ward from samples of their handwriting. He offered to demonstrate his ability on ten samples of writing provided by the psychologist. The latter gave him samples of eight of the patients and two different samples written by the other psychologist who worked on the ward. The second psychologist was subject to mood swings at times, and the head psychologist picked out a sample written when he was "up" and another sample written when he was "down." Needless to say, the handwriting "expert" bombed! Not only did he diagnose the actual patients in ways which provided no help, but he also refused to believe that the two samples from the assistant psychologist were written by the same person, and he was convinced that both samples were from severely disturbed individuals.

Themes, Not Specifics

As I have written earlier, astrology is the only one of the subjects discussed in this book in which I have extensive experience. In the other areas, I have a smattering of knowledge only. But with my mutable dilemma, I do enjoy exploring new areas. I have collected a fair number of books on all of the fields being covered, and have found the same general tendency in most of them: an attempt to be too precise in guessing details. To list some examples from texts on graphology, a loop formation on the upper stem of the letter "p" is supposedly a sign of a peaceful nature, and looped stems on the letters "d" and "t" are described as a sign of a supersensitive nature, a touchy person who takes things personally and is easily offended or hurt.

As with palmistry and astrology, there is a germ of truth in such statements, but they are both too sweeping and too specific, assuming "good" or "bad" details in the life from a single trait in the writing. The "probable truth" behind such statements is that individuals who tend to write with rounded curves, including all kinds of loops on all letters as well as rounded tops or bottoms on letters such as "m" and "n," tend to be more soft and/or sensitive and/or gentle people. Sharp, angular formations, in contrast, fit a more assertive, penetrating, sometimes aggressive style of approaching life. But I personally doubt that we can know from the handwriting whether the individual is primarily sensitive to personal needs, self-absorbed and perhaps vulnerable, or whether the individual is sensitive to the needs of others and basically just kind and generous.

The rounded formations in handwriting seem to me somewhat like "water" in a horoscope. An emphasis on water in a chart may point to a person who is dependent and mostly focused on personal security, or it may mark a person who plays "mother and savior" to the world. Personal self-confidence and faith in a Higher Power contribute to the difference, and individuals may move from the "baby" state to the "parent" state as they grow.

Similarly, small margins, crowded words with little space between them, and sharp cut-offs on words rather than a continuation extending out from the last letter, are sometimes associated with being careful or thrifty and sometimes described as selfish, lacking in generosity. The antiquity of interest in handwriting as a key to personality is shown by a quotation from Suetonius, a second-century Roman historian, that "Augustus Caesar's meanness could be plainly read in his tight script." p.174 in Klara Roman's *Encyclopedia of the Written Word*. Yet it is quite possible to be thrifty in the sense of avoiding waste yet at the same time to be generous.

Another example involves the slant of letters, with some books describing varying slants in the same writing as an indication of versatility in emotional expression while others state flatly that such writers have emotional conflicts. Some subjects might enjoy their varied expressiveness and feel it is under their own control, while others might feel driven and disturbed by it. When the analysis tries to be too specific on details, just as with astrology and palmistry, it will be wrong fairly often. Errors are likely whether the limited focus is on individual details in the writing or on individual details in the life expression of the subject.

A Wholistic Approach

The handwriting analysis books done by Europeans who have studied the subject in university courses and have done extensive research themselves point out the need for a wholistic approach to the subject. Many different components in the writing need to be considered and integrated, and there are positive and painful ways to express the consequences in the life. Among the most helpful authors in my experience are Klara Roman, educated in psychology, who came to the U.S. from Hungary after extensive scientific research in handwriting analysis, and Werner Wolff, a student of depth psychology and later a college professor in psychology. Wolff's book, *Diagrams of the Unconscious*, has 500 references in its bibliography, many of them only available in German.

Since my own experience with handwriting is very limited, I am inclined to offer whatever I say as a "theory," needing to be tested. But at least in this area, in contrast to palmistry, numerology and astrology, a sizable amount of research has already been carried out. We are beyond the "anecdotal" stage of the other subjects. I also feel under less pressure to present a full coverage of the basic principles of the subject since they can be found in books such as those by Roman and Wolff. I do want to offer a brief overview of the theories, and I assume that readers of our book will use the samples to test their own theories of handwriting analysis.

Factors to Consider

Among the possible tools used in graphology, we can consider size of writing, pressure on the page which can be partly noted by seeing to what extent there are ridges raised on the opposite side of the paper, shading, shaping (such as roundness versus angularity), slant (of letters toward the right or left or vertical and the slant of the whole line of writing), spaces (margins, between letters, words, lines, etc.), the size of the three basic "zones" including upper and lower loops and the middle part of the letters, speed of writing, rhythm, connectedness, precision with details, originality of letter shapes and more. Signatures are a study in themselves, sometimes appearing quite different from the balance of the writing. Flourishes and underlines tell us something. As is apparent from even this partial list, the subject is not something one masters quickly and casually.

Moods

One other point made by the more thorough authors involves the currency of handwriting. Our writing expresses our feelings at the time that we do it, and a sample written at another time, under different circumstances, may be surprisingly different, as my erstwhile teacher could have discovered if he had not been so rigid or insecure that he was incapable of accepting that some of his theories were wrong and needed revising. Our writing changes as we change. Some of our character is basic and enduring, but other parts change as we grow or simply have short-term fluctuations depending on our current state of mind. Handwriting analysis does not predict the future except to the extent that we can guess that a given character is likely to produce related events somewhere along the line.

Handwriting is also subject to cultural influences, and the country of origin of the writer should be considered in an analysis. Of course, in the occult view, we are born where we fit. It is not a "coincidence" that German writing tends to be more angular. Some books describe angular writing as an indication of a critical mind while rounded writing is seen as gullible — another example of trying to be too specific. Being gullible may accompany acceptance of other people and what they say at face value, or at least being kind enough not to disagree openly. But if the writing is small and legible, implying control and thoroughness, this may offset the "trust in other people" suggested by the soft, round forms.

Size

Perhaps the preceding is sufficient introduction to the topic to let us proceed to a brief survey of the principles. As just indicated, size is one of the important variables. My limited experience suggests that small size is somewhat similar in meaning to letters six and ten in our astrological alphabet, with a tendency toward self-control and restraint, thoroughness, precision, and the general Puritan virtues. To some degree, handwriting analysis seems more logical and deducible from simple "common sense" than the rest of our approaches to understanding people. It "makes sense" that writing characterized by careful limits would mark a person very aware of "limits" which are symbolized by earth in astrology. Security or the lack of it may also be an important issue for people with small writing, which implies that water in some form might also be found prominent in the writers' horoscopes.

I would expect large writing to be associated with some kind of fire emphasis, perhaps supported by air, since it is said to indicate an expansive and expressive nature, with some diminution of self-control. The self-confidence might produce a very effective person, or it might be overdone and lead to overconfidence, too much spontaneity, and to rash or headstrong tendencies. The writing of most people will fall in the middle rather than at either extreme. The great bell-shaped curve of science offers its ubiquitous definition of what is average or "normal."

Wolff cites interesting studies of children in which 86% of the depressed children made very small drawings suggesting overcontrol. Feeble-minded children, on the other hand, made very large drawings showing a lack of control over their movements. Rejected and deprived children generally used only a small part of the available paper, usually the bottom part. The connotations are almost suspiciously obvious: a feeling of being low man on the totem pole, lacking the right to occupy much space, tense or "on guard" against potential pain from the world.

Pressure

Pressure is another important variable in handwriting. In the book of another psychologist who specialized in handwriting analysis, Dr. Hal Falcon suggests a rating scale from zero to ten based on the number of carbons which the writing can produce. Writing which would produce five carbons is classed as #5 pressure. The pressure can be seen as ridges on the back of the paper as well as indentations on the paper underneath. Falcon associates pressure with power (including willpower), energy, drive and competitive spirit. He finds that most successful people in executive positions write with a 5 or higher pressure. He claims that average intelligence and the drive shown by pressure are more likely to rise to the top than a very high IQ combined with laziness. I'm sure that pressure or drive is one of the keys to success, but advise caution in giving too much weight to any single variable. Long strong "t" bars and other straight, strong strokes in writing are additional keys to the potential for drive, enthusiasm, confidence, etc.

Space

Space, whether between letters, words, lines or between the writing and the edges of the paper (margins), is often but not always related to size. Small writing tends to accompany small spaces, as an indication of thrift and precision or care, the avoidance of waste. But it is possible to find writing with small letters but with wide spaces between letters, words, and/or lines. As an opposite tendency to thrift, conservation, caution, etc., such spaces could suggest more generosity or extravagance or openness in some other form.

Open Letters

One of the theories found in many traditional graphology books but unsupported by research involves letters being left open which are normally closed. An unclosed "a" or "o" is said to indicate a talkative person who cannot keep a secret, while the closure of one of these letters with a loop or double loop is supposed to be a sign of a secretive or even deceptive person. Dr. Falcon, mentioned above, found this theory inaccurate. He described a salesman who hardly let him get in one word to the salesman's five but who firmly closed all his letters. I suspect that open letters are more connected to speed of writing, as are "t" crosses which start to the right of the "t," and "i" dots which are thrown in to the right of the "i." The writer is too eager to move on to go back all the way.

Speed

Speed of writing is one of the important variables and is an obvious common sense correlate to speed in other areas of the life. Like large writing, I would speculate that it goes with fire (perhaps supported by air) in the horoscope, with many interests and/or impatience or eagerness or enthusiasm, etc. Sometimes writing is so fast that it is almost reduced to a wavy line which can be nearly illegible. Have you studied the signatures on many M.D.'s prescriptions? One is likely to be a bit impatient at having to do again something routine which has been done so often in the past. The technical name for such writing is "threading" or "threadlike."

Rhythms

Rhythm is somewhat related to speed, since fast writing is a bit more likely to be rhythmic than is very deliberate writing. Again, there is a common sense correlate. Flowing writing seems to go with easy-flow motions, often with love of rhythmic sports or dancing. It may also be associated with other forms of artistic ability or appreciation.

Shading

Shading is also said to be commonly found in the writing of artists, and to be associated with sensuality. As with astrology, we can use a love of pleasure connected to the physical world to collect posses-sions which we admire, to indulge the appetites or to create beauty. In a corresponding horoscope we would look for a fixed emphasis and possibly a prominent letter seven or twelve.

Slant

The degree to which letters are slanted is one of the controversial tools of graphology. Some texts class writing which slants forward as extroverted; a back slant as introverted; and vertical writing as in the middle — ambivert. As mentioned earlier, variable writing is often described as a sign of a disturbed individual. As readers must know by now, I would strongly advise using neutral words such as versatile and checking the life of the person to see whether it was experienced as a problem. Some graphology texts associate the for-ward slant with emotions, stating that the more it leans forward, the deeper or more intense the emotions. They consider the back slant a sign of repression or coldness. Others write that the forward slant accompanies a tendency to express the emotions while people with the back slant have deep emotions but hold them in and are hard to understand.

Falcon believes that the back slant is as emotional as a corresponding forward slant, but his word for such individuals is "choosy," versus "ardent" for the equivalent forward slant. The description of the back slant is of a self-oriented if not selfish per-son, while the forward slant is described as generous. Falcon's angle for "coldness" is just slightly to the right of vertical.

Despite my limited experience with graphology, I have seen enough to know that a vertical or near-vertical slant is not a sign of coldness or of lack of emotionality or generosity, or (another interpretation) the head controlling the heart. I have friends who write almost vertically who are deeply emotional; one very embarrassed about her frequent crying spells. She is also very emotionally expressive. The closest I have been able to come to a description of the vertical to back-slanted writing is a tendency toward self-consciousness which may range from being overly self-absorbed at the expense of others (Falcon's interpretation), to someone who is self-contained and likes to be alone, to someone who is highly self-aware and self-analytical (the "head ruling heart" concept).

Wolff divides movements into centripetal (back toward the self) and centrifugal (out away from the self) which comes close to what I have experienced. The little hooks which are sometimes seen at either the beginning or the end of letters could be included in this interpretation as an attempt to grasp at something and pull it back toward the self, to gain or maintain possession or for more mental processing. Wolff also suggests that a forward slant indicates more action and a backward slant more reflection, a kind of outer versus inner orientation. The interconnectedness of different factors is seen in the association of fast writing with a slant to the right. Reflection certainly requires at least a temporary slowdown in the action.

The variable slant (as already described) can operate in both directions. We would need to talk to the person or observe the life to find out whether the variability was experienced as a problem for the individual or for associates.

The general slant of the lines of writing (which should be done on unlined paper) is associated with the general emotional tone at the time of writing: up for hope or optimism and down for depression or discouragement or when physically tired. As already indicated, such traits can vary in writing done at different times while in different moods. For thorough analysis, one should have several samples done by the same person but written at different times.

Garlands and Arcades

Another set of theories which are found in many texts but which I find questionable involve differentiations between garlands and arcades. Arcades are the "normal" form of the "m" and "n" with the tops rounded and the bottoms sharp points. Garlands are the reverse; the same letters (and others with similar potentials) made with rounded bottoms and sharp points at the tops so an "n" looks like a "u." Some authors consider the garland a sign of a friendly, sociable personality while the arcade is put down as showing a lack of spontaneity. In another text, the arcade is associated with a nonaggressive, cooperative but sometimes gullible nature.

A study cited by Wolff throws doubt on the issue unless we are prepared to believe that left-handedness is associated with a specific type of personality. In the research cited, 80% of the left-handed subjects wrote with arcades while the right-handed subjects included 40% with arcades, 40% with garlands, and 20% angular. Since some studies have found left-handedness correlated with exceptional artistic and mathematical ability, often with considerable originality, along with (sometimes credited to) more connectedness between right and left sides of the brain than is common for males, I suspect the whole area is another attempt to be too specific on details.

Wolff comments that there have been some studies associating more curves and few edges with people who are fairly well-adjusted, slightly passive and introversive but affectionate with a tendency to lack confidence, have a fanciful imagination, be emotional and dependent but competent and productive. Individuals with many angles and few curves, on the other hand, were more overtly aggressive, assertive in negativistic ways, outgoing, with realistic interests, initiative, and a low level of adjustment. A variety of models in psychology would fit this collection of traits, including a fairly close fit to the concept of outer-directed versus inner-directed individuals. But of course, one can be inner-directed and still well-adjusted enough to get along with other people with minimal aggression.

Three Zones

Another area of mixed interpretations involves the division of handwriting into three zones. Most texts associate the **upper loops with mental activity and/or spiritual aspirations; the middle zone with practical affairs in the daily life; and the lower loops with either emotions or physical appetites** (including sex) or with material interests such as money and possessions. Distortions involving the lower loops sound very much like the fixed dilemma in astrology. As usual, many authors try to be too specific in their interpretations, but the problems might involve emotions, money, possessions, appetites, power; learning to give, to receive, to share, or to attain self-knowledge and/or self-mastery. Problems are suggested if the loops are excessively short, long, wide, cut off near the bottom of the stem, etc.

I feel the need for more experience in this area of handwriting analysis. The descriptions of the zones are almost too pat, too obvious to be trustworthy, and I am suspicious of the details offered in most of the texts. But there does seem to be some truth in the general principles. The "t" crossing floating above the stem of the letter does seem associated with a tendency to have the head in the clouds some of the time. Long loops are often found with large rhythmic flowing writing in individuals who love dancing or other active, somewhat sensual and attention-getting avocations. If both upper and lower loops are approximately the same length and not far from the height of the unlooped letters, the individual is considered well-balanced. A very large middle zone is supposed to indicate a very practical person with less emphasis on either mental-abstract or on emotional-sensual matters. I don't seem to attract that kind of person into my life, so I have not been able to test the theory so far.

Connectedness, "T" Bars and "I" Dots

A number of other theories exist, including an association of connected writing with a logical mind while disconnected writing (involving breaks in the middle of words) is supposed to show intuitive ability. Since it is possible to have high ability in both talents or in neither of them, the theory is questionable. Precision with details seems a little more solidly based as a key to careful, precise individuals. Examples would include placing the dot exactly over the "i" and crossing the "t" at the right height and with a bar no longer than the stem of the "t". Such writers might be careful and/or conventional.

Individuality and Showmanship

Individuality, on the other hand, is suggested by unusual forms for the letters. Of course individuality might be expressed in positive creativity or might be rebellion against convention without offering anything better to replace it. One of the too-specific old ideas associates Greek letters with writing talent. It is possible that in the days when writers were still taught Greek in school in being educated in the classics, such an association existed, but I have not observed it in modern writers. To repeat what has already been said, the cultural context of the writer must always be considered. Cultures vary and they change over time. The current trend is toward simplicity in writing, with capital letters almost like printed ones with an avoidance of frills and flourishes. But ornate flourishes can still be seen, with their implication of showmanship, expansive urges or artistic interests.

Signatures

Many texts emphasize signatures and the letter "I" as special keys to the individual's sense of personal identity and ego. Large capitals, especially with flourishes and underlining, are theoretically connected to some tendencies toward exhibitionism or narcissism — someone naturally dramatic, who wants to be noticed and admired. We again think of a fire emphasis in astrology, especially involving letter five: Sun, Leo or the fifth house. But Wolff suggests that the underline is a form of support (presumably indicating the individual feels the need for such) and that the overline plays a directive role. When working with historical material, it is important to know whether flourishes and extra lines were an approved part of the cultural milieu at the time and place of the writing. Very small capital letters in a signature may indicate humility or self-doubt. But any unusual forms might also be an attempt to make an impression or a need to feel unique.

Get the Whole Picture

At the risk of boring readers through repetition, remember that all the factors have to be integrated to arrive at an accurate understanding of a person. One detail is not enough to say anything! Wolff reports that in the numerous experiments done by Max Pulver, one of the foremost experts in Germany, they failed to get results when there was too much emphasis on individual "signs" in the writing. They were only successful when they looked at the whole picture.

Perhaps enough has been said to cover the general principles, and it is time to turn to our seven subjects. Again, I have to apologize at the start for the inadequate data sample for some of our subjects. To take my own advice, I should have several pages of writing done at different times. But we will do what we can with what we have and perhaps by the time this book goes to publication, we can include additional samples.

Ms. One

Looking first at Ms. One, our impression is of large writing, with a wide right-hand margin and usually considerable space between words and lines. The writing slants forward and looks as if it were done rapidly. There is a fair sense of rhythm in the writing but the pressure is moderate except on some of the "t" bars and the cross-out lines on one word. The general slope of the lines is just slightly downward. Most of the upper loops and a few of the lower loops are quite long in comparison to the middle zone of the writing. There are many rounded formations in the letters but some angularity.

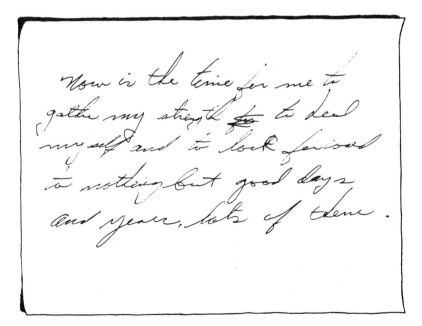

In general, we get a sense of a warm person, reaching out to life and others, with high aspirations or mental interests which might overshadow the practical side of life. There seems to be a danger of inadequate power to achieve the head and heart goals. I get a sense of the mutable dilemma, of wanting more than is possible. If the theory is accurate (it is still an ''if'' as far as my experience is concerned), the breaks in the middle of four of the words could point to an intuitive nature which would fit the sensitivity suggested by the rounded forms of many letters. Again, the flow, speed, rhythm, size, all fit an enthusiastic, creative, eager, sometimes impatient person but the lack of pressure and relatively smaller middle zone would suggest some sort of lack in the area of physical energy or personal confidence. Obviously, the contents of the handwriting sample points to personal tension. I'm glad that the astrological, numerological and palmistry analyses were written first, to avoid any influences from choice of subject matter in the handwriting samples.

In spite of the size and speed of the writing, the details are handled. One ''i'' dot is almost over the letter and another is just a little to the right. The ''t'' crossings are mostly normal though one starts just at the stem of the letter. But the ''t'' bars do stay on the low side, unlike the soaring upper loops, again fitting our possible conflict between aspirations and anxiety about reaching the high goals. But there is hope. The forward-looking slant to the letters fits the contents expressed in the brief statement.

There is more variation on the lower loops than in the rest of the writing with some long and slender, some broken off and incomplete, several forming whole or partial triangles. Dr. Falcon would interpret the low crossing of the return loops and the partial returns on the lower loops as a sense of denial or lack of fulfillment in the material or sensual area. This might mean financial pressures, lack of material security in other forms, desire for more shared physical pleasures with others, etc. We can see some small hooks on the initial letters of several words, supporting a sense of need to hold on to security in some form. The writing gives us a sense of reaching for the stars, for the future, but feeling the need of something to cling to. Are we looking at a graphology version of the freedom-closeness dilemma or security versus risk and change?

Since we are protecting the anonymity of our subjects, their signatures will not be included in our book, but I do have them and can comment on similarities or differences from the balance of the writing. Ms. One's signature is basically similar to her other writing except for the capital letters of the signature being somewhat larger than any of the other letters. The first letter of the first name is the largest single letter in the sample: very round and flowing, yet with a small hook at both the beginning and the end of the letter. The letter is made with a single sweep of the pen. The first letter of the last name is equally tall but not as wide, but two upper loops in the last name soar even above the capitals. A "t" bar in the signature is about three times as long as any in the rest of the sample, and the "i" dot is a slash that is almost vertical but sloping up and to the right. There is a suggestion of power and determination in the long "t" bar and the slashed dot and a longer final extension at the end of the last name. Also, the letters are somewhat more angular. Only the capital of the first name, a loop at the beginning of the capital of the second name, and two letters in the middle zone are truly circular. The signature seems to be reaching for strength, again like the content of the message. We hope that Ms. One is finding her good days and years.

Mr. Two

Turning to Mr. Two, we see that he has chosen to copy a paragraph from a metaphysical writer rather than to make a personal statement. In contrast to the far-right slant in the writing of Ms. One, Mr. Two's letters are just slightly to the right of vertical. Depending on which of our texts we believe, Mr. Two may be more reflective and less active, less emotionally expressive, or more self-contained and inner directed in some way. The writing is highly legible with rounded forms and nicely dotted "i's" and crossed "t's." Mr. Two looks well-organized, careful and thorough, but also basically kind and thoughtful with the round forms.

The middle zone is well-developed, suggesting a person able to cope with the material needs of daily life. In spite of the choice of a metaphysical quotation, the upper loops and stems are not very high, so Mr. Two would seem to have his feet on the ground. The connected writing also supports a logical and practical mind. Many of the lower loops are longer than the upper ones, adding emphasis to the emotional or sensual area of life. The practical nature might hold indulgences in check and live a lot in the imagination, but it is interesting that Mr. Two picked a paragraph about sensual indulgence for his handwriting sample. Since I don't believe in chance, the choice would point to the area as an issue in the life. The spaces between words and lines would fit a fairly open, expressive individual but the narrow margins suggest thrift to support the general feeling of a thoughtful, careful, competent person. Power is not emphasized in the writing, so Mr. Two may live a lot in his logical mind.

"From the 28th year to the 35th year one comes into moral responsibility for his actions and appetites. If he develops any negative appetites or selfish habits, such as vulgarity in speech, dishonesty, adultery, or the excessive use of drugs, alcohol, or tobacco — these will produce etheric scars which may remain for life. If these appetites and habits are not resolved before the 35th year, they are carried over into the next life and will appear as certain defects and weaknesses.

In spite of the nearly upright writing, there is a nice flow and sense of rhythm which would fit good physical coordination and potential artistic talent in some form. An interesting variation appears in the signature with the last name separated into four pieces. We wonder whether he is pulled between his "feet-on-the-ground" side and a growing identification with the intuitive side of life? Since the breaks appear in the family name, is there a family member who shares that interest or has opened Mr. Two to that area? Or does he feel separated in some way in his family relationships? In spite of the rounded forms in the general writing, the upright letters and careful execution show a need to integrate the friendliness and kindness with the ability to see flaws in life. But it seems likely that Mr. Two can handle life successfully.

Ms. Three

Turning to Ms. Three, we note that the writing has some similarities to Mr. Two but the slant is somewhat more to the right. Our varied theories might suggest that this slant means moderate tendencies toward action and outreach to people. But the final strokes of several letters curve back toward the left, indicating attention directed inward toward personal needs or feelings. It is unfortunate that all writing samples were not done with the same writing instrument to permit accurate comparisons. The writing in Ms. Three's sample looks heavier, but the type of pen might be responsible for the suggestion of greater intensity. Of course, one's choice of pen would be a significant clue to character, but Ms. Three writes she is not using her customary pen. The writing is also slightly smaller than Mr. Two, but still well within a normal range.

> Dear Bill,
>   Without benefit of a desk or my usual trusty fountain pen I will answer your request by writing part of our wedding ceremony which was composed almost entirely of scripture.
>   "Thou shalt love the Lord thy God with all thine heart, and with all thy soul, and with all thy might."
>   "Trust in the Lord with all thine heart; and lean not unto thine own understanding. In all thy ways acknowledge him and He shall direct Thy paths."
>   "Have ye love one for another even as I have loved you."
>   "In quietness and confidence shall be your strength."
>   With this ring I Thee wed... to pledge my

Like Mr. Two, the middle zone of writing is dominant, fitting a practical person who is focused on coping with the everyday world. The lower loops are mostly somewhat longer than the upper loops, so the emotional-imaginative and/or sensual-physical areas of life are also important but not excessively so. The loops are narrow, with some letters such as the "p's" written with the return stroke superimposed on the downstroke. Though there is a good flow to the writing, it looks mostly controlled, neat and legible. Other indications of a careful, thorough person include the precision with details such as "i" dots almost always placed above the letter or just slightly to the right, and "t" bars mostly short and at a normal height on the stem. A hint of impatience shows in one bar starting at the stem of the "t." Several bars, including the top line of four capital "t's," slant up to suggest optimism.

The letter forms are mostly rounded, including "m," "n," "o," "a" and the middle zone part of "p," "g" and "d," but the "e's" are mostly very narrow. At this point in my understanding, I am not prepared to speculate about a meaning for narrow "e's" except to note that they fit the generally narrow upper loops. The upper stems of "d" and "t" are unlooped, while "h" is either unlooped or with a very narrow one. We might theorize that the writing points to a kind and basically friendly person but with the aspirations kept cautious and under control by the practical nature.

The close spacing of the words and lines would also fit a careful, thrifty person, yet there are very wide margins. The combination is the opposite of Mr. Two who had wide spacing between his words and lines but very narrow margins. Perhaps they are both conscious of limits but are handling the available resources (material or emotional or time or whatever) with different priorities. The close spacing between the lines is especially noticeable since some of the lower loops run into the line below their own line. Reluctance to waste space may translate into a more general avoidance of waste, or to some other variety of security needs. Another related clue comes from the small beginning lines on some (but far from all) of the initial letters. In the words beginning with "a" and "o," some letters are started at the top of the loop while others start at the baseline, rise to the top of the letter, then retrace to make the circle to return to the top to join the initial stroke. The latter movement is much more involved and time-consuming, and suggests possible caution or deliberation about starting things. Letters which start at the top and plunge quickly around the circle have a feeling of more readiness to just plunge in: rather like diving in a pool without testing the water first. The "knots" on some of the "o's" and on two capital "T's" and a capital "H" may be another sign of conservatism or security focus, some kind of holding-on and holding-in. Also, except for the capital letters, all the letters in the words are connected: another possible indication of a logical mind. Mostly, the writing of Ms. Three gives a sense of a water-earth emphasis, a solid citizen, practical, careful, controlled, thorough, kind and helpful but not flamboyant or exhibitionistic.

I have only the first name of Ms. Three's signature, but it supports the balance of the writing. The initial capital is close to the same size as the letters with upper loops, and the whole name is simply done without any ostentation. If the self-image is also shown by the handling of the personal pronoun, the capital "I," they seem much like the signature; fairly narrow, of moderate height and simple form but with loops unlike the capital "T's" and "W's" which are close to printing style.

Mr. Four

Continuing to Mr. Four, the writing size is slightly smaller than our preceding samples but still well within a normal range. There is much less sense of control and much more sense of speed in the forms as in the "i" dots like dashes, along with more angularity. Yet some of the "t's" and "d's," normally unlooped letters, do have their upper stems looped. The combination suggests a mixture of sensitivity and assertion, but, of course, we have to look at the life to see whether the sensitivity is manifested in consideration for others or more in self-protection. The letters mostly slant toward the right, suggesting a life of action and outreach, though some are close to upright for attention to the self. The contents of the handwriting sample suggest that Mr. Four sees himself as a person of action rather than of words.

The wide spaces between words and lines and the good margins might offer further support for a casual or confident or defiant approach to life, unlike the closer, more controlled forms in the last two samples. Most of the initial letters of words start at the top of the form, rather than with an approach from the baseline which was noted in the sample from Ms. Three. This occurs even with the initial "m's," "n's" and "w's" where it is less common than with initial "a," "o," "c," "t," etc. One gets an impression of someone willing to "jump into things." The upward slope of the lines also would fit someone with some confidence about the future. But the "t" bars are mixed: some high and some low. And the "knots" or inner loops on most of the "a's" and "o's" along with a number of "tied t's" where the bar is made in a single sweep without lifting the pen, point more toward awareness of security needs. Perhaps we are looking at a graphological manifestation of the "security versus risk" dilemma? In spite of the speed of the writing, the details such as "i" dots and "t" bars are handled with precision, pointing to personal competence and thoroughness.

Though Mr. Four's pressure seems relatively light, suggesting only moderate drive or energy, some sweeping "t" bars seem forceful and assertive, as do the unlooped downstrokes of some final "g's" and "y's." In other cases of these letters which extend below the base line of the writing, the lower stems start a return loop but stop far below the baseline while one "f" ends pointing back toward the left which is theoretically the self. Dr. Falcon would say that there was some dissatisfaction in the area of material or sensual desires.

The moderately large capital "I's" support some degree of self-importance (or a desire for it?), as do the capitals in the signature. The first letter of the first name is distinctly larger than the middle initial or first letter of the family name, theoretically an indication of personal self-esteem, perhaps of a need to match or go beyond the level attained by the family. A full signature made at a different time than the balance of the handwriting sample was done with considerably more pressure than the main sample. The sense of energy and drive is very visible in the pressure, the rhythmic flow and the speed of the writing. The sense of an active, "take charge" individual comes through clearly in this separate signature.

Ms. Five

Moving on to Ms. Five, we see that she has chosen poetry by Emily Dickinson to present her handwriting, a highly suitable choice since the first impression of the writing is its artistic quality. The letters are rounded, flowing and rhythmic with unique flourishes on most initial capitals adding to the sense of grace. The lower loops are moderately long, a few of them widely rounded or triangular, but many stop the return stroke before reaching the baseline. The love of beauty may be more imaginative, in the mind and emotions, than expressed on the physical, sensual level. But there might be a love of dancing and music as well as poetry. The light pressure and the rounded forms of the letters supports a gentle quality in the life, again making the choice of Emily Dickinson poetry seem highly appropriate.

The right slanting letters fit someone actively reaching out to life and others, though the final strokes on some of the letters curl up and turn slightly back to the left as a possible key to attention directed back to the self. The relatively long upper and lower loops as compared to the middle zone of the letters may be telling us that much of the action is in the mind. But the middle zone is not deficient, so there should be adequate capacity to handle everyday affairs. Many of the "i" dots are actually short dashes, testifying to the speed of the writing, but they are above the "i's" or just slightly to the right, and the "t" bars are appropriately placed, so attention to details is good. If disconnections between letters in the words is an indication of intuition, it should be fairly important in the life. Many of the "m's," "n's" and "p's" and some of the letters with lower loops such as "g," "j" and "y" are disconnected from the letters which follow them.

Spacing is fairly wide throughout the writing: between words and lines and margins. Many authors associate such space with artistic appreciation and/or ability. It might suggest that security or waste are not major issues, or it might simply show the feeling for harmony and balance which astrology associates with a strong Libra or Venus. I would expect the horoscope to show some form of prominence for Venus and/or Neptune. Even the signature has wide spaces between the three names.

The initial capital letters of the names are similar in size and perhaps slightly stronger in pressure than the balance of the writing. Only the family name has an unusually formed capital. If the flourishes on the capitals of the Dickinson poetry are a sign of dramatic tendencies or showmanship in the nature, it seems more connected to the artistic interests than to the self-image. The capital "F" in the paragraph about astrology is similar to the flourished letter in the family name. Except for the capital "S," other capitals in the paragraph are mostly simple, rounded forms of printed letters. The capital "I" in the poetry is formed by a small loop at the top followed by a simple downstroke, theoretically an indication of a modest person. It is interesting that the contents of the writing samples include some very sensitive, emotional poetry while the chosen prose is seemingly impersonal and factual. There are no capital "I's" in the paragraph on astrology. The adjectives (personal values?) included in the paragraph involve long life, action, ambition and comfort. Action and ambition could be fire goals, but the balance of the writing implies they are more likely to be goals than actualized achievements. A Venus emphasis in the horoscope would fit the artistic writing and the value placed on comfort.

The overall impression of the writing suggests a sensitive artistic and gentle person; "tender" is the word emphasized in one of the Dickinson poems. The dreams may outreach the limits of the possible on occasion, but the clear, smooth, flowing style and care with details should indicate an individual able to meet and handle life.

Ms. Six

Looking next at Ms. Six, we see distinctly larger writing, with some words also showing moderately strong pressure. A fire emphasis, quite possibly backed up by water, looks like a good guess for the horoscope. Many of the upper and lower loops are average in comparison to the general size of the writing, but some sweep much further up or down, suggesting a mind that at times might get overextended and struggle against the limits of the ordinary world. The contents that speak of a "race against time" would fit that kind of pressure. A possible "mutable dilemma" in the horoscope including considerable versatility, might also be suggested by the variety of "t" bars: some standard types, some tied by a continuous stroke that swings back to cross the stem in a standard way, some just touching the stem and continuing forward, and some just represented by a slight curve in an upward stroke. A few high crossings would also support an eager approach to life backed by optimism. Yet the lines tend to slope just slightly down. The down slope may be too small to be meaningful, but might suggest a touch of anxiety or discouragement about reaching the high goals.

The letter forms are mostly rounded, fitting a generally unaggressive person, a "people person." The right-hand slant also supports an active outreach to life. With the large size in general, we might suspect some natural showmanship, and this is emphasized much more in the signature which has very large captials and more of those sweeping upper and lower loops. The capital for the personal name is larger than any other letter in the sample, so we can suspect that personal self-esteem is important to Ms. Six, that she needs an emotional response from the important people in her life, perhaps more than the average person. The capital "I's," theoretically one of the keys to our sense of self, are also interesting. An extended loop to the left suggests attention to personal feelings and needs, perhaps introspection or self-analysis.

In general, the spacing between words and lines fits the general size of the writing, and there is a good left-hand margin, so there is minimal indication of tension over holding on or holding in. But there are some "knots" or inner loops in some of the "a's" (including a capital "A"), "o's" and "p's," so if these forms are connected to security issues, they are certainly present in the life. The sense of free flow and rhythm is strong, which might mean love of dancing or other forms of physical movement. But the lower loops are as varied as the "t" bars, ranging from a downstroke which does not return at all, to a partial return that cuts across to the right side of the stem or stops just short of it, to a partial return which turns back to the left side of the letter, to a normal full return to the baseline of the writing. One gets a strong sense of versatility or love of variety in the varying forms, but there is also ability to handle details with properly dotted "i's" even though some of them are displaced to the right, showing the speed of the writing. So, leaving Ms. Six with a sense of warmth, enthusiasm and energy, we move to our last subject.

Mr. Seven

The first impression received from the handwriting of Mr. Seven is of the strongest pressure of any of our subjects. The sense of intense active energy coming from both the pressure and the strong slant to the right seems appropriate to statements which both feature "joy" in their contents. "Joy" is a fire word, where Venus is more like the laid-back word "pleasure." Mr. Seven is or certainly tries to be joyful. Drive and determination are also suggested by strong "t" bars, some very long in addition to their strength.

The moderately large letters and spaces between words and lines as well as the left-hand margins seem compatible with an open, flowing, expansive nature. But the letters within the words are more cramped, many almost on top of each other, so somewhere there is a sense of caution and concern with security or control. It seems possible that self-control or control of the personal life is an important issue. With many upper loops soaring above the middle zone of the writing, the aspirations described in the contents of the writing are clearly visible, and we might suspect a mutable dilemma conflict between the ideals and the limits of the everyday world. But the strong faith and optimism of the contents of the writing are visible in the upward slant of several of the lines, and both signatures slant up, one at a 45° angle. If, despite the metaphysics, anxiety or discouragement occasionally rear their ugly heads, as is suggested by the downward slants of some of the "t" bars, Mr. Seven probably sends them packing.

Since Mr. Seven is our only subject who was born in another country, I am not sure whether cultural influences might be playing a role in the letter formation. There is a mixture of round and angular forms fitting sensitivity but also a capacity for assertion. If the mixture is effectively integrated, success in life seems likely, when the ability to "zero in" is added to the drive and energy. One wonders whether the metaphysical statement emphasizing the "now" is important to Mr. Seven as a counterbalance to an inherent tendency to race ahead. Our favorite quotations are so often keys to our personal goals rather than to achieved positions. But we certainly hope that Mr. Seven and everyone else can abide in a state of joy in the eternal "now."

CHAPTER TWELVE
PSYCHOLOGICAL EVALUATIONS
by Helen Ewald, M.A.

All the subjects of this book took a standard personality inventory test. This particular test was chosen for its ability to ascertain general information about the normal personality rather than focusing attention on clinical issues, as do most psychological tests. The material which follows is the writer's interpretation of the data provided by the test results for each subject. These test results, together with age and sex of the subjects, are the only information available to this author at the time of writing this chapter.

In actual practice, such tests are always used by psychologists in conjunction with a personal interview, except when the test is used for research purposes. The interview provides a wealth of corroborating information by direct questions, observation of demeanor, dress, body language, voice and innumerable subliminal clues. Making an interpretation without this additional and extremely valuable information is like working in the dark, and not a little frightening due to the great potential for misinterpretation.

In a personal interview, rapport is established, empathy is utilized and a mutual, caring interaction takes place (hopefully). Since this analysis is being done "blind," the information is presented without any of the softening or qualification which would naturally take place in a face-to-face consultation. This text has been written from the point of view of one psychological professional to another, or one professional for his/her own notes. **The test results would NOT be presented to a client in the manner they are presented here**.

It is important to recognize, also, that these questions were answered at a specific time in the life of each participant. Their answers are strongly influenced by the current issues in their lives, some of which may be totally forgotten by now. We all have "good days" and "bad days" with mood swings which make us temporarily optimistic or pessimistic and affect the way we see ourselves and everyone and everything around us.

However, since this is the only information available to us at this point, we will have to assume that the data is valid and reliable, in order to make any worthwhile deductions from it. As a reminder of the questionable nature of the resource I will often point out that the interpretations are only possibilities. When I make flat statements, it is to avoid overloading the text with conditional terms rather than to be dogmatic about the validity of the statement.

Therefore, at the outset, let me share my personal firm conviction that these are merely **descriptions of pure energy** which is experienced by all of us and expressed through us, each in our own unique way. We can express our weltanshauung through a major or a minor key, or a combination. Once we really **hear** our melody, we can change it if we don't like it. Undoubtedly some of the circumstances of our lives are beyond our control. Other than that, what we do with these circumstances — how we react to them and the life decisions we make based on our response to life events and the subsequent results of our decisions — all this is up to us. In this respect we each create our own life.

As a therapist it is not up to me to judge another's song — its content, its melody, its quality. Simply being a sounding board which permits an accurate reexperiencing, reinterpreting and reevaluation of one's song, together with exploring other possibilities and options, seems to me to be the best way to help another sing her/his own unique melody in the chosen key.

Case One, Female - Age 50

This looks like the profile of someone who does not feel very good about herself and "toughs it out" in the world. At the time the psychological questionnaire was answered, Ms. One was carrying a lot of frustration and anger, much of which was probably turned inward as self-attack. The inner tension thus produced could manifest in such problems as sleeping difficulties, addictions, physical illness or accident-proneness.

I would expect her to have a rather cool and reserved demeanor.

She seems to be self-sufficient and self-reliant, with little need for other people. She doesn't expect much from others or trust them very far.

It appears that she is quite conscientious and persistent, and tends to be a perfectionist. She is quite bound by tradition and social convention. These feelings are in potential conflict with another part of her which would like to dump all that and live like a free spirit.

There seems to be a tendency to displace her conflicts or project them onto others. Thus, she might yell at her husband or kids when she is unhappy with herself, or because she feels abused by her boss at work. Getting along with people can be difficult, for she probably often feels irritable and has trouble restraining herself when she gets frustrated. Jealousy could be an issue for her. She is quite capable of expressing her displeasure directly in no uncertain terms. She has plenty of additional ammunition from buried anger and resentment which has a way of popping out inappropriately.

I would expect her to have a facile way with words. She probably enjoys fighting and arguing. She could also be very witty and a lot of fun. My guess is that this is a side of her that most people don't know, because she is unhappy much of the time.

Despite her expressiveness, it appears that she has a lot of bound-up energy which could contribute to a general feeling of discontent and unhappiness. She also seems to experience an extraordinary amount of general anxiety, as well as slightly more feelings of guilt than the average person.

The test indicates that she is conscientious, persevering and determined, dominated by a sense of duty. She tends to be a perfectionist with a deep concern about moral standards and rules. She is also quite conservative and resistant to change. It is difficult to reconcile this with other information which suggests someone who is bold, venturesome, uninhibited, and can handle stress well; and other scores which describe one who is impulsive and careless of social rules, is self-indulgent and in general follows her own urges. It suggests considerable inner conflict and identity confusion.

One wonders how her early life may have have contributed to the conflicts and unhappiness revealed here. Perhaps she experienced criticism or rejection from one or both parents. Could this be an example of a square peg pounded into a round hole? Could this have been a naturally exuberant child who was tamed by a very strict, nonnourishing upbringing? It seems that this woman has developed a harsh conscience which has taken over the job of keeping her inner child in line, and probably keeps her miserable and largely ineffectual in the process.

It is possible that she had little experience of acceptance, tenderness and touching, especially in the very vulnerable early years. She may have been abused or neglected. Whatever her experience, her emotional pain and scars are still affecting, perhaps even dominating her life.

My guess is that she does not love or accept herself, and almost certainly cannot open herself to receive love from others. Thus her basic emotional needs would continue unmet. Therapy to build her sense of self-worth and self-esteem and help her resolve some of her conflicts should be very helpful after she gains sufficient trust in her therapist. She could also benefit greatly from learning how to nurture herself.

She would probably be most successful and content with work that would not present her with abrupt changes or demanding decisions or constant interactions with people — perhaps something like accounting, computer work or even outdoor work. She has better than average intelligence, enough to do just about anything she wants to. In addition, her IQ is probably higher than the results show, since high anxiety tends to reduce the IQ score. The major concern in job-seeking would be to find work that would be the least stressful.

Ms. One tells us that she has a problem with lack of energy. This is probably due more to self-blocking and dissipation of energy rather than inadequate basic vital energy. I suspect she will have ample energy for whatever she wants to do once she gets out of her own way. It is likely that she is quite judgmental and critical, and probably the person she is hardest on is herself.

In general, it looks like self-blocking has pretty largely soured this life. However, it could be that she is just somewhat cool, detached and formal in dealing with other people; solemn, independent-minded and assertive. She is conscientious and dutiful, and concerned with moral standards, as well as being adventuresome and able to take risks. She has the courage of her own convictions and lives according to her own rules. Her enthusiasm and energy, together with her resourcefulness and self-sufficiency, may enable her to override her frustration level part of the time and give her some good feelings about herself.

This is a maximizing of the profile, and would be a place where a therapist might intercede to help this woman see another side of life; to help her mobilize her strengths and reassess her weaknesses so she doesn't feel so overwhelmed; to show her a direction in which she can move to create a different picture of reality that will give her more pleasure and satisfaction with conflict resolution. This woman has a strong personality, enough energy to make some dramatic changes, and intelligence to see the way.

Case Two, Male - Age 34

The first thing we might notice about Mr. Two is his ability to dominate the scene wherever he is. He is the kind of person who tends to be chosen for leadership. He is capable, self-confident and loves the limelight. He also has a lot of drive and a strong need to be in charge. He could be stubborn and controlling. He is sophisticated, poised and worldly wise, with an appreciation of the arts, travel and cultural advantages in general.

Despite all his drive, with power in reserve, there is a soft, warm, tender side to this man. He is kindly, gentle and indulgent with himself and others. He is exceedingly trusting. Being too trusting can get one into a lot of trouble, but Mr. Two is not gullible; he is very much in charge of his life, with a resourcefulness that has probably proved trustworthy in many potentially dangerous situations. Although he is a law unto himself, it is unlikely that he would ever be mean or underhanded. He is not hostile and does not anticipate hostility from others.

There are a number of contradictions in the test results that are a little difficult to tease out. We are told that he is very mature, constant in his interests, goal oriented; able to adjust to reality despite his feelings; emotionally detached and disciplined; responsible and reliable. Yet there is another side, equally strong, that is emotional, changeable and expedient; that ignores social rules and obligations; that is rather lazy, demanding and impatient. Of course, this just makes him human, but integrating these sides in a workable way could require some clever orchestration.

There is more. Although he seeks attention and admiration, and enjoys being in the center of activity, there is nevertheless a very strong urge to distance himself from others, withdrawing into himself and cutting off communication. This is a conflict which could have serious consequences in his career as well as in his relationships. It is not certain just why he withdraws; it could be that he gets tired putting himself out so strongly, and retreats for refueling and centering; it could be that he has a fear of intimacy and needs to protect his vulnerability.

He seems to be able to ask for help and affection on occasion, which suggests he can admit that he is vulnerable and has needs. Yet, one suspects that when his need is greatest may be the time he chooses to withdraw into his cool, incommunicable stance. If he has learned to share his vulnerability, as well as his strength, with significant others, his potential for gratifying relationships is much greater.

He seems to have very definite ideas about how things should be done, and may stubbornly insist that they be done his way. This is another issue that could get him into trouble in his work, and play havoc with egalitarian relationships. A somewhat balanced sharing of power is necessary for a wholesome relationship. If one person wields all the power, the other is relegated to a dependent-child status and resorts to manipulation. This usually turns out to be unsatisfying for all concerned.

There is a rebelliousness that suggests the possibility of some unresolved issues with authority figures. His need to be in charge is so strong that it could be difficult for him to work in a subordinate position. His supervisors, as well, would likely be frustrated. There are many kinds of work for which he is admirably suited, including art, law, research and any kind of administrative work.

Lest I give the impression that all life is a power struggle for Mr. Two, let me reassure you that he has an easygoing, tolerant, understanding, permissive side. He can be cheerful, resilient and affectionate, sensitive and intuitive.

He has a general mental alertness and a lively imagination, and is an astute, analytical thinker who enjoys intellectual pursuits. He likes to experiment and has the potential to be very creative. He may be a political liberal, concerned about social issues.

One thing that may be uncomfortably low is his ability to take pleasure and enjoyment in life. There appears to be a significant lack of enthusiasm and pure abandoned fun. On the contrary, it seems that his outlook is very serious, sober and solemn. Perhaps he needs to be more physically active — to get out of his head and into his body. The test does not tell us how physically active he is, but does suggest he has an affinity for mental activity. Turning up his fire a bit could brighten Mr. Two's life a lot.

This man has such a number of very strong opposing traits that he almost seems like two people: one sensitive, easygoing, tolerant and relaxed, absorbed in thought, uncommunicative and remote; and the other aggressive and competitive, critical and judgmental, demanding to be in charge and in the center of things.

He has tremendous potential that is not easy to manifest, for integration of many diverse energies would be necessary. He may already be doing a good job of this, considering his high test score in emotional stability and maturity.

It will be interesting to see how Mr. Two resolves these issues and reconciles the different aspects of his nature.

Case Three, Female - Age 36

This seems to be an exceptionally bright, very mature young woman who would be almost certain to get any job she applied for. Although slightly on the cool and reserved side, this is nicely balanced by her good cheer and enthusiasm.

Considering her unusual intellectual ability, she is not very assertive or competitive. However, there is a good balance between dominance and submissiveness which probably makes her easy and comfortable to work with. She has the ability to be a leader, but may lack sufficient assertiveness to push herself forward into a leadership role.

She is quick and alert, talkative and expresses herself well. In groups she would be an active participant. She is quite gregarious, and is likely to have many friends. We see her as spontaneous and outgoing, eager to be in the center of activity, and with a strong interest in the opposite sex. She may consider herself an emancipated woman.

She is affectionate, kind and gentle. She needs and wants attention and affection in return, and can become quite demanding and impatient if it isn't forthcoming . She also has a rich inner life and may be artistic or theatrical. She loves drama and the arts, and dislikes rough occupations and crudity or hostility in any form.

With the intelligence, energy and intuition which Ms. Three has in such generous measure, she has the potential to be very creative. The prospects for this are enhanced by an apparent willingness to experiment and change, and the ability for critical evaluation. Her resourcefulness and self-reliance are also a great help.

What could stand in her way is a possible lack of sufficient self-discipline, willpower and drive to accomplish her goals. She might prefer to adopt an artistically Bohemian lifestyle; but with her power and energy she would need to be doing something that seems worthwhile and that challenges her abilities in order to feel good about herself.

Ms. Three is insightful concerning herself and others, and can also maintain the separation and emotional detachment needed to be a good therapist. She is alert, resourceful and ambitious, and will probably do exceedingly well wherever she focuses her energies. This young woman seems self-assured enough to be unconcerned about the approval or disapproval of others. On the other hand, she is an open-minded, original thinker, with the inner strength and resources to follow her own path. She has little concern for society's standards, and prefers to live by her own rules. She may have a concern for social issues, and be on the cutting edge of social change. She has the potential to offer valuable and insightful comments and criticism to a group discussion. And she probably plays an excellent game of bridge. In other words, she has considerable executive ability and can accomplish a great deal with relative ease.

She should enjoy good health; she appears to be relatively free from the emotional stresses which often lead to physical problems.

Her relationships would be rewarding because she is at ease with herself and others, and is affectionate, cheerful and energetic. A little more warmth and sharing of her own feelings and a little less detachment could transform her experience with significant others.

The only reason she might be unhappy with her work is if it is insufficiently challenging or worthy. It appears she has the ability to do anything she chooses, and she certainly has the ability to explore new possibilities and weigh the options.

Her parents have every right to be proud of her. Considering her inner strength and apparent high self-esteem, it is probable that her parents provided a secure environment with support and nurturance in her early life.

Ms. Three looks like a bright and shining star, with the sky (or outer space?) as her limit.

Case Four, Male - Age 54

Upon meeting this man one might find him to be unusually sober, quiet and reserved, and very reticent in emotional expression. Not only does he not need other people much, he may actually avoid personal contact. Parties would probably be his least favorite thing in the world.

It thus almost goes without saying that Mr. Four does not invite intimacy. It would take a real effort to draw him out enough to really get to know him. He is somewhat shy, but this might not be so easily recognized because he has a competent self-reliance and independence together with a gruff, tough manner which covers up his vulnerability very effectively even to himself. He has few fears or worries.

It would be hard for him to admit that he needs anyone. If he is married, lack of interest in personal, physical and even sexual involvement could be a great frustration to his wife.

He probably is also a very masculine, macho man, with a brusque demeanor which wards off unwelcome intrusions. He could also be quite vigorous physically, an outdoorsman type who loves nothing better than backpacking alone in the High Sierras for weeks at a time.

He is very intelligent and uses his mind creatively in problem solving and decision making. He also prefers intellectual entertainment, and is probably his own best resource. He enjoys competition, and bridge or chess could be his favorite way of socializing. Otherwise, he is probably happiest with his nose in a book, or hiding behind a newspaper, or deeply involved in teasing out the answer to some challenging intellectual problem.

This man learns very quickly, and would not be likely to have the patience to be a good teacher for this reason, as well as because of his personal remoteness. He could do well as a research scientist, an accountant, a computer programmer, or anything where exacting, creative work is needed without the necessity of dealing much with others. He is very good as his own boss because he has plenty of energy and self-discipline to be self-starting, the insight to know what takes priority and how to do what needs to be done, and the determination and perseverance to see things through to the end.

He is capable and successful at his work. He enjoys responsibility and handles it well. Decision-making comes easily to him; he can gather and evaluate the facts while others are still trying to figure out what the issues are.

He is absorbed in ideas, theories and intellectual pursuits to the degree that we might suspect that he may tend to disregard practicality. The test tells us that he is controlled and self-disciplined, with an orderly mind and a persistence that will carry him through to the end of the toughest assignment and may border on compulsivity. Therefore, it appears that he could easily become so absorbed in work that he would skip meals, forget appointments, and perhaps work straight through too many nights in disregard of his health and well-being. He has an exacting willpower, and keeps his emotions under tight control.

An important factor in this man's makeup is a kind of tough-minded realism which rejects illusion or sentiment. He is logical, practical and focused. He is very strong in these traits which we think of as masculine. This probably is another indication that the imaginative qualities on which he tests very high have more to do with problem-solving ability and intellectual creativity, and less to do with the absentminded impracticality also found under the same category.

Finally, let us take another brief look at the emotional aspect of personality. In addition to a distinctly reserved demeanor, we find that despite Mr. Four's tough and unruffled appearance he is rather easily annoyed and carries some resentments. He probably experiences periods of low energy and fatigue; he may never suspect that the strain of keeping his emotions tightly controlled is sapping his energy.

A number of answers to the questionnaire contribute to the picture of a person with a serious outlook on life, one who gives little attention to pleasure and fun or the opposite sex. If these factors were any lower, they would indicate a potential danger, under stress, of psychosomatic problems.

Finally, we find that Mr. Four has a good balance between tranquil relaxation and high-drive tension, although he might be more comfortable with a little less tension. Nevertheless, he has been able to maintain thus far the strong, capable, man-in-control image without undue discomfort or damage. And it is probable that he wouldn't even consider changing.

Case Five, Female - Age 54

This is a highly intelligent woman, but probably no one knows it — perhaps not even she herself. Her weltanschauung is slightly but consistently off-key.

We find another aloof, somewhat withdrawn person with a cool and unapproachable manner. She is quiet and serious, cautious. The test suggests that she withdraws under stress; that she shies away from personal contact and tends to be uncomfortable in social situations.

We are also told that she is often annoyed and frustrated, and feels she has a lack of energy. Since we get the impression that she is quiet and generally uncommunicative, it seems likely that the low energy results in part from the load of frustration and anger which she carries because it has never been released satisfactorily. She probably often feels that life, especially because of the people she has to deal with, is just too heavy. She may be prone to sulk, and probably has bouts of depression.

The picture of her inner and outer struggles is rounded out with information that she is somewhat nervous, impatient and restless, as well as clinging and dependent. She needs attention and affection as we all do, but has never, it seems, learned how to get them. This could be a major source of trouble, for it makes one too needy and demanding in relationships, driving away the very persons we need most for nourishment and to give us a sense of being valued and loved.

More positive possibilities from these same test responses are: here is a person with a cool, no-nonsense manner, with little emotional expression. Although she is somewhat changeable, fearful and resentful, she is accommodating and cooperative with other people. She is shy, modest and retiring, and has a serious outlook on life. She is quiet and uncommunicative, but conscientious, reliable and dependable. She is introspective and intuitive, and perhaps a bit unrealistic and impractical.

The reality is probably somewhere between these two descriptions, or a combination.

The rest of the profile tells us that she is shrewd and insightful regarding herself and others; poised, worldly and socially aware; ambitious, efficient and capable of doing demanding, exacting work. She can discriminate between the essential and extraneous issues involved in making decisions. These qualities are doubtless of great value to her career. However, despite these significant abilities, she seems to feel quite insecure, and may be covering a lot of inner discomfort under a brusque, efficient demeanor.

We find Ms. Five at the top of the scale in self-sufficiency and resourcefulness, which tells us she has well-founded confidence in her ability to take care of herself. From this we would also suspect that she rarely takes others into her confidence even when she is troubled; she probably makes even very difficult life decisions without discussing the issues and options with anyone, or seeking feedback. This would contribute to feelings of isolation and loneliness.

We are told that this woman is conscientious and considerate of others. She keeps her feelings under control, which must often be quite a struggle. She could be compulsively orderly and fastidious. She is concerned with etiquette and her social reputation, and so probably behaves in a conventional way. The opinion of others seems to be very important to her, and "What will people think?" may be a significant determinant of her behavior. This could be another frustration for one who likes to see herself as independent and self-directed.

Considering all of the above, it is surprising to find that she carries a level of tension and anxiety that is only high-average. If this category were higher, it would be a good bet that that she has some kind of stress-produced illness, such as heart or nervous problems or an addiction. Although she seems fairly reconciled to her problems, health could still be a danger area.

A little therapy could be a real blessing to this woman. She could use some help in communication skills so that she might learn more effective ways of seeking what she wants and needs from others, and thus get her dependency needs met. Assertion training to give her acceptable ways of discharging anger would enable her to be accommodating when she really felt like it, and to say "No" and make it stick when she didn't. This would multiply her options in difficult situations and make her a lot more comfortable with other people. With fewer frustrations to repress, she would find herself with much more energy to spend.

She has so much potential, and she is so close. And yet, the sense is that it just doesn't quite work out right.

Case Six, Female - Age 52

This is an extraordinary woman who challenges the limits of the test in three categories: intelligence, emotional stability and relaxed composure. In three other categories she scored within one point of the limit: freedom from social inhibitions, self-assurance and self-control. The scores show wide swings, and almost all of them are in the direction of superior health and a super personality.

There is a category that we haven't mentioned before, called the "Need to Look Good" scale. Ms. Six tips the scale here at ten also, which indicates the test-makers suspect that it was important to this subject to make a good showing. She certainly is bright enough to fake the "right" answers. (Supposedly no faking is possible in intelligence.) However, in interpreting the tests of people I know well, some of the most honest, generous and kindly people get a high score on this scale, suggesting that they are just too good to be true. At this point it is impossible to know whether the test is prejudiced, or if this subject is really very close to perfection.

Going through the test in more depth, we find that Ms. Six is good-natured and easygoing, warmhearted and at ease with people. We are told that she is trusting, accepting and relaxed in relationships. One would deduce from this that she has many friends. She would take the initiative socially, sexually and emotionally. She would easily and naturally achieve whatever measure of intimacy she desires, and her relationships would be mutually rewarding. There is no evidence of any need to manipulate others.

She could be easygoing to the point of lacking drive and ambition, except that we see that she also has high standards for herself. She is disciplined and as precise as the most demanding perfectionist, without evidence of the strain and tension that such high standards usually produce. Is it because her abilities are so great that she can meet these ordinarily unrealistic demands with ease?

A person who scores at the top of the maturity scale could be expected to be the ultimate in emotional stability, with a well-rounded, fully developed personality. She would be untroubled by fears and anxieties. She would be able to see how to proceed in an emergency and be able to respond with quiet confidence. Her inner stability would probably be contagious, bringing a sense of peace in her presence. Her calm assessment and acceptance of reality is characteristic of highly educated and sophisticated people who never doubt what is the "right" thing to do in any situation. She seems to be untroubled by guilt.

We are told that she is spontaneous and open; direct and uninhibited, willing to take risks. She freely throws herself into her activities and likes meeting people. She probably loves drama, travel and new experiences. In groups she participates freely, often as leader. She handles stress and grueling emotional situations with an extraordinary inner strength.

With all this going for her, it is not surprising to learn that she is essentially fearless, confidently unconcerned about the approval or disapproval of others; and prone to simple, uncomplicated action and behavior. As mentioned before, there is no sense of the need to manipulate others that the disempowered express. Manipulation usually results from a sense of weakness, and this appears to be a powerful woman. A high degree of self-sufficiency and independence are to be expected.

On the other hand, we are given information that opens up some other possibilities: she could be demanding and impatient, attention-seeking and flighty. She may be somewhat critical and judgmental of others, her sensibilities offended by crudity or any lack of refinement.

She is probably introspective and intuitive, with a rich inner life. It is probable that she has a conservative temperament and finds change difficult. She could be prone to religious moralizing. She is persistent and sees problems as challenges to stay with until they are solved. She is very responsible, and keeps her promises. If operating less optimally, these same scores could indicate compulsively rigid behavior in an attempt to live up to a perfectionist ego ideal.

As can readily be seen, some of this material is inconsistent with our expectations from the rest of the pattern. It is important to remember that the same characteristics can be realistically interpreted as positive in one situation and negative in another.

It would be easier to believe that some of the negative interpretations of the foregoing paragraphs are applicable, if only because it is hard to believe that anyone can be as nearly perfect as Ms. Six seems to be. We wonder what she does with her anger over the inevitable (it seems) frustrations of life. Does she have no resentments? Does her openness of expression prevent a buildup of these and other negative emotions; or perchance are they so vigorously denied and buried so deep that she doesn't really feel them?

However, if the negative interpretations were appropriate, one would expect anxiety to be higher, indicating tension and frustration from striving for an impossible goal, or stress and fatigue from trying to keep turbulent feelings repressed. Instead, we find Ms. Six scoring at the bottom of the anxiety scale, which tells us she is about as relaxed and tranquil as one can get and still maintain enough tension to breathe and pump the blood necessary to keep one alive. This test has no measurement for less stress, for more ease, for letting it all hang out and going with the flow, than is indicated for this woman.

In light of all this, it is surprising to find an indication of considerable dependency, humility and submissive docility. To be so modest and retiring with all the power and strength shown by the rest of the test, truly sounds like Ms. Six is a saint — and perhaps she is.

Case Seven, Male - Age 64

All the other subjects of this book tested average or below on the category which measures personal warmth and the experiencing and expression of emotions. It is interesting that the highest score in this category should be achieved by a man rather than a woman, and an older man at that.

We tend to think of men as being walled off from their feelings — their feelings of vulnerability, in particular — and expressing their feelings of anger and aggression to the exclusion of nearly everything else. Here is a man who is very much an exception to this rule. Not only is he good-natured, warmhearted and easygoing in his relationships, but we would expect him to be humble and gentle, diplomatic and accommodating rather than competitive, aggressive and stubborn. We also find it likely that he is intuitive, imaginative and artistic.

There is the possibility of dependency, conformity and passivity. There could be a deep immature insecurity with an impatient seeking of help, attention and sympathy. These less desirable aspects are pretty well ruled out in Mr. Seven, however, by his end-of-scale scores in self-assurance and self-sufficiency, indicating a cheerful self-reliance, as well as a deep sense of peace and security which comes from recognizing that he can solve his own problems, make his own decisions, and live comfortably with the results. This is corroborated by other indications of relaxed composure.

This man seems to be very serious and sober in his outlook on life. He tends to be quiet, introspective and rather self-contained; somewhat slow and cautious. This is difficult to reconcile with the high score on warmth and expressiveness, and other scores which would indicate a gregarious, dauntless, spontaneous person who is socially bold. This incongruity could indicate a "Walter Mitty" personality with a lot of power which has not yet seen expression in the outer world to any great degree. This power can be the wellspring which sustains the inner man to keep life exciting and satisfying and relatively impervious to outward circumstances.

The above pattern could also apply to a person whose life had changed, one who is reliving experiences from a past which was much more active, challenging and thrilling than the current daily routine. If this is his situation, Mr. Seven would do well to get out more and get more involved with others to feel more alive. With his natural gift for relating, he would bring energy and cheer to himself and others by becoming more active and sharing his rich inner life.

There are some other possibilities that should be mentioned. We find the suggestion of somewhat concrete rigid thought patterns, and a certain timidity added to a slow cautious demeanor. These are all qualities which are a natural part of the aging process, and could begin to be a discernible factor by age 64.

We see that he enjoys people and can work well with them. His quiet, nonaggressive manner indicates he is probably much more comfortable in a supportive role in groups, rather than in a position of leadership.

It is surprising to find so much of the spectator, simply accepting what is, in a man with so much emotional stability and inner security, and with such a high ability to take bold risks, except perhaps in someone of low social status. If Mr. Seven were a black man, for example, this would all make perfect sense, for society offered little encouragement or opportunity for the bold, uninhibited and powerful young black man in the 1940s and 1950s. On the contrary, considering him threatening and dangerous, society was repressive and actively hostile. It has opened little enough even now. The need to conform in order to survive could explain this unusual combination of boldness and submissiveness or nonresistance.

Another possible explanation for this pattern could be that Mr. Seven is a deeply religious man of sincere humility. He might be a minister, a missionary, a teacher or a social worker. It appears that he has a lot of power which he is careful not to abuse or misuse, and probably rarely uses.

So far as health is concerned, people with high self-sufficiency are prone to coronaries and stroke. They tend to take responsibility for the world upon their shoulders and then collapse under the intolerable burden. It is possible that Mr. Seven has experienced and survived this with a profound effect on his personality and his life.

Whatever his circumstance, Mr. Seven seems to have made his peace with it.

SECTION TWO

CHAPTER THIRTEEN
CONSCIOUS AWARENESS
by William Wrobel

The purpose of using any system of character analysis must ultimately be a practical one: to gain knowledge of your essential nature, and to apply it constructively in your life. Without knowledge of your nature, you cannot live intelligently, or certainly in best fulfillment. Knowledge, not ignorance, is power. It is only through knowledge of the nature and laws of your being, and then applying what you know in action, that you can liberate yourself from illusion and confusion, and begin to create a more fulfilling destiny. A familiar sequence of causation follows:

CONSCIOUSNESS→THOUGHT (belief system)→BEHAVIOR→
HABITS→CHARACTER→DESTINY

Destiny is how you consciously use your energies directed by will. You create your experience (as you sow, so shall you reap). But to reap abundantly or intelligently, you need to be more conscious of your method of sowing. You need to be self-aware. Here astrology, numerology, etc., can help as diagnostic tools of self-awareness. However, no diagnostic tool can ultimately define you. Consciousness, the creator of all systems, is far greater than any system. Also, there is no one "real" level of selfhood, just as you are not merely defined by your skin color, nationality, nor by what you say and think. The systems employed here, then, are simply parentheses of identity. It is a meaningful game of Let's Pretend you can be defined, a series of "models" meant to simplify your complex or multidimensional psyche.

Astrology, numerology, palmistry and graphology are pragmatic tools of divination which serve as lights or "cosmic lanterns" along the path of unfoldment. If you are a counselor, you help others help themselves by offering information as a means toward self-awareness. Whether you use conventional psychotherapeutic tools, including hypnosis, or whether you use unorthodox methods such as astrology makes little difference if the end result is genuine helpfulness and healing. The ultimate test is pragmatic — Does it work? Does it help? All exploratory techniques are meant to aid in realizing your strengths, weaknesses and potentials, and to show alternatives on how to use your energies constructively on the path of growth, expansion and evolution.

Admittedly, you may prefer to employ those speedier tools which offer the greatest promise of clearly assessing the nature of self. Here we enter the domain of the so-called "psychic sciences" or ancient arts such as astrology and numerology. Such tools show the inner dynamics of character in this lifetime, though not necessarily one's present state of evolutionary development. As given earlier, there are no limits to the psyche (Gr. "soul"). However, the psyche does **represent** itself as an astrological natal (birth) chart, say, or as numerical "vibrations." Your natal chart is a symbolic representation of yourself, conceptualized as a complex symbol system. The psyche is innately creative and thus it can represent itself in any of many ways. It can also dimensionalize itself and manifest as a living symbol — e.g., the physical body.

To clarify a point, the phrase "psychic sciences" is a misnomer, as I would prefer to call them **gnostic tools**. Gnosis (Gr."knowledge") relates to the inner nature of phenomenon (Gr. "appearance"). Hence we speak of dia**gnosis**, an attempt to ascertain the truth behind an effect, form or symptom. Life is more than what it appears or seems to be on the surface. Similarly, a horoscope is a dia**gnostic** tool of character, a blueprint or inner knowledge of an entity (person, place, event). That entity likewise is far more than what it appears to be.

Now, the options of your directive (decision making) are limited pragmatically by your knowledge (*gnosis*) and conscious awareness. The more you know yourself and become intelligently self-aware, the more you can consciously affect changes in your life and create a constructive, happier destiny. Here astrology and other *gnostic* tools can be invaluable aids, but any system of unfoldment can apply to the principle of power-bestowing knowledge.

Ignorance closes off many options and probable destinies. In our

Western culture particularly, we have become lost in a psychic fog, out of touch with the primacy of our own inner experiencing. Hence we look to others for answers. In that stage of development we become outwardly-oriented, yet it is the start of an **inward** journey of self. Thus the psychic sciences or *gnostic* tools, as well as all other exploratory techniques, serve as entry doors to unfoldment, personal development and knowledge. It is the knowledge of your power: the power of your consciousness creating effect and form (appearance). It is the knowledge of the laws of your being, which recognizes consciousness as the source of power, thereby not projecting power away "out there" (germs, the past, money, planets) due to ignorance, the root of fear. Ultimately, as mystics tell, it is the knowledge of Consciousness (God, Macrocosm) manifesting as you (human being, microcosm), the energy of which you direct as you freely choose.*

The numerological "readings" are largely a compilation of the interpretations given by two numerologists. One is Susan (Stephanie) Joseph; the other is Sylvia Abraham, a "New Age" teacher, lecturer and counselor, who operates the Cosmic Lantern Bookstore in Long Beach, California, with her husband. Their system of numerical interpretation is quite similar and compatible. Their interpretations are mostly not "blind" since some of the case studies were somewhat known by either one or both of them, as will be noted in each particular case presentation. In fact, Sylvia actually gave face-to-face readings to four of the participants (Mr. 2, Ms. 3, Ms. 5, Ms. 6). The numerological methodology following illustrates the methods used by Stephanie and Sylvia to set up the numerological charts. Portions of the numerological analysis of Ms. One offer additional material on how to construct Pinnacles and Challenges based on month/day/year of birth, Personal Year, etc.

Numerological Methodology

Each letter of the alphabet is assigned a numerical value, as the following chart shows:

---

* For a fuller exposition on the mystical, metaphysical and psychological interpretation of astrological symbolism, refer to my upcoming book, *Mystical Astrology as a Wisdom Science*.

1	2	3	4	5	6	7	8	9
A	B	C	D	E	F	G	H	I
J	K	L	M	N	O	P	Q	R
S	T	U	V	W	X	Y	Z	

Have before you the full name **as written** on the birth certificate. In determining the **Soul Urge** (sum of the vowels in a name), begin by assigning the appropriate number value above each vowel. The letter "Y" is also assigned a vowel value if it is placed between two consonants; whereas, if a "Y" has a vowel next to it, it is a consonant. Here are some examples. (Number values for vowels are written above the letters; number values for consonants appear below the letters.)

$$\text{EYE} \quad \text{MONEY} \quad \overset{7}{\text{MANY}} \quad \overset{7}{\text{HYDRA}}$$
$$\underset{7}{\text{EYE}} \quad \underset{7}{\text{MONEY}}$$

In determining the **Personality** (sum of the consonants in a name), begin by assigning the appropriate number value below each consonant. The number values of the following sample name are shown in their proper positions:

$$\overset{7 \quad 9\,1}{\text{SYLVIA}} \quad \overset{6 \quad 9\,1 \quad 1}{\text{ZODIACA}} \quad \overset{3 \quad 5 \quad 6 \quad 6 \quad 7}{\text{NUMEROLOGY}}$$
$$\underset{1 \quad 3\,4}{} \quad \underset{8 \quad 4 \quad 3}{} \quad \underset{5 \quad 4 \quad 9 \quad 3 \quad 7}{}$$

The vowels total (Soul Urge) is $7 + 9 + 1 + 6 + 9 + 1 + 1 + 3 + 5 + 6 + 6 + 7 = 61$. For numbers of more than one digit, the digits are added together until a one-digit sum is reached. Thus $61 = 6 + 1 = 7$.

Next, determine the subtotals of the vowels and consonants of each subname, reducing it by addition. The total of the combined vowels and consonants is the **Name/Expression** number. The total of the Soul Urge and Personality numbers should also be that same Name number. Returning to our sample name, the subtotals are as follows:

$$\frac{17}{8} \quad \frac{17}{15} \quad \frac{27}{28}$$

$$\frac{8}{8} = 16 = 7 \quad \frac{8}{6} = 14 = 5 \quad \frac{9}{1} = 10 = 1 \quad \begin{array}{l} = 7 \text{ Soul Urge} \\ = 6 \text{ Personality} \end{array} = 4 \text{ Name}$$

Next, set up an **Inclusion Table** which shows the quantity of each number in a name. Each "box" in the nine-box grid format is assigned its proper number values as follows:

1	2	3
4	5	6
7	8	9

Returning to the same name, count how many 1's are in the name and insert that quantity in·its proper box; count how many 2's are in the name and insert that quantity in its proper box, etc. After you complete that, insert the sum of each of the three rows and three columns.

```
     7   9 1            6   9 1   1              3    5    6    6   7
   SYLVIA             ZODIACA            N U M E R O L O G Y
   1    3 4            8    4     3             5    4    9    3   7
```

4	0	4	8 Individual
3	2	3	8 Family
3	1	3	7 World

```
10 3 10
P E M
H M E
Y O N
S T T
I I A
C O L
A N
L A
  L
```

The total number of letters in the sample name is 23. Check your results against this number by totaling the Inclusion Table numbers. They should match (= 23).

The **Life Path** is derived by adding the month, day and year of birth. The number values of the months are given below:

January	= 1	April	= 4	July	= 7	October	= 1
February	= 2	May	= 5	August	= 8	November	= 2
March	= 3	June	= 6	September	= 9	December	= 3

Ms. 1 — September 17, 1933 becomes:
      9 + 1 + 7 + 1 + 9 + 3 + 3 = 6 Life Path
Mr. 2: 1 + 2 + 1 + 1 + 9 + 5 + 0 = 1 Life Path
Ms. 3: 1 + 1 + 1 + 9 + 1 + 9 + 4 + 8 = 7 Life Path
Mr. 4: 1 + 2 + 2 + 1 + 1 + 9 + 2 + 8 = 8 Life Path
Ms. 5: 5 + 3 + 1 + 9 + 2 + 9 = 11/2 Life Path
Ms. 6: 7 + 3 + 1 + 9 + 3 + 1 = 6 Life Path
Mr. 7: 1 + 2 + 1 + 4 + 1 + 9 + 1 + 9 = 1 Life Path

Regarding the background information on each participant, my approach was two-pronged: first, request each person to complete a questionnaire regarding background, goals, values and current issues in the life; second, conduct an oral interview, meant to clarify details and issues not adequately established in the returned questionnaire material, and to gauge the response to Zip's initial interpretation. The interviews were conducted usually in the subjects' homes. Each individual had read and signed a release form. My revised questionnaire appears in the appendix. Its primary purpose was to reduce any possibility of self-consciousness and "rushing" often involved in direct interviewing, and to allow the participants to write or tape as much or as little as they wished. My overriding intent was to fully dimensionalize each subject, to derive ample feedback on how the participants themselves saw their own lives.

Now, there is no great pleasure in delving into personal backgrounds, but I was asked to perform this task. However, the risks involved in self-disclosure were significantly minimized since each participant is anonymous. Often what a person **says** is one of the most untrustworthy sources of presenting clues to the inner nature of the person. Yet anonymity allowed the participants the opportunity to look within themselves with candor. They present their self-image and judge themselves by what they say and believe about themselves. We are free to define ourselves, and we create our own boundaries. And what they revealed to me often was quite revealing to them, especially after they read a draft of their verbatim statements for their personal editing before publication. "Is that what I said? Is this how I label myself?"

Instead of just an external assessment of character through astrology, etc., we are presented with an internal assessment of character from the point of view of the person's own words, behavior and subjective responses to those external assessments. The intent was to accurately understand their motives, outlook, and observe their behavior, and they in turn disclosed their thoughts, words and deeds. We then perceived their chosen mode of life. For the sub-jects, I am quite sure it was highly educative, and even unsettling at times for some. Once again, the pragmatic dictum is: Know Thyself. The unexamined life is wasteful, for we may devote time and energy to essentially painful or empty activities, habits, fears and addictions. The greater the degree of self-knowledge, the less we will need exterior methods of assessment and aid, and the more we will live moment-to-moment in freedom and joy.

Read not to contradict and to confute nor to believe and take for granted, but to weigh and consider — Bacon

CHAPTER FOURTEEN

MS. ONE

Introduction to Ms. One

I first met our "lady of passionate depths," as Zip correctly surmised, in late February 1983. She had an appointment with me to discuss her horoscope. When she entered my apartment, I felt an energy surge penetrating the place. Her aura, on a sentient level, was dynamic and highly charged, and when she spoke I immediately noted the clarity, strength and quickness of her voice. She was quite a talker, I found out later, as she passionately discussed her recent life events in vivid detail. Ms. One can patiently listen, but when it's her turn to talk, watch out!

When I scanned her chart, my eyes fixed on the intense Mars in Scorpio rising. It was an astrological verification of my initial impressions as she walked in. It wasn't until the end of our meeting that I responded to inspiration and asked her if she would like to participate in this book as an anonymous case study. She consented with great interest. I explained that she was the very first person I had asked, the "perfect" person to lead off because of her Mars on the Ascendant — a double statement of "letter one" emphasis in a chart. The only other combination which would be the purest is a Mars in Aries on the Ascendant, but I was not prepared to put an ad in the newspaper! I was quite happy with the Mars in Scorpio rising that the Universe directed to me, especially since Mars is naturally a co-ruler of Scorpio, a fascinating theme mixture in its own accord.

Ms. One signed the release forms. After a vigorous chat together for a while, Ms. One left to cook dinner at home. It wasn't until seven months later in October that we met again for the book-related interview, with a follow-up interview two weeks later to discuss her response to Zip's initial interpretation. During those seven months she had "mysteriously" disappeared due to surgeries, unknown to me, but as it happened, Ms. One is here now to present her following story.

Ms. One's Background

[In this section I will largely employ Ms. One's own words, collected and freely connected from various interviews. Sections in brackets and boldface are my own words, meant to introduce clarifying or missing data unavailable as direct quotes.]

Ms. One:
"My father left when I was a baby and I think the first time I saw him was when I was 12 years old. My mother worked at the canneries and we lived at Terminal Island at the time. We had fish and rice every night, but I didn't know we were poor. I didn't feel like we were poor. But my mother did the best she could, and she kept us together. We always stayed alone. I have an older brother and one older sister, and although my sister was older, I always felt I was older. When we were little she would say, 'Mother is gone all the time; she doesn't love us.' And I said, 'Yes, she does! That's why she's gone, because she's working all the time.' Isn't that rational? But my sister couldn't see that. And my sister was always mad because my mother also did housework for doctors and movie people, and a famous producer wanted to adopt me and my sister. And my sister has never forgiven my mother for not letting him. He didn't want my brother, just the girls. But in those days she did really well and she shouldn't feel guilty that she didn't do good enough. My mother was a very strong mother. She's a lot like me. All the years I was growing up I never saw my mother buy herself any clothes or spend money on herself.

"My parents divorced when I was a baby, but I had a stepfather that my mother married when I was quite young. He was a terror. He was physically brutal to my brother, a little bit to my sister, and not very much to me. They divorced when I was 12 and she then remarried — someone she had known as a friend since we lived on Terminal Island. He was just fine; a kind, wonderful man. I called him 'Pop.' He was crippled and he owned a garage. In fact, when he first got hurt he was quite wealthy. But he broke his neck and he was going to die, and his wife left him; but he didn't die, he lived. He and my mother divorced when I was 19, and he just died last year. But my mother divorced the 'brutal one' because he was so cruel to my brother — the love of my mother's life. That's when my mother started drinking, and I didn't like the drinking. She still drinks to this day. She had a bar for thirty years.

"Probably the biggest negative about my mother is that, although I always knew that my mother loved me, she was never showy. She was not a lovey, huggy person (she is now) but I always knew that she loved me. The last time I saw her she just cried because she wished that she could've done more for us. I told my mother, you know, that my mother's mother died when my mother was seven years old, and my mother was kicked around from one place to another. She was not raised with love and attention. I never had that huggy love, so when I had my kids I overly did that so that my kids would be lovey, huggy, affectionate people, which they are. You see, I don't believe in that song and dance of people whining, 'Oh, I was beaten when I was a kid, so I beat my kids,' or 'I didn't get any love so I can't give love.' That's bullshit. That's not being a grown adult and mature. But my mother let me do anything. I mean, like with art, if I painted the front room purple when she was at work, she would come home and say it was wonderful! Or all summer we'd camp out in the backyard and take all her dishes and pots and pans and do stuff, and she'd just say that's great.

"I never felt pretty or cute or popular when I was a kid. I was a loner child and I always enjoyed being alone and playing by myself. I could've gone into sports if I wanted but I didn't. But I always thought I could do anything. The main reason probably why I never really went into anything is because my mother always worked and we were alone a lot, and I didn't have anyone to push me into anything. I was never assertive; I was never strong — only later in years. I would more or less keep quiet. For instance, my sister all through the years would always get money from my parents and do different things. And for me, for some reason, there's just something in me that I have to do myself, that I have to take care of myself. My sister always had more clothes that I did. I would ask Pop — which was the stepfather during our teenage years — for new shoes or a sweater or something, and he would say no. So I would tell my mother and she said, 'You know Pop; you have to beg him.' And I said I don't beg from anyone. I won't. And all the years I was raising my kids I had hard, I mean, really hard times. I mean, there were times when I was alone when my kids couldn't start school on time because I didn't have any money to give them school clothes and stuff because my husband was off running around somewhere. But I always had to do it myself. I had to. I ask only once. Maybe sometimes I'll ask twice, but that's it. That was the same way raising my kids. The rule was, I'll ask you once, then twice, and God help you if I have to tell you three times.

"I got married to my first husband when I was 15. I was married to him for four years and I had two children from that marriage. I just married him to get out of the house. There was no real love there. It was just infatuation. When I then married my second husband, my whole family disowned me for a while because they thought my first husband was wonderful and that I shouldn't have left him.

"I had not only my two kids but his two kids that I raised. I had one little girl that passed away as a baby from a heart condition, and that was very hard on me. And I like made a deal: I can accept this but all the rest of my children had to be healthy. And I truly believed that, and it has been. I raised six children. When I first got pregnant with our first child, everything was wonderful. Then I had the baby and she died, and my second husband couldn't handle that and left to join the army. When he came back we went back together. You know, in the courtship time, he was wonderful. And then as soon as we had a child, then — our early years, if I wrote on that, would be a horror story. He was abusive. I was what you would call a battered wife. He drank. I had my nose broken at least four times. I had my tailbone broken twice. I had ribs broken and my left arm. One time I was beaten up so bad that I had to tell the kids I got in a car wreck, or else I would tell them that I was washing the walls and fell off the ladder. My husband would say, 'I drink and I don't know what I'm doing.' He never hit me in front of the kids. I'll give him that. But he knew what he was doing. There was a part of him that was dingy, that was nutty. Every day I would get up wondering, Will he get up and be mean or would he be kind? A lot of it was his upbringing. I divorced him two years ago. I feel sorry for him. I don't hate him. I care for him still. I care what happens to him because he has been my husband for all those many years. I love him, but I don't want to have a future life with him.

"I stuck it out because I hate to fail. My first marriage didn't work and I hate to lose. It was like a failure. It's like I have to do whatever I say. If someone says I can't do something, that's just wonderful with me because then I will do it! I stuck on because I did all the raising of my kids. My husband didn't care what they did as long as they didn't bother him. He never took them places, never did anything with them, never corrected them. The only time he ever said anything to them was when he was mad. So I had to be the smoothing-over person. He wasn't a good father but he never abused them. They still love him. But I felt pretty helpless because what my husband did was, he always skimmed off the top of the money. If he had $150 he took his drinking money and his skydiving and having a good time, and I got what was left. Whatever he gave me, if the bills weren't paid, he was a crazy man. I was waitressing for twenty years and he was an I.D. longshoreman — at the time just getting the extra work. And in those days you got no assistance. If you tried to get any welfare or anything to help you through, they said, 'Oh, you can't take care of your kids? Oh, we'll just take them!' So it was the idea of having a little bit of help and him being home sometime or me not being able to make it. All my money went for rent and food and clothes and the babysitter. I worked from 6 PM to 2 AM, got home at 3 AM, got up at 7 AM to take care of the kids; and for two years at that time I also worked 11:30 AM to 2:30 PM for lunch. I kept every bit of that money to buy my first house. And then I quit work seven months' pregnant. Right after my son was born, they came to the house and said he hadn't been making the payments, and I lost the house.

"No one can go through all those years of the mental 'Is he going to get up to kiss me or kick me?' and working and fixing the house, paying the bills and keep the peace. I did it but I don't know how I did it. All the street kids in the neighborhood hung out at our house because they thought we had the happiest home going. In all appearances we had this wonderful, happy home. The kids thought it was so wonderful. But I made it wonderful. What I did after all those years was impossible, physically impossible, but I did it. I was so put down. I mean, he treated me so bad, and he said, 'You can't leave me because no one would ever want you. I'm so bitchin and you're so homely. I don't know why I spent my life with you. You have to stay with me because no one would want you with the kids.' And I believed it. He had me brainwashed. I believed him and I couldn't make it financially with that many kids.

"At one time I just mentally couldn't handle it. I was always so strong and I always wanted to keep everything happy. But he just pushed me to a point where 11-12 years ago I tried to commit suicide. I was drinking tea and taking two pills each. I took over fifty pills.

It should've killed a horse, they said! They don't know why it didn't kill me. I have a strong constitution! But from that time on he improved a lot. That was his changing point. He came home and locked himself in the bathroom and cried during the three days I was in the hospital. The kids were shocked: our father, hard-as-nails Dad, was in the bathroom crying. He was not as coldhearted as we thought he was. I told him, it could've been your claim to fame that after so many years you drove someone to lose the will to live. That's what it was. I lost the will to live at that point. He would purposefully do something to make every day miserable. But I didn't fight him. I would try to protect myself and that kind of stuff, and I made him leave a lot of times. But I never really argued with him. I just suppressed, and that wasn't my nature. I repressed it to keep peace and have a happy home.

"Finally the stress over the years made me sick. I had gout, bursitis in my shoulders, and arthritis in my hands and back. I did electronic assembly, and then I sold furniture as my arthritis got worse; I did lighter things.

"I discovered a lump September 27, 1979. I went for a complete checkup at a cancer center to have the lump looked at. [**The condition was misdiagnosed as benign. Actually she had squamous cell carcinoma, the most dangerous of all cancers, according to another doctor. Surgery was performed May 12, 1980, to remove the lump. The cancer had spread and several major surgeries were performed over a long period of time.**]

"Two years ago in November I had a tumor in this leg and at the time they thought I would have to have my leg amputated. They wanted me to sign papers to do that, and I said no. The cancer had grown to the nerves and the muscles and other areas. I just feel that if you give them information, they get too cut happy. Five doctors said that they had to remove my colon, urethra, vagina, right leg, all the lymph nodes from my legs, back and pelvis, and do a vulvectomy. I said bullshit! Others did a lot of that but not all of it. I was told that I was arrogant and forward. I said, 'I could not care less. I'm not here for a popularity contest. I don't want you to like me. I just want you to be a good doctor.' My body is sapped. My last surgery was September 20, 1983, and I had five surgeries within 51 days. I feel good now and I have a lot of energy. But I think about having three more operations and it depresses me. It made me mad about those doctors. I said, I'd like for you to have a hole in your stomach. I'd like you to go through a few surgeries. It would probably do you good! — to know what the other person is going through. They're cold: 'Oh, yeah. Let's cut it up here and go through there, and let's do this and cut that.' I'm suing the cancer center for $3 million. It's not malpractice so much as gross negligence. But I'm not suing the wonderful doctor that did my major surgery or the ones taking care of me now.

"But I'm a survivor. You just do what you have to do. What I can't stand is people who are weak and who are crybabies. The thing of it is, if you can't take anything that happens to you in your life and find something positive out of it, then you might as well go blow your brains out right now, you know? I know that it has been bad but I'll tell you, I know how lucky I am because you should see some of the people in the hospitals. I know a 29-year-old woman next to me who had cancer in the spine. They can't do anything for her, and she has a 3-year-old baby. So you can't feel sorry for yourself when you see all that going on. And it's easier for the person who's sick than it is for the people around them. It would be harder for me if one of my kids were sick.

[**Ms. One divorced her husband two years ago right after her first surgery. It culminated in a release of pent-up emotions.**] "We had a fight you would not believe. Every place he went I busted out the windows and was after him! He got into his car and I broke all his windows. He was lucky to get away. I had so much rage that I had held in for so long. He was not supportive. His idea of support was to go around and get a girlfriend. He wants me to come back, but I told him, 'You are the way you are. You should keep doing what you're doing. If what you do makes you happy, do it. Be my guest.' It's the same with anyone. I'm not going to change you. If you really want to be with me, you'll be with me. If you don't want to, and leave, then see ya — don't let the door hit you on the ass! I'm not going to put a gun to your head and say, 'You be a good boy!'

"I feel so free now. I gave my husband the house, and I took the money from our cabin and bought a home up north two years ago near my oldest daughter. I just thought that it was time for a change. I always wanted to live in the country, so I figured it was as good a time as any! My house is in an old Episcopal church built in 1900. It's just perfect. My neighbor is supposed to help me get an antique shop open. He's a 39-year-old retired architect I was seeing, a Scorpio. He has a sense of humor like I do. He said I'm 49 going on 15! He's seeing someone else but that's all right. He said he didn't want to deal with my situation right now, although he calls me at the hospital. But I'm seeing two different men — the Scorpio and an Aries, a man I ran into that I knew when I was 12 years old.

"I feel I'm getting everything I want: living where I want. It seems like life is really simple now. I think I got sick to show me that my life has been in the wrong direction. I haven't been doing the things that I wanted to — things for myself. Everything happens for a reason. If this sickness had not happened to me, I would not have changed my life because the best time of my life is right now. I don't really look at the surgeries as horribleness. It made me change my life. I would've been the same here, putting up with the same bullshit, just going on and on and on. Probably the reason why I have so much energy is because my energy was stifled so much during my married years that I'm like reborn, starting to do all the things I kept saying, 'Someday . . . .' I forgot that all my kids are going to grow up and go away and I'm going to have to live my own life. I didn't look that far in the future. Now I don't have to do anything except what I want to do. I am happy. Never in my whole life have I ever been able to do what I wanted to do. Now I'm Number One. I want to write a book. I've been keeping notes ever since my illness started. I have maybe fifty pages of notes. I thought I'd take some classes when I go back north.

"I feel so free. When I go over the hills to town to shop up north, and I'm all alone with my Willie Nelson tapes going, I laugh all the way! I felt like I have lived under so much stress that I had to make a complete change. And that's what I did. And when I'm up there, I get up in the morning and I do what I want to do. And I do just what I want to do because in my whole life I've never been able to do that. I'm going to get my settlement and I'm going to have a good time and go everywhere and run my antique shop."

Numerological Analysis

In this section I will partially compile the interpretations of Ms. One offered by our two numerologists, Sylvia and Stephanie. Material not in quotes is partly a summary of ideas contributed by them, and partly expanded observations by me directly, especially when astrological correlates are discussed.

Now: Of the three names given Ms. One at birth, the rundown of her major number patterns are as follows:

Soul Urge (vowels sum)	=	7
Personality (consonants sum)	=	11/2
Name/Expression (name sum)	=	9
Life Path (month/day/year sum)	=	6

Her 7 Soul Urge (how she identifies or sees herself) is described by Sylvia: "She has come to learn, to study, to analyze, investigate herself, and to have faith and trust in her own nature. As a child, there could've been an aspect of shyness, being like a wallflower, quiet, or perhaps not feeling proud, feeling that she is not a superior person. Or she can be a lady who does think that she has all the knowledge, has a superior mind or is a superior person."

The Soul Urge is often referred to as being "hidden." It is, in other words, that private conception of oneself or inner motivation that most people aren't even aware of. Number 7 is an introverted number, inward-turning, associated with keeping one's thoughts to oneself usually. It also possesses a "water" quality, being emotionally oriented or subjective, functioning on an inner, deeper level. In terms of awareness, it can be quite analytical and investigative, searching for "superior" information — including spiritual comprehension and insight. The keynote of number 7 is study, understanding, and wanting the best, whether the superior, materially oriented life (keeping up with the Joneses) or the superior, spiritually oriented life (being in the world but not of it). In Ms. One's case, since she has no 7's in her name, the 7 principle is definitely a lesson area, as we'll discuss later in the Inclusion Table section.

[Parenthetically, number 7 is occultly the number of consummation or perfection of a major phase of development — e.g., the 7th and final symbolic Day of Creation in *Genesis*. Metaphysically, it represents the evolutionary goal of union of the fourfold, mortal personality with the threefold, immortal Soul (4 + 3 = 7). If multiplied (transmuted), 4 X 3 = 12, it indicates the number of completion in the manifested universe (the perfected unfolding of the twelvefold zodiacal qualities in each person). The occult symbolism of number 7 in terms of spirituality can therefore be seen with its reference to a "superior" or perfected state of being. Number 7 was regarded as the most sacred number by the ancient philosophers and astrologers alike (e.g., reference to the Seven Sacred Planets).]

Ms. One's Personality (how other people see her or how she impresses them) is the 11/2. The 2 Personality (consonants reduced to a prime number), in astrological correspondence, is the Libra and/or the Cancer focus — a relationship emphasis wanting union, cooperation, harmony and security. In Ms. One's chart, both rulers of her first house of identity (or "persona" for some astrologers) are in Libra and Cancer signs. Sylvia conceptualizes the number 2 as principally a Cancerian emphasis.

"The 2 Personality shows the mothering quality," she suggested, "the quality of being passive and receptive, to be able to get along with other people, be a mediator. She shows that she wants to be a survivor, that she wants to have security and safety around her."

The 11 Personality (unreduced consonants from the subtotals), on the other hand, is a "master number" or higher expression of the number 2 principle. It denotes a transpersonal focus rather than a personal/interpersonal emphasis; a visionary, idealistic leaning, dedicated to a higher purpose than one's personal concerns. In terms of the Cancerian aspect of motherhood, it can manifest as, say, being a mother to the world (Ms. One's Moon in the tenth house) after or during the rearing of one's immediate family.

Ms. One's Name number (also frequently called the "Expression") is number 9. The Name/Expression is the second most important major number next to the Life Path. It is calculated irrespective of how you formulate the Soul Urge and Personality numbers, and many differing methods of determining those subsidiary major numbers exist in practice. The Expression is the total name and represents your essential vibration, and it represents the talents and potential of your present character — how you naturally express yourself. Some numerologists call it the "Destiny" number, similar to the Life Path, which you must manifest as your mission in life. In this section of the book, the consensus is that the Name/Expression is what you principally are, and secondarily, what you are "destined" to express, say, on a higher, more rewarding level, contingent on free will.

Number 9 is the number of completion, the "world," humanitarianism and long distance travel. It can also indicate the martyr/victim, feeling burdened if selfless giving and helping becomes excessive and spills into the savior role, becoming the Atlas attempting to save the world. The 7/2/9 major numbers combination suggests the potential for professionalism (7/9 mixture — e.g., law) connected with partnership and/or the home (number 2). It's an intuitive, helping combination that could manifest professionally in the wider world as counseling and consulting. Number 9 is also associated with creative talents and artistic ability.

Ms. One's Life Path number is 6. The Life Path is considered the most important of the major numbers as an indicator of character. It represents your central-growth goal or destiny, the life direction you need to follow for best development. Unlike the Name/Expression, the Life Path cannot be changed in a court of law. Number 6 refers to responsibility. Its main characteristic is service and the desire to be needed or wanted, whether serving as a cook and housekeeper or serving in community activity. It is the responsibility for home and marriage, to create and maintain harmony, peace and love. It is the number of the heart. Marriage, home and family responsibility would be a definite lesson for Ms. One, however, since she is missing a 6 in her name. A missing number is often called a "Karmic Lesson," requiring extra focus in handling the principle represented by that number. Since Ms. One is missing four numbers, three of which represent her major numbers, "she has set herself up with a lifetime of big lessons," as one numerologist speculated. We'll discuss the missing numbers in order of their appearance below in the analysis of the Inclusion Table (a table in box format derived from the letters in a given name which shows the sum of each letter value.)

Inclusion Table

8	3	0		I	11
3	2	0		We	5
0	0	3		They	3
P	E	M			
11	5	3			

Eight 1's connects the theme of power, authority, control and money (number 8) with the area of personal action, ego and independence (number 1). Astrologically, it corresponds to her Mars in Scorpio rising, an identification with power and intense self-will or willpower.

"She's expressing her ego or will in an 8 fashion," Stephanie elaborated, "being that 1 is the number of the ego. Eight is a power number and wants authority and control, and the person can get very frustrated if the power isn't expressed. Eight can be a difficult number because it is into power and it's easy for it to be misused or misdirected. But she doesn't understand the 8 principle because there are no 8's in her name. It's definitely a big lesson for her. Negatively, number 1 can be selfish and number 8 can be ruthless in getting the power. But since she has no 8's, and being that she is a 9 Name, I would say that this lady would probably take it out on herself instead of taking it out on someone else. If she represses her power, her body can suffer as she fights against her instincts — hurts and cuts and accidents and surgeries. If she projects it out, someone else might be ruthless to her and, in that sense, be cruel to herself. But they can be fighters if they wanted to. She needs to be in business or have a healthy power outlet."

Sylvia added an observation: "She has four missing numbers which, of course, is not an easy life to bear, but she has those eight 1's which indicates that she came to live her life and to have the strength to cope with it. Having the eight 1's and 6 Life Path, there would be a tendency to be involved either in the medical profession, in healing/helping, or, if she's not careful, to victimize her physical self and then be a martyr and victim of illnesses."

As an intensity point, then, or strong characteristic, the eight 1's are heavily accentuated. An indomitable will is likely, though not necessarily a self-centered direction of will since the 2, 6, 9 major numbers suggest a giving, relationship-oriented person. Yet whatever a task or job entails, even despite seemingly impossible odds, the person is likely to state, "It will get done!"

Three 2's connects pleasure/communication/creativity with the area of partnership and relationships. It can manifest in varied ways: enjoyment of conversation, pleasure and comfort in partnership, scattering in associations, etc. Three 2's deals with communication and fun in relationships, while two 3's (a similar combination) deals with passivity/sensitivity/partnership in the area of communication. The number in each box in the Inclusion Table would represent the verb or the action-carrying dynamic. With three 2's, you express your relationships in a 3 manner; with two 3's, you express communication, creativity and the lower mind in a 2 manner.

The missing 3 is a Karmic Lesson. Stephanie explained: "It is learning how to have the joy of living and be expressive and creative and communicative. She has three 2's, 4's and 9's, so the 3 is a major emphasis in how she expresses her life. She has come here to learn how to express and enjoy herself through relationships, through work and balance, and in the world, talking and meeting with people, being creative in the world." A Karmic Lesson usually means the tendency to overdo, underdo or displace the energy involved. For example, if not consciously handled, a missing 3 can either deny oneself reasonable pleasures and happiness in life, or overindulge in areas of one's choice.

"Three 4's," Sylvia explained, "indicates that she would like to be involved with a man who is very creative, into pleasure and enjoyment. Also she would like to find these qualities in the work, to want pleasure at work, and finding some sort of work that is creative or involves communication."

Two 5's connects partnership/sensitivity/motherhood with the area of sexuality/changes/freedom (number 5). The numerologists mentioned the tendency of this combination for passivity, and sometimes even manipulation, in the area of sensuality and changes. Two is under the average for the number of 5's in a name. In some cases for women, sex is principally seen as a method of desired motherhood, secondarily for pleasure.

The missing 6 is a lesson regarding responsibilities — often quite loaded — toward marriage, family and community. Often much service and dedication is asked with little seeming reward except the satisfaction of accomplishment and doing a job well. Sometimes with a 6 Life Path also involved, accepting responsibility unconditionally without resentment may be a major issue as a condition of developmental karma and means of growth. Eight 1's, however, illustrates the strength of will to carry out responsibilities faithfully.

The missing 7 is significant in Ms. One's pattern because of her 7 Soul Urge. Number 7 is connected with understanding, either learning through the negative consequences of experience (the hard way) or learning through observation, thinking before acting, and paying attention to the early warning signals of unrewarding activities (the easy way). The missing 7 may indicate a challenge of correct evaluation and a weakness of "common sense" in which a person may undergo the so-called "repeat syndrome" in which painful or empty experiences recur over and over again. The 7 vibration often requires sufficient alone time to engage in healthy, honest introspection. The missing 7 may mean the fear of being alone in many cases, and in other cases a person may retreat into a shell of excessive introspection. It can indicate displaced faith, insufficient trust, not heeding the future consequences of present behavior, or arrogant faith in one's own present knowledge and perspective. However, the missing 7 does exist and is "good," a functional dynamic in Ms. One's character. It may signify an incentive to be open and receptive to life's experiences. It may mean the inner drive to fill the void of the missing 7 in terms of being the seeker for higher knowledge, wider truth, actively reaching out for those books, teachers and experiences that will serve as a stimulus for learning and growth.

The missing 8 is often considered as a lack of self-confidence and feeling of inferiority in terms of handling the material world — money, business, physical security, etc. Ability may exist in handling the practical necessities of life, especially after training and experience, but inner doubt and worry may be the dynamic. It may reflect as an overconcern on money, power, authority and health. Money is often given an inordinate priority in one's value system; survival and financial safety are uppermost in one's mind. Managing money and handling business dealings effectively may be primary issues in the life until the person feels the power and competence in his or her own hands.

"Three 9's," Sylvia observed, "indicates the desire to be happy in the world, finding pleasure in the world, likes to communicate, get around, see others and talk with the world." This combination suggests a fire-air extroversion and social outgoingness. Giving and interacting with the world will be performed in a number 3 manner — talking, writing or diversifying one's service to the world, being a Jack (or Jane) of all trades.

Stephanie briefly focused upon the totals of the Inclusion Table's rows and columns: "She also has a three in the World Row (sum of boxes 7, 8, 9), similar to the three 9's, therefore she can talk in the world, travel, and be creative. She can also be scattered. Her 3 in the Mental Column (boxes 3, 6, 9) is a creative mind and a quick mind, but it can also be a scattered mind that wanders all over the place. She has 5 in the Emotional Column (boxes 2, 5, 8), so she's up and down emotionally. Her emotions are changeable and active. In the Family Row (boxes 4, 5, 6) is a 5 showing changes in the family. She can live away from her early family, would want to get away to be free. The 11 in the 'I' Row (boxes 1, 2, 3) and the Physical Column (boxes 1, 4, 7) can show prominence because 11 is a master number and it is a more-than-average number in those places. She can become known for something that she does, good or bad; if bad, she can be used or abused."

Stephanie continued with an observation on Ms. One's birthday, a subsidiary core indicator of character similar to the Life Path number. "She was born on a 17 day, which ends up being an 8, so again with her Birthday she has come to learn business, to be powerful and self-confident and in control — but realizing that the major control you have in life is over yourself, self-control, and not over other people or overcontrolling yourself."

The numerologists then focused upon Ms. One's **Natal Imprint** — primarily the **Pinnacles** and **Challenges** based on the baseline numbers of her month/day/year of birth. Born September (9) 17 (8), 1933 (7), her baseline numbers are 9-8-7 (= 6 Life Path). **Adding the first two baseline numbers** (9, 8) results in the 8 **Pinnacle** above the baseline; **subtracting** the first two baseline numbers results in a 1 **Challenge** below the baseline. The first Pinnacle and Challenge is the 8/1, therefore, lasting from birth until the end of her 30th year (36 minus 6 Life Path = 30). Number 9 is the number of completion and the numerological cycle of humanity. Four Pinnacles and four Challenges are in effect: 4X9 = 36. **Adding the second and third baseline numbers** (8, 7) results in the 6 **second Pinnacle**; **subtracting** the second and third baseline numbers results in a 1 **second Challenge**. This 6/1 Pinnacle and Challenge is a **nine-year cycle** starting on her 31st birthday until the start of her 40th birthday. **Adding the first two Pinnacles** (8, 6) results in the 5 **third Pinnacle; subtracting the first two Challenges** (1, 1) results in a 0 **third Challenge** — lasting (nine years) from age 40 until 49. When you **add all the Pinnacles** (8, 6, 5), the result is a 1 **Super Pinnacle** at the very top of the Natal Imprint; when you **add all the Challenges** (1, 1, 0), the result is the 2 **Super Challenge** at the very bottom of the pattern.

Natal Imprint

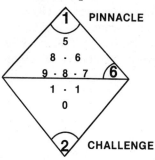

Sylvia discussed portions of the overall pattern in relationship to her Inclusion Table: "As we said, she doesn't have an 8 in her major numbers, but the eight 1's is a very powerful statement, saying, 'I'm going to have the power and control in my life and I'm never going to let anybody else tell me what to do or how to do it or when to do it. She's a rebel in this way, and we see the first Pinnacle and Challenge being the 8 over 1, so it's again showing the rebellious-ness doing what she wants to do, and then perhaps feeling sorry about it because of that missing 7, not having the common sense, and then getting involved in some situation like getting married early or sexually involved young or having children young. That 1 Super Pinnacle is saying she must be in charge, doing what she wants to do. Her focus is definitely into doing her own thing, money, power, or whatever it is that she is striving for. Of course, if she feels that her husband has to provide the money and authority, then it could be problematical."

The first Pinnacle and Challenge, then, suggests that ego, self-will and independence (number 1) is challenged by environmental (Pinnacle) factors relating to money and power (number 8) — e.g., being poor, controlling parent, etc. The 6/1 second Pinnacle and Challenge suggests again that self is challenged by the 6 theme of home, family or community responsibilities. On a positive, developmental basis, it can mean using stumbling blocks as stepping-stones, strengthening independence and competence through the test of responsibilities. Currently Ms. One is in the final Pinnacle and Challenge, the 1 Super Pinnacle and 2 Super Challenge (although undertones were felt throughout her whole life), suggesting that she may finally be doing what she really wants, but she is sensitive about it regarding relationships and partnership and perhaps the home

(2 Super Challenge). That 1/2 pattern involves a Self-Other balancing act, requiring compromise, teamwork and equality.

At this writing, Ms. One is 50 years old. **Adding her 6 Life Path to her present age** would result in a 2 **Personal Year** beginning on her 50th birthday (5 + 0 + 6 = 11/2); that is, 5 + 0 (her present age) + 6 (her Life Path) = 11/2 Personal Year. A 2 year involves partnerships, relationships, the issue of security and motherhood, and sensitivity. She has 2's in her name, so it shows ability to handle that particular year vibration. The three 5's involved in the first four months of her Personal Year (5 baseline first number, and the 5/5 first Pinnacle and Challenge) may mean many changes — e.g., the 5 theme of the physical body, freedom, moving.

Year Imprint

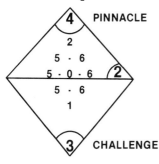

Finally, but certainly not least in importance, we refer back to Ms. One's Natal Imprint and its 9-8-7 baseline. The first number (9) of this 9-8-7 baseline is the **First Cycle**, called the Formative (or Developmental) Cycle. It would end approximately on her first Saturn return in transits (or, for some numerologists, after her first lunar return in secondary progressions), both occurring at age 28-29 generally. The second number (8) of this 9-8-7 baseline is the **Second Cycle**, called the Productive (or Accomplishment) Cycle, lasting until her second Saturn return around age 59. This 8 Productive Cycle is an emphasis on material, practical affairs, business, money, power, etc. The third number (7) of this 9-8-7 baseline is the **Third** or **Final Cycle**, sometimes called the Integrative Cycle. This 7 Final Cycle in Ms. One's pattern will begin approximately in her 59th year (second Saturn return). This period is likely to be reflective and best spent in a nature setting, near water, or wherever is conducive for understanding, learning and introspection. It can be a good period for writing, being with grandchildren, settling down with a calmer, more relaxed disposition. It is basically a time for being alone, to be at-one-ment with greater aspects of one's beingness. In Scripture, the 7th day of creation was the day of rest (renewal and reflection). It can be a period of being by oneself in meditative silence, becoming as the archetypal "wise old woman."

Ms. One Responds to Zip

Ms. One stiffly settled upon the couch, smiling. Her previous surgery was only a month ago and she brooked her discomfort well. Two weeks earlier she completed a lengthy interview with me despite her healing pains, and this time she demonstrated far greater vigor and willingness to continue. I was impressed with her toughness. Before I started with the follow-up questioning of Ms. One's response to Zip's initial interpretation of her chart that she read within the last two weeks, she showed me a photo of her taken 23 years ago, wearing a skydiving outfit.

"My husband jumped for years and I tried it. I really liked it. He jumped me and he was shaking, but I wasn't. He said that if anything happened to me, my family would never believe it! But a lot of people jump because they want to show someone or prove something. I wanted to jump just to see what it was like."

I shortly asked her if she felt that Zip's analysis was accurate.

"A lot of it was right on," she answered. "I read it twice and I was going to go back to it again because the medication I'm on makes it really hard for me to concentrate on reading."

"Do you see yourself as a lady of passionate depths, as Zip said?" I asked.

"Oh, yeah. A lot of people I don't like," she replied, such as phonies, "and if I don't like them, I won't have anything to do with them. If I like people, I really like them. I had a real bad temper when I was very young, but I learned to curb that. I mellowed."

However, in response to my question about her outspokenness, Ms. One recounted an incident about a decade or more ago between herself and an intruding neighbor who volunteered to state that one of Ms. One's sons was "no good."

"I was mad but I calmly said, 'What makes you say that?' And she said, 'Well, he's got real long hair and wants to go to Haight-Ashbury.' And I said, 'Well, you've got orange hair and you look like a hooker! Look at the way you dress. Every time you bend over, your ass shows!' And she goes, 'How dare you!' And I said, 'How dare you come in my home and tell me my son is no good. Maybe my son has long hair but inside he's a good person.' "

Her forthrightness shows in many ways. I asked her what really turned her off.

"Hassling, fighting, selfishness," she answered, clearly and directly. "Anytime I see an injustice or someone having a problem,

I have to say something or do something. I can't **not** get involved."

She is an unblinking fighter when necessary, however, especially when locking horns with so-called medical authorities. As she spoke, I scanned her chart and noted her Mars square Saturn.

"Many doctors treat you like a bad child. In the hospital they would say that I didn't accept authority. What authority? 'Oh, my authority,' the doctor would say. And I said, 'You don't have authority over me. I have authority.' Doctors tell me what to do, but I have the authority. If I want to do it, I do it; if I don't, I won't. You know, I took care of my kids and I did all the things I had to do. No one now has authority over me."

I noted her tenth-house Moon and the ruler of her fourth-house Uranus, in her sixth house of work and service, and I inquired if she was a professional mother.

"I did all the raising of my kids," she answered, stating that she also worked on the outside to buy food, clothing and pay the bills for the family. "I had all the responsibility. In all the years I was raising my kids I only bought necessities. I never spent money on myself. I don't know why, but I would feel guilty. I would buy good clothes for the girls, save all my tips during the week and spend maybe $100-$150 on a dress for my daughter, but I would spend $10 at the most for myself on pants. I always felt guilty spending money on myself."

She taught her kids cleanliness, good manners and learning to get along with each other. "I always told them, if sisters and brothers don't love each other, don't ever expect anyone else to. My husband said I was always too strict with the kids. None of my kids have ever talked back to me, swore at me, because they knew I'd knock them right through the wall. I didn't have time to play games. So I was really strict and hard on my kids, a strong disciplinarian, in some areas, but real liberal in others — I'd listen to anything. Although I was huggy and lovey and close to my kids, sometimes I feel like I didn't give them enough emotional support when they were teenagers. Even though I was strong, I was weak in a certain way because there was so much to do. But probably the main thing is, I never ever would let the kids say, 'I can't' anything. That was one of my very pet things. If anyone would say, 'Do this,' and they'd say, 'I can't' without trying, I'd just want to strangle them. And I think that is the main thing, that they realize that they **can** anything."

Was she a parent to mate or vice versa, as Zip considered as one possibility?

"Definitely," she replied emphatically. "I always said I had seven kids, not just six. He's still a child mentally. He never ceases to amaze me. He's so immature. But, of course, it's partly the way he was raised."

As I noted the idealism factors tied to partnership, I asked Ms. One if she always felt the need for a mate and if she is adjusting well to her present divorced state — despite the fact that she is convalescing in her former husband's home with her adult children around.

"It has been hard for me to be alone. I love being alone but not all the time. But you know, even with all the years I was married, I was really alone a lot. I mean, you can be around fifty people and still not be close. He would get up and he could hardly wait to get to work and then later have a good time. So he was gone most of the time."

Ms. One mentioned that if she could do things over again, perhaps she would train to be an attorney. At this point in her life, she plans to return to her new home in the mountains after her final surgeries.

"Now I don't have to do anything except what I want to do. This is the time of my life where I'm going to do what I want to do. I want to go home, paint my church and open my shop. From now on I'm going to do, without hurting anyone, everything I want for me for a change. I may be crazy but I'm going to be crazy happy.

"I'd like to take psychology. I'd like to be a social worker, a psychologist. I'm seeing a young woman psychologist right now up north. They're like babies. When we started talking about stuff and I went into details, she was shocked. The worst thing that probably happened to them was maybe the car breaking down on the freeway or something. I thought she would never shut up crying. But I feel I could be a good psychologist because I've been through pretty much. There's no way that you can ever really know something unless you've been there. Book learning is just book learning. I can work maybe as a hospital counselor because I know I've been to the very pit. About everything there can be, I've been through."

CHAPTER FIFTEEN

MR. TWO

Introduction to Mr. Two

When I originally met Mr. Two, I was quite impressed by his natural articulateness. He projected such a mental quality; yet, I was impressed, moreover, by his responsive, almost vulnerable eyes, suggesting not a cold intellectuality, but a sensitive intelligence ready to be vocalized.

"I'm a big mouth, but basically I am a quiet person," he paradoxically once said.

He is gay, but, as he asserted, "I represent no one but myself."

After I had obtained and examined his horoscope, I later asked him if he would be interested in participating as an anonymous case study for this book. He consented, signing the release forms, which allowed his questionnaire and interview comments to be publishable. However, as with all the participants, he had the freedom to edit his material in the first working draft in case he had second doubts about wanting certain previous statements published.

Mr. Two did edit extensively, realizing clearly now my intent to rely heavily on quotations for accuracy. Part of the difficulty was his surprise at how detailed and revealing his interview statements were once he read its written form. Part of the difficulty also stemmed from the dichotomy, in most cases, between the spoken word versus the written word, and that the formal, written style is greatly preferred over verbatim of the vocal style. This is understandable, but also allowed for in the nature of this presentation.

However, for these and other reasons, I will make an unusual approach in this case study only: I will almost exclusively rely on Mr. Two's written answers on my questionnaire. With the other cases, I have combined the enlightening interview material with the questionnaire material for a fuller presentation, especially in light of clarifying material given in the open question-and-answer format of the interviewing context. This case study will be rather abbreviated, as a result, but all the informative data given will indeed suffice. It should prove interesting to view background information from a questionnaire context, and I will also insert clarifying data unavailable as direct written quotes.

At any rate, let us proceed with Mr. Two's presentation of his background and approach to life.

Mr. Two's Background

Mr. Two:

"I was the fourth of six children: two older half sisters, an older half brother and two younger sisters. It was my understanding that I was raised until two by my second older sister, and I had to be broken at age two of calling her 'Mommy.' For a long time, I maintained a dependency on her, calling for her, during illness, rather than my mother. Both parents worked.

"Early memories are more negative than positive. I feared my father and grew to giving one thing importance — staying out of his way! His abuse was harsh and confusing. The whole air of the environment was one of fear. He dominated everything. And even when he was gone, everything was done according to whether, 'What would Dad think when he gets home?' Everything had to be checked out first. I remember being at a total loss for understanding what was being done to me and why. My memory is that we all suffered under him.

"At eight, my mother left the family for another man. My oldest sisters had already married and my brother joined the Navy. This left my two younger sisters and me. A year later my father brought us to [**another state**] where I grew up and went to school."

[**In response to the question, "List and describe the major, impactful events of your life, and why."**] "I have been the 'major event' of my life, with all due respect to other people. This view has to be balanced with the fact that until the recent past I tended to share and often lose my identity with others in relationships.

"The events are often historical facts I consciously feel detached from. Other events are internal, and I have a vivid emotional memory of them. Listed briefly:

"A. In early childhood — the family discord.
"B. Discovery of my sexuality (homosexual). The alternate expression (very early) and suppression was a driving force in my life.
"C. Personal inner fear and inferiority and public achievement to a high degree. In junior high school I was named one of the top ten students of the city in which I lived. High school found me named president pro-tem of the mayor's youth race-relations council, and winning awards in school for sports, forensics, etc. But my internal dissatisfaction led me to quit high school three times. Finally I got my diploma through adult school at night.
"D. Along with the above, I was active in church. I always used to run away to Sunday school [age 7] rather than go to a ball game with my father. Through high school I found myself in the pulpit often, and handling missionary efforts. I received a great deal of acclaim, but felt slightly phony because I knew how short I was falling of accomplishing what I could, blocked by my lack of internal concentration.

"At 18, the draft and Vietnam had a big effect on me. My spiritual views led me to conscientious objection, and many church 'friends' labeled me a tool of Satan for such views. This was not totally the case but more so than those who supported me. I left the church."

[In response to the question of describing one's own characteristics and qualities.] "I most like my mind. My ability for detail and depth. My intuition. My ability to sense others' needs often even before they sense them. I am very outgoing, but I am an extroverted loner, a thinker whose doing is frustrated by laziness and procrastination. I can be very persuasive, but detest the need to 'sell' anything."

[In response to the question, "How do you feel other people see you?"] "People's views of me depend on the context of our interaction. I am seen as charismatic by some; difficult, moody and hard to reach by others. Severely intelligent, and a patsy. Other people say [in completing the statement "He is a fine human being, but —"] 'He's too analytical, cold, distant; also, a sucker for other people's intentions. Too philosophical.' But I don't believe we can pretend to answer this question objectively. Truth is often subjective."

[In response to the question on what affects him and what

motivates him.] Pettiness affects me. It's distressing. An unbidden smile affects me. I may not remember it, but I know I am touched and changed.

"What motivates me?! Food, sex and the need for meaning!"

["**List three or more things or conditions you want most out of life.**"] "Peace, understanding, love."

[**In response to his greatest challenge in life.**] "Myself. I give me such a bad time. I asked [**an older sister**] what kind of a child she thought I was. She said, You were always so serious. You took everything to heart. Everything that happened just destroyed you."

[**His definition of success.**] "To sail through every day and get my mind out of the way."

[**Significant health problems and operations.**] "Sun poisoning at age 3-4. Hepatitis, age 23. Emotional distress: in adolescence diagnosed as latent schizophrenic, age 18.

[**Jobs held.**] "16 years old — liquor store stock clerk.

"19 years old — supply stock clerk in hospital.

"23 years old — machine operator at book bindery.

"25-33 years old — waiter. I love my customers."

Numerological Analysis

Of the three names given Mr. Two at birth, the rundown of his major numbers is as follows:

Soul Urge (vowels sum)	= 5
Personality (consonants sum)	= 1
Name/Expression (name sum)	= 6
Life Path (month/day/year sum)	= 1

His 5 Soul Urge (how he identifies or sees himself) is described by Stephanie: "A 5 Soul Urge is someone who is very restless and wants to move about and change. It can also be sexually involved — a lot of sexual desire — since number 5 is the number of the five senses and the physical body. He possibly will travel domestically more so than internationally (number 9) since 5 is the number of domestic travel."

Another hallmark of number 5 is freedom. Mr. Two's Personality (outer expression, how other people see him or how he impresses them) is the number 1, which also contributes to the freedom theme in his overall pattern. Of the four major numbers (core indicators of character), three are freedom-oriented: his 5 Soul Urge, 1 Personality, and 1 Life Path. Number 1 is the number of self-will and independence — doing one's own thing.

"We see that with those 1's involved in his major numbers," Sylvia observed, "that this is someone who has come to be independent, stand on his own two feet, and get involved with his own sense of identity. It is a very interesting aspect of a person who really wants to be a person on his own terms. On another level, the major 1's can talk about someone who can be very selfish or very I-oriented, wanting to do what he wants to do."

Mr. Two's Name (or "Expression") is number 6. The keynote of number 6 is responsibility and service. As given in the earlier case study, the Name is the second most important core indicator of character, next to the Life Path, in terms of relative power. It represents your essential vibration at birth, your talents and qualities — how you naturally express yourself.

"The 5-1-6 combination of major numbers," [**Soul Urge, Personality, Name**] Stephanie suggested, "usually shows someone who needs to be out working in public service of some sort. The 6 Name in itself is someone who is into the responsibility of home and family, whether the immediate nuclear family or the community family in which we belong. Usually people who have a 6 in the major numbers have something to contribute to the world. But he is missing a 6 in his name, so he has set up a grand lesson to learn in dealing with responsibility, and learning about love and harmony." Shortly we will discuss the missing 6 in the Inclusion Table section.

As given, Mr. Two's Life Path is the number 1. As the most important delineator of character, the Life Path signifies your growth goal or destiny, the life direction you must follow for best development. His developmental direction is one of true independence and constructive self-will in action. Otherwise, its undesirable expression can be painful self-consciousness in its excessive "me"-orientation, aggressiveness, repression (blocked number 1), or struggles with unresolved dependency needs. In its constructive fulfillment, the number 1 can manifest, for example, as the trendsetting pioneer or leader.

"The 1 Life Path," Stephanie added, "along with the 1 Personality, indicates that he can be a leader. With the responsibility focus of his 6 Name, leadership seems to be something that is going to be very important in his life: to be a leader rather than a follower, and someone who is given a leadership or management position so that people know that there is someone there to depend on and look up to — to get people started."

Born on the twenty-first, his Birthday numbers reduce to the number 3, the number of creative self-expression and communication. As a subsidiary core symbol of character, the Birthday is somewhat similar to the Life Path in terms of potential life direction. It may also suggest a mixture of both the Name qualities and the Life Path: a natural, yet developing expression of self. Its astrological correlate is Gemini and Mercury — e.g., Mr. Two's Gemini rising (identification with the mind, ideas and communication). His Mercury, ruling his Gemini Ascendant, is in the sign of serious, cautious, responsible Capricorn. Perhaps the developmental aspect of the 3 Birthday in Mr. Two's case is to develop more the lightheartedness characteristic of number 3, or being non-judgmental of relationships (more on this later when we discuss his four 3's in the Inclusion Table section).

Attention was next focused upon Mr. Two's Inclusion Table (diagram in box format derived from the total letter values of a name).

Inclusion Table

3	0	4	I	7
1	1	0	We	2
3	3	5	They	11

P E M
7 4 9

Three 1's in his name connects communication, mind and pleasure (number 3) with identity, self-will and independence (number 1). As Stephanie commented: "He has three 1's, and that's someone who enjoys talking about himself. The person wants to go out, talk, have a good time." Since the number in the box is the action-carrying "verb," he will likely express his identity and individuality in a number 3 manner — e.g., chattering, writing, reading, wanting to enjoy himself, perhaps being scattered or versatile. Again, his Gemini rising appears to fit this description.

The missing 2 is a Karmic Lesson. The number 2 area of women, relationships in general, and partnership is a lesson or challenge area, requiring extra focus in handling.

"The missing 2," Stephanie explained, "is learning how to be gentle and diplomatic, to deal with women and understanding relationships in general. Number 2 tends to soften a personality considerably, so that it is easier to get along comfortably in relationships. Missing 2, then, is a great lesson of trust and tactfulness in relationships. Along with the missing 6, I would say he has or had a lesson to learn in dealing with women, learning how to understand them and the female principle, and being responsible for any such relationship that he might have in terms of having commitments to."

Oftentimes, the missing 2 can indicate an oversensitivity to the opinions and feeling of other people (e.g., Mr. Two's Libra stellium in the Leo/fifth house). In other cases, lack of consideration may be evident. Also, if number 2 relates to the mother (female), nurturing figure, a lesson concerning her may play a role in the life. The missing 2 can additionally refer to the issue of passivity in the nature — too much, too little or in the wrong place.

Four 3's ties work, discipline and limitation with the area of communication and enjoyment. "With four 3's," Sylvia said, "we can either be critical and judgmental of our mind and creativity, or we are doing it in a very balanced way."

The potential manifestations of this combination are varied: the detailed, orderly mind; measured, deliberate speech; critical, flaw-finding; biting communication, etc. It is interesting to note that Mr. Two's Mercury in Capricorn in the eighth house could reflect the four 3's. Also, in the eighth-Scorpio house, Mercury can accentuate good research abilities — the methodical, structured, thorough mind.

One 4 connects identity, self-will and independence with work, father, men, order and balance. He will choose to relate to number 4 areas on his own terms and be the kind of man he chooses. It shows an innate understanding of work requirements and keeping within limits — e.g., punctuality.

One 5 unites self-will and identity with the area of sex, sensuality, changes and freedom. Again, he is going to express the number 5 areas on his own (number 1) terms. Since three to five is the average number of 5's in a name, perhaps one 5 can indicate a self-imposed myopic limitation of life's experiences, staying on a prescribed path, disinclined to make changes often — or changing too frequently before experiences can be fully assimilated and integrated within self (again, the extremes of "too much" or "too little"). Another speculation is going along the loner (number 1) path, or being truly independent and self-reliant in number 5 areas.

The missing 6 is another Karmic Lesson. It is an important lesson since Mr. Two's Name/Expression is a 6. The missing 6 is a challenge around home and community responsibility, service, love and harmony.

Sylvia commented on this in a face-to-face session with Mr. Two for this book: "You don't have any 6's in your name, and the 6 is your Name total. So we're seeing a person who has a need to be needed, and sometimes with that we can have a tendency to put other people's needs ahead of our own. And yet here we have the independent operator, the person who wants to be free! — at the same time, allowing the other person to 'make' you responsible for his or her problems. So instead of living your own life, you could martyr yourself in some way because of other people's needs. So the missing 6 adds to the lesson of how to be responsible for yourself instead of you having to be so responsible for other people."

Three 7's connects communication and creative self-expression with the area of study, the higher mind, and spirituality. It suggests a pleasure of communicating what one knows.

"We see the three 1's, the three 7's, and the three 8's in the Inclusion Table," noted Sylvia, "showing a lot of creativity here. The 6 Name is a creative number, and his birthday — the 21st — totals a 3. So we see a lot of potential here to do something in a creative way, particularly with communication or artistic endeavors in some way. The creativity of the 3 involves the mouth and the throat, as it relates to those parts of the physical body. We can talk about just food and pleasure, what we take into our mouth and we enjoy through the five senses. But when we do that on a higher (7) level — that creative ability — then we do something that we put out into the world where other people can enjoy and experience. Also, three 7's says, 'I want to be happy learning.' "

"People with three 7's," Stephanie added, "can be into a lot of different fields of study and knowledge. They can be mentally creative in an analytical sense. Good investigators. The more 7's you have, the greater that ability. With three 7's, they could be good speakers often. Three 7's would be communication on a higher level, such as religion and philosophy." As an astrological correlate, perhaps Mr. Two's Sun and Jupiter in Aquarius in the ninth house would fit (the Sun rules a portion of his third house).

Three 8's combines communication, creativity and pleasure with money, power, authority and control (number 8). It can mean a deeply probing mind (Scorpionic); attacking communication or words used as weapons much like a Scorpion's sting; the need to integrate passion and power with noncoercive reason, etc. The person may want money for books, pleasure and creative projects, or squander it in a flippant, scattered manner.

Five 9's is an Intensity Point or concentration focus since the average number of 9's in a name is two or three. It connects sex, sensuality, freedom and changes with the wider, transpersonal world. These are two movement and travel numbers in combination which can indicate scattering because it says, "I want to be free in the world, to go, to travel." Nervousness and restlessness may be manifested in the life.

Sylvia briefly focused upon the totals of the Inclusion Table's rows and columns: "The 7 in the 'I' Row (sum of boxes 1, 2, 3) and 7 in the Physical Column (boxes 1, 4, 7) show that we're very involved with religion, metaphysics or whatever we choose to think is superior. We want to study, to learn, and we want to understand what life is all about. That 11 in the World Row (boxes 7, 8, 9) shows that you have come to be prominent in the world. Number 11 is a master number, and it says, 'I have come into the world to learn how to be a teacher on a higher plane.' The 9 total in the Mental Column (boxes 3, 6, 9) indicates that mood swings are possible, trying not to be a martyr in some way, or feeling depressed in some instances. The 4 total in the Emotional Column (boxes 2, 5, 8) indicates that in some ways you have closed off that emotional expression. Number 4 can be a critical/judgmental number. The 2 in the Family Row (boxes 4, 5, 6) is trying to have the control, or being manipulated in the family. And through your experience with your mother and father, you know what that trip is all about."

Natal Imprint

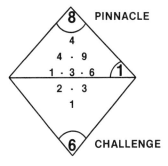

Attention was next placed upon Mr. Two's Natal Imprint, which is primarily the baseline and Pinnacles and Challenges based on the month/day/year of birth. Born January 21, 1950, Mr. Two's baseline numbers are 1-3-6 (= 1 Life Path). His first Pinnacle and Challenge is the 4 over 2, ending at the conclusion of his 35th birthday (36 minus 1 Life Path = 35). This pattern suggests sensitivity (2 Challenge) about work, father, males in the environment (4 Pinnacle). It can also indicate a challenge between father and mother, since number 2 can symbolize the mother or female figure. Its astrological correlate may be Mr. Two's Moon opposite Saturn closely squaring his Ascendant, suggesting a strong impact on personal action and identity. Note in the illustration the first baseline number (number 1) coming in between the 4 over 2).

"The 4 over 2," Sylvia observed, "shows that in some way you had this feeling of coming between your mother and father, and feeling responsible in a way for what happened when they separated. There's a tremendous amount of sensitivity in this pattern, and it won't change until you reach 36 years old." Mr. Two agreed with her assessment of the parental situation.

The second Pinnacle and Challenge (9 over 3) is a nine-year period beginning on his 36th birthday, which suggests involvement with creativity and communication in the world. Pleasure, happiness and self-expression may be challenged (3 Challenge) in the environment (9 Pinnacle), if constructive creativity is not mobilized. The combined 4-9-4 Pinnacles suggest dealing with men, work and balance in the world. It is the potential for selfless giving, humanitarianism, or martyrdom, limitation and fear if the 6 Super Challenge is not handled wisely. The 8 Super Pinnacle and 6 Super Challenge are lifelong themes, indicating the potential for a great deal of power and responsibility — money, authority and control earned through his own efforts, or attracting power figures (particularly men with the 4 Pinnacles) in the environment, thereby learning how to handle power. His Personal Year starting on his 34th birthday in 1984 is also an 8 (3 + 4 + 1 Life Path = 8). As the Year diagram shows, its own Super Pinnacle and Super Challenge is a 6 over 6, so responsibility, service and power are the themes of that year.

Year Imprint

```
      /6\  PINNACLE
       3
     7 · 5
    3 · 4 · 1  /8\
     1 · 3
       2
     /6\  CHALLENGE
```

Returning to the 1-3-6 natal baseline, Mr. Two is presently within the number 3 Accomplishment (or Productive) Cycle, which began approximately at his first Saturn return at age 29. The 3 Cycle (the "3" in the 1-3-6 baseline) centers around the theme of pleasure, indulgences, communication, creative self-expression, or perhaps scattering and loss of direction. Commencing on his second Saturn return (approximately age 58-59), Mr. Two will enter the 6 Final Cycle (the "6" in the 1-3-6 baseline). Once again, the theme for this final period is responsibility, harmony, service, family and love. If responsibility and commitment is reconciled with freedom and self-will (major numbers theme), then this Cycle can hold quite a fulfilling potential in terms of satisfying service and welcomed harmony, peace and love.

Mr. Two Responds to Zip

I will briefly summarize Mr. Two's comments on the astrological and numerological "readings." First of all, Zip's idea of his freedom/closeness dilemma attracted his attention, and he felt it was very accurate. He mentioned the past tendency of attracting others who, because of their own emptiness, projected their power upon him for their fulfillment in a relationship. The power issue was involved since he would often attract aggressive, pushy people who were perhaps weaker-appearing people initially.

Mr. Two read for me one of his favorite passages of Zip's interpretation: "Helping is best done in a professional framework. In peer relationships, it is an invitation to disaster for one person to try to save another who should be an equal." He felt that that statement probably summed up his biggest lesson in the last decade. He is learning to help people help themselves rather than taking responsibility for their emptiness. He asserted that there's no savior complex anymore (being one's brother's keeper to an excessive degree), nor being excessively vulnerable to their crises: "Within the last couple of years I've started coming out of that. But I remember most of my life, around any friend or family member, if they were going through their own hell, I felt like I was drowning. I almost started suffocating for air — emotional air — of some kind."

He admitted his judgmentalness of people, yet he can be quite generous to friends and family. He has a close tie with his mother. But this judgmental process, he felt, was part of holding off others at arm's length (freedom/closeness issue again). I asked if the gay lifestyle had a built-in freedom/closeness dilemma — e.g., is commitment and exclusivity among male gays the exception rather than the rule? Much of the difficulty, he answered, has to do with the particular individual's total acceptance or not of his sexual identity. A significant stressor is feeling dichotomized by one's homosexual expression outwardly and one's inner rejection of such behavior by a disapproving conscience and cultural taboos. Such an internal conflict happened with Mr. Two, and it contributed to severe depression experienced between age 16-18. He was labeled as latently schizophrenic. Part of the depression was also due to existential issues — e.g., there must be more to life than pettiness and power struggles. He contended, however, that he resolved the internal conflict during his mid-twenties, accepting his gay lifestyle as a valid and good expression — a characteristic, just as race or height is a characteristic (sexual identity being secondary to being a person). He is living by himself, but he is not lonely. He likes the idea of one-to-one intimacy, but not in terms of a closed system. Presently he is exploring new avenues of meaningful, satisfying work, donating time and energy to community service. Renewed schooling and training is part of the future picture.

CHAPTER SIXTEEN

Ms. Three

Introduction to Ms. Three

Similar to the previous subject, I met Ms. Three at Sylvia's bookstore less than two years ago. For several months our relationship was friendly in an impersonal way, merely a sparse acquaintance. As her student, she occasionally participated in Sylvia's monthly psychic faire as a tarot card reader. As the months passed, Ms. Three began to share with me and others a series of lectures given by Mr. Seven. My initial impression of Ms. Three was also a lasting one. I gleaned a sensitive and sensual quality about her, but not delicate in a vulnerable, weak manner. She had a tough, independent and restless undercurrent, yet her whole demeanor spoke of **feelings**, particularly inward-turning, as though she readily identified with her emotions. She had to be a prominent water child, I felt, yet with a mixture of fixity to represent that touch of enduring self-will about her.

Finally I examined her horoscope and smiled as I noted her Moon in Cancer on the Ascendant, slightly into the twelfth water house, and her Scorpio focus in the fifth house adding depth, strength and intensity. For purposes of this book, I wanted at least three or four charts with a planet in high focus, particularly conjunct the Ascendant. Already I had a Mars rising chart and a Neptune rising horoscope, and I felt that the Universe provided me another chart with a prominently-placed, yet different, planet. Ms. Three agreed to participate as an anonymous subject for this book. Weeks before my offer, however, she had asked me to briefly delineate her current secondary progressions. I was struck with the uncanny precision of timing of her progressed Moon aspects, as she verified in terms of recent events in her life. As the actual ruler of her Cancer rising, Ms. Three's Moon played a prime role as a noteworthy indicator of ongoing astrological unfolding of character. The time of birth recorded on her birth certificate was quite precise since events corroborated Moon-angle contacts.

Now, let us focus on her past and current background.

Ms. Three's Personal Background

Ms. Three:

"I was born in the Southeast, raised throughout several states. We moved lots and lots, from Florida to three cities in North Carolina to Virginia. I got used to being the new girl in town. It didn't bother me; I always seemed to make new friends.

"I never knew my father's parents. I did know my grandmother, who was a really neat woman. She was an artist, a painter. I never knew her husband because she divorced back before the depression years. The story goes that my grandfather wanted her to be a neat housekeeper and entertainer. He was a businessman and wanted her to be the ideal housewife and mother, but he would come home and my grandmother would have her paints all over the place. She would be painting, the house would be a mess, and there wouldn't be anything to eat. So she had to decide between making him happy or continuing in her art. And so she continued in her art! She married again — a Baptist preacher — but she was a real free spirit. She traveled until she was in her eighties, and she was always going around visiting her children, doing her art. She lived until 88 or something. She was a neat woman.

"I had a sister who was younger than I was, and she died of pneumonia when she was very young, like a year and a half. I have one brother who is five years older than I am. I always got along with him. We were really close when we were growing up, and he was very supportive, took care of me a lot and treated me well. We were just real close. Once he went to college and started teaching in college, I didn't see him much because I left home and I ended up being in different places. I wasn't in the same town, but we always kept in touch. Until the past seven or eight years I saw him quite a bit. Now I see him once or twice a year. I think my brother is a very intellectual man. He's a bookworm. He likes to study all the time. He always has his head in a book and he likes to talk intellectually. He uses his mind a lot and he's basically a loner. But he took it real hard — our childhood with our mother being ill and then dying, and not having a close relationship with my father — although he had a closer one than I did.

"Perhaps the event of most impact in my life was the chronic illness of my mother who, from the time I was five until she died when I was seventeen, suffered heart disease. As I grew, I hoped in the skill and healing of the human physician. My only peace was away from home, in school, playing, practicing dance and piano, or in church (Methodist). My mother died when she was in her early forties.

"My father was not home very much. He did about the same thing I did recently, except he serviced computers instead of sold them. He was at work most of the time and did some traveling. He was basically very good to me until my mother died. Soon after, he remarried and my stepmother said within a few months that it's either her or me living under the same roof. So I left. My father was pretty weak in that he let her control his life regarding his children. She kept up with her own children, but I was a threat to her, so my father basically didn't see me from the time I was seventeen or eighteen until the present day. I guess it has been fourteen years, and I hardly know what he looks like or anything. As you can imagine, it didn't give me much respect for men. I would say that he wasn't real warm or real supportive in that way! It seems like he just changed when this new woman came into his life. After he withdrew his emotional support and everything, I went through several years of bitterness toward the fact of not having a family and not having anybody to go to for Christmas and all that.

"At seventeen I left home and became independent, learning survival in the world since my father withdrew all financial and emotional support. I worked my way through college [**B.S. Education, thesis away from Master's degree**], and I taught the third, fourth and fifth grades for three years. After that I left and worked as a flight attendant for a year. I liked travel and the spontaneous, unplanned lifestyle. A 'personality trait' I like is my strength in adapting to constant changes.

"Then I met my former husband and I got married, longing for home, family and financial security, giving over my self-responsibility to my husband. It was an illusion I went through; not love but dependency and expectations that another person was able to provide my happiness, and secretly resenting his failure to do so. I followed the course of my mother and became critically ill. I had chronic, active hepatitis which led to internal hemorrhaging very near the point of death [**major surgery vein shunt**].

"We had decided to get married very quickly. I thought he could take care of me and I was tired of being alone. We didn't really know each other, and unconsciously I picked somebody that was critical. His numbers are 8/8, and he's not what you call warm and loving. He's a Gemini and has two sides of his personality: one side is really mean, and the other side of it is a fake sweetness. He treated me like a child in a lot of ways and didn't give me respect. I guess I was in the state of mind then when I didn't love myself or think much of myself. On the outside world, he was very talented and we went into business and had a business type of relationship. That's when I was a clothing store owner and manager, and that lasted only a few months. Hated that. Business became a real strain on him because he wasn't that successful, and he started smoking pot. He got real heavy into marijuana and he smoked it every day, which of course led to absolutely no communication between us. We didn't have a closeness. The last straw was when he hit me on more than one occasion (removal of my spleen in 1981). I divorced my husband after being married seven years. I guess I realized that I wasn't **that** bad of a person that I should go walking back in. And I caused myself to be ill from all the tension and stress, and not facing up to things. And then when I was ill, except for a short period of time, he wasn't even very warm and loving about that. So there wasn't really much there.

"It was in 1978-1979 that the most significant change in my life began. I began to study Christian Science. For the first time I began to see the power of thought, that disease manifestations were a result of negative thinking and assumed powerlessness over the physical body. Having spent years in contemplating the authoritative, seductive intellect of the physician, I went through an inner turmoil of the metaphysician versus the physician, succumbing to my sexual instincts and began a love affair of passion with my doctor. I then realized my own idealizations and concept of my doctor as a seductive figure of intellect dealing with the physical and emotional body. My recognition of this came after going to tarot readings. I studied tarot, involving myself in it very deeply. These studies, with the persistent guidance of my teacher, led to an understanding of how I had thus far shaped my life.

"I am now engaged to be married in December 1983. [**She has indeed married on December 3, 1983.**] I am happy for the first time in my life because I have begun to trust, to share in love, which is a new and peaceful experience. He is an inspiration to me. Our mutual love of nature heightens our vision and brings us closer together. I am now in a love relationship where we are both dedicated to our spiritual lives. However, his life and family has been built around the structures of the Catholic Church. In times of 'emotionality' I feel that the structures of Catholicism rise before me like walls separating me from that harmony with him. I am going through an interview and big ordeal with the Catholic Church because it means a lot to my fiance inside to later have a marriage take place in the Church — to be 'validated.' There are Catholic rules and regulations and things I have to go through about my past, contact people and everything.

"I feel real good about his family. There are a lot of responsibilities with a large family, so I'm learning to just keep up with them, their birthdays, etc. They're very, very supportive of each other in all ways. They keep in touch and support each other through times of crisis. So I'm seeing a responsibility and giving and taking and loving and sharing there. So it's something I'm getting used to, but I like it. It's real important and real satisfying.

"Motherhood is in the plans for my career, but I also realize that I need more than staying at home all day. Teaching is definitely a focus. I do like teaching and that interaction with people."

[Until July 1983 Ms. Three worked full-time as a computer sales representative for a Southeast firm, making calls by car within a California regional area. She quit after six months due to internal corporate politics and power struggles with a boss. She moved back to the Southeast in late August to be with her then fiance, a Cancer rising with a Libra-Scorpio stellium in the fourth house, born in 1957. Recently she has completed volunteer work with the handicapped, reinvested in a grand piano, taken dance lessons, and studied metaphysical/ mystical literature. Her father died in April 1984, after a reconciliation with her at her wedding. Presently she is busy teaching grammar school children full-time.]

Numerological Analysis

Of the three names given Ms. Three at birth, the following are her major number vibrations:

Soul Urge (vowels sum)	= 11/2
Personality (consonants sum)	= 3
Name/Expression (name sum)	= 5
Life Path (month/day/year sum)	= 7

Our final participant, Mr. Seven, also has the same Soul Urge, Personality and Expression numbers, so the reader may wish to compare the numerological analysis of his major numbers with Ms. Three's analysis since the presentation is somewhat different. In Ms. Three's case, I will utilize in verbatim the readings presented by our two numerologists, Sylvia and Stephanie.

Sylvia commenced her analysis in direct consultation with Ms. Three for this book: "What we see with a 2 Soul Urge is a person who comes into life, especially a female, who sees herself as the mother, a person who needs a relationship, who wants to get along with other people, and who feels a definite need for tenderness, gentleness, caring and sharing. A 2 Soul Urge never sees oneself as alone but through the relationship with another person(s).

"The 3 Personality shows other people that you are a very creative lady, communicating that you are into pleasure and having a good time. It can also show that you are involved with children.

"You are a 5 Name. Whenever I see a 5 in an open position in the major numbers (Personality, Name and Life Path), I always see that as a sexual person, someone who vibrates sexuality, and brings other people into their life because of that constant change and variety. There's that physical sense. So you can be good at sports and all kinds of activities that require physical action. People with an open 5 can be terrific salespeople. The number 5 wants to go out there to mingle with other people and have a lot of changes and variety. Sometimes that variety can mean escapism.

"The 7 Life Path, which is your birth total, says that you've come in to learn, to be into awareness, study, to learn from life and get one's life together. The number 7 can deal with law in some way. You can also get involved with drugs and pills. So the 7 Life Path indicates that you have come to learn to be spiritual, to come into awareness, wanting a better education, wanting better things in your life, and to be progressive in terms of having a superior life.

"Now, the number 2 is the survivor: 'I need safety and security; I need to feel protected.' You can try to get that security from another person. That's the way you've been most of your life. But you'll never feel secure until you learn that you yourself are your own means of survival. If you have faith and trust in your own nature and in a Higher Power, which is that 7 potential, then survival is something you can take for granted, and there's no fear."

The following is Stephanie's presentation of Ms. Three's major numbers: "The 11/2 Soul Urge can be someone who vibrates higher ideals, wanting to help mankind. Simply on the number 2 level it can mean being dependent, cold and passive, into manipulation on the negative side, or else it can be someone into motherhood and nurturing, into teamwork. She has a 3 Personality so she could be seen by others as rather nice-looking, pleasant and congenial. The 3 Personality is a good salesperson, actor, actress, good at expressing oneself and very magnetic. It can also be into the illusionary aspect of the number 3 in which they might think themselves as being something they're really not. She has a 7 Life Path, coming in to be involved with higher knowledge. The 7 is the number which bridges the physical mundane world into the spiritual. It can be people who like to be by themselves, study a lot, may be very intuitive and insightful. She also has a 7 Super Pinnacle in her birth pattern, so that's someone who wants the best in her environment, to either rise above the mundane world or get into the social climbing aspect of the world."

The numerologists then focused their attention upon Ms. Three's Inclusion Table (table in box format derived from the total letter values of a name).

Inclusion Table

1	0	5	I	6
1	7	1	We	9
1	0	3	They	4

P E M
3 7 9

Ms. Three has one 1 in her name, a double statement of the independence/self-will issue of number 1. Since the average quantity of this number is 3, it indicates a weakness or challenge regarding identity, action or doing one's own thing. Its probable manifestation is learning to be independent and striking a healthy balance between self-will and the will of other people. Often it shows as week self-esteem in the early stages.

The missing 2 in her name can be problematical since any missing number is often referred to as a "Karmic Lesson." It requires a conscious handling of that area or principle of life. Since Ms. Three is also missing the number 8, this necessitates an extra focus in understanding the ramifications of that particular combination, as our numerologists will now expound.

Sylvia: "We see a missing 2 and a missing 8 in the Inclusion Table, and together it indicates someone who is looking for a rich or capable person to support you so that you can feel that safety and security. The missing 2 is talking about how I don't understand the female principle, or how I didn't have a good role model for being a mother, or I'm attached to my mother. Yet with the 2 Soul Urge you're identified with the mother in many ways. The 2 says I have come into the world to make relationships, to bring other people closely into my life, yet I may not have very much trust in the other person and may have fear in a relationship with that missing 2. It can mean a conditional relationship instead of being equals. With a 2 Soul Urge you have come to be a mother, but you don't have any 2's in your name. So being a mother to you is a frightening experience. You've always been cautious of that because you always refer back to how you were raised. But you are not your mother. And you were mothering adults instead of mothering children whom you needed to mother.

"The missing 8 indicates learning about money, power, authority and health. It informs us that she can have a lack of self-confidence with power. Often we see people with a missing 8 worrying about money constantly, not so much that they need it to spend particularly, but to have it to feel secure. With an 8 in the name a person acquires money in order to spend; missing 8's acquire it to feel secure."

Stephanie: "She has a 2 Soul Urge with a missing 2 and she's missing an 8. This usually signifies people who want a partner who is powerful, who has money, and can take care of them. Princess Diana of England, I must say, is also missing the 2 and the 8, and I think she's the perfect example of someone who wants a partner who has the power and the money to provide the security she feels she needs."

Five 3's in her name is an Intensity Point since the average quantity of that number is two or three. This combination connects the number 5 theme of changes, freedom and sexuality with the area of expression, communication and enjoyment. It is an emphasis of restlessness and changeable creative expression, which is great for sales work and being on the go. Creative pleasure outlets may be sought, including sensual indulgences. Plenty of imagination may be on tap, and even sexual fantasies and travel daydreams entertained in the mind. The need to channel her restless creative potency is highlighted so that she doesn't scatter and diffuse her energies.

One 4, however, suggests that she inherently understands the principle of balance and discipline. This combination ties the self-will principle of number 1 with the area of work and order, so another theme may be identification with work, choosing a structured, responsible job, etc.

Seven 5's is definitely her prime intensity point since the average number of 5's in a name is usually no more than three to five. Sylvia elaborates: "The seven 5's says that I need to investigate sex and my physical body and five senses; I want to travel, to learn through travel. That's why you really got involved with going to Egypt, Alaska, etc. Also it can mean being the religious ascetic because they feel that getting involved with their sexuality is not superior. You are a Scorpio, however, and Scorpio is definitely focused into sexuality.''

One 6 indicates that she understands responsibility, though it may be on her own terms (number 1 principle), capable of dealing with obligations to home/family/community.

One 7 suggests that she is naturally capable of analyzing in a common sense manner. It ties the principle of self and action with truth, learning, higher knowledge, research, and perhaps spirituality. Astrologically, it may be paralleled with her Mars in Sagittarius. Often this combination indicates a need to be alone periodically, to withdraw, go within.

The missing 8 has already been explained. However, mention may be made regarding the need to realistically handle the practical necessities of life: how to make and manage money, satisfactorily handle power people in the life, etc.

Three 9's combines the number 3 principle of communication/fun/creativity with the area of wider humanity, the world and long-distance travel. It indicates her desire to have fun and pleasure in the outside world, to chatter with diverse people and to be creative in the world.

Stephanie at this point examined the various sum totals of the rows and columns constituting the Inclusion Table format: ''In the 'I' row (boxes 1, 2, 3), which totals a 6, she can be a responsible person — and she does have a 6 in her name. It shows how responsible she needs to be for herself. In the Family Row (boxes 4, 5, 6) she has a 9 which shows that she can be a martyr in her family or, if she rises above that, wanting to be helpful and giving. The 4 in the World Row (boxes 7, 8, 9) shows that she can be boxed in on how she approaches the world (judgmental and critical of what other people do in the world), or she can be very disciplined. She has a 3 in the Physical Column (boxes 1, 4, 7), so she does want to enjoy herself, to have a good time, be creative. She might also be a little scattered with that. The 7 in the Emotional Column (boxes 2, 5, 8) reinforces wanting the best for herself. She might be very analytical emotionally, or she might make people feel that she thinks of herself as being better than they are. The 9 in the Mental Column might show she feels put upon, suffering mentally. On a higher expression, since number 9 encompasses all the numbers, she might be thinking the very highest thoughts about mankind, into helping others.''

Another indicator of Ms. Three's character is her Birthday number. "She has a 19 birthday," Sylvia offered, "which can be a difficult birthday for she will experience all the events that can possibly happen. Numbers 1 through 9 include all the numbers and there are a tremendous number of experiences to go through intensely, being also a Scorpio child." Her birthday reduces into the number 1 which suggests a long journey leading to true independence and self-actualization, if we consider that number 9 subemphasis. Maturity manifested as personal (number 1 theme) professional service to humanity (number 9 theme) is suggested as being potential.

Natal Imprint

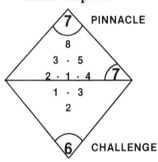

Born November 19, 1948, Ms. Three has a baseline of 2-1-4/22(= 7 Life Path). Her First or Developmental Cycle is the number 2, which would end roughly on her 28th or 29th year (e.g., her Saturn return). It emphasizes the focus upon mother, partnership and sensitivity in relationships. If a sense of deprivation exists from childhood experiences, dependency would be a powerful issue, whether sought through parents or partner. Her second baseline number or Productive Cycle is the number 1, which would last until approximately her 59th birthday (second Saturn return). This period requires action and self-motivation, being independent or a leader/pioneer. It is the polar opposite (partner) of the previous 2 cycle, requiring individuation and personal attainment in the world. The Final Cycle is the 22/4 (her year of birth 1948 = 22/4). Limitation, work and/or balance is its keynote. Ideally, the 22 may indicate a specialist or master builder geared toward universal endeavors.

Ms. Three's first Pinnacle and Challenge is a 3 over 1 which ended at the completion of her 29th year (7 Life Path subtracted from 36). The 1 Challenge can denote struggle in asserting self or clearly individualizing self; doing what she wants to do is challenged. The 3 Pinnacle during that developmental period, nevertheless, may indicate happy outlets, such as the development of creative potential and communication skills. Presently Ms. Three is in the second Pinnacle and Challenge pattern, the 5 over 3, ranging from age 30 through 38. The 5 Pinnacle suggests changes, freedom, travel, sexual/sensual focus, frequent contacts with the public. The 3 Challenge may show tension relating to communication and pleasures (e.g., indulgences).

Year Imprint

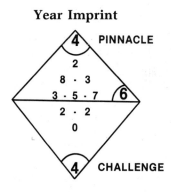

As she approaches her birthday in November 1983, she is finishing her 5 Personal Year. A 5 Personal Year is often considered a "pivotal" year within the nine-year cycle, expressing as a period of change and variety. [**Ms. Three's divorce finalization, traveling in her work, job changes, move across the country, engagement for another marriage.**] After her birthday in November 1983 (or, in some systems, starting January 1, 1984, until December 31, 1984), she will enter a 6 Personal Year which carries its theme of responsibility for home/family/marriage/community life. Starting at age 39, she will enter the third Pinnacle and Challenge pattern of 8 over 2, a period of sensitivity regarding money, power and authority. A financial partnership is hinted, or a partnership/control theme, suggesting powerful material accomplishments and, if she is not careful, potential for power struggles (an 8/2 period could be problematical since she has no 2's and 8's in her name).

Finally, let us briefly match the preceding numerological analysis of Ms. Three's major numbers with the astrological correspondences in her chart, although many of them can be inferred. For instance, the 2 Soul Urge nicely fits the Cancer Moon/Ascendant with its Libra dwad, as well as the Libra/Venus stellium in the Cancer/fourth house. The Scorpio strength contributes to the number 2 theme (Cancer/Libra mixture) of relationships, partnership, sensitivity, sharing and caring — the interpersonal theme. The 5 Name/Expression can symbolize the full Leo/fifth house, including its natural ruler, Sun, in that house; the degree of Leo identity tied to her first house; also the Sagittarius (freedom fire) undertone connected with number 5 since Mars, key to self, is in the sign of Sagittarius widely conjunct Jupiter, natural ruler of Sagittarius. The 7 Life Path may have its astrological correlations primarily with that Mars in Sagittarius conjunct Jupiter (search for Truth or higher awareness), and perhaps Moon, ruling the Ascendant, in the Pisces house since number 7 is traditionally associated with water (and spiritual overtones).

The 3 Personality, the least important of the four major numbers (core character indicators), is also less evident in astrological parallels. Perhaps a correlation can be made with Sun/Chiron, Mercury, and various asteroids domiciled in the openly expressive fifth/Leo house.

Leo-Sun is the vital, expressive will-force to do something creative with your source energy, so that you can "shine." Numerologically, number 3 is the prime key to creativity and pleasure, and adding number 5 to it would certainly contribute to a restless, creative fire-air persona seen by the world. Ms. Three, then, might display her instinctive drama and show(wo)manship, e.g., Mercury (number 3) in the fifth/Leo house. However, I place the greatest emphasis upon the Life Path foremost, then the Name/Expression. Methods by various numerologists of determining what exactly are the vowel (Soul Urge) and consonant (Personality) totals of the name and what they mean are too varied, and even contradictory, to warrant extra emphasis on the Soul Urge and Personality as "infallible" indicators of character. We can only present a method and test its theory.

Ms. Three Responds to Zip

Since I could not interview Ms. Three face-to-face (she presently resides 3,000 miles away), and she is also beyond shouting distance, we communicated by letter and cassette. Her response to Zip's reading was overwhelmingly affirmative.

"Zip's interpretation was very accurate," she wrote. "I think she was pretty much on the mark."

As given in her earlier text, her mother did indeed play a crucial role in Ms. Three's upbringing, the Piscean parental figure (Moon in Cancer in the twelfth house and Neptune in the Cancer/fourth house). Although the information Ms. Three offered was quite sketchy about her mother, the overall impression was that of a victim (ill) mother, acting as a role model of what not to do in that area.

As a creative outlet during that period, however, Ms. Three focused on music and dance. "Fine Arts" was listed in her completed questionnaire as a major interest.

"I love dance, particularly ballet," she explained on tape with a Southern drawl. "When I was about four or five years old I started ballet class and piano. Then my parents couldn't afford both, so they wanted me to take piano instead. I hated giving up ballet, but I didn't have any choice. But later on, a year or so, I started twirling the baton, which is pretty similar to dance. I did that all the time, winning contests, and became a majorette in school. I did a lot of stage acts where I was performing in both music and ballet. Then, later on as an adult, when I lived in Atlanta, I started ballet again. I love that kind of expression. And I love just plain going-out dancing. It makes me feel good. I think it's a whole lot of fun."

I asked Ms. Three about her creative ability in terms of heightened imagination and perhaps Piscean daydreaming. I personally noted her Saturn in Virgo in the third house of mind and communication square Pallas in the Pisces house, widely square the Sun, actual ruler of her third house.

"I like to read, study, drink wine, dream. Now I realize it's more important to act. I have in the past been basically a thinker. Now I'm a doer. You can sit there and dream and study and think about things for years and years, and never get around to doing anything. Lord knows there's a lot of people who do that. That may be my Pisces focus, but, more, I think the reaching of more and more of that ideal thing, wanting to be free."

At this point, the discussion led into the combined issue of independence, sexuality and power struggles.

"All my life I have sought freedom," she continued. "In the past I was involved in a power drive with men. I have had struggles in every 'man-woman' relationship, quickly seducing men into a bond, and then running from it. I had always seen a man as someone to seduce under my power, but not as a friend. And I was ignorant of harmony with a partner in the home and feared a man's constant presence as a limitation of my freedom. There was much past self-criticism and looking for flaws (always that desire for the ideal). So I attracted a mate who criticized me constantly.

"I've been through my times of 'lust' and using most of my energy that way. The greatest truism of Zip is that inner challenge to have pleasure and master the appetites. Mastering my appetites is the biggest thing. I love wine. I do use wine as a drink to relax from anxieties.

"I have now begun to learn that freedom demands inhibition and discipline so that I can move in harmony with Universal Life. The universe is completely disciplined so that all its parts interrelate and work together precisely to maintain perfect balance and harmony. Freedom, as I understood it in the past, was in actuality turning my back on the harmony out of laziness, fear, etc., and it brought about self-indulgences, repeated experiences, ups and downs, highs and lows."

As given, Ms. Three is now married with a younger man, "experiencing cooperation, sharing, trust and love." They committed their relationship in marriage on December 3, 1983. I asked her if she was prepared to be a mother, and did she always want to play the mother role.

"Yes, I always wanted to be a mother. Ever since a child I wanted to be a mother. But then I went into this not being able to get into a decent relationship with a man. I then became so independent and I became more identified with my role as a stewardess or sales representative or whatever. I never developed love with a man that brought about the desire for children — I mean, mutually. So I think that it's basically that relationship problem I had in not trusting men and all that kept me at 35 years old not having any children yet. However, I still want children, and so does my husband (one of each, a boy and a girl)."

I then asked Ms. Three if she indeed had, as Zip ventured "above-average psychic ability."

She chuckled on tape. "I can read tarot cards real well! I feel very psychic with my husband and feel that he is psychic. It's almost like nothing's hidden. I know how he's feeling and almost what he's thinking. And I know he's the same toward me. I know that all I have to do is be open to it and not be selfish or thinking about myself, and I can pretty much sense other people's feelings and situations. But I'm not real interested in just being psychic. I think it is a step up to the goal that you're really reaching for.

"My goal — unity," she concluded in her questionnaire.

[Tragic update: Ms. Three passed away on Tuesday night, about 10 p.m., June 25, 1985 — struck by a car while crossing a crosswalk in Long Beach, California.]

CHAPTER SEVENTEEN

MR. FOUR

Introduction to Mr. Four

I first met Mr. Four through his wife, a lovely, witty lady who regularly attends a class we both share. It is a metaphysically oriented class which I reluctantly had to miss one week, so I asked her to cassette record it. The next afternoon I drove to her spacious suburban home to pick up the tape. There I met Mr. Four; actually, I first met his astrological chart! I immediately noted his Virgo rising and grand trine in water houses: a nice earthy, stable, security-oriented, responsible status-quo individual was my initial impression. I wanted him for this book, and I asked his wife to act as an "agent" to intercede my request for me. Initially he offhandedly declined since he is a nonbeliever in astrology, but thanks to his wife's gentle persuasive ability, he agreed to participate as an anonymous case study.

Finally I did meet Mr. Four in person at his home on October 20, 1983, for an interview. My neck stretched a bit as I was greeted by this very tall, handsome gentleman. He was quite courteous and personable as he led the way to the dinner table as the site for the interview. After preliminary ice-breaking chit-chat, I first asked him why he agreed to do the book after all.

"Just because my wife suggested it, and I thought it might be interesting," he replied, with an even tone of voice.

I then asked him if indeed he was a skeptic regarding astrology and numerology.

"I'm familiar with the fact that they exist and a lot of people believe in them. I think skeptic is probably the closest to the way I feel, though it doesn't exactly fit. I'm not a nonbeliever — well, that's not necessarily right either! Maybe I am. I have an engineering background and I expect to be able to prove things, and everything that I believe can be proved. And astrology and numerology are areas that can't be proved. They're not scientific. They're hypothetical areas with a lot of hearsay and a lot of opinions, but nothing to me that's really solid.''

I beamed. ''You're just the man I wanted for this book! I wanted at least one person with a prove-it-to-me attitude.''

''Obviously there are a lot of mechanics involved in astrology,'' Mr. Four continued, ''because people calculate very carefully where the stars and planets are at any particular time. They have charts that tell them how to calculate where particular planets are at certain times. So what? I mean, to me that doesn't say anything about a person's personality or future. To me it just doesn't cut. But I still understand that a lot of people believe in it and I can't fault them for it. If they want to believe it, fine. To me it's like a religion: if they want to believe in that, that's their bag. If they want to believe what it tells them and interpret things so that in a convoluted manner it comes out the way they want it to be, that's fine. But I don't think it's necessarily accurate. I think it's conjecture, or coincidence — let's put it that way.''

Thus began a pleasant three-hour interview, a mixture of sober realism and humor, candid disclosure and a fun interchange of divergent beliefs. Mr. Four now discusses his background as follows.

Mr. Four's Background

Mr. Four:
''I was born and raised in Los Angeles. I have two older sisters, one and two years older than myself. Both of my parents are living. I never felt deprived. We were fairly comfortable financially, but my mother taught us all how to not be wasteful. Mother was the one who raised all three of us. As far as discipline goes, she was the disciplinarian. If we really got out of hand, Dad was the backup! And one thing you didn't want to do was to get into Dad's bad graces! He administered the spankings. But they were for particularly naughty things the kids had done. I don't have any recollection of being a rebel. I'm sure I was unruly. I'm sure I rebelled against my mother's authority. I think all kids do. It's the nature of kids! But I don't have any real vivid memories of being a rebel. I suspect I was spoiled to a certain extent. My sisters told me I was!

"My mother taught me manners and helped me with schoolwork when needed. She taught kindergarten before she got married. Mother was more the teacher, and she was the one who got us to go to church. Dad didn't go to church. I think in a great respect I'm taking after him right now. And I think, looking at him now, he didn't need to go to church! But both of them were my examples of morals and social behavior. My mother had played much tennis as a girl and in college. She was fantastic. She could beat most of the best men players at a club where we were members. I learned to swim well there and also played paddle tennis. I got very good, and I made friends there that I still see regularly.

"My father is an engineer and a fairly accomplished mechanic. He was the first in the family name to graduate as an engineer. His dad and grandfather were both lawyers. He broke the mold. He was a civil engineer at graduation and he got into more mechanical things as his career went on. I thought he was great. I was always interested when he would work on the cars or fix something around the house. He had a small machine shop for a number of years where he and his partner — an ex-midget-race-car mechanic — designed and built carburetors and ignition systems. They built a small race car for me using an old but powerful four-cylinder motorcycle engine. This turned out to be about midget-race-car size and was very fast — much faster than they had really planned. I don't think he necessarily taught me mechanics, but at least he probably kindled my interest in cars. He used to work on the cars in the garage at home and, of course, he had a shop. But I think it was my own interest in mechanics that got me more interested in cars. I know the first job I ever really had was after classes when I was going to high school, taking motor scooters out of the crate and assembling them, making them ready to run.

"I was never really a very good student. I never really enjoyed school. I didn't like it. Too much bother. There were too many things that I thought were unnecessary, for one thing, that I never used in my whole life, like history! That kind of thing just turned me off about school. Too much work having to learn things that I don't want.

"My most significant health incidents were having my tonsils out when I was 11, and having kidney stones about 11 years ago. I have been told I have a heart murmur and was classified 4-F for the draft. I try not to eat too much and I try to walk as much as I can. I deliberately walk fast. I enjoy walking, but I hate to run! I don't like to get out of control, so I drink in moderation. My mom and dad rarely drank.

"One major impact in my life began when I was introduced to a woman whose father was one of Hollywood's most famous makeup men. We didn't hit it off very well, but her dad was super. One day I asked him how I could find out if my singing voice was worth trying to do something with. He asked the head of a studio's music department who recommended a voice coach. I went to him, and liked him, and began voice coaching lessons. This guy was super. First of all, he didn't claim to be a teacher. He said that there's no such thing as a voice teacher. You can't be taught to sing. It's got to be there as a talent, and he could coach me to bring it out. So I liked his attitude right off the bat. I think I had been going sporadically for two or three years when a buddy of mine and I decided to quit our jobs and go to Europe before we got tied down by marriage. I was 25. We went by boat and I was asked to sing at Gala Night in the first-class dining salon. This was definitely a first for me. I practiced two days with their French ship orchestra — 12 piece — the biggest one I ever sung with, and we finally got down to four tunes that I knew and that they could play. Then the big night came and I had to use a microphone for the first time. There were about 250 people eating and talking and clinking silverware and glasses, and waiters were everywhere. But I started to sing and got about one-fourth of the way into my first song, and the place became very quiet! That's pretty complimentary. This was a tremendous thrill for me because that was an unconscious compliment of a very high order from everyone in the room.

"I met a girl on the boat, and she said she would get me a job singing in Paris. After I had toured Europe for four months, I called her to say goodbye. She said I couldn't leave — she had a job for me singing in a hotel for two weeks. Unfortunately, I was out of money and couldn't stay two weeks more in Paris. I had no idea what the pay was. It's such an uncertain industry. I also bought a 1955 VW Bug over there and I worked very hard with tricky negotiations to get my car on the boat at a good price. But that's one of those things where I wondered what I would've done if I had taken that job. Where would I be now if I had stayed? I have nothing but good memories of that trip through Europe, and a lot of good pictures (I am also pretty good with a camera). But I've done several singing engagements since then. I was in a show down at a club two years ago, a Cole Porter show. I did a solo with dancers behind me. I enjoy show tunes and light opera. Gordon MacRae has the kind of voice where I imitate his qualities somewhat. If I would practice and get my voice back in some kind of shape, I wouldn't feel too reluctant to continue. It's just a bother; too easy not to.

"Goodlooking women turn me on. But I was shy with girls. I was too bashful, but I opened up a lot when I went to Europe. That was one of the best things that I ever could've done. That really helped me. I wish that I knew more girls, but I just never knew how to approach them. My wife and I dated on and off for several years. I would just disappear without saying anything, and then I'd start dating somebody else. I guess that suited my fancy at the time. I finally decided I didn't want to run around anymore. I was 31 or 32 when I got married. I'm reasonably happy. I think it would be better if my wife and I were interested in more of the same things. I think maybe more sports. I'd like her to get back out and get some exercise and take up tennis again. She definitely has a physical limitation that she has to be careful about. She's got a good brain, she's artistic, and she likes to do something with that. She's definitely not tied to the house. She is very independent. She has taken jobs that would take maybe two or three days a month that she can do here in the house. She likes to do that kind of thing where she can bring it here and work on it at home. It gets her out of the rut.

"I love to drive and enjoy automobile-based competition. I participated in many sports car rallies and other events for about three years before I was married. I had a sports car for about six years. My wife and I went on a couple of rallies in my sports car after we were married. The first time we went, we won it. The second one we entered, we got second place. Before we went on the third one I said I didn't want any third placement, so we didn't go. But she didn't enjoy it because she had to navigate and she's not into that kind of precision and thinking, and I was out of work for too long when we got married and the cost was a factor, so I stopped rallying.

"My wife seems to have gotten much more active in metaphysics in the last 4-5 years. I guess it's all right. I sometimes think she takes it too much to heart. I tend to stand back and say that's for somebody else. She used to try to get me to use some of the techniques that she had learned and thought were great. She got me to go to a couple of lectures or meetings of some sort. As far as I was concerned, they were probably good exercises in how to relax. Beyond that it didn't do a thing for me. It was power of the mind, I guess. It was just too far out for me to even accept as a good yarn! I don't think there's anything that is going to make me believe that my mind will control anything else. I don't think that's possible. Things happen either by chance or just because people make them happen.

"I have two boys. I have expectations for my boys, and the possibility that I feel right now is that they're not doing what I think they should be doing as far as their achievements go. Our oldest boy did poorly in school, but the last two years of high school he was on the Dean's list. I guess he's doing very well at community college. My youngest son still has some maturing to do, I think. He is sort of drifting. He's not really doing anything that has any particular goal or any field that he seems interested in getting into. That concerns me. I'm afraid I tend to be more emotional about their actions than my wife. During the day things sometimes get pretty tense at times too because until you've had teenagers — and other people have told us the same thing — you don't understand how messy they are, how they do their own thing. And it's amazing how they know everything in the world at the age of 20! But I'm very proud of the things that I have. It hurts me to have someone else damage it or degrade it in some manner, things that I have worked to earn and feel very proud of and take very good care of, like my car. I covet things, I think. I like nice things that I earned and bought.

"My jobs have mostly been in engineering related work. I have an A.A. degree plus further studies in mechanical engineering, statistics and quality control. I spent one summer driving a large bulldozer and thoroughly enjoyed it. For about one and a half years I worked in real estate and was only mildly successful. For the fun of it I would like to drive a tractor again, but I do like my present position as Director of Quality Assurance for the American branch of a Japanese company. I think what I like is that I am respected for my knowledge, experience and judgment.

"Only recently within the last 10-15 years has the issue of security ever bothered me. Security was not a concern when I was young. There was no theme about, 'We have no money for that.' But after getting married, having a family this size, this house and getting to the age where it's not as easy to get a job, yeah, security is in my mind. The need to provide for my family motivates me. I hope my present job will last for more than a couple of years. You see, I worked for three companies that either went out of business or moved out of state, and that terminated my jobs real quickly! I don't like that feeling. It's very uncomfortable. But that's not imminent in my present job. I enjoy it. I'm responsible, directly or indirectly, for the quality of the products that we put out the door, and that involves all suppliers. I really enjoy the people I work with. My new boss and I think the same way. His philosophy is the same as mine. And I had more than just a couple of my people tell me that they thought I was the greatest boss they ever had. That's an ego-booster. Maybe I'm too easy. I may be too soft on them. I am somewhat impatient and intolerant of errors by my family, but I don't dwell on mistakes by those who work for me near as much. I think other people see me as a very capable, pleasant person; trustworthy, responsible, conscientious. If they are close friends, they probably see my picky side. In the fields I think I know, I am a bit of a perfectionist. I'm sure my wife would say 'Whoo-boy!' to that!

"We have an organized department at work. In quality you've got to be organized. You've got to have rules and you've got to follow the rules, otherwise the rules are no good. It's an axiom: Do the job right the first time and you won't have to do it over again. That's one of the philosophies that we try to instill on our production people. At least with my people, they have to be qualified to do their job, or they won't be doing that. They understand their job, they do it, and I can rely on them. The Japanese philosophy of business is a little different from the American. They've got a much higher stress on quality. To them, quality runs the company. But I doubt if I'd want to run the whole company, and I would have severe reservations about going into business for myself. I don't want to go beyond what I don't understand, because then you're in real dangerous ground. Too many aspects about business that I don't know about. Marketing is something that I just don't really know about. It's not my bag. I am somewhat outgoing, but nowhere near the typical salesman type.

"I really enjoy doing things where I use my hands and use my brain to work things out. I like projects. I can be happy alone if I have some activity I like to keep me occupied. I'm not bored easily. I usually find something to do. I'm building some cabinets in the garage right now. It's a sense of accomplishment; it's something you can see that I've done. I think in pictures. I have to be able to form a mental image of a situation or the action happening in order to adequately remember something. I have to visualize it. I think I have a creative mind. I'm not artistic. I don't appreciate paintings and things the way my wife does. It's got to have form to me! You know, it's got to have something I can recognize. But I appreciate well-designed things. I'm artistic as far as mechanical design goes. My other interests are building model cars, trains, boats; electronics; any work with my hands; driving and hiking.

"The one thing we probably enjoy the most outside the house is travel. A couple of months ago we rented a motor home on a trial. We've never done that before. I just love that kind of thing. I used to belong to the Boy Scouts and we went camping all the time. I am a camper at heart and I like to hike, but I haven't done any of that for quite a number of years. But we rented a motor home and drove up the coast to San Francisco. We took the boys; they wanted to go. I thought that was great. I thoroughly enjoyed it. I thought it was a lot of fun, and my wife did too. We just took it easy."

Numerological Analysis

Of the three names (and "Jr.") given Mr. Four at birth, the rundown of his major numbers is as follows:

Soul Urge (vowels sum)	= 7
Personality (consonants sum)	= 4
Name/Expression (name sum)	= 2
Life Path (month/day/year sum)	= 8

His 7 Soul Urge (how he identifies or sees himself) is described by Stephanie: "The 7 Soul Urge is usually a loner, but not in the same sense as the 1 Soul Urge. The 1 is a loner as far as having their own way, being in an independent field such as sales, being the pioneer or their own boss. The 7 needs to be alone for their solitude, reminiscing, meditating or thinking. The 7 is often the deep, deep thinkers, and investigate themselves and the world. The 7 prefers to remain aloof and detached from most people, stand back and observe and analyze. The 7 wants to live above the mundane world and live instead in a high class world — either highly material or highly spiritual — which is 'superior' to them. People who are major 7's usually feel that they know a lot of things. Number 7 is the most mystical of all the numbers — the bridge between two worlds."

As given in our study of Ms. One, who also has a 7 Soul Urge, the Soul Urge is "hidden" in the sense of being one's private perception of oneself, or inner motivation, that many people aren't aware of usually. Number 7 is a subjective, internalized number, focused on keeping one's thoughts to oneself, learning, striving to understand. Shyness or reticence is common with a 7 Soul Urge, especially if supported by other introversion factors.

His Personality (outer expression, how other people see him or how he impresses them) is a 4. Sylvia commented: "The 4 Personality is someone who can be very organized, stable, into routine, and works with the arms, legs and back. Numbers 7 and 4 are the two

242 Seven Paths to Understanding

critical/judgmental numbers in numerology, so they sometimes can be seen as very rigid, critical or perfectionistic people." So a keynote of number 4 is structure, order, predictability and balance. It denotes a solid base approach to life, disciplined and realistic; a scientific bent. It also represents limitation and law; also, fear and guilt on an emotional level. Its astrological correlate is the work-related earth (practical realist/materialist) signs, Virgo and Capricorn.

"The 2 Name," Sylvia observed, "says that he's a person who has come into the world to survive. It's talking about how 'I want to be involved in a relationship,' and how he wants safety and security in the world." Here she relates number 2 to a Cancerian flavor — its characteristic need for rootedness and emotional/physical security (e.g., Mr. Four's Capricorn planets in the fourth/Cancer house, including the ruler of his Ascendant). Number 2, then, is interpreted as a mixture of Libra and Cancer, both desiring union and harmony and relationship. Partnership and cooperation as equals can also be highlighted (e.g., Libra in Mr. Four's first house of identity).

His Life Path (primary growth goal or destiny) is number 8. The Life Path is designated as the most important core indicator (major number) of character because your month/day/year of birth is unalterable. It represents the life direction to be followed for optimum personal development. The 8 Life Path suggests an emphasis on money, power, authority and control. The person tends to go into business or assumes an executive/managerial power position in an organizational structure. The 8 vibration is involved with the practical, physical necessities of life, including money and earning a living. The drive for power and security is often sought through the power of money and/or the power of position and prestige. It can thus be ambitious in its desire to make an impact on the world. On the other hand, if the familiarity and stability of the present status quo is uppermost in priority, then risk-taking ambitions may be voluntarily limited for fear of losing known security. Overall, number 8 is a materialistic (earth) vibration. On an inner level, it can also be seen as the Scorpio drive for power of self-mastery.

Next, the numerologists centered their attention on Mr. Four's Inclusion Table (a table in box format derived from the total letter values of a name).

Inclusion Table

5	2	2	I	9
2	3	2	We	7
1	1	6	They	8

P E M
8 6 10

Five 1's connects the theme of changes/freedom/sexuality (number 5) with the area of self-will and individuality (number 1). "With the five 1's," Sylvia noted, "he can be very quick, wanting to be free, to have variety, and get into sex. It says, 'I need to be free to do my own thing.' " Astrologically, it can be correlated with Mr. Four's freedom emphasis of Moon in Aries, and Venus, ruling his first-house Libra, in Aquarius; plus it can be tied with his Leo/fifth house focus — e.g., the ruler of his Ascendant conjunct the Sun, and co-ruler of the first house in the Leo house.

Two 2's emphasizes the dominant number 2 pattern in his Inclusion Table with his two 3's, two 4's, and two 6's also involved. Number 2 is also his Name/Expression number. This can show as passivity and sensitivity in the nature, needing security and a partner or relationships in his life. Number 2 is a feminine (passive) principle, people-oriented (detached or intimate; clutchy or arm's length), friendly and sometimes manipulative. Its Libra focus can be into appearances and looking good.

Two 3's indicates that he expresses communication/creativity/fun in a 2 manner — passively and/or with a partner. The inclination toward passive arts is suggested since it ties creativity with comfort and pleasure.

Two 4's in his name is often a control combination, wanting to be boss. Equality versus control may be an issue, similar to the Libra/Capricorn square. Positively expressed, it suggests cooperation and partnership in the work; job teamwork; working with mate in some project; comfortable, passive work.

Three 5's connects fun/pleasure/self-expression with sexuality, sensuality, changes and freedom. The person usually enjoys sex, or at least likes to talk and read about it. The person wants to be happy with the physical body, to indulge with the senses, have a good time. It also shows a quick, creative mind with a hint of mental restlessness and versatility.

Two 6's ties partnership with home and family responsibilities and service to the community. It indicates that he needs a partner, a mate. It is very much a marriage-oriented combination.

One 7 connects self-will and independence with understanding and learning. It may mean analysis and study on his own terms, learning what he wants to learn. It shows common sense, good ability to analyze and comfortableness in being by oneself.

One 8 connects self-will and individuality with power, money and material reality. It is an identification (number 1) with authority and control, saying, "I can do what I want with power and money." He expresses those areas on his own terms and initiative.

Six 9's is an Intensity (concentration) Point since the average number of 9's in a name is two or three. This is the combination of responsibility (number 6) in the world (number 9), suggesting humanitarian service and professionalism — e.g., medical, healing/helping work, social work, etc. Also this is a combination of two of the three creative numbers in numerology (3, 6, 9) in which he can potentially make his name known in some creative venture [**e.g., Steven Spielberg, born December 18, 1947, with a 3-9-3 baseline, has his Natal Imprint totally dominated by 3's, 6's and 9's**]. Creativity is additionally seen with his Birthday number being a 3 (2 + 1 = 3, born on the 21st of December). December is also a 3 month. Number 3 is traditionally associated with the creativity involved with the mouth and throat — e.g., singing, platform speaking — as well as good mental, conversational ability.

Sylvia commented briefly on the totals of the Inclusion Table's rows and columns: "The 9 in the 'I' Row (sum of boxes 1, 2, 3) speaks of wanting to be out in the world. Number 7 in the Family Row (boxes 4, 5, 6) wants to come into a family to make his life superior, wanting a fine house, fine clothes, eat fine food. He has an 8 in the World Row (boxes 7, 8, 9), so he wants to make money and have power in the world. He has 10 in the Mental Column (boxes 3, 6, 9) which indicates that he has a very powerful, fantastic mind. The 6 in the Emotional Column (boxes 2, 5, 8) is talking about his caring and responsibility. The 8 in the Physical Column (boxes 1, 4, 7) also talks about making money. He's not going to work unless he makes good money at it or has the power and authority."

Natal Imprint

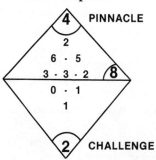

Attention was then focused upon Mr. Four's Natal Imprint, which is primarily the baseline and Pinnacles and Challenges derived from the month/day/year of birth. Born 12/21/28, his baseline numbers are 3-3-2 (= 8 Life Path). Since I described the process of deriving the Pinnacles and Challenges in Ms. One's case, please refer back to that. Now: Mr. Four's first Pinnacle and Challenge is a 6 over 0, lasting until the end of his 28th birthday (36 minus 8 Life Path = 28) which suggests a strong home and family focus.

Responsibilities are involved, but relative harmony is indicated with the zero Challenge, and he does have 6's in his name (zero Challenge can mean all the challenges or none). From age 29 until the start of his 38th birthday, his second Pinnacle and Challenge is a 5 over 1. This pattern suggests a lessening of personal freedom and variety due to marriage, say, or other commitments. Independence and self-will (number 1) is challenged by changes in the environment (5 Pinnacle). The next nine-year cycle period is the 2 over 1 Pinnacle and Challenge ending at his 47th birthday, indicating a strong personal involvement with partnership and/or relationships in general. Again, self-will is challenged by relationships or need for security, but it is a good period for forming relationships. From age 47 on, the Super Pinnacle and Super Challenge are in direct focus, although they form the undertone of his whole life — the 4 over 2. It suggests a sensitivity in relationships (number 2 Super Challenge) or in the home base, and dealing with a work/discipline environment (4 Super Pinnacle). It denotes a security-orientation.

Year Imprint

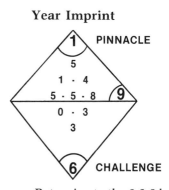

Commencing on his 55th birthday in 1983, Mr. Four's Personal Year will be a 9 (5 + 5 + 8 = 9); that is, 5 + 5 (his present age at 55) + 8 (his Life Path) = 9 Personal Year. This is a year of finishing and completion — letting go of the outworn features of his concluding nine-year cycle, preparing for the upcoming 1 Personal Year of new beginnings. The dominant number of 5's in the pattern suggests the likelihood of changes and even travel.

Returning to the 3-3-2 baseline of his Natal Imprint, his First Cycle (or Life Path Period) is the Formative or Developmental period of his childhood and early adulthood, ending approximately at his first Saturn return at age 28-29. This number 3 First Cycle shows the pleasure and lightness focus. Self-expression and creativity is highlighted, as well as social activity with the people immediately around him. Its danger is overindulgence and scattering of forces. His Second or Productive (Accomplishment) Cycle would end approximately at his second Saturn return (age 58-59). It is also a 3 Cycle indicating creativity and enjoyment once again. His Final Cycle is a 2, indicating an emphasis on partnership and home base security. A stronger focus on supportive relationships in general is indicated, and perhaps even greater passivity or being laid back.

Mr. Four Responds to Zip

Mr. Four leaned over his copy of Zip's initial interpretation and leafed through a few pages.

"I would say that it's probably 10% to 20% correct as far as my own interest and leanings go," he mentioned, still scanning the pages. He also stated that he had difficulty understanding it due to its technical language, confessing that he's unfamiliar with astrology's basic nomenclature.

"She's totally wrong about my parents as far as that goes," he continued. "But I didn't read it twice, and I think I should have." He then mentioned, however, that he was impressed with a hand-writing analysis he had several years ago by a friend.

I looked quizzically at my own notes. Perhaps if I discussed his chart themes in a different light, Mr. Four might upgrade the percentage of accuracy. I first asked him about Zip's first theme focus: the mutable dilemma and the potential conflict between high aspirations and the limits of what is realistically possible.

His eyebrows furrowed. "Only when I find there are projects I want to do, and the immediate time isn't there to do it. It takes time to get them all done. But I don't think so. I'm not sure if I really understand that question. I don't feel that I ever had any goals that are unachievable."

I nodded attentively and then inquired about any challenges in the area of schooling, learning, siblings or communication, since Saturn and south node of the Moon, both lesson areas, were domiciled in the third house, with Saturn square the Ascendant. He started to answer that he got along well with his sisters and, as he stated in the earlier text, he never really liked school. However, he tied my question with another I posed: Does he have the "Capricorn" tendency of being reticent about his feelings?

"I think probably to a great extent, yeah. In a lot of situations I think that's true. I don't have the words at my command to really express it at the time, so I keep quiet. The words don't come to mind right away. Later they might."

"But you seem to be communicating very well and openly in this interview with me," I offered.

"Well, there's no stress. In an argument or confrontation, the words aren't there. The words I want aren't there. I'm not given the time to work out the phrases that I want, so I just shut up! Or else I come out with something that's irrational. So it's not being able to express myself at the time the way I would like to. I am probably a better listener than talker. Also, unless it's something I really understand, like mechanics, I don't like to get into arguments. Discord turns me off. I would rather sit back and just let other people talk about politics and religion and that kind of stuff because it's not anything that I'm interested in. So therefore I don't search out knowledge in those areas.''

His explanation interested me because it shed light on his disinclination to debate abstract, philosophical concepts: both the true south node of the Moon and Saturn are in Sagittarius in the third house. As I looked at that, I noted his Mars opposite Sun and I asked Mr. Four about his earlier statements about his impatience.

''Yeah. I am not as patient as I think I should be. It's interesting that at work it's a different thing. Here at home I'm impatient if it's going to cost me money. When I see that it's going to be expensive, I'm impatient. And I guess I'm picky about a lot of things. But at work, generally if it's the first time around for somebody making whatever the error is, you explain to them. I don't have too much trouble having patience then. Usually there's never a second time. So it's a different kind of situation. At home the teenagers do the same rotten things over and over again! But at home I raise my voice, and on rare occasions I may pound on the table — something for emphasis. I have a hard time containing myself sometimes. I don't feel bad because I'm out of control. I don't think of it that way. I just think that I shouldn't have yelled.''

Mr. Four's Uranus is in his seventh house of partnership, so I asked him if he approached friend as mate or mate as friend.

''Oh, yeah. How in the hell can you be married with an adversary!''

I laughed. However, I noted, physically brutal marriages do exist and are maintained. With Virgoish Vesta also in the seventh house. I inquired if he attracted a mate as worker.

''Well, that's hard to define. I think I've got perhaps some very old-fashioned notions about what a wife should do. I think she should take care of the house, personally. If I'm out all day long earning the money, working to take care of the family and provide the living amenities, I don't want to have to worry about coming home and vacuuming the rugs. I think the house should be run by somebody, and if I can't be here all day to do it, I think my wife should. Not that she should have to be here all day to do it. But it's her responsibility to do it as time permits. She does it, but I don't know if she agrees! It's an old-fashioned idea. I grew up in a family that was exactly that way. I mean, my dad made the money and my mom took care of the house. I make the money and she takes care of the house.''

I noted his Moon in the eighth house, and I asked if he was looking for mother in a mate or playing mother to mate, so to speak.

"Well, I don't think we have to tie it to a mothering quality, but I think somebody needs to do the housework, and my wife is the other half of the partnership.''

Mr. Four's wife is a 29° Cancer rising, Moon in Capricorn, Sun-Mercury-Jupiter-Pluto in Cancer, born in 1931. She is a 5 Life Path, 8 Soul Urge, 7 Personality and a 6 Name, missing 2's and 7's in her name. Taurus, the tactile/sensual sign, is located in Mr. Four's eighth house. Does he like to touch and be touched in regard to mate?

"Yeah. That's right. But I'm not always satisfied in that area. I would like to get some more closeness back in our lives.''

Quite spontaneously, with no prior intent to ask for his beliefs on metaphysical issues, my inquiry about his "earth" desire for predictability led to deeper issues.

"No, life is not predictable,'' he replied, "but I think that lends interest to the whole thing. If everything were predictable, how dull it would be! I don't think life is **that** predictable. There are certain things that are constant-like that I've got to believe are going to be there tomorrow, like the sun coming up. Or staying out there where it is. I don't want it any closer!''

"Do you believe in a supreme being, in God?'' I asked.

"Yeah. I believe in God, but I don't have any visualization for that. I don't go to church. I don't think I need company or leadership to worship God. I don't believe that any Supreme Being controls the planets. That's all in the control of physical laws. We can explain the motions of all the planets and the various bodies in the universe by rigid physical laws. So I don't believe anybody needs to control that. It's done by the nature of magnetic attraction and gravity. And I don't believe in reincarnation. I don't see any need for it. The whole evolution of the Earth tells me that that's not right. As far as I'm concerned, where a person is born is strictly by chance and where their parents were. Maybe the guy's father had a job in New York, and so he was born in New York. I think people live lives because some genes got together.''

"Do you believe in an afterlife,'' I asked, "and being in a nonmaterial state of existence?''

"I'm very split on that. I don't know why there should be an afterlife. You know, you've got vague mental pictures of people floating around. I don't see any need for it. I don't see any reason why there should be."

I posed to him his deathbed scene. Wouldn't he be bothered? He answered, wondering why anyone should have to come back, and that if he becomes nonexistent at death, he wouldn't be capable of being bothered. So I asked him, **what if** there was another life?

"If there's another life, I can only assume that I'm not in my first one. Then why don't I know something about some other life? Why is this life any different than what I had before? Why should it be? What's the reason for coming back? I don't see any reason.

I smiled, and asked if he has such existential discussions with his wife.

"No," he answered, amused. "She talks me out. She just has many more words than I have, and I just can't express myself satisfactorily."

"Do you believe in karma?" I asked, being the last question.

"I'm not sure what that really means. I think you achieve according to your efforts. I don't believe in mind over matter — the belief that if you think hard enough about something, it's going to happen. I think that if you're going to have this attitude of your mind controlling things for you, you've got to do things to help it, physically. If you want to lose weight, you just can't say in your mind that you're going to lose ten pounds in the next two months. It just doesn't happen. You've got to do something physically to make it happen. In other words, you use your mind-thoughts to control what you do, like less food intake and more exercise. You plant in your mind the idea that you want to lose weight, then your mind has to constantly feed back to you and tell you what you have to **do** physically to lose that weight. Your mind can't make it happen all by itself. I believe that **you** have to make it happen, and your mind can be the trigger and the constant reminder. Nothing magically happens. I think you've got to apply yourself.

"In other words," Mr. Four concluded, humorously, "you can't decide you're going to win a tennis tournament, and lie down on the bench and go to sleep! You can't do that. You've go to go out there and practice."

Shortly afterward, Mr. Four escorted me outside to my car. We chatted for several more minutes and he shook my hand, announcing that he thoroughly enjoyed the interview. I concurred, thinking to myself as I waved goodbye that perhaps a basic need for any human being is to feel genuinely **listened** to and appreciated.

CHAPTER EIGHTEEN

MS. FIVE

Introduction to Ms. Five

I first met Ms. Five over a year ago, a faithful student when I taught an astrology class at Sylvia's store. I admired her friendliness, considerateness and her eagerness to study a different approach to astrology. Indeed, she had studied astrology for over eighteen years.

"But I haven't studied it intensely," she pointed out, "except when I first started. When I first became interested, I used to sit up in the kitchen until two or three in the morning reading it. Then it leveled off. But I'm fascinated with astrology. I really believe in astrology, but I think it takes a very talented and gifted person to interpret it to a good degree of accuracy. There are a lot of amateur astrologers running around who don't know that much, but a good astrologer is pretty hard to find. Yes, I love astrology. It's exciting to me and I think all the answers are there to our life."

As you may note, her approach to the subject contrasts considerably with our previous participant, Mr. Four. Of all the other participants, only Mr. Seven has a working knowledge of astrology and numerology. I mused, therefore, that it might prove interesting to have Ms. Five follow Mr. Four in the case sequence of this book. She consented appreciatively to participate in this book project.

Last summer I handed her the questionnaire for her to complete in written form. There was no rush for it to be finished. A few months later, I incredulously was the recipient of seventeen single-spaced typewritten pages of the completed questionnaire! Most of the participants submitted the equivalent of only one or two single-spaced pages. So I thanked Ms. Five for saving me some work and interview time.

Let us therefore proceed with Ms. Five's story, utilizing her questionnaire material exclusively.

Ms. Five's Background

Ms. Five:

''I was born and raised in [**a large city in California**]. I have one sister who is two years older than me [**January 6, 1927**]. We were an upper middle-class American family and did the usual things an average American family does. We observed the holidays, went on picnics, went out to dinner, traveled a lot on short trips. We always lived in a comfortable and pleasant environment, and always had enough money for a happy and enjoyable existence.

''I would say that basically both parents raised me fairly equally; although I would have to say that my mother [**January 15, 1900**] exerted much more authority and more time in the upbringing of my sister and myself. My father would have the final 'say so,' but my mother and father always seemed to get along very well, and I am sure they were always in love. I sometimes have thought that my father loved my mother more than she loved him. He was a very shy, dreamy and rather romantic man in a quiet fashion. My mother often told me that she could have been just as happy had she never married. She was a great club woman and greatly enjoyed the company of other women, but I'm sure that married life and being a mother meant a great deal to her.

''I believe that my father was the finest man I have ever known. I never knew a more honest, kindly, unselfish, devoted family man and father and patriotic person than my father [**July 11, 1895**]. He was raised on a cattle ranch. He was very, very shy around men and women alike, and I am sure that his marriage to my mother was a very fortunate happening for him. He might have lived a very quiet and lonely and unhappy life without my mother and my sister and I. He loved us all dearly and equally, and was proud to be a husband and a father. He worked hard all his life to support us in comfort and was always happy to do it. He dearly loved nature and his country. He served in the army during World War II, for which he was very proud. He greatly revered his mother and all women. He did not have a good relationship with his father who treated him rather badly, and openly favored my father's younger brother. But my father overlooked all of that because he was a good and kindly man. He was basically raised by his mother.

''My mother was an entirely different type of person. She was brought up in an upper middle class Baptist family, and was basically a strong-willed, self-confident, efficient, and rather business-oriented person. Social life and standing were always quite important to my mother, and before she came to California at age 23, she was an executive secretary, a tennis player of some note, and a popular church-oriented girl. She had boyfriends but greatly enjoyed the company of a group of four girls who ran around together for several years. After her marriage, she became involved in a lot of women's clubs and became an ace bridge player. She belonged to the church, church groups and the choir. She had a fine singing voice. Down through the years, my mother had her own business and was always adept at making money.

"My one sister, sad to say, has never liked me except perhaps on isolated occasions. As long as I can remember, she has picked on me, ridiculed me, criticized me, and has rarely showed any closeness, affection, or love to me. Since my parents' passing these past two years, our relationship has deteriorated somewhat, and the hate I feel from her sometimes is overwhelming. I fear for my health due to the stress, and I try to stay away from her as much as possible. I can remember all through my childhood trying to get along with her, be friends with her; but it never worked for long. Many times I would have to run to my mother or father for protection, which I'm sure infuriated her all the more.

"I do not feel either of my parents ever expected too much of me. I think they always thought I would get married and have a family. They never seemed to take very much of a personal interest in me and my hopes and expectations. They never talked to me about what I should take in school or what I wanted to do with my life, and this was always a big disappointment to me. It was as though they never thought of me as a developing human being, but only as a child they needed to protect and bring up. I felt that they were too busy with their own lives to think about my emotional growth and also, they had little knowledge or interest in the basics of psychology in general, let alone child psychology.

"My mother was overprotective and overpossessive of me and my sister alike, but mostly toward me since I was the younger. I enjoyed her attention when I was quite young, but as I grew into my teens I felt smothered and at times resentful. She seemed to favor me to my sister, and even when I was quite young I knew this was wrong and unfair. And, of course, it resulted in serious problems with my sister, both in her relationship with me and in her life to come. My mother did a lot of unwise and dumb things which caused serious repercussions for my sister and I, and which probably have affected us adversely throughout our life. I realize that she meant no harm to us, but she was simply very uninformed and uneducated along psychological lines. And so, I would have to say that my mother had a negative effect on me in large part. My problems with my mother occurred when I was in my teens, but during the last thirty or so years we have had a very pleasant and trouble-free relationship.

"I always deeply loved and greatly admired my father. When I was quite young we were very close. I was Daddy's little girl. I was called 'little sister' for many years, and I'm sure my life script was 'the good little girl.' I adored my father. He was always sweet and calm and easygoing. I really can't ever remember him losing his temper, and I loved him for that. He always had a sweet smile on his face and was such a happy man. He was very strong and protective of his family, capable of doing almost anything to help us, from cooking to cleaning house to repairing almost anything. He had no bad habits and rarely got sick. He was very good to my mother, and very rarely did they have any kind of argument. He was a wonderful driver and we made a lot of short trips throughout California. He worked on the same job for 35 years and never complained about a thing connected with that job. He was a driller. I can remember worrying about him when he had to go out in the middle of the night, and it was my job to fix his lunch and coffee. He made a point to be very impartial and equal with his affections and attention to my sister and I. I greatly admired him for this.

"As I grew into puberty my father drifted away from me and closer to my mother. I felt bad about this but I was very busy growing up. I have always greatly admired him as being a very honorable, sensitive, intelligent and loving man. My only adverse criticism of him is that he almost always went along with my mother's ideas and wishes, even if he knew them to be wrong or unwise.

"My mother's parents were a very important part of my childhood. I spent a lot of time with them in their big apartment house. I especially adored my grandma, a kindly, unselfish, hardworking, serious-minded, religious woman and, I would say, the backbone of America, pioneering type woman that made this country great. I was not nearly as close to my father's parents. They were divorced by the time I was born, and both lived quite a ways from us. But we did travel quite often to see both of them, and I particularly loved and admired my father's mother. She was a small, thin, delicate little lady who was a writer, a poet, and a naturalist.

"When I was nine or ten years of age I almost died from a

ruptured appendix and resultant peritonitis. It was a small miracle
that I lived. I spent three weeks in the hospital, and the following
year I had to have surgery to remove the pieces of the appendix
which were scattered around in my stomach. But the most impactful event of my life was when I was about 12 or 13. My best friend
lived across from me with her parents and two sisters. Down the
street were two boy friends whom we went around with. I wasn't
getting along too well with my mother. It was a critical age. She was
being very restrictive and did not like me spending so much time
across the street with my friend and her family. I think she thought
we were drinking or smoking or misbehaving with the two boys.
Actually, we were just listening to records most of the time. One
day when I was in class in junior high, a clerk from the principal's
office came into the class and told my teacher that I was to report
to the principal's office at once. I was mortified. I was sure I had
done nothing wrong. I was always a very well-behaved student. I
went down to the office scared to death and was told by the principal that I was to report to the Juvenile Department downtown at
the police department. It turned out that my mother had called the
juvenile authorities and said she thought I was getting into trouble
across the street and that I was a behavior problem, and she could
no longer control me. The authorities were wonderful to me, and
after talking to me and to my friend's mother on the phone, they
realized that it was all perfectly innocent, and reprimanded my
parents for ever turning me in over nothing. I'm sure they could see
what a shock this was to me. And it truly was. I did not speak to
my mother for two years, or to my father for one year. I am sure
this incident had far-reaching psychological effects on me — and
probably physiological. I wanted to totally understand my mother's
motivations for her actions and also totally forgive her. So, I decided I must go to college and study psychology. I should mention that
during those two years I did not talk to my mother, she sent me to
a psychiatrist once a week for several months. After he suggested
shock treatments I did not go back to him.

"It is hard to remember the exact sequence of events, but I do
know that my health suffered for years as a result of this incident.
Nothing too critical, just lots of little underlying and mysterious
symptoms. I had trouble with my periods; in fact, they stopped
altogether for about three years. I became very thin and went to
several doctors trying to find out what was wrong. I have never
weighed over 110 pounds since that time of my life, except once in
my teens I weighed 127 pounds. When I was about 19 years old,

I only weighed 90 pounds. I wasn't sick, but generally just weak.

"Nevertheless, nothing really daunted me in those days. I graduated when I was 16, went to city college for 2 ½ years, and enrolled at UCLA in 1950. I worked my way through it for two years with a little help from my mother, and maintained a "B" average. I took a vast variety of classes, but mainly psychology. I was in a very idealistic period of my life and wanted to help all the children of the world.

"Another impactful event of my life occurred in 1971 or 1972. I have been going with a man for about four years and felt I was very much in love with him. He was in the Merchant Marines and gone most of the time. He started to suggest that I drive back to another state with him and that we would take an apartment together. This whole idea went against my rather old-fashioned morals about these things, but I was in love. I agonized over the whole thing for months while he kept writing me letters about it, trying to convince me. Finally, I decided to go with him. It was a difficult decision for me, for I was so closely tied to my home life. I quit my job, packed as many things as I could take, gave my keys to my father, etc. He, however, changed his mind at the last minute and without an 'I'm sorry.' It took me months to get over the disappointment.

"There was a period in 1970 or 1971 in which I was involved in four automobile accidents in a three-month period, none of which was my fault. I was not physically hurt in any of them, but pretty much shook up emotionally.

"I have held a vast array of jobs since I was in high school, and even before. Most of them have been office jobs, and most of them have been of a fairly short duration. Probably my first job was working as a clerk in my mother's dime store. After I graduated from high school, I worked during the summers as a typist at the phone company and as a typist-receptionist for a wholesale house. While attending the university, I acted as a Mother's Helper for three different families, and worked in the library and bookstore to support myself at college. After I left the university I worked as a secretary for an insurance company; then as a secretary for three attorneys; then as a secretary for one attorney; then as a secretary-girl Friday for someone else, etc.; a series of jobs I worked. Through a temporary agency, I obtained a position at an investment company as a Girl Friday, where I worked for about three years, off and on; and this was probably the longest I stayed at any one job. The jobs I preferred were secretarial with the most variety of duties and responsibilities.

The jobs I liked least were the ones on which I just typed or ran a machine most or all of the time.

"I would say that I am a dichotomy in temperament. Basically, I am a very happy, easygoing and sunny person who is most always smiling and cheerful. But, at the same time, there is a sadness within me, made up of a million little regrets and disappointments of what might have been or what should have been in my life. I am thankful most profoundly for the many opportunities and conditions I have been blessed with; but, at the same time, I feel that my life in large part has been somewhat of a waste, and that I could have and should have lived a much more productive and important and happy life had I made different decisions down the road.

"I was told once on a job that my greatest asset was my pleasant disposition and even temperament. People seem to be comfortable around me. They seem to know instinctively that I am very slow to anger, that I am kind and understanding, and that I am extremely sympathetic. I dearly love people and love to communicate and interact with people of all types. But, I also love to be alone and seem to **need it** every now and then to refuel my body and emotional being. I really do get worn out very easily and find I have to be quiet for a while and be by myself. I could spend days by myself very happily just reading, thinking, walking, looking at flowers, listening to the radio, cooking and talking to myself occasionally. This is my dichotomy (one of them). These past three or four years, companionship and relationships have become more important in my life, and I know I wouldn't want to spend my life entirely alone — that I need a man to relate to and share my life with. I wish I had realized this much earlier in my life.

"I can be very outgoing. Full of enthusiasm. Charming. And dramatic. In fact, quite often dramatic! I believe, in my heart, I should have been an actress, or on the stage, probably, or in radio. I would have to say that I am onstage quite a bit of the time...Loner? Oh, yes. In many ways I am a loner. Always have been, in fact. I can remember back in high school, hanging out by myself a lot. I always had several casual friends and at least one good fried, but basically, I was a quiet, 'in the background' type of person. I still prefer to be alone and go places alone most of the time.

"Artistic? Yes, I would say that in many ways I am artistic. In fact, in some ways, it rules my life. I seem to have a great need to create each and every day, and I have always had an overriding desire to beautify the environment. Since I was a very young girl I have been involved in sewing, cooking, gardening and a little painting. I think my joy in creating a beautiful landscape or a delicious and nutritious dinner are among the strongest motivating forces of my existence. Also, I believe I have a rather poetic mind. Even though I have not written any prose, per se, I have always delighted in forming literally beautiful sentences, and I have always found that my thoughts quite often form themselves into poetic frameworks.

"Musical? Oh, yes. I have played the piano since I was about ten years old, and I have always loved to dance. I went steady with two professional dancers and entered professional dance exhibitions several times, with some success. And, I enjoy singing but have not done a great deal with that.

"Competitive? Not really. Perhaps in a very low-key sort of fashion, but not to any degree that I am aware of. Money, power and fame have never played much of a role with me to any extent. I think there is a part of me who would like to be famous. I would really like to be looked up to and admired for my intelligence and some important contribution I might make in this world to help people live better lives. I'm not sure why. Maybe because I have been put down by my sister all of my life, or because my father was so overly modest about his attributes.

"As I have said, creativity and beauty motivate me greatly. A great turn-off for me is rudeness and inconsiderate behavior by anyone. I have always gone out of my way to be courteous and considerate of everyone around me, sometimes to the point of bothering my family. I seem always to have to apologize for anything that does not seem quite right to me. I cannot stand to run the risk of hurting someone with a hurtful sentence. Also, I am particularly turned off by people who are rude to children or elderly people.

"I should say I am also turned on by the past: old houses being preserved, antiques, old movies, old cookbooks and kitchen utensils, garage sales, museums of all kinds. The past is very important, just as important as the present or the future. It is our roots.

"Am I happy? Yes and no. I realize I have a lot to be thankful for. I've lived a long and varied life, and have a million wonderful memories, which are like precious jewels to me. But yet, for many reasons, I am unhappy. I regret that I did not take the time and interest to get married when I was much younger. It seemed that I was not very interested or concerned with getting married when I was young. I had a great overriding need and desire to go to college and to learn a great variety of subjects. I remember thinking I needed to thoroughly prepare myself as a person first. I wanted to be the best wife possible. Also, I regret that I did not make more of myself career-wise. I've changed jobs too often. I've never stuck to one thing long enough to be a big success at it.

"I believe my basic weakness is disorganization. I don't always try hard enough. I daydream a lot and I often put off until tomorrow what needs to be done today. I seem to want to have everything 'just perfect' before I make my move. And so, I all too often waste valuable time waiting for that perfect moment to act or trying to set the perfect stage for action. I think I am simply afraid I will make some wrong move and get stuck in some irreversible position or lose some ground already gained. I am afraid to take chances, especially in jobs. I think I am very shy in some ways, and probably afraid I will fail and be rejected. Another probable growth area problem is that in many ways I am stubborn, especially when I think I am right. I don't always trust others to do things right, and more than often prefer to do them myself. Another big problem is that I'm a great collector. I have many stacks of books and magazines and articles. I have parcels of old love letters, boxes of all kinds of sentimental trivia, etc., etc. I really cannot bear to throw out anything that I might need someday. All this, of course, adds to the confusion of my life, my mind, and to my inefficiency. I have too much detail in my life, perhaps. I believe this is one of my major challenges — to get organized and to simplify my life.

"The thing I want most out of life is peace of mind and knowing that I am fulfilling my destiny here on Earth; to live a meaningful and constructive life; to be free of emotional entanglements. I would like to leave this Earth a better place for my having been here. There is so much I want to do and I'm afraid I won't live long enough to barely tap the surface. That is my greatest regret in life — time wasted and lost. And, I want very much the companionship and love of someone I love and who loves me, and with whom I can really be myself. I have rarely had that type of relationship in my life, certainly not with the two principal relationships of my life (March 15, 1931, and April 24, 1927). I would love to have total emotional intimacy within a relationship of mutual love and respect.

"My ideals are to live the finest life we can here on Earth. I believe in God, for our life is truly a miracle. My church is in my heart. I believe in a hereafter. I believe our souls go on to another place. I believe we are here on Earth to learn certain lessons. My study of astrology has strengthened this belief. I believe in love. We must try to see the good in people and cheer them with a smile and words of praise whenever possible. We should not be overly critical and gloomy. This brings people's spirits down and inhibits their motivations.

"My definition of success is to have a meaningful and constructive job, to be involved in a loving relationship (preferably married) in which I can truly be my real self without fear of losing my partner or causing an argument, and to be helping other people in whatever way I can. Success also means to have a lovely home — however modest — and a garden. It also means to have enough money and time and good health to travel. Success means peace of mind.

"If I had no fear I would go back to college and get my degree. I would also take up a course in theater arts with the goal of being in a stage play someday. I would inquire about jobs on cruise liners with the idea of getting a secretarial job on a cruise ship. It has always been a dream of mine to sail off to faraway ports of call, especially the South Seas. Most of all, the thing I would wish to do if I had the nerve would be to tell my boyfriend (March 15, 1931) that I would like to get married someday — maybe not for five or six years (and maybe even for only a day or a week) — but someday. I would truly like to be married, but my life must first be totally organized (my projects, my hobbies, my possessions, and my intellectual pursuits). I know this has been a lifelong goal of mine.

"As previously stated, I had an appendectomy when I was about ten or eleven, a year after a ruptured appendix. Before that I had my tonsils removed at around six or seven. When I was about 43, I had an operation to remove an ovarian cyst which took quite a toll on me. I was pretty weak for about a year after that. A major health problem I've had all my life has been my teeth. I've been going to the dentist since I was quite young and have had a 'million' teeth filled. I attribute this to my rather poor diet when I was young — all the candy and sweets I ate.

"As for additional information, I have unbelievable patience. I believe I could wait forever for something I believed was worth waiting for. I am very much against quick changes of any kind. I think out things very carefully before I make a move. Quite often, I think things over for too long and the opportunity passes me by. I think I am afraid I will make the wrong move and get stuck in something which will be difficult to get out of, especially in reference to jobs. It is extremely difficult for me to do things on the spur of the moment. I seem never to be quite ready to go out somewhere without advance notice. I have missed many fine trips and events because I felt I wasn't quite ready.

"I believe that tact and diplomacy are my strong points. I have a keen sense of responsibility and my word is as good as gold. I am a very peace-loving person and usually take the stings and barbs of criticism rather than start an argument over it. I am a very romantic person and always have been. I love romantic songs and movies and poetry. I strongly believe relationships and marriages should retain their romance forever. I love to cuddle.

"I believe the finest thing I have done in my life was setting my job and my personal life aside to take care of my parents these past three and a half years as their health was declining and they could no longer take care of themselves completely. It was my chance to help repay them a little for all their good deeds, and I really felt needed for the first time in my life."

Numerological Analysis

Of the three names given Ms. Five at birth, the rundown of her major numbers is as follows:

Soul Urge (vowels sum)	=	1
Personality (consonants sum)	=	4
Name/Expression (name sum)	=	5
Life Path (month/day/year sum)	=	11/2

Her 1 Soul Urge (how she identifies or sees herself) suggests someone being her own person. "Her name starts with a 1 and she has a 1 Soul Urge," Stephanie observed, "which is someone who is independent and who wants to do one's own thing — to basically live on one's own terms. Such people can also show the pioneering spirit, going out and starting things in motion. Basically, however, they are loners; able to interact with others, but they still prefer to remain individuals at all costs."

The number 1 is the number of the self-reliant individualist, a freedom number, which can often be self-oriented, if only by insisting to remain the independent operator. Its astrological parallel is Aries/Mars/first house and other keys to identity and self-will. In Ms. Five's horoscope, it may be tied to freedom-oriented Aquarius in her first house, with its ruler, Uranus, in the independent sign of Aries.

Ms. Five's Personality (outer expression, how other people see her or how she impresses them) is number 4, the Personality number of our previous participant, Mr. Four. This is the number of work, order, structure, discipline, father and other male figures. It can show stability and balance if the number 4 principle is understood and mobilized, or it can show imbalance, judgmentalness, fear or guilt if not mobilized constructively. The missing 4 in her name may suggest a challenge regarding work and accomplishment, or father and men, as will be discussed later in the Inclusion Table section. The astrological equivalent of number 4 is work-oriented, pragmatic earth (Virgo and/or Capricorn; Vesta and/or Saturn). Note Ms. Five's Capricorn rising, with its ruler, Saturn, in Capricorn widely conjunct her Ascendant. If the Ascendant/first house can be construed partially as being one's "persona," then perhaps it can relate as the 4 Personality (although as given earlier, I put less emphasis on the Personality number). Her Taurus grouping, being earth, may also contribute, if only in terms of stableness and being tied to property and possessions.

Her Name or Expression is number 5, the number of change, freedom, sex and sensuality. (Note that Ms. Three also has a 5 Name, as does Mr. Seven.) As her essential vibration in terms of natural expression, number 5 is particularly oriented toward human living in its basic physical and emotional context. Its astrological correlate is the fixed quality (focus on the physical/material world), but particularly its fire component, Leo/Sun. Leo shares the "changes" and dramatics aspects of number 5, although not the freedom characteristic usually associated with it. In many cases, number 5 is associated with another freedom-fire sign, Sagittarius (sometimes associated with Aquarius/Uranus). Jupiter/Chiron/Sagittarius are expansive and vital and freedom-oriented, but once again, number 5 is more associated with material living (physical body and the five senses) than with a mental (mutable) orientation. Note the Ms. Five's Sun in Taurus is conjunct Chiron, and more widely, Jupiter.

At any rate, her 5 Name suggests a freedom-loving, dramatic, sexually and/or sensually-oriented lady. The **urge** at least to be active, to travel, to risk, to want variety is likely with her nature. She can be a stimulating companion, an entertainer, quite talented and versatile. The 5 Name can also manifest as restlessness, being overindulgent with the senses, too materialistic; or, if the 5 energy is blocked or rigidly controlled instead of disciplined to moderation, the person can feel quite frustrated and "fixed" about self-imposed routine and status quo, but inwardly preferring excitement and risk in life (change versus stability conflict).

Ms. Five's reduced or prime Life Path is 2. As the most important core indicator of character, the Life Path is one's major growth goal or destiny to be followed for best fulfillment. The number 2 is the number of partnership, relationships in general, mothering or dependency needs, and the female (passive and receptive) principle. Unlike the 1 Soul Urge's identification with independence and "Self," the number 2 is involved with the "Other," wanting to be close and caring, a companion — to share life with someone (e.g., partnership or motherhood). Both her 1 Soul Urge and 5 Name are freedom-oriented, but the 2 suggests that personal, intimate involvement with other people is her primary growth need. A Self-Other polarity is evident or independence versus dependence (freedom/closeness dilemma) with these major number patterns. The missing 2 in her name points to a challenge in the area of relationships and/or dependency. The astrological correlate may be her Mars in Cancer in the Libra/partnership house squaring Venus in Aries — stress with the issue of equality, dependency and independence. This will be discussed shortly in the Inclusion Table section when the missing 2 is focused upon.

Ms. Five's Birthday is a 3 (born May 3), the number of enjoyment, communication and the mind. As a "minor" rather than a "major" indicator of character, it is nevertheless another facet of her life direction. It suggests a friendly, creative nature, oriented toward pleasure and comfort. A mental quality is indicated, with perhaps a tendency to scatter and be interested in diverse subjects. A ruler of her first house (Uranus ruling Aquarius) in the third house and Aries there, plus Mercury in Gemini may be the astrological correlates since number 3 relates to Gemini/Mercury most comfortably, as well as, perhaps, a tinge of Taurus/Venus for pleasure, indulgence and artistic ability.

Attention was then focused upon Ms. Five's Inclusion Table (diagram in box format derived from the total letter values of a name).

Inclusion Table

2	0	2	I	4
0	4	4	We	8
1	0	1	They	2
P	E	M		
3	4	7		

Two 1's connects partnership, relationships, nurturance/dependency with the area of self-will, identity and independence. It repeats the Self-Other theme. She will express her identity or ego in a 2 fashion — e.g., being tactful and accommodating (Libra traits), passivity about her actions, etc. Number 2 is the number of sensitivity and vulnerability, so she can be quite sensitive about her ego, especially in terms of relationships affecting her.

"Two 1's," Stephanie explained, "can be passive and diplomatic, but not terribly assertive. It softens the personality and softens the disposition where the ego is concerned. Such people can come on very quietly or sweetly, but they can be wishy-washy or cold and manipulative sometimes because of security needs or dependency needs."

Two 1's can also frequently show as an identification with the mothering urge — to take care of, nurture and protect. Since two 1's is under the average for the number of 1's in a name, it can indicate weak confidence, needing other people to motivate oneself to act (being reactive), or excessive vulnerability to how close others such as one's mate (number 2) respond to oneself. Learning to be truly self-reliant may be an issue, despite the 1 Soul Urge which says, "I want what I want."

The missing 2 is a Karmic Lesson, requiring extra focus to handle that area of life. It is a challenge of handling partnership/equality, relationships, mother, nurturance/dependency and passivity in the nature. It is usually a lesson in trust and sensitivity (e.g., easily hurt feelings). A missing number manifests as doing too much, too little, or displacing the principle of that number. Being too other-directed can indicate low self-esteem; being too inconsiderate or manipulative can lead to loneliness and alienation from others; being vulnerable to everybody's opinions can lead to thin-skinned weakness and fear of closeness. Since Ms. Five's Life Path or growth goal is the 2, it is a particularly highlighted lesson area. A common displacement manifestation is playing parent or boss in a relationship that should be equalitarian. As given earlier, Ms. Five's Cancer in the seventh house of equal relationships, plus south node of the Moon conjunct Juno, the marriage/equality asteroid, Mars in Cancer in the seventh house square the Midheaven, and Moon trioctile Mars can indicate the astrological equivalent of the parent/partner theme in stress.

Two 3's connects partnership and passivity with the mind, communication and creative self-expression. Passive, comfortable or familiar arts and modes of creativity may be preferred. To speak in a 2 manner — pleasantly, diplomatically, agreeably, apologetically — is likely, as well as communicating in a sensitive, vulnerable way. Usually it shows an enjoyment and ease of being social and talking with people. Domestic creativity may be emphasized, such as gardening, sewing, cooking, etc.

The missing 4 is another lesson area involving father, men, discipline or work — or all of them! In the work area, it can manifest as the workaholic or overdrive person, the self-blocker, or displacing the work ethic (e.g., making a job of relationships, being critical toward men in general, etc.). Ms. Five does have a 4 Personality and can impress people as being dependable and capable; however, internal stress may be felt in terms of job dissatisfaction, not sticking to a job long enough, and so forth. Laziness and procrastination may also be a missing 4 issue. On an interpersonal level, understanding men and the male principle may be a lesson, its roots perhaps stemming from the relationship with the father — the first man in most women's lives. Astrologically, the missing 4 can possibly be correlated with the south node of the Moon in the tenth house of father and career, and Saturn, key to father and work, in Capricorn quincunx Vesta. The missing 4 is a lesson around reality-testing, control, balance and learning through consequences (Capricorn principle).

Four 5's connects males, work and limitation with the area of sex, sensuality, changes and freedom. It repeats the theme of Ms. Five's major numbers with her 4 Personality and 5 name. The 4/5 mixture is not an easy blend usually. For some people, it can mean a Victorian approach of restraint regarding sex and sensuality (inhibitions, fears, conservatism, sexual blocks). For others, it can mean a balanced and prudent approach to number 5 areas. It can manifest as being critical and judgmental toward one's physical body, or being realistic and disciplined in maintaining its health. This combination unites work with changes and freedom, so a variety of jobs is possible or a career with variety and change built-in. Travel in one's work is another possibility.

Four 6's combines work, father, males and discipline with the area of home, family or community responsibility, service, and love and harmony. "The four 6's," Sylvia commented, "indicates a problem potential in dealing with responsibilities. Perhaps she would have critical and judgmental attitudes about committing to a marriage situation, feeling that being married would be a limiting experience. People with four 6's often don't want the responsibility of marriage because they think it's a prison or a burden."

This is the fear of marriage responsibilities and commitment, feeling "boxed-in" (the 4 or square shape) about it. Another possibility is the importance of father in the continuing domestic family scene — e.g., ongoing responsibility and service to one's father or other male figure. In terms of work, it can manifest as a penchant toward interior decorating, say, or housekeeping.

One 7 connects identity, self-will and independence with study and higher (or superior) understanding. The person is able to be alone comfortably, to analyze, and to be the seeker of Truth. It also suggests learning on one's own terms.

The missing 8 is a lesson area regarding money, power, authority or health. Learning to handle the practical necessities of life in a satisfactory manner may be an issue. There may exist an over-concern about money or health. Poor or unrealistic financial judgment may be evident, or fear of lack.

"One 9," Sylvia said, "indicates that she deals with the world on her own terms, wanting to be independent in the world." Since one 9 is less than the average number of 9's, it can indicate less concern for the world at large, except at occasions when it affects the individual personally (number 1). It says, "I choose those with whom I'm going to associate with." Focus tends to be centered on personal and interpersonal areas rather than with humanity (humanitarianism in action).

Next, the totals of the Inclusion Table's rows and columns were briefly commented upon. Number 4 is again accentuated with 4 as the sum of the Individual row (boxes 1, 2, 3) and the Emotional Column (boxes 2, 5, 8). The four in the Emotional can indicate a rigid control of emotions which she can dam up, critical and judgmental feelings toward self and other, or balanced emotions disciplined by higher aspects of the self. The 4 in the Individual adds to the identification with father, work, realism or self-blocking.

Sylvia commented on the self-blocking possibility: the inhibition potential . . . of the number 4 focus (4 Personality, missing 4, four 5's, four 6's, and the 4 in the Individual and Emotional) indicates that she could have had a lot of fear and guilt about her life as a child, and that she can put barriers around herself, not allowing other people into her life for fear of being hurt.

Stephanie continued with the other Inclusion Table totals: "She has 3 in the Physical Column (total of boxes 1, 4, 7) so that shows she wants to enjoy herself physically, or she can be very scattered. In the Mental Column (boxes 3, 6, 9) she has a 7 total, someone who could be into higher knowledge, metaphysics, or someone who can be into social climbing, classics, higher forms of music or other 'superior' activities. The 8 in the Family Row (boxes 4, 5, 6) shows the control of money or power she wants in that area. She has 2 in the World Row (boxes 7, 8, 9) which can mean being passive with the world, or being diplomatic and tactful."

Natal Imprint

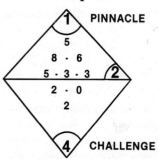

PINNACLE

5
8 · 6
5 · 3 · 3
2 · 0
2

CHALLENGE

The numerologists then focused upon Ms. Five's Natal Imprint, primarily the baseline and Pinnacles and Challenges derived from her month/day/year of birth. Born May 3, 1929, her baseline pattern is 5-3-3(=11/2 Life path). Her first Pinnacle and Challenge is the 8 over 2, which ended at the conclusion of her 34th birthday (36 minus 2 Life Path=34). It suggests sensitivity about relationships and mother (number 2 Challenge) regarding power or money in the environment (8 Pinnacle). It can indicate problems in the home caused by internal power struggles, particularly involving the mother and/or female figure(s).

"The 6 over 0 second Pinnacle and Challenge," Sylvia said, "indicates that she was going to be in some sort of responsibility, and that she was going to be taken care of in some way." The focus on relationships, sensitivity and the home/mother is highlighted with the 2-0-2 Challenges, and it reflects the 2 Life Path is terms of needing a partnership or relationships in order to reflect herself through another person. The 5 over 2 third Pinnacle and Challenge, which began at age 44, suggests changes (number 5) in relationships and being quite sensitive about them (number 2). Her Super Pinnacle and Super Challenge is the 1 over 4, repeating her Soul Urge and Personality numbers. It reiterates the same theme of self and father, self and work, self and men, self and discipline.

"She has a 1 Super Pinnacle," Stephanie said, "so she can be in some leadership position, which is very good for her since she does have a 1 Soul Urge. But again, she does have to deal with balance and discipline with the 4 Super Challenge."

Ms. Five's first baseline Cycle (or Life Path period) is the 5, which lasted until her first Saturn return, approximately age 28-29. It suggests a developmental period of wanting to be free to explore life, sensuality, changes. Her Second, Accomplishment Cycle, is the 3, ending approximately at her second Saturn return at age 58-59. It supports her 3 Birthday in terms of wanting to enjoy life, indulge, pursue mental and creative activities, and perhaps be a bit scattered in the process. Her Final Cycle is also a 3, suggesting a focus on pleasure, social activity and creative pursuits, or it can be an aimless and indecisive retirement period. In its best fulfillment, the 3 Final Cycle points to seasoned creative self-expression and joyful living.

Ms. Five Responds to Zip

I visited Ms. Five early one evening last September to pick up her completed questionnaire. She had already read Zip's initial interpretation draft, and I brought along my Panasonic recorder for a short interview session. Since the background information she provided was so thorough, the interview was of short duration. My standard first question was to gauge her overall response to Zip's reading.

"Everything is true, what she says," Ms. Five answered. "The interesting thing she picked up was my relationship with men. Half the time I'm the little girl and half the time I'm the mother. What Zip said about my relationship with men is true: I do treat them like a father or a son."

I inquired if her male friend of nine years enjoyed that arrangement.

"He likes it. It's all right and fun and carefree, but we really don't get down to the business of a mature relationship. He avoids commitments completely, so he likes this carefree game we play. We even talk baby talk."

"What if he suddenly popped the question one romantic evening?" I posed to her.

"I'd probably be a little scared but I think I'd be ready for it this time. I think I'm a little scared of marriage, but I'm getting to the point where I can be ready for it. There's a small possibility he might ask me to marry him someday, but I'm really not counting on it. He's very much afraid of commitment of any kind. He likes his freedom. He likes our relationship because we get along. And it's comfortable for me. We still have a lot of our own free time. I think that's the main reason I've never gotten married, because I like a lot of free time. I like to alternate. I like to have a relationship, and then I like to go back to my home base and do all the intellectual things I want to do and all the creative things. I want time to cook and do gardening, read a lot, and think about a lot of things. You can't always do that in a relationship."

Later in the interview, she picked up on the marriage theme again.

"I would like to get married some day. I really feel that every girl should get married once in her lifetime, if only for a few months. I want to experience that special thing of being a wife. I really want to get married. Maybe not right away, but in a few years. I don't think it would be a good idea to marry my present boyfriend because he's so critical. He will never love me in the way that I love him. It's sort of an impersonal thing with him — Moon and Venus in Aquarius. And this bothers me. I really don't feel secure with him, and that's kind of a bad thing for a Taurus."

In the earlier numerological session, it was suggested that perhaps she idealized her father to such an extent that no other man could live up to his standards. Ms. Five replied that that may be partially true but "it won't make me appreciate men any less." A main reason for not marrying was her 1 Soul Urge free choice, and "waiting for the right man to come along. . .and I was afraid of being tied down seven days a week to a man."

Ms. Five agreed with Zip's supposition of idealizing the father. "I do idealize my father and always have and always will. And I pattern my ideals after him."

I hypothesized a situation in which in a past life they may have been intimately connected. Did she agree?

"That's entirely possible because I feel that I'm an extension of my father more than just being a daughter. I look like him, I have the same personality and the same temperament. And I know that since his health had failed and I started to take care of him, sad as it was to see him go downhill, I've done the most important thing in my life: just taking care of him as though I was a mother. This gave me a great sense of satisfaction that I could finally do something for him after all these years. He did so much for me.

He died just the year before (September 12, 1982). "I still feel very sad but I'm getting adjusted to it. He was 87. He was a wonderful, wonderful man. He was very special. I feel like I'm carrying him within me and will for the rest of my life. He was such a dear, shy, gentle man (Moon in Pisces). I really felt that he needed to be taken care of in some ways. He was so shy, and he had feelings of inferiority that stemmed from his childhood because his father favored his brother. But I just felt that he sort of needed me. He needed my love and support. We were very close when I was little. Then as I grew up through puberty, we kind of separated, and he became very close to my mother. I had problems with my mother and he always sided with her. They were always very close. But then these last years we've gotten closer, especially after my mother passed away, and he really needed me."

Ms. Five commented on her current situation with her older sister and her father's house (where both of them presently reside).

"I'm trying to buy the house away from my sister. I don't get along with my sister. In fact, things are much worse with her than ever. It's very difficult with her now. I'm under more stress now than when my father was going downhill. It is terrible because I can't deal with her. She's such a strong force and she's taking over everything. She's running the house and doing what she wants to, and I just can't cope with it . . . [**Update: her sister died in August 1984, six months after terminal cancer was discovered.**]

"My family and my home have been the center of my whole life. Even when I went away to college for two years, which is the longest I had ever been away from home, I just chucked the whole thing one day and moved back home when I was close to getting my degree. I just couldn't stand being away for another minute and I had to come back home. Some strong force drew me back. I gave up everything. Then I went to business school to become a secretary. I regretted it many times in a way; in a way, I haven't."

Did she feel a sense of self-blocking and perhaps low self-esteem regarding her past?

"I think highly of myself in an intellectual way, and yet there's some basic thing that I don't even understand. It must be an emotional thing that I can't put my finger on that gives me this low self-esteem. My father had it too. He was a wonderful person, yet basically he had a feeling of inferiority. I do know there's a lot of love in me, but sometimes I fall back from people. I've been told that."

I inquired about her 5 Name/Expression, wondering if indeed she would characterize her life as one of changes and freedom.

"I feel changes are coming over the horizon. I feel a sense of freedom now that I never had in my life since my parents have passed away. And I'm sort of becoming an adult now because I was always the little girl with them. I was always treated like a little girl all my life. Now, I always had a lot of boyfriends and a lot of jobs. That was my variety. Some of my relationships were very serious, but I just wasn't ready to get married. I always found something wrong with them and reasons to break off from them. There was something funny about them that I didn't like. I didn't like the way they kissed or whatever! Also I had a vast variety of jobs. There was something wrong with every job. But the one thing I stuck to was my house. It has been hard for me to leave home. It is my base of operations. I can do my thing there. I can create, cook, work in the yard. I'd hate to have to move away somewhere."

The number 5 quality also expresses in terms of her being "very emotional." She added: "I love to be dramatic and talk a lot. I can talk for hours about my boyfriends. I love to talk about romance and love. But I won't live with a man who won't marry me." In terms of the sensuality aspect of the number 5 vibration, she replied that she prefers cuddling to sex, being turned on by a good kisser and by romance.

I noted Vesta in the fifth house of procreation quincunx Saturn in the twelfth house, and I asked Ms. Five if she ever wanted children, her own or adopted.

"I never seemed to want to have children, and I know the reason why: because I would want to devote all my time and energies to my husband because I'm a very romantic person. I just want to be the perfect wife and the perfect sweetheart to him. And I know that if I had children, I would be spending a lot of time with them. But for the last few years, I'm feeling differently. I seem to want to be a mother more than ever. I'm mothering everything now. I mother plants, animals, everything. I was always a mother to some extent, but I never had a great desire to have children as a lot of women do. It's the big thing for them. And I really wouldn't want to adopt. But I would like to have another little parrot again — my child! I had two birds that were like little children to me. They both died recently."

Finally I asked her if she wanted to work as a teacher. "I never wanted to be a teacher in a classroom. But Zip said something that's quite interesting: that I could be a teacher in an unorthodox situation, teaching far-out subjects, such as standing on a street corner talking about astrology, which I do often with neighbors. I love to talk to people about their charts. So I never wanted to be a teacher, but I wanted to be a counselor. I wanted to be a psychologist or a psychiatric social worker, child psychologist or some kind of a family counselor. I always wanted to do that because I think I have that capacity to bring people together, to bring peace."

CHAPTER NINETEEN

MS. SIX

Introduction to Ms. Six

It is interesting how the Universe does indeed respond to a need, especially when you consciously visualize its fulfillment with strong intent. Of the seven potential case studies, I purposefully wanted one to be a professional woman, edging toward the healing/helping field. As it happened, an acquaintance indirectly led me to Ms. Six, mentioning that he knew a woman counselor utilizing analytical psychology and hypnotherapy. I promptly phoned her that evening, introduced myself, and briefly discussed the upcoming book. Stating that I was considering her as a candidate for selection, she agreed to disclose her full birth certificate name and birth data.

Her chart patterns intrigued me, particularly the active twelfth-house focus and Jupiter rising. Considering the succinct overview of her background that Ms. Six described over the phone, the chart did indeed fit, and would serve, I felt, as an excellent case study. So I contacted her about my go-ahead and she consented to participate in the book project.

Ms. Six's Background

Ms. Six:
"I was born in Illinois in the bedroom of my grandmother's house. As far as I know, I was an easy birth. I was very much wanted, most particularly by my mother. I came into the world surrounded by love. After the first four years in my parents' home in Illinois, we then moved to Indiana for a short time, maybe a year. My father

took us back to our grandmother's and left us there for several months. He then returned, picked us up, and we returned to Indiana. We moved to several residences in that community in Indiana. We moved a lot. I was always the 'new kid' — the new, different kid — in school, moving from one area of the country to the other: Midwest to South to far North to West.

"I spent summers with my grandmother and my grandfather, my father's parents. My mother's parents had passed on, and she was reared by her aunt and uncle. I adored my grandfather, the one positive male in my life. In fact, my summers with my grandparents was a highlight. I was the first grandchild and the first great niece. I was surrounded by a great deal of love and attention.

"My mother is a very positive person; an intelligent lady, well-educated, with a marvelous sense of humor. She was in all true sense of the word the nurturing mother, always very positive. She opened all kinds of worlds to me. She was a reader, and I became a reader. Therefore, we sought education besides school, reading in the home. I chose beautifully when I chose her! She was very definitely a very positive role model. She carries all roles. She is my best friend. She is a confidant, carrying secrets to her grave, and gives wise advice only if asked. She is very much the role of mother — nurturing mother, not interfering mother. We call her our little matriarch. She's a five-foot redhead. I used to kid her that she's the mother of the four of us — my three children and myself. She was born January 3, 1910.

"My father, on the positive side, was open in many ways. I was treated both as daddy's girl and his boy, being the only child — no brothers or sisters. Looking back, I think perhaps I tried to get my father's love. I didn't feel he loved me as I was loved by other people, mostly my mother. I didn't feel the love from him I needed ever, although I think he loved me as much as he was able to love. Father had problems. He was an alcoholic, which I didn't realize until I got older. My father expressed volatile, frightful anger. He scared me to death with his anger. Yet he would go at times without drinking, and when he did, he had a very sweet nature. His alcoholism didn't interfere with his profession (as superintendent of a plant). He was born March 20, 1904. My father was dominant, but he was a very weak man covering with a show of strength. He was also very work-oriented. I think I felt I had to do things right. My father joined the service toward the end of the war and went overseas. That would be an impactful event of my life.

"The year before, my mother had an automobile accident, her

face crushed on the steering wheel. She was found by a farmer, and apparently was able to tell him where she lived, although she has no recollection to this day of the incident. He brought her home instead of taking her to a hospital, and left her with me. I was approximately ten years old. By this time, her face was horribly swollen and bloody. I immediately put her to bed and called my father at work, and called the ambulance. They came and picked her up. By this time she was in shock. It was probably the most fearful thing that ever happened to me. She was unconscious for two weeks. We didn't expect her to live. In fact, after it was decided that she would live, it was thought that she would not be either of sound mind or be able to function. She was, in fact, written up in the medical journals as one who had experimental procedures done on her. She even kept all of her teeth.

"My parents were divorced when I was entering my senior year, much to my pleasure. In fact, I probably helped it along a bit. I almost gave her an ultimatum. She would've waited until I graduated from high school. As it was, it was at the end of my junior year. Drama was my major interest at the time, and dance. In fact, I was onstage dancing at 2½, and from there I was giving musical readings. I was given lessons in dancing, which I adored. After I graduated from high school, I went to a university. I also entered a modeling school, and I took a secretarial course so that I could help pay through college because my father wasn't going to do it. I did work on television, an original 'Queen for a Day' model. I did a lot of PR work, a little theater, and I did quite a lot of dancing.

"However, a year or so later, I re-met the youngest son of friends of my parents. I was then married for almost 25 years — all of them unhappy. I reared three children whom I adored (boy, girl, boy). As the women are wont to do in my era, I did my duty: put my husband first always. I feel duty very, very strongly. I feel commitment very, very strongly. I was reared that one must do one's duty. I still feel that I am the kind of woman who feels that her man comes first. That is me besides my era of training and besides the role models I had. I am absolutely not a woman's libber in any way. If a woman works as hard as a man, of course she should be paid the same. But that's humanistic, not woman's libbing.

"My former husband is an Aries, born April 7, 1921. Everything I have ever read about Aries-Cancer said, good heavens, don't do that! Good heavens, I did that! A most unsatisfactory relationship on all counts. It was a negative relationship for 25 years. It was all psychological: my idealism. I was so idealistic. I represented my dream to everybody, and if I wanted it to be so, I could make this happen by not acknowledging negatives, by constantly working with it. And then his psychiatrist would say I'm doing a beautiful job — just keep on doing what you're doing. It was the burden of responsibility: you can't walk out on a man. But I was so overruled. I had all of the responsibility with none of the authority. That became my favorite phrase. But I chose a weak man who covered with a show of strength. He once told our minister, 'I can't put God first because money comes first.' He also had a love-hate relationship with his mother, and therefore with women. He was totally and absolutely selfish and lived his life as a single man. I don't mean by that he had affairs constantly. It was just within his thinking. His mother interfered in a subversive way. It was just those two against the world. It was a very sick relationship. He was jealous of family and friends. We had very little social life, and when we did, it was with friends he would accept in our life, and maybe once a year. I don't believe in fighting, however. There were issues faced at times which got heavy. But I'm a talker. I overtalked. That was a fault of mine.

"I finally became a nonperson in my own acknowledgment of me. In attempting to cope with an extremely negative life, while choosing to remain in it, I began to lose touch with me. I was holding in anger and holding in frustrations of all kinds. They manifested as physical symptoms, as we humans do! During the negative time I manifested colitis, arthritis, migraine headaches, had the uterus removed, knowing all the time that I wasn't living my life correctly or I wouldn't have had those symptoms. I haven't had them for years. During a trial arrangement with him, I got up one morning, and said, 'This is it. I can't do it anymore.' The summer wasn't working out as we had planned. And he was doing absolutely nothing to contribute to help this marriage go along. So I got up and opened suitcases. I said, 'This is the day. I can't take it another day.' And very seriously — like the movies! I've been divorced for eight years. But it has been a tremendous learning experience for me. I've allowed me to come to terms with me and with life in a very positive and productive way. I've given time for me.

"I have always been one of those people to whom neighbors and friends would confide. I've always done that, but I didn't think of it in terms of a profession until my family was reared and I decided to live life as a single person. I decided I was going to go back and get my degree — go into the mental health field. Besides dance and being a mother, that interest has always been there also. I just didn't think of it as a career until family was finished. First I'll get psychiatric social work and then go from there. A dear doctor friend of mine suggested I go to a certain doctor's talk. He's the first medical hypnotist in the United States. And I studied and trained under him. I knew exactly what direction to follow. I stayed up a lot of nights and weekends! I existed on four to five hours' sleep.

"I do not believe in drugs of any kind in therapy except in very extreme rare cases such as hysteria/psychotic. I can accomplish more under analytical counseling with the use of hypnotherapy than I can at a clinic. It is against my beliefs and values to use drugs. Also, I'm eclectic. I use what is needed for that patient at that time, be it hypnosis, be it gestalt, be it transactional analysis, be it past-life therapy or whatever. I have a very logical, scientific mind, and I'm constantly checking and double-checking. You have to be careful of people who are just hypnotherapists. Sometimes such people graduate after only six weeks of training, and they call themselves hypnotists. Sometimes, under selective circumstances, I use past-life therapy as an adjunct. It doesn't matter if I can't prove it. What matters is that I do it on a professional level, and it's a help to certain clients and they feel better.

[Ms. Six and associates formed a professional association which does research and therapy concerning hypnosis and past-life regression. Ever since at least her early teens, she felt that she always had an "inner knowing" about reincarnation. She has clairsentience psychic ability, which she utilizes only in counseling, and only when invited.]

"I have stifled that because I have no right in your mind. I'm very selective when I need to do it. I rarely tell them what I can see. I don't let them know about their defenses because I want them to find it out. I don't want to put words in their mouth or thoughts in their mind. And sometimes, I wait and see, and ask myself, Am I right? There is that scientific test and checking.

"Now: as for characteristics, I have a very even temperament and a good sense of humor. I'm extremely patient, very tenacious, outgoing. I'm not a loner; I enjoy people. However, I enjoy my own time, and up until this time, I have in fact always needed a certain amount of alone time. I have always had to have quiet time and crawl into my little crab shell, I guess. I don't need it now. I'm presently in a relationship with a man whom I adore and with whom I'm in love totally. In this relationship I'm being fed now where before I was being drained. Instead of a weak man, I am now having a beautiful love relationship with a very strong man. And I love it, adore it, enjoy it and encourage it!

"I am musically inclined only in the dance, not with instrument or vocal. Competitive? No. Consequently, I'm not a very good tennis player. One must need to win to be a good athlete. I have a very logical, scientific mind, yet I do believe in the metaphysical. I was reared a Methodist and a summertime Baptist! Finally I came to an age through the years where I didn't apologize for my thinking or for my beliefs. I do believe that there is a Supreme Being, and I am spiritually inclined. Parapsychology fascinates me. Metaphysics in the scientific vein is most interesting to me.

"I'm motivated by happiness and pleasure around me. I'm turned off by anger and loud noise. In fact, I don't like the new loud punk music. Am I happy? Deliriously so! I'm very happy because I'm living my life almost exactly as I would like to. I've worked very hard on me, developing who I am today. I've learned a lot from life, and I'm conducting my life as nearly to the way I wanted it as possible. I tend to become a procrastinator when it comes to business things. I detest writing letters; I'd much rather phone. I don't like doing figures. I can be more self-disciplined in exercising my body, even though I walk and bike. Even though I'm high energy, I do flow. Also, I am a nurturer, and I have need of home. I'm striving now on achieving a home which I can nurture. I love to keep house. I am looking forward to a long future with my present relationship, and when that continues to be — to total fulfillment — then I will at that time be totally happy.

"I value honesty and communication. You can't have one without the other one. Respect with myself and of my mate are important. What is success? One is successful when one is living one's life so that you can say you're happy. I don't care if you're a ditch-digger or a president of a bank. If you feel at peace and are content and happy, then you are a success. You must be true and honest to self. It really doesn't matter what other people say or want from you or for you in the long run. It's important, but one must be true to oneself to be successful. The last fear I conquered was the fear of rejection. I live basically with the 'prefer' approach to life rather than demanding."

Numerological Analysis

Of the three names given Ms. Six at birth, the rundown of her major numbers is as follows:

Soul Urge (vowels sum)   = 1
Personality (consonants sum)   = 1
Name/Expression (name sum)   = 2
Life Path (month/day/year sum) = 6

Her Soul Urge (how she identifies or sees herself) and Personality (how others see her or how she impresses them) are both the number 1. In a face-to-face session with Ms. Six, Sylvia commented: "Your inner and outer are similar. You're in life to really do your own thing, to be independent, wanting to do what you want to do."

The 1 is the number of the independent ego, being the pioneer, standing on one's own two feet, and the self-reliant individualist. Astrologically, it relates to Aries and cardinality: the self-initiated drive for freedom of action. Action and overt events are highlighted, as well as a high-energy, "on the go" approach to life. The number 1 can be the natural loner and quite "me"-oriented, being the leader or trendsetter in terms of entrepreneurship. On a negative standpoint, it can show as impulsiveness, headstrong willfulness, and even aggressiveness. If blocked, the number 1 can manifest as depression, head problems, accidents and surgery.

However, Ms. Six's Name (also called the "Expression") is a 2 — the number of relationships rather than the self-will and independence emphasis of the number 1. The Name is given a greater emphasis than either the Soul Urge or the Personality, derived independently of whatever system is used to ascertain the Soul Urge and Personality. It describes a person's overall characteristic vibration or natural "expression." As given in earlier case studies with a major number 2 emphasis, the number 2 relates astrologically to a Libra and/or Cancer focus: partnership or dependency/nurturance(baby/mother) focus. Both want closeness, union, comfort and harmony in a relationship context. Sylvia views the number 2 as expressing, in a strong person, the Cancer-mother, along with the corollary drives for security, safety and survival — very much protective, nurturant and home-oriented.There appears to be a Self-Other polarity with the major 1 and the major 2 combinations. The astrological parallel of this combination may indeed be Ms. Six's Cancer rising (first-house cusp) — identity, self-will and action tied to closeness and nurturing. The freedom aspect of number 1 may have its astrological correlate with Moon, ruling the Cancer rising, in the freedom sign of Aquarius, plus Jupiter rising. The nodes of the Moon in Aries-Libra also parallel the numerological Self-Other polarity. The intense Cancer stellium and Cancer Ascendant seem to support Sylvia's treatment of the 2 Name as the Cancer person at heart.

Ms. Six's Life Path (primary growth goal or destiny) is the number 6. The keynote of number 6 is responsibility and service. "The work that she is doing — counseling — is good for a 6 Life Path," Stephanie observed, "because it can be into healing and helping people; service of some type, such as nursing or other medical work."

"The 6 Life Path," Sylvia added, "shows a person who has come into life to learn about responsibility for home, family, marriage, work and service in the community, and love and harmony."

The numerologists next focused their attention on Ms. Six's Inclusion Table (table in box form derived from the total letter values of a name).

Inclusion Table

3	1	1	I	5
0	4	1	We	5
2	1	2	They	5

P E M
5 6 4

Three 1's connects creative self-expression, communication and enjoyment (number 3) with self-will, identity and independence (number 1). She expresses her individuality and does her own thing in a number 3 manner — e.g., talking, writing, enjoying self.

"You have three 1's," Sylvia explained to Ms. Six, "which means you like to dress nice, look very pretty, take care of your hair and nails. Like me — I have three 1's — you like to talk and be creative and communicative."

One 2 ties identity and individuality with partnership, relationships and motherhood/security. It shows an understanding of the female (passive, receptive) principle, and an ability to make friends, to get along with others. It indicates the trait of tactfulness, diplomacy and understanding the other person's sensitivities. She will likely express relationships in a number 1 manner — as an individual with her own sense of identity (unless blocked), or relating to others on her own terms.

One 3 combines self-will/identity/independence with the area of communication/pleasure/creativity/children. It can show as an identification with the mind, an independent mind, a direct and active style of communication, etc. She understands self-expression, pleasure and creativity, and demonstrates them in her own individualistic way.

The missing 4 is the only missing number in her name: a "Karmic Lesson." It requires extra handling in successfully coping with that principle represented by the missing number. Number 4 represents the male principle, father, discipline and order.

"The missing 4," Sylvia observed, "indicates that you came in to learn about men and having a positive role model for men. For some women, it can mean being lazy, expecting a man to fulfill them. Or they can be the workaholic, which then becomes a problem because they need to balance work with play. There's no one thing that's that important in your life that you have to spend 24 hours a day at it. The missing 4 means putting yourself in balance."

"Four 5's ," she continued, "can mean having a limiting experience with one's physical body in some way. Such people are looking for ways to better it, finding fault with it. They may feel guilty about pleasure, or be balanced about their physical appetites."

This combination connects realistic limitation and order with the area of sex, sensuality, changes and freedom. If not constructively handled, it can mean inhibition in any of the number 5 areas — sexual blocks, restricted freedom, fear of changes, etc. If constructively handled, it can mean discipline and balance regarding freedom, travel, changes and physical appetites. Number 4 can suggest "being boxed-in" or critical/judgmental (right versus wrong, or good versus bad programming), so it requires conscious handling not to slip into its undesirable expressions. Otherwise, number 4 can manifest as fear, guilt, repression, demands rather than preferences. Its positive handling is healthy realism and structure: Knowing what you can do, can't do, and have to do (borrowing Zip's statement on the Capricorn principle).

One 6 joins self-will and individuality with responsibility and service. It shows that she understands responsibility, can accept or reject a given responsibility depending on what she chooses to commit to. Since her Life Path is a 6, it shows good ability to fulfill her life mission successfully rather than being challenged with a missing 6.

Two 7's connects relationships, partnership and perhaps motherhood with understanding and the higher mind. It can manifest as cooperative ventures of higher learning, passivity or sensitivity regarding knowledge, wanting superior relationships (idealism), idealizing motherhood, etc. It may indicate counseling or consulting in the "best" way possible — e.g., state-of-the-art counseling techniques, use of metaphysical tools, etc.

"One 8," Sylvia explained, "says that you're not as aggressively interested in money, only to the point that you'd like to have it to spend! It would be very nice to have an open-ended checking account! But having power, money and authority is a natural flow for you."

Two 9's ties relationships and nurturing with the wider world. Since number 2 frequently involves a one-to-one mode of interaction, while number 9 involves a one-to-many mode of interaction, changes of associations are suggested. On the other hand, she could interact with the world as a friend or partner: personable, motherly, diplomatic.

"On the negative side," Stephanie said, "they can manipulate the world or be sensitive to everyone. But she understands the world, and she would likely want a partner when she deals with the world."

Stephanie continued with a brief overview of the totals of the Inclusion Table's rows and columns: "She has 5 in the Physical Column (sum of boxes 1, 4, 7), 5 in the Individual row (boxes 1, 2, 3), 5 in the Family Row (boxes 4, 5, 6), and 5 in the World Row (boxes 7,8,9). All those 5's signify a person who probably is on the go a lot, who likes to travel, doing different things. She can be really nervous or in a hurry, into a lot of changes and freedom in those areas. The 6 in the Emotional Column (boxes 2, 5, 8) can show as someone expressing emotions in a very responsible, harmonious way. The 4 in the Mental Column (boxes 3, 6, 9) shows that she can be closed-in or boxed-in with her mind, or she can have a disciplined, scientific mind."

Ms. Six's Birthday number is a 3, the number of creative self-expression and communication. The Birthday is a subsidiary core indicator of character, considered to be similar to the Life Path, though not a "major" number (primary core indicator). Number 3 has its astrological parallel with Gemini: mind, communication, curiosity, lightness, humor, scattering, social. The highlight of number 3 is happiness and the joy of living. It suggests a buoyant, creative, friendly nature.

Natal Imprint

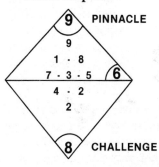

The numerologists turned their attention to Ms. Six's Natal Imprint, which is primarily the baseline and Pinnacles and Challenges derived from the month/day/year of birth. Born July 3, 1931, Ms. Six has a baseline of 7-3-5 (= 6 Life Path) pattern. Her first Pinnacle and Challenge is the 1 over 4, ending at the conclusion of her 30th birthday (36 minus 6 Life Path = 30). It suggests that self-will or independence was challenged by work, father, boss or other male figures. Presently Ms. Six is experiencing the 9 Super Pinnacle and 8 Super Challenge, which suggests power and authority in connection with the world. Its highest expression is being the selfless channel to mankind in a professional context or other power position.

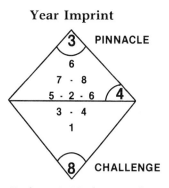

Year Imprint

Stephanie explained Ms. Six's Pinnacles and Challenges: "The 1-8-9 in her environment (Pinnacles) can be someone who is involved a lot with other people's problems, giving a lot to the world. The 4-2-2 Challenges show her sensitivity with relationships, men and power or money with the 8 Super Challenge."

Stephanie continued with Ms. Six's 4 Personal Year, which began on her birthday at age 52 in 1983 (5 + 2 + 6 Life Path = 4). "In her yearly pattern, she is in a 4 Personal Year, which is interesting because that's the only number she is missing. So she will have to be dealing with the male principle, men in her life, discipline, hard work, limitation and balance. The year's Super Challenge is an 8 which means she will have to deal with matters concerning money or her health. She has a 3 Super Pinnacle, which means she wants to enjoy herself, have fun, communicate in her environment."

Ms. Six's baseline, as given, is the 7-3-5 in her Natal Imprint. Each number represents a lengthy Cycle (also called Life Path Period). Presently she is in her number 3 Productive (Accomplishment) Cycle, concluding approximately on her second Saturn return (58-59th birthday). The 3 Cycle denotes creative self-expression, communication and children. Her Third and final number 5 Cycle suggests a varied, changeable "retirement" period. Movement, activity, travel and freedom are the hallmarks of a 5 Cycle.

Ms. Six Responds to Zip

Ms. Six does not fit the traditional physical description of a "typical" Cancer woman, despite her Cancer Ascendant and stellium. Amused, Ms. Six agreed as I conducted the interview in the spacious living room of her apartment.

"Funny thing. You read usually about Cancerians being round-faced and full. I don't fit any of the physical features of the Cancerian at all. However, I love to cook; I like to work on the garden. I like pets, but I don't want the responsibility for them now, although I had them all my life — from monkeys to everything except birds. I have three storage bins filled to the brim! I once had five acres of a 5000-square-foot house with a barn."

Presently she rents an apartment by the ocean, although she will shortly leave due to the traffic noise factor when counseling clients. She prefers not to open an office. [**Update: she just purchased a small house in the vicinity**.] I then asked her if she did indeed fit the Cancerian focus of being a mother.

"I love to nurture. I adored being pregnant. I adored the birth experiencing and witnessing. And I adored my children. One son at age 32 still desperately wants his father's love, but I can let him be that way. I have an open and honest relationship with my kids. Also, when Zip mentioned idealism and wanting to be the perfect mother to perfect children, oh, yes. I did battle with that. They showed me. They turned out not to be perfect!" She smiled. I asked her to elaborate on this idealism issue and the "parent/partner" theme which Zip observed.

"I emulated to the point that one year I finally said to myself, 'I am not my mother.' I have to learn who I am and deal with it — with who I am, rather than constantly measuring myself against perfect mother because I was not going to make it. I am not going to be perfect like she is. So, therefore, it has to be OK with me not to be perfect!" Ms. Six's mother is also a 6 Life Path. Her Soul Urge is a 5; 4 Personality; 9 Name with missing 2's and 6's.

Did a "risk versus security" theme manifest in her life?

"Security has been very important to me," she answered. "Not necessarily a financial one, except in terms of my children. I always knew that I could make it in this world. It's the survivor thing. Security in my surroundings and home situation was where my security needs manifested. I was extremely domesticated."

Ms. Six admitted that, despite her tremendous mothering urge, she nevertheless was torn originally between having a family and being committed to her dancing/drama probable life direction. When she saw *Chorus Line* onstage, she felt a "top of the head regret." To conclude the Cancer theme, I asked if she was a mother to the world.

"Definitely," she concurred. "I acted as teacher, healer and house mother in institutions. I've done all three: counselor/mother/teacher."

Turning to another chart theme — perfectionism — I inquired, noting her Saturn-Vesta in Capricorn conjunction in the Virgo house, if indeed she once had the "need to do everything flawlessly."

"Very definitely," she answered vigorously. "I could not make a mistake. I was helped through that by my former associate. He would say, 'Look, it's not the first mistake you ever made in your life, and it's not going to be your last, so what's the big deal?' But oh, yes, I mustn't do things wrong. I must do them right always. But the perfectionism is not strong anymore — just a little tinge in there. I have trained myself over the last two years to not be so intense on life, to be not so exacting."

"So you were a workaholic, then?" I asked.

"Yes. I have been most of my life. Most of my life has been racing a clock. Time is an element. However, I organize and schedule properly. I don't just race around in a tangent. I'm methodical. I can be a workaholic. That's why I'm playing now, realizing that I never played before in my life. I was doing almost nothing but playing for the last two years. Now the work is creeping back in, so I have to watch it."

I scanned her chart and commented on her mutable, mental focus, including the nodes of the Moon across the third-ninth houses. She mentioned that she could lock herself up in her room for days when writing. She has written under a pseudonym.

"I've always been a reader, always been a writer, and always been a student," she confirmed. She also confirmed that she had an excellent memory when I mentioned her Mercury in Cancer conjunct Pluto being rather absorbent. Its opposition to Saturn-Vesta reflects the logical, scientific mind that she referred to earlier.

Next I asked if she was idealistic about love.

"Oh, definitely. This has been my pattern. That's still a basis for me. I've just learned to look at it differently and to accept realism about it much more healthfully than I have in the past. But I am tremendously romantic. I'm enjoying a relationship now with a man who is very romantic and satisfies that need within me."

I hypothesized a rating scale of home, mate and work. Ms. Six, after a brief deliberation, considered home/mate unity and family "...first and foremost. Then the extension of myself in my practice."

She has women friends, but dislikes hen parties. "When we are out socially, instead of joining the women talking about babies, bridge parties and shopping, I want to be over there with the men because they're talking about really interesting things. I enjoy talking with men more than women, except on a one-to-one basis with those women I have chosen."

As I concluded the interview, Ms. Six and I were again discussing the merits of hypnosis. She recounted how five years ago she underwent cosmetic surgery on her ears with the use of hypno-anesthesia.

"I had no creases in my ears. They were Dumbo ears!" she laughed. The surgeon was amazed at the drugless operation with no bleeding. In fact, Ms. Six overheard him incredulously stating, "I don't believe it!" So her associate had to return and reinstate a deep hypnotic state before Ms. Six regained full conscious awareness during the surgical procedure.

At this point, I left, resisting the inner suggestion to quip that I was indeed "entranced" by our interview!

CHAPTER TWENTY

MR. SEVEN

Introduction to Mr. Seven

Stephanie Joseph and I first met Mr. Seven on Easter Sunday, April 3, 1983. I learned about the gentleman from a monthly newsletter mailed by a New Age/metaphysical center, announcing his weekly Sunday inspirational lectures. The location of that Sunday's talk was nearby a friend's home where we enjoyed an early afternoon brunch. With time to spare, and acting on impulse, we decided to attend Mr. Seven's two o'clock service. The session was already over an hour in progress as we sheepishly tiptoed to the patio of the facilities. I donned my wool, blue sweater to brace the cool, occasionally brisk wind. The bright afternoon sun glared my vision of the two men and four women seated around the grated, circular patio table. We apologized for being late.

"It's never too late," Mr. Seven responded amiably as we sat, stroking his white bearded jaw.

His topic was "Being Spiritually High but No Earthly Good." He resumed the conclusion of the lecture with an emphasis on grace and gratitude, whether "saying grace" at meals, say, or penning "With blessings" upon the memo line of a personal check as you paid a bill. A suggested expression of gratitude was then offered: "I bless and pronounce good this bounty of my kingdom (consciousness) which I have brought forth in this hour. I dedicate this kingdom and its bounty this day and henceforth through the expression of my own loving thought, loving word and loving deed."

Thus began a weekly ongoing interaction in which I attended his lectures, both to experience his message and also to satisfy my curiosity about the speaker of the message. This latter point applied especially after he signed the release form in late April, consenting to participate as a subject for this book. I wanted to see him in action, or "live," so to speak. I also made it a practice to cassette record his lectures. Portions of the background data given in this book, in fact, were gleaned from these recordings. In the classes he would offer information when asked, or he would spontaneously portray a personal life episode as a means of illustration of some point. As a result, I probably had a greater opportunity to know Mr. Seven better than any of the other participants.

Mr. Seven's Background

Mr. Seven:

"I was born in a very well-to-do, upper-middle-class family in Ireland. My father was an interesting man. He started out his life living with his family, and then he went off to the priesthood. He quit the seminary by 'shimmying down the sheets,' to quote himself! He split the seminary while he was in Italy, and he then lived in Italy for the next seven years where he became an artist. Then he came back to live in Ireland and started his profession from there. He used to lie on his back and paint ceilings. He was a frustrated Michaelangelo! But actually, he did it very well.

"I'll give you one thing that he did, and that will sum the whole thing up. He went to his club once at Christmastime, and he won a goose in a raffle. My father was beautifully dressed and he didn't know what to do with the goose, and he couldn't find anyone who could do anything about it. So he asked the doorman at the club for a piece of string, and he tied the string to the goose's neck and dragged it home through the snow. And then he got my mother out of bed and said that the goose needed to be prepared because he wanted to take it to the orphanage the next day! So there they were, the two of them, sitting up in the middle of the night down in the kitchen preparing the goose. My mother put it in the oven, left it there, and by the time they got up later in the morning it was cooked. So he was not 'normal,' do you know what I mean? He wasn't crazy or anything, but flakey in a nice sort of way.

"So my father was a person with an artistic background. My mother was a person with a scientific background. She was a nurse — what was known in those days as a General Nurse. In addition to this, my mother was heavily into metaphysics — folk metaphysics. She knew that, generally speaking, medicine alone didn't know enough about the human body to heal it. My grandmother — my mother's mother — died before I was born, but she was the local country healer. You see, the folk religion existed side by side with the Catholic Church. The 'other-world' living was very well set in the community. My grandmother, who was a 'God-fearing' Christian, had her children collect herbs in the field, and she would boil them, mix her concoctions or whatever she did, and then went out and did her laying on of hands.

''I grew up in the last great Victorian family. My father was the head of a household that can trace its lineage back over 900 years. Our family home had been in our family for seven generations. And because I was who I was, I was known in town; not me, I was my father's son. One of the lessons I had to learn at a very young age was the recognition from who I was family-wise into being what **I** was. The whole of my orientation up to age 15 was totally based on my family position in society. My father registered me for boarding school the day I was born! That's the way it worked. He died when I was ten; he died in September and I was ten in December. If my father had lived, the chances are in human terms that today I would not be standing here. I would at this particular point in my career be getting ready to retire from the British foreign service. That's where my father saw me going. My father didn't demand that we be like him. The only thing he demanded was that he decided that by the time we were five years of age what our careers would be, and I am the only one who did not fulfill it. He wanted me to be a lawyer — an international government lawyer — and work in the foreign office in England.

''My parents expected excellence in activity and a joy in the obligation of service to others. This was the example set by them, not what they 'told' us as children. I was the youngest; I had four brothers and one sister. Our first duty in every instance was to be of service. My father instilled this in all his children, particularly the boys. You were not doing anything for yourself. You were doing it as part of the service because of who you were. My father and his father before him and his father before him raised all their children on the basis of obligation to the people. In fact, the family motto was, 'To Serve with Excellence.'

''We all had particular chores. My family job was to clean everybody's shoes and boots. That's how I got my pocket money when I was a small kid. I got six pennies per week. Two pennies went in the church basket on Sunday morning; two pennies went into savings; the last two pennies I was allowed to keep and spend.

So everybody had obligations; everybody had chores. And you had to carry them out. There was no excuse. The only reason you couldn't carry it out was because you were sick in bed. Also, once your task was assigned, there were no alternatives.

"Both parents were united in all matters related to our upbringing. You could never split my father and mother. You could never get one to say yes, and the other to say no, because as soon as you ask one, the first question was, 'Have you spoken with your father?' or 'Have you spoken with your mother?' You couldn't divide them. And they never argued in our presence. They always agreed with each other, and they never challenged each other in our presence. So, in that sense, there was no split in the discipline. My mother was not easy on me and my father tough, or my father easy and my mother tough. It didn't work that way. But the point was, what they were after was not to discipline because they 'said so'; they wanted you to discipline yourself. That was the whole object of the rearing. Problems were not encouraged. My mother never solved our problems. My mother's response was 'Life is hard. So you fell out of an apple tree? Why did you fall out of an apple tree? You can't fall out of an apple tree if you're walking along the ground. . .etc.' I learned patience the hard way as a child. My mother deliberately taught all her children to be patient. She made them wait for something that there really was no need to wait for. But her purpose was to teach them patience: You can't have this now — go do something else in the meantime! So my mother had tremendous patience, and you had to have tremendous patience around my mother! The other thing, besides patience, that I learned from my mother (who was a Scorpio/Sagittarius cusp, by the way) was to distinguish between being secretive and being discreet. My father was a perfectionist. He was a Capricorn. What did I learn from my father? Very simple: 'Always ask' if you don't know how to do something.

"The family was a united unit of common activity and team endeavor. I remember only one 'fight' in my family in all my childhood and all my teen years between two of my brothers. In one sense, I can't relate to people who talk about having problems in childhood. I don't relate to that on an intimate basis. I didn't envy anybody. I didn't want to be my brother. I didn't want to do the things my brother did. We were all very different and very independent. I'm not really sure if we were close knit. We were all so damn independent, although I was the maverick in the family. We were not close emotionally; we were only close physically. And I would say for me it worked out fine. You see, we were taught very young not to be emotionally dependent. Emotional relationships were very low on the scale in my family. That's how we related. We were never dependent on our mother. She didn't take care of all our needs. Most of our needs were taken care of by the people who worked for my parents. Therefore, she didn't play the role that is apparently expected of a mother in America. We didn't have that sort of a mother. Yes, we went out with our parents; we took walks, we made trips, various things like that. But my mother did not take care of us in that sense.

"My education started at home. I started with a tutor from age four to six. From age six I went to a regular day school. Then I went to boarding school from age eleven until I was seventeen. Why would I object? You went to school. You had no choice. And you were expected to do well in school. And you did do well in school. You paid attention. You learned.

"Now, I had a lot of information on my previous incarnation when I was a child because I came in very open. [**In his previous incarnation he was telepathic on a sporadic, hit-and-miss basis, but his clairvoyant ability flowered right at the start of this incarnation**.] I had the kind of parents, particularly the kind of mother, who didn't block what I was expressing. It was, 'Yes, yes, dear. We all have it' kind of attitude, not 'Oh, gee. He's wonderful,' or 'He's a freak!' Instead it was, 'Yes, yes. I know . . . Now did you do your homework? Have you cleaned your shoes?' That's where my mother was with it. It was totally acceptable to her. But I had a great problem as a child sometimes in knowing how to deal with some of my memories because what I would do, I would start to tell something and I would suddenly realize that the people had gone silent because obviously I had lied. But I was telling the truth because I was talking about my childhood in the previous incarnation. And it took me a little while to get the filing cabinet organized.

"I think what helped me at a very early age when I was about five years old, a lady came to visit my mother. She visited regularly; she was a friend of the family. And she visited one afternoon to have tea after we've just been back from a vacation. And the lady came in, said hello to my mother, and before she could say anything to me, I said, 'Yes, thank you. We had a wonderful holiday!' A little while later my mother gave me the best put-down she ever gave me the whole of her life. She said, 'I know very well you knew what she was going to say, but it is still polite to allow her to ask the question before you give the answer.' I mean, she put the psychic thing in perspective for me right away. I've never forgotten that. To her, she was not impressed with my psychic ability; she was very impressed with my lack of good manners! I was not aware, incidentally, at that particular time that I was doing anything that anybody else didn't do. I thought all kids did it. It wasn't until much later in school that I found out other kids couldn't do some of the things I could do. In fact, I got my nose punched over it! That really taught me. I kept saying, 'Yes, you can! Everybody can do this!' This other kid got really mad because he couldn't do it, so he punched me in the nose! I shouldn't have argued with this kid anyway. He was about three sizes bigger than I was. It shows you I wasn't very bright!

"From a very early age I had an awareness of what my destiny in this life was. When I was still only five years old, I went into the dining room, took all the chairs away from the dining room table, and arranged all these chairs in the dining room. Then I climbed up on a stool and was giving a speech to the chairs! My mother came home, and I had to put all the chairs away and spend the rest of the afternoon in my room 'meditating'!

[**Mr. Seven has a seriously impaired left leg, although he now limply walks without a cane.**] "My present disability dates back to when I was fifteen years old. I had a very bad automobile accident. I was riding a bicycle and I was hit by a car. And the gentleman who hit me apparently had been to the golf course on that Sunday morning at ten o'clock, and by four o'clock in the afternoon he played his eighteen holes at the bar. I went across a green light around four-thirty or five o'clock, and the guy who hit me, he didn't even know there was an intersection, let alone a light. The first time he saw me was when I was lying on top of his hood looking through the windshield at him. However, the end of that story is that it cured him of his drinking, and it put him in a mental home, which is kind of sad.

"They put me in a hospital, and I was medically unconscious until, I believe, Wednesday evening. During my period of alleged unconsciousness, I had what was known as an involuntary out-of-body experience with the recognition of personal immortality. I just found myself suddenly poised above looking at the bed and a group of people standing around it, with one of them holding my wrist. I was dying, apparently. Medically, I was dying. Because the nun said I was almost gone, I decided right then I wasn't going anywhere. Incidentally, I didn't hear her saying it. I was aware of her saying it, but I didn't hear it. It was almost like reading her thoughts than hearing her voice. At the same moment, I also made the recognition that that was my body on the bed. Listen to the language: that is my body, not 'that is me.' At that moment I became aware that my body and I were not the same. I was sort of eight or ten feet back. And the next thing, I made the recognition that if that's my body, then I exist independently of my body. The next part of my out-of-body experience I can't tell anybody, not even my nearest and dearest. Thirty-five minutes later I came back. I didn't ask anything that night. The following morning when the nun came around for her rounds, I said, 'I'd like to talk to you privately, Sister.' [**She returned twenty minutes later and Mr. Seven recounted his experience of remembering, in his out-of-body state, her stating that he was almost gone**.] I knew she was agitated because she started to play with her beads! She decided that this was a job for a priest, and when I spoke to the priest about it, he almost asked to be moved to the foreign missions! He was a regular, secular clergyman attached to a local parish church, and he was appointed to the local hospital as a chaplain. He was a great guy to come in and pat you on the back and say you're getting well, and that you'll be up to play football next week. Marvelous. But as far as spiritual guidance and theology was concerned, forget it. He knew the Ten Commandments, I guess, and that was it. Fortunately I found my 'guru,' to put it in those terms. But that was the death of my fear. When you have that experience and suddenly realize, 'Hey that's my body, and I'm not dependent on my body,' and you follow this up with many years of research, examination and meditation, and put it all together, you recognize that there's nothing to fear.

"In the hospital, I decided I wasn't going anywhere in response to a nun. But following that is a closed chapter in which there was another communication which was not on the earth level. As far as I am prepared to say, it necessitated a decision. There was a job to do sometime, now or later. It's not quite the realm of choice. It's more a round of sequence. What you can do, you can take a vacation now, and when you've finished your vacation, you can put your nose on the grindstone. Sometime or another you're going to have to damn well do it! Despite what Tony Newley says in his play and musical, 'Stop the World, I Want to Get Off,' you can't. So what you can do, you can slow down or delay a particular assignment. But we're all here for the duration! There's no going back. We've all come into this incarnation, and every incarnation, with assignments — not given us, but assumed by us. Some of us are only in the stage where we are only learning in this incarnation to be what we'll really be in the next incarnation. Our assignment at this particular stage is to be in school.

"Let me give you an example from my own experience. You can take it as valid or invalid as you choose. In my immediate previous incarnation, I had a tremendous desire to be a teacher. But at that time I wasn't looking to be a spiritual teacher. I wanted to be a teacher in a regular school. In the family I then belonged to, one did not go to work. The sons of gentlemen didn't work. They hunted, they fished, they wenched — but they didn't work. So I was not allowed by my family to become a teacher. Well, fortunately or unfortunately, the 1914-1918 World War intervened. And like all patriotic people at the time, I rushed off. Dummy! And, of course, like all brave young men (they were expected to be brave and collect medals as part of the deal), I was interested in getting medals. And in order to get a medal I got myself 'killed.' The only thing, I took two other soldiers with me that didn't need to be taken. I was a young first lieutenant, and I took a sergeant and a private with me. Totally uselessly. It was an absolutely stupid move. I took them to stop, I think, a German battalion. So I didn't make it as a teacher at that time, but I did this time. Yet for many long years, probably until I was about 33-34 — which is a long time, a couple of centuries! — I carried in my consciousness a knowledge of my previous incarnation, and also some of the acts during that incarnation which, 'karmically' speaking, was the cause of my mishap in this incarnation. During those years I made extremely good physical progress. But when I made the recognition that there was no enduring connection between the two, my physical progress accelerated. Medically speaking, that 'shouldn't' have happened — but it did. I function better today than I did when I was thirty, physically. We are what we believe ourselves to be.

[After boarding school, Mr. Seven attended a university for five years, graduating with an M. A. in sociology and a D.D. in theology-philosophy. During this period, he continued his investigative work in the occult and enrolled in the extracurricular college of psychic science within the university. Between 1942-1946 he worked in executive government service, principally a wartime administration job with the government. Concurrently he was persuaded to teach two sociology classes a week at another university. He also taught separate classes on metaphysical/spiritual subjects, as requested by the students. In May 1945 he married his first wife, but in early autumn 1953, they divorced.]

"She was an artist. In fact, I married an artist's artist. She was a puppeteer, made her own puppets, put on her own puppet plays, was a portrait painter, and a child photographer. So you know, I married my father! My first wife had a wanderlust — not for men; just a wanderlust. While we were married she took off and went to Spain with a donkey and traveled through Spain, doing puppet shows in villages. She was right to do that, and I wanted her to do that, and I admired her for doing it. But I felt that I was a limitation to her. I was because, when she was in Spain, she was feeling guilty. Then she went to India to do something similar, and she was feeling guilty. She felt that she should be home. We had a parting of the ways. There was no enmity. . . . It was an intellectual relationship, by the way. We were both heavily intellectual at that time."

[In 1946 Mr. Seven went to France to work as a United Nations correspondent for a year, employed by a newspaper. He returned to the British Isles to eventually work as a lobby correspondent until 1952, functioning as an interviewer and features' writer. He then moved directly into the self-development field, being self-employed up to the present moment. In 1952 he cofounded a "residential self-development center."]

"The center was situated at a manor house — a fifteenth century country manor house — in England. It had 36 rooms and stood on 155-acre grounds. I stayed with the organization for three years. I was one of the founders, but I was not interested in continuing the work. I felt I had done what I needed to do. It was an eclectic organization because we were taking the best of everything and blending them. We were also publishing at the same time. Then I went into full-time individually organized lecturing and so forth — exactly what I'm doing right now. I used an agent for part of the field work, but he didn't get all my work, only probably two-thirds of my work. The others came by referral. I did this from 1955 to 1962 primarily in the British Isles. From time to time I would take limited assignments on a consultant basis with individual companies and maybe stay with them for three months while we put the program together. I did a lot of radio and television work. I also did some feature writing, articles for newspapers and magazines, primarily in the area of self-development. Then I came to the United States for the first time in June 1962. There were all sorts of reasons for moving, but primarily I was responding to my own inspiration.

[He married his present wife of thirty years duration in December 1953. She is a Sun in Capricorn and works as an accountant and financial consultant for a prestigious financial consultant service. They have a son born in 1956, also a

Sun in Capricorn.]

"We have all chosen a lifestyle. I knew that my job was sort of a teaching role. I selected to teach. I haven't selected to just teach from my own home, sit back in my living room, and have people walk through the living room and then out the back! I've also made the recognition that I must go places. In other words, I actually made a joke years ago in the early sixties. I was talking with somebody, and I said, 'Have Speech, Will Travel.' Boy, I should never have said that! You wouldn't believe it, but within three months I had invitations from people and organizations that I never even knew existed. But the point was, having made that statement that I was prepared to do that, all the facilities to do so were provided: the car, the money to buy gas, buildings were put at my disposal, people were prepared to do things to make it work."

[Between June 1962 and the end of 1964, Mr. Seven was kept busy with various matters, as well as adjusting to his first years in the United States. In 1965 he collaborated with several other professionals and staff members of a prestigious East Coast university, engaged in a special drug rehabilitation program for college dropouts. Meditation techniques were utilized in the program, and Mr. Seven taught twice a week for two years at a twenty-four room mansion on five-acre grounds donated for the holistic drug-rehabilitation program. Currently it is a college of psychic science. Also in 1965, Mr. Seven was invited to do a popular radio program in Philadelphia. On one of the shows he met a young male psychic, which foreshadowed a long-time working collaboration.]

"We discovered that by bouncing off each other we could magnify what both of us did. We both became better at what we did by bouncing off each other. We did several programs like that. Then we had an idea. We decided we would go out and try to do what we had done on the radio show in a public auditorium. First of all, we would talk and lecture and answer questions on ESP, and then we would demonstrate. In that sense, it started to get 'theatrical.' In 1969 we put an entirely new program together which we did at the Fillmore East in New York. We put on a multimedia program including New Age music with a band, film, 14,000 slides with a three-screen, backscreen projection, and 'psychic demonstration.' That worked well and it hit the stars. We didn't know it would take off the way it did in terms of audience response. Then in the following year, he and I collaborated to write a whole new production which was called 'Occultism in the 70s.'"

[During this general period Mr. Seven also worked in prisons teaching inmates meditation techniques. He continued his lecture tours and private counseling. In terms of characteristics and interests, he discontinued smoking 25 years ago, and is a vegetarian. Besides once owning German shepherd dogs, another interest was collecting and restoring antique furniture. Recently he hosted his own brief radio show. Currently, Mr. Seven has completed a book based on his esoteric lectures.]

Numerological Analysis

Of the four names bestowed upon Mr. Seven at birth, the rundown of his major number patterns is as follows:

Soul Urge (vowels sum)	=	11/2
Personality (consonants sum)	=	3
Name/Expression (name sum)	=	5
Life Path (month/day/year sum)	=	1

The 2 Soul Urge (how Mr. Seven identifies or sees himself) suggests a strong relationship orientation, whether viewed astrologically as Libran partnership or as the Cancerian nurturing/dependency expression. Sylvia sees the 2 as more the Cancerian security focus, baby or mother. Nevertheless, both Cancer and Libra want closeness and relationship, although Libra represents the equal partnership theme of togetherness. However the number 2 is interpreted, it is a focus on wanting to be involved in some type of relationship; the Other is intimately associated with Self, wanting to share and to care. It is the number of pairing, duality and polarization (male-female, positive-negative, etc.). The 2 Soul Urge characteristically wants union, cooperation, harmony, peace and comfort in relating. It is interesting to note that Mr. Seven's Mars, as a key to identity, is in the sign of partnership, Libra.

Unreduced to a prime number, Mr. Seven's Soul Urge would be number 11, the higher vibration, in one sense, of the number 2. This "master number" can be viewed as a transmutation of the energy of the number 2 once that vibration or principle has itself been mastered. In other terms, the principle of the 2 is personal/interpersonal, while the principle of number 11 is unmistakably transpersonal (Aquarius-Uranus-eleventh house/Pisces-Neptune-twelfth house mixture). Number 11 is related to inspirational knowledge, ESP, illumination, intuition, and perhaps spiritual discipleship. Stephanie mentioned that its vibration can manifest as rising above the common human condition through the practice of meditation. **Any** person with any number vibration can benefit from meditation, but the number 11 vibration may characteristically utilize it as a natural "high." True to its astrological parallel of Mr. Seven's Neptune rising, number 11 can also be unrealistic, dreamy and too idealistic. If its constructive potential is channeled, Mr. Seven can indeed become a "master" in some manner.

His Personality vibration (outer expression, how other people see him or how he impresses them) is the number 3. Stephanie, herself a 3 Personality, spoke on its meaning: "He's got a 3 Personality, which is one of the nicest Personality numbers one could possibly have! It can even be more expressive than a 5 because the 3 is the number of joy, happiness, good times, theater, dramatics, communication, and the person usually expresses himself or herself very well. They often dress well, and they have a pleasant demeanor about them." Sylvia added that his 3 Personality shows the ability to express a highly creative side of his nature, into talking, enjoying himself, being childlike or childish, depending on his state of maturity. As the number of self-expression, the 3 adds to social proclivities, wanting to communicate, enhancing the 2 Soul Urge. And since the 3 refers to the mouth, it can even indicate a person focused into related indulgences: eating, gossiping, etc.

Sylvia then commented on his 5 Name/Expression: "The 5 Name indicates that he is a very freedom-loving person in some way. It can show a very attractive man with a lot of sexual energy; wanting to go, wanting to experience his physical body and five senses." The Name or Expression number denotes your prime overall vibration, or personal energy pattern. Most numerologists agree that it represents talents and latent action, how best or naturally you express yourself.

Esoterically, number 5 is the number of "Man" (male and female) or humanity — e.g., the five senses, the occult "5th" principle of mind or *manas* (Sk., the root of "Man" as thinker); and, the five principles of humanity, the microcosm: Atma (will), Buddhi (love-wisdom), Manas (mind-intelligence), Astral (emotions-desire), and Sthula (physical). The pentagram, or five-pointed star, is often the glyph used in depicting humanity — i.e., the head, the two outstretched arms and two outstretched legs. In occult philosophy, an Initiate of the Fifth Degree is the Aseka Adept, or master of esoteric knowledge, a perfected man. A less idealistic expression (inversion) of the number 5 is typified by the unenlightened materialism of this number of humanhood — egoism, license, competition, indulgence in excesses, possessiveness. A "higher" expression in terms of good humanhood is constructive freedom in earthly pursuits and quality of earth living combined with rich quantity. For the Initiate, the ultimate freedom keynote of number 5 would be spiritual freedom, the state of pure consciousness unencumbered by material limitations. But the normal keynote of number 5, however, is changes, movement, freedom, travel and variety (not ignoring, as mentioned earlier, the sexual/sensual aspect of number 5). It is also the number of the salesperson, public relations, people contact and the platform speaker (especially adding number 3 to its energy).

Mr. Seven's Life Path number is 1. The Life Path, once again, is primarily one's growth goal or destiny. It is considered by most numerologists as the most important major number because it is unchangeable; you cannot go to a court of law to change the fact of your date of birth, unlike your legal name. The Life Path shows your basic life direction which needs to be materialized in action. If you are missing that particular number in your name, then it may mean a greater challenge in satisfactorily manifesting the principle of that number.

"The 1 Life Path shows that he came into the world to stand on his own two feet," Sylvia commented, "to be an independent person, and to pay more attention to his own needs rather than to see himself exclusively through the other person. So he acts with the 2 Soul Urge, seeing himself involved with the other person, and yet the 1 Life Path indicates that he has come in to learn how to be by himself and do his own thing."

However, as Stephanie stressed, "It may not be difficult for him because he is a strong personality since he does have five 1's in his name. That can be an ego problem with many 1's, but he still has the strength he needs to be independent. A 1 Life Path is usually someone who needs to be a leader, someone who can start things, take pioneer action, opening up new vistas and doorways, and then go on to other things."

Attention was then placed upon Mr. Seven's Inclusion Table (a table derived from the letters in a name which totals the quantity of each letter value). He possesses all of his numbers which, according to our two numerologists, can mean boredom and the inner drive to manifest an almost undefinable "more" in life. This can signify either a more materialistic or "worldly" manifestation, or it can mean being bored with what the mundane world has to offer (especially to a major "11" or "22" individual), therefore expanding one's options in nonmaterialistic ways. At any rate, he does not innately lack some sort of functional understanding of each of the nine numbers or principles or "boxes" in the Inclusion Table (representing areas of life activity).

Inclusion Table

5	1	4	I	10
1	5	2	We	8
3	4	5	They	12
P	E	M		
9	10	11		

Five 1's reinforces the dominant number 5 principle expressed in his Name: the freedom aspect, ego, sexual magnetism, changes and travel, etc.

One 2 suggests an understanding of women, the feminine principle, and getting along with other people — although perhaps on his own terms (principle of number 1 in the area of number 2). As Sylvia commented, "The one 2 shows the ability to make friends and enter relationships on his own terms, and being identified in the relationship as a person who has his own ego and his own identity."

Four 3's in his name connects the theme of structure, order, discipline and work with the theme of communication, creativity and fun. This can manifest as being detailed and efficient in the functioning of his concrete mind (e.g., astrologically correlated by his Virgo Moon in his third house); being boxed in or critical/judgmental about his creative, communicative abilities; critical, flaw-finding, sarcastic speech; imbalance or balance regarding work, play and recreation, etc.

One 4 shows an understanding of the male principle, order/form/structure, and the capacity to be self-disciplined, although in his own way (the number 1 principle).

Five 5's again reemphasizes his major number 5 theme. Astrologically, it can conceivably be tied in with his Sun (Leo principle) in its own house in the freedom sign of Sagittarius (freedom aspect of number 5 in numerological terms). Again it shows the vibration of someone wanting freedom to come and go, wanting to express himself physically in travel, sex or sensuality. It is a double-freedom emphasis.

Two 6's modifies Mr. Seven's freedom disposition and strengthens his 2 Soul Urge expression. Two 6's really needs a partner, desiring to share responsibilities rather than facing life alone. It can sometimes mean passivity — e.g., let the marriage partner handle the finances, say. Sylvia added an observation: "In many ways we can see him hopping back and forth between wanting a partner, wanting the other person in his life for whatever reasons versus the attitude, 'I can do it by myself; I can stand on my own two feet.' So he can be caught between those two polar aspects of his life.''

Three 7's in Mr. Seven's name connects the lower mind and communication theme with the area of the higher mind, study and spirituality. There is an inherent ambivalence in that combination since number 3 is normally open, expressive and communicative while number 7 is often meditative and reclusive, preferring silence to chatter. The key, of course, is balance and moderation, or to blend them constructively — e.g., enjoying to communicate (the 3 principle of pleasure and talking) on higher aspects of life, such as philosophy, religion, metaphysics. But that combination often suggests a natural pleasure to communicate what one knows, and/or enjoying to learn ''superior'' studies.

Four 8's connects the work/discipline/limitation theme with the area of money, power, authority. This can manifest as being critical/judgmental about those in position of authority and control; burdens or responsibility in handling money, or even wealth; illness or disability in one's functioning or learning efficient functioning; working hard for financial security or for authority, etc. The 4/8 combinations are often inhibitive or serious, similar to Capricorn/Scorpio combinations.

Five 9's unites two travel letters together, wanting to be free (number 5) in the world (number 9). World travel is suggested; scattering is possible since both numbers are restless movement numbers. If number 5 is expressed on a higher level in terms of the ''initiate,'' as given earlier, then humanitarianism and being a world/spiritual teacher is possible. (The 5/9 combination is also often associated with flight attendants.)

Mr. Seven's birthday (the 14th) also reduces into the number 5. The Birthday number is a subsidiary expression similar to the Life Path, but nevertheless an important indicator of character. An analysis of the unreduced Birthday number is subject to various interpretations and theories. Number 14, however, contains the subemphasis of its components (numbers 1 and 4), adding their coloration to the overall vibration of number 5 (freedom and change).

Next, Stephanie concentrated on the sum totals of the rows and columns in the Inclusion Table format: ''In the Physical Column (boxes 1, 4, 7) he's got a 9 which is someone out in the world, perhaps preaching and teaching; negatively, he can act as a martyr. He's got a 10 in the Emotional Column (boxes 2, 5, 8) which means that he can be very emotionally intense, overwhelming, dominant, powerful.

The 11 in the Mental (boxes 3, 6, 9) is someone who can be very inspirational or idealistic. He has a 10 in the Individual or 'I' Row (boxes 1, 2, 3), another way of saying that he can be famous, well known in some respect. The 8 in the Family Row (boxes 4, 5, 6) shows the power and the authority he may want in that area or experienced in the past. The 12 in the World Row (boxes 7, 8, 9), similar to 9 in the Physical, shows that he's there for the world, that he is making himself known."

Natal Imprint

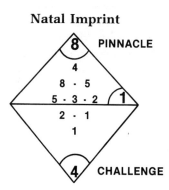

Let us now consider briefly Mr. Seven's Natal Imprint pattern (the baseline and Pinnacles and Challenges derived from his month/day/year of birth). Since he is of foreign birth, the day is recorded first on the birth certificate, the month next, then the year, forming the 5-3-2 baseline (= 1 Life Path). Mr. Seven, once again, was born December 14, 1919. As seen in the illustration, number 8 is prominent in the overall pattern with two 8's in the Environment (or Pinnacles above the baseline); also number 4 plays a role in connection with the 8's. Physical limitations, illness or inner restraint is often associated with the 4/8 combination. On another level, power in one's work, self-imposed order and structure, and self-discipline may be suggested. The number 5 Pinnacle added to that combination suggests changes and freedom in one's work, and perhaps fluctuations in power, authority and money. The 2-1-1 Challenge pattern implies sensitivity in relationships; personal self-will and independence may be challenged. Again it reinforces Mr. Seven's major numbers duality — his 2 Soul Urge counterbalancing the 1 Life Path, or the Self-Other polarity.

At this writing (November 1983), Mr. Seven, age 63, is presently in the last few months of his number 1 Personal Year (6 + 3 + 1 Life Path = 1), which inaugurated a new nine-year cycle beginning on his birthday, December 14, 1982. Since Mr. Seven is a 1 Life Path, the 1 Personal Year accentuates the desirability to plant seeds for this new cycle, to set a new creative process in motion. It is a year of new beginnings, new directions, a fresh start of a cycle. Looking at the Personal Year imprint in the illustration, 9/3 is the first Pinnacle and Challenge of his 1 Personal Year, spanning the four-month period from his 1982 birthday until April 14, 1983. Including its baseline numbers, the overall pattern is a 6/3, 9/3.

Year Imprint

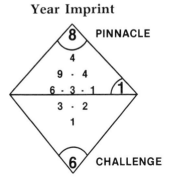

Sylvia elaborated on that pattern: "We see this very creative pattern, but he might have had some sort of a problem with communication, or maybe not being as happy or comfortable as he wanted to be." The next four months until August 14 is symbolized by the 4 Pinnacle and 2 Challenge. "Then we have the ability to be focused on work and home," Sylvia continued, "but being rather sensitive, caught up in a relationship, having to deal with the other person in a sensitive way."

Returning to his natal baseline numbers (5-3-2 = 1 Life Path), Mr. Seven is presently in his 2 Final Cycle — i.e., his third baseline number (2). The Final Cycle usually begins around the second Saturn return (approximately age 59). Mr. Seven's second Saturn return occurred in mid-1979.

"A 2 in the last cycle of life is not a very active period," Stephanie concluded. "It's more or less someone who's starting to wind down, sit back and enjoy the fruits of their labor, or work in comfort." It can also indicate a greater emphasis on staying at home base, being closer in partnership and relationships, into comfort and security.

Mr. Seven Responds to Zip

Mr. Seven sipped his brewed tea and leaned back snugly into his armchair. His whitish hair and trimmed beard contrasted sharply against his black shirt and slacks. He waited alertly as I prepared to ask him questions regarding Zip's analysis of his horoscope. I scanned my notes and began with an inquiry of why he previously commented that Zip's observation of his "search for ultimates" was only approximate or off-center.

"I'm not **driven**," he replied. "I don't have to teach; I don't have to write. That's what I do. That's why I took 20% off. I have no problem in goofing off!"

I looked at him quizzically. Didn't he mention earlier that he felt he had to accomplish a mission? That his destiny was to teach? Wasn't he, in that sense, driven by that purpose?

"Not now," he answered. "Not any more I don't. At one period

I thought it was. And I want you now to hear me with your golden ear on this: it really doesn't matter to me if I don't go to teach on Sunday. I'll go, and I'll enjoy going, and I'll enjoy being there. But if something were to intervene, it's OK. No, I don't have goals anymore in that sense.

"At one time, like a lot of other people who get in the 'unfoldment business,' I went through the phase that I had a mission or a task or a destiny. We have a lot of fancy words to describe it. I don't have that any more. I haven't had that for years. I guess it probably came to an end in the early seventies — from the time I came to California, without a doubt. I mean, I was quite prepared to sit on the beach for the rest of my life and watch the girls go by! The only thing I do now, I do what I am **asked** to do. So my only goal, in that sense, is to do what I am asked to do. You see, they ask me to do the lectures; I don't ask them. And if it turns out that we're not going to have it, fine. Marvelous. I'll read a book; I'll go shopping with my wife; I'll listen to music; I'll take a walk. Whatever I do, I'll enjoy that. It's almost living each moment as it comes."

"What gives you real pleasure in life?" I asked.

He paused. "This is going to sound very strange: everything I do," he replied, intently. He had listed "music and theater" as interests in the completed questionnaire.

"If I go to the theater, I enjoy it; if I don't go to it, I'm not sorry. I don't miss it. If I watch a TV show, I enjoy it; if it's not something that I would want to enjoy, I don't watch it. I enjoy everything I do, otherwise I don't do it. It's the same about eating. I eat what I enjoy, and the other things I don't eat."

His response led me to ask a relevant question: If indeed he is living moment to moment, did Mr. Seven integrate his former high aims with the limits of reality, as Zip suggested?

"Zip is right on that. Very accurate. I think now in terms of comfort and convenience. I pursue comfort — and I don't mean luxury. I pursue **not** being pressured. I pursue being comfortable in what I'm doing whenever I'm doing it. I think I made a crack once in class: if I have to hurry to do it, I don't do it. I don't run. We were taught as children not to run. You only ran when you were in the area of recreation or play. Not only did you walk, you walked slowly. We always left in more time than it was necessary to get there. We never had to rush. Our church was fifteen minutes from our house, and we left a half an hour before the beginning of the service. On the way there was time to pause and look at the clouds, listen to the birds. 'Oh, did you hear that?...Be quiet a moment...Isn't that beautiful, boys?' So I guess it's the pursuit of comfort and ease, which comes down metaphysically as the maintenance of harmony, the flow of harmony.''

In terms of value systems, is that one of Mr. Seven's priorities, then?

''We only have one priority in life: to remember who we are at all times — 'I Am. . .I shall not have strange gods before me,' as Scripture says it. There is only One Source of all expression. Secondarily to that is being prudent in our commitments. You never make a commitment unless you're 1000% certain of being able to fulfill it. You'd be better to say, 'I don't know; I will talk to you later; let me check that out.'

''I had a problem at one time with commitments to other people. I was what my mother had referred to — silver-tongued! 'Oh, yes, yes! I'll take care of that.' Do 28 hours work in 24 hours. So I made commitments I was not able to fulfill. In other words, I opened mouth and inserted foot! I was not able to fulfill them and thereby suffered by not doing so. I didn't realize what I was doing at the time, and I learned the process of what happens when you promise or commit and don't fulfill it. When I commit to you, I commit to God. It's as simple as that. You cannot expect to commit to God, so to speak, and break the commitment, and then expect God to commit to you and not break it. You can't expect to commit to life, break it, and then expect life to still deliver. So I was the one who said, 'I'll take care of it!' I was the volunteer. I would do anything. Unfortunately, most of us get out of it by breaking our commitments. That's when we get into trouble because now what we have aborted is the creative process. Then we say, 'Nothing goes right with me anymore.' The reason is because you've had too many abortions. So now my hand never goes up; I never volunteer, and most of the time I say no. I don't even say I'm sorry. I say, No, I'm not prepared to do that.''

I asked Mr. Seven to elaborate on this issue.

''At one time, the world needed me, and only me, to save it,'' he recounted, amused. ''There was nobody else. Obviously. I was **the** Atlas, not an atlas. **The**. The man! And incidentally, with no helpers! I solved that in the early sixties. I was on the Maryland turnpike, beating it down to Baltimore on a Tuesday afternoon. I pulled up at one of the restaurant rest centers there. While I was sitting there I saw this guy come rushing in. He wanted a take-out order, and he was looking nervously at his watch: 'I want six coffees and four sandwiches. Make it quick, will you?!' And I looked at this guy, and I said, 'Wait a minute. I do that!' But I do it on a different level. By the time I went back in my car on the turnpike, I was changed — a change in consciousness. What I did was cut my schedule in half. I made the decision that I was not going to take on any additional commitments, and I was also going to complete as easily and as quickly and as smoothly and as kindly as possible such commitments I had with people at that particular time.

"So I guess my mission," he continued, summing up, "was just to help, and that my job was sort of a teaching role. I now know why I chose parents because there I was really disciplined and drilled into help and service. That's why I chose them. And you move into a sign vibration according to your individual needs. Let me give you an example. I happen to know the birth data of my previous incarnation. What I really needed to develop were two things: One was perfection of expression, and the other was patience. I've knocked the patience, and I'm now starting on the perfection of expression. But in order to do that, I came into a condition of incarnation in which I have my Moon in Virgo. That gives me the opportunity to work on the perfection of expression. I'm also a Sun in Sagittarius and Leo rising which gives me tremendous energy to do the perfection work."

What does "perfection of expression" mean to Mr. Seven?

"I think the easiest way I can answer you is the coming into the awareness of what the soul needs and not what the body wants — or the 'me,' the personality. What we're really concerned with in an individual incarnation is entering at the point of time and space and relationship which provides the opportunity to do that which is the next step of growth in our ongoing soul evolution."

As given earlier, Mr. Seven's awareness of his previous immediate incarnation had its roots during early childhood. When he was in his late teen years, he began to comb parish records to check the accuracy of his childhood memories of the past life. Chiefly through regression, he determined the identity of that incarnation, verified by local records. In the previous life he was born English in 1887. I have the date and place of that incarnation's birth, but no precise time is available. However, both Sun and Mars are in Aries in a wide conjunction. The fascinating aspect of that incarnation's numerological pattern with Mr. Seven's is that the four major numbers (Soul Urge, Personality, Name, Life Path) are **exactly** the same. The baseline and Inclusion Table are different, as to be expected. In this lifetime, Mr. Seven assumed the vibration of a Mars in Libra rather than its polar opposite, Aries.

"Aries is tremendously impulsive," Mr. Seven explained. "Aries rushes in where fools fear to tread, not just angels! But I had two delightful Aries women help me deal with it in this life. One was a developed or progressed Aries, the other not developed at all. They provided me with an almost vicarious opportunity to deal with my own Aries. When I would look at one of these ladies, I would say, 'Oh, so **that** is what I do.' "

With the Aries (impatience) issue resolved, this left, as Mr. Seven mentioned, the need to establish "perfection of expression." As a teacher and counselor of spiritual psychology and mysticism, the method of purification or perfection was chosen: identifying the three-dimensional personality ("me") with its "I" or multidimensional Higher Self, which in turn is the microcosmic expression of the Macrocosm (God, Universe). Mr. Seven's philosophy follows the ancient *gnostic* tradition or belief that we are essentially spiritual beings (immortal, eternal, free) descended or expressed in bodily form (lower or denser vibratory manifestation). "Man" (male and female) is the prodigal son (personality or Lower Self) who ventures off in a pilgrimage (evolutionary stages of development, twelvefold Zodiacal Cycle of Life) into the "far country" of the manifested worlds. Stated differently, humanity is the "seed" planted on the Earth, destined to fully unfold (manifest, actualize) inherent deific Power and Life. This is achieved through the process of reincarnation (successive bodily lives) connected by karma (cause and effect). Thus the goal is to awaken to one's true identity and to establish conscious oneness with God.

Such a philosophy could loosely be termed Theosophia, the Ageless Wisdom, Brahmavidya, etc. It holds that each individual, as a microcosmic reflection of Deity ("Word made flesh") is a god-in-the-becoming, an embryo deity meant to manifest potentiality as actuality, latency of divinity into potency of divinity; learning the art of manifestation that the Macrocosm displays as the Universe. However, lost in the roles within the earth drama, caught up in the externals of phenomenal existence (maya, the world of effects), Man as human being (Prodigal Son) has temporarily forgotten his or her spiritual origin and heritage and has become lost in the illusion of separated self-existence (Sk. *"Ahamkara"* or "false sense of I"). As a result, Mr. Seven continually advocates the practice of meditation (true yoga), or "practicing the Presence," as a method of achieving conscious, if but temporary, union with one's Higher Self (and ultimately God). Perfection of expression, then, would steadily increase as one's self becomes more and more integrated or unified.

"It is important to communicate to all," Mr. Seven wrote in the open statement section at the end of the questionnaire, "that God is individual consciousness and that it becomes creative individually when we become aware of this fact."

On this point, Mr. Seven offered an invocation in class: "I surrender body, mind and soul here and now. Let there not be me and mine, but thy alone be now me." Mr. Seven continued: "You say, 'Be thou me' because then the me becomes **perfected**, and the me now doesn't have any problems because the 'I' is now in total charge."

Hence, the overriding dynamic of Mr. Seven's behavior appears to be the personal identification with the infinite (astrologically represented by Neptune, key to the ultimate, conjunct his Ascendant). The key is right identification: **not** "I am expressing as God, and I can do anything I will," but rather, "God is expressing through me as an individualized being." In other words, **you** are not expressing as God; God is expressing **as** you. Mr. Seven refers to this as being God-in-action, and the primary conscious method of tapping into the Source is meditation. Meditation, simply put, is the art of being still and receptive, listening to the inner voice within. Perfection of expression (manifestation) would be far more likely if you meditate before you take important action in the outer world. A special stance toward living then ensues: "I am in the world but not of it," which becomes the key to practical spiritual living. In other words, instead of the "me" being a helpless victim in the world of creations, the "me" now identifies itself as the "I" which is the creator of its creations in time/space. By assuming responsibility for your creations **consciously**, you then learn to perfect the nature of your creations or manifestations.

Joel S. Goldsmith, a now deceased, modern Jewish mystic whom Mr. Seven holds in high esteem, defines mysticism in his book, *Conscious Union with God*: "The true meaning of mysticism is any philosophy or religion that teaches oneness with God." I asked Mr. Seven if he was always involved with mysticism and intuition, despite his psychic performance background.

"I think I was more involved in the mystical aspect in this incarnation than what people normally refer to as the psychic. I pursued mystical knowledge rather than pursued psychic ability. Yes, I stood up on a stage and demonstrated it, but my psychic ability works best on a one-to-one basis in consultation. But the psychic tends to be confined to events, more often catastrophe than anything else. Unfortunately, most people who start to discover their psychic ability tend to look for forecasting, foreseeing the future; whereas being intuitive is knowing what to do next."

Does he nevertheless check his progressions or transits for his own life?

"I no longer involve myself in any of the so-called occult sciences in my personal activity," Mr. Seven replied, matter-of-factly. "I used to take very close note of my biorhythm chart, my numerological chart, my astrology chart. The only thing I still do is buy Llewellyn's astrological calender. I may glance at that from time to time just for personal reference. I'm quite capable of functioning without those tools. I always know what to do next." Recently, however, because he was involved as a case study for this book, he has briefly inquired about his progressed chart.

My attention was then fixed upon Zip's analysis of the family relatedness issue, especially in connection with marriage. On one level, Mr. Seven felt that the issue of teamwork was a close mark in Zip's interpretation, but the "emotional" bonding was considered only weakly approximate.

Mr. Seven explained. "It seemed that it was talking about close relationship, but this is not a closely related family. Therefore, it is only approximate. My wife is totally independent. She's not dependent on me and I'm not dependent on her. She makes very good money. She's a very competent and skilled lady. In fact, she can function very well without me at any time. That's what makes the relationship good."

I noted the freedom/closeness issue mentioned by Zip. As given earlier, Mr. Seven attracted an exceptionally free soul as his first wife, who traveled extensively to other countries to do her own thing. Did the freedom/closeness dilemma extend into his present partnership?

"I don't think so," he mused. "I don't think I ever felt pressured in that sense in relation to my wife. I don't ever think I lacked my space, that I didn't have my space in relation to her."

His wife is an 8° Capricorn Sun, Moon-Pluto in Cancer connected in a wide grand water trine with Uranus and Saturn; her Venus is conjunct his Eros in Aquarius, and her Mars is conjoined his Mercury in Sagittarius. Mr. Seven hinted that his wife dealt with the space issue in relation to him.

"But she became very independent of me," he added. "I was more independent of her to begin with. What happened apparently, by process of osmosis, she became independent of me. It rubbed off. I didn't make her become independent, but she saw what independence did for you." Numerologically, in terms of her own sense of freedom, she has a 5 Life Path and a 5 Personality (and a 3 Soul Urge and 8 Name/Expression to complete the picture).

A five-year period of adjustment to each other's individuality and habits ensued after their marriage. Mr. Seven admitted that the challenge, in large part, centered around his "chauvinistic" attitude. "It never occurred to me that anybody else near me didn't want to do what I wanted to do. I would go and book seats for the theater, and I find out that my wife didn't want to see that. She wanted to go to the theater, but she didn't want to see **that** damn play. Or I'd invite people whom I knew she was very fond of, but she didn't want them that night. I had no right to invite them over that night. So I was learning all those things, and there was a lot of them to learn! But we're not talking about monumental disagreements. We never had any big, fundamental problems."

I then asked Mr. Seven if there was a "like father, like son" relationship going on with his only offspring.

"He's totally unlike me," he announced. "My son is not following his father's example — not that he should be, by the way. At this particular time he's on a completely different path of unfoldment. He's on the materialistic path of unfoldment. This is not a condemnation, you understand. Our interests are not opposed; they just move in totally different directions. An agreement on independence would be the bridge of connection between us. I'm surrounded by my son because there's something in me I haven't yet resolved. There's nothing wrong with my son. He's got a materialistic outlook, but that doesn't mean there's anything wrong with him. I have never given him one lecture; I have never chastised him. As my son puts it when he talks with me, he said, 'You know, I'm a deprived person! You didn't leave me with any complexes when I was growing up!' So every time I hear him make a statement of the nature of a materialistic outlook, inside I think to myself, "You too are the Father's expression.' That's all I do. And he's coming around. When he's ready, he'll ask."

As given earlier, besides his father, Mr. Seven's wife and unmarried son are both Capricorns. Why does he seem to attract such earthy vibrations into his intimate environment?

"I would say probably — I don't want to say need, since it's not a need in the ordinary sense. I think it's my recognition of earth being the outer expression of the spiritual. And they keep me in touch with that. I'm sure that I can take off and fly off quite easily without any difficulty, but I have to deal with those people every day at that level. I've got to deal with my wife every day as a progressed

Capricorn. I have to deal with her as she is right now, and my son."

I noted to Mr. Seven that he was 37 when his son was born. Why the wait?

"I was never interested in the reproduction of me. I mean, a lot of men can't wait to have a son so that they can make the son do all the things they failed to do. I guess I do so much in my life that I want to do that I'm not interested in my son doing it for me. I was too busy living."

With all the potential charisma and sexual magnetism shown in Mr. Seven's astrological and numerological charts, I couldn't help but ask him if, at least in his earlier unmarried days, he was a "woman's man" or "man of the world."

"Sex was always second or third on the totem pole. I was into people, not girls. Most of my girlfriends were friends anyways. The fact that they were a different sex didn't make any difference. And I always associated with interesting people. If she was not personable, and if she was not intelligent and well-educated, I was not interested. Sex was there, and I think it was healthy. If I took a woman out for the evening, I wanted to spend a nice evening, conversing, and if we ended up in bed, that was OK. But that was not the object of the evening. So, in that sense, I didn't sleep around."

Zip wrote that Mr. Seven may need a rooted home with the Scorpio in his fourth house, and I asked him if he owned any property and if he was preparing for a financial crash of the world economy perhaps in 1988 that even he predicted.

"I don't prepare for anything," he answered matter-of-factly. "Since 1951, when I sold my last house, any property I ever had since I always had it on lease. I'm not interested in owning it. I don't have credit cards now, and I don't have credit either. I pay cash for everything. I have no savings account nor life insurance. I don't need it, and my wife is not dependent on me. For the last fifteen years or so I always get what I ask for, but I only ask for what I need! You can only drink from one cup; you can only sit in one chair at a time. I literally always have what I need. One doesn't have to concern oneself with one's needs. They are taken care of, but only if you know what your source is: have ye not a care for tomorrow what you shall eat and what you shall put on, for your heavenly Father hath knowledge of your needs — as Scripture says it. That's the state of grace."

I scanned his chart and noted the Taurus/Scorpio nodes of the Moon, with the south node (lesson area) in Taurus in the tenth house, and Saturn, another lesson indicator, in the Taurus/second house.

Did Mr. Seven have a lesson to learn regarding giving or receiving or handling money?

"I was all into giving at one time and did not know how to receive. Very very heavy in my early life into giving. We were trained as kids to give, trained to serve. What I learned later was not to take, but to allow other people to give. Many years ago I would refuse adamantly to take any 'reward' — in money or services — for anything that I ever did. In those days I had a very adequate income from other sources. In a very short number of years, the income from all sources totally dried up. I had become a remittance man at the hands of my wife! I didn't think that was kosher. What I did, I refused the bounty of the kingdom, and you can't refuse a part of the bounty, you can only refuse it all. Now, people like to have a guideline. I say, I have received between this and that amount, and I've also received nothing. Now I found that the recovery rate among the nonpayers was extremely small. And when you get something for nothing, because of our culture, it's not worth anything. So I quote a sum between this and this which is the truth that I have received in the past for my services. I say, 'If you cannot do this, it's OK. I would like you to do what you can. And if there's nothing you can pay, then I want a commitment from you. I want you to promise yourself that you will do something of some value that approximates to the figures I've given you for somebody else.' That way they are not getting it for nothing. You must give, you must outpour, you must manifest in order to receive."

To sum up, the hallmarks of Mr. Seven's current life are simplicity of expression, detachment of personal possessions, a dedication to service (responding when asked), enjoyment and humor in the present as the point of power, ministration by voice and pen of mystical knowledge, and devotion to the practical unfoldment of spiritual principles. By my observation, such seems to be the mode of life reflected by his conduct and example. However, he realistically cautioned a class recently on the danger of totally, unjudiciously accepting the beliefs proposed by anyone in the "Truth" business.

"You don't buy my particular trip at this particular moment," he explained. "In the final analysis, your own inner feeling must be your guide. Otherwise, as soon as you have found him or her or it as your guru, you set up a false god. You buy into a form of idolatry. It's saying, 'I'm denying my own experience, and I can only reach God through that guru.' Then we lose touch with divinity. We lose touch with our own indwelling divine self. Jesus said, the kingdom of God is within you — not outside of you. If I make you

my guru, I'm divided: I'm unworthy, I'm unknowing, I'm just 'un'
— ! The whole direction has to be inward. Once you go inward,
then what you express on the outside will be changed. So we've got
to be extremely careful not to set up a dependency on the outside.
As St. Paul said, 'Prove all things.' '' (Thess.5:21)

SECTION
THREE

CHAPTER TWENTY-ONE

REVIEW AND WRAP-UP
Ms. One Revisited

After reading Ms. One's personal statement and life history, I am impressed by the extent to which she lived out a fire conflict with water and earth. The passion, the importance of relationships, but also the need to work were all there in her life. The rising Mars was clearly a major key to her life, and she did, as I had suggested was possible, swing between self-blocking and projecting her power to the point of being beaten by her husband, or undergoing repeated surgeries, and then occasionally exploding and attacking her tormentors. She is now living out her Mars in a constructive way, finding she can be independent and "do what she pleases," but the need for love is still part of her nature and somewhere, somehow, a compromise has to be reached. Ms. One is aware of the ambivalence now, and is seeing two different men even while she enjoys her freedom, so we hope she is on the way to that compromise.

Unfortunately, a person with a fire-earth emphasis often ends up as an "Atlas," carrying most or all of the load, hating dependency, and expressing the water through nurturing others. Yet, we still have dependency needs and they can add to the danger of illness if that is the only way we can let other people help us.

The horoscope indication of a strong mother playing a major role in the life of Ms. One was certainly true. The details, as Ms. One gave them, included a working mother, herself an "Atlas" figure attracted to "victim" husbands; one with a strong desire to do the right thing but one who eventually became a victim herself. Neptune is usually involved in some way with the house of the parent when we have one who retreats into alcohol. Neptune symbolizes the search for infinite love and beauty and the person with that hunger may start as a savior and too often end as a victim.

The potential of divorce and one parent playing both roles, as shown in Ms. One's chart, was a repeated experience for her. The blood father wanted his freedom (fourth-house rulers in Aquarius and Aries), and the second had health problems (Uranus in the sixth house). The third-house Saturn also expressed as the feeling of being parent of her siblings even though one was actually older than Ms. One, and in her lack of formal schooling. It is common for Saturn in or ruling the third or ninth houses to have limiting reality factors (often money) block early education, but when the individual has an inquiring mind, he or she may often return later for more education. However, Saturn's placement in Aquarius can often indicate a person who is more interested in unconventional subjects and prefers to learn in her own way.

The lack of education and early plunge into marriage and a family probably played a major role in keeping Ms. One in jobs that did not do justice to her potentials. With fire signs or fire planets in the earth houses, work that requires physical energy, action, is common, and feeding people fits the tenth-house Moon and node. But the warmth and expressiveness and desire for variety could also help her in a sales job. Antiques would be a good choice where Ms. One could emphasize the beauty that her offering would bring to the home of the customer.

When I wrote my original interpretation of Ms. One's horoscope, I noted that her progressed Sun was about to cross her natal Ascendant, so I was not surprised to hear that she had made a major change, moving to another part of California. Her progressed Ascendant has also passed her progressed Mars by now. They remained conjunct each other for many years of her life, maintaining the issue of tremendous strength and self-will (Mars-Ascendant) confronting the Scorpio need for a mate and danger of giving the power to the mate. I hope that Ms. One has learned to express her fire outwardly now, in healthy assertion and competition, rather than blocking or projecting it. Her progressed Sun is also past the square to natal and progressed Saturn. They were trioctile in the natal chart, showing conflict between those parts of the nature, some variation on the conflict between fire (self-will and self-confidence) and earth reality limits whether in the form of natural law, authority figures or our own conscience. When we move from a conflict aspect in the natal chart to another one in the progressed chart, the challenge in the life can be intense. These aspects among others were symbolic of Ms. One's final struggle with her husband, gaining the strength to leave him, but experiencing the consequences of the frustration and anxiety in the form of illness and surgery. With the progressed MC now coming up to progressed Jupiter, there could be a strengthened faith and understanding of how personal attitudes and actions shape our lives, and how we can change them. We trust that some of the lessons are learned by now, and that better days are ahead.

NUMBERS

Looking at Ms. One's numerology in the light of her life experiences, I am mainly impressed by the accuracy of my original speculation that so many "1's" above the line (in the form of vowels) with only one below (in the consonants) might indicate individualistic urges which would be very difficult to bring into manifestation. The combination of vowel "1's" without consonant "1's" looks very much like fire in the horoscope blocked by earth and/or water awareness of realistic limits and need for security and to do the "right thing." As indicated above, Ms. One has her fire Sun in an earth sign, her fire Mars in a water sign, and both of them in conflict to Saturn, our primary earth planet, in addition to other fire-water and fire-earth combinations mentioned in Ms. One's original analysis. If a person with the fire-earth steamroller potential and the power struggle potential shown by conflict aspects involving fixed and cardinal factors, represses or projects the power, we get the attacks from the world (husband) and the surgery until we learn to express ourselves in healthy ways.

HANDS

In general, I think Ms. One's palms and handwriting also add useful ideas to our understanding of her life. The writing especially seems to me to repeat the danger of aspirations that were not being realized at the time the writing sample was made. The palms suggest immense strength and energy while the writing lacks pressure and force. The palms are more indicative of Ms. One's true capacity while the writing fits the period of temporary physical weakness following major surgery. One of my favorite mottoes states that "Life is not an 'either-or,' it is an 'and.' " I think our different models are clearly complementary in the case of Ms. One, with the handwriting especially useful as a key to contemporary feelings at the time the writing is done. The results on Ms. One's psychological questionnaire were also highly contemporary, picking up her struggle with resentment and frustration, and the low energy after the surgery. Interpreting a complex, psychological profile is as much an art as interpreting a horoscope or a palm or any of our other models of human nature. I did not look at the results of the psychological questionnaires until after I had done all my own analyses using the horoscope, numbers, palms and writing, but I was impressed at how helpful the psychological profile proved, used as an adjunct to the rest. Of course, a proper psychological approach would say the reverse. Isn't it remarkable that these fringe systems can supplement a "scientific" method of character analysis. I wonder how long it will be before we will see centers in which all of these tools can be freely used?

Obviously, all the tools remain abstracts until we look at the life of the subject. The person is living out those abstract principles, manifesting them in concrete details in the life. Once we understand the principles which are shaping our lives, we can change our details. We can express the principles, satisfy the drives and desires, in more fulfilling and more effective ways. I'm sure that Ms. One with her strength, idealism, warmth, and basic common sense, will be able to make a better life for herself in her future days and years.

Mr. Two Revisited

The facts of Mr. Two's life seem to mesh well with the general picture we got from his horoscope and his numbers. The freedom-closeness dilemma remains an ongoing issue, but he reports that he has learned not to play savior in his personal relationships. Since progressed Mars remains conjunct his south node of the Moon for quite a few years, it may take time to work out the compromise between personal will and a committed relationship. Life is a juggling act for all of us, and sometimes it seems comforting to know that we are all trying to resolve some of the same basic dilemmas.

I am always interested in finding out how the issues shown in the horoscope connected to parents have actually worked out in the life. In the case of Mr. Two, the Pluto in Leo and Saturn in the Leo house turned out to be a dictator father with the critical Virgo (Saturn's sign) added to the need to dominate. It is interesting that on Mr. Two's psychological questionnaire, his highest score was on the need to dominate. I do think that we come where we fit, and that Mr. Two had a chance to learn from his father not to take power over others. As far as his horoscope shows, the main theme is a tremendous need to resist being controlled by others rather than a desire to have control. But when we have the rulers of the first house, including Mars, the natural ruler, in letters seven or eight (sign or house), we may swing between being swallowed up in others, trying to keep all the power (sometimes done by picking weak people), and retreating from closeness, as I pointed out in the initial chart interpretation. Mr. Two's psychological evaluation described an impression of him as "two people," one sounding similar to his description of his father, the other like its opposite; father used as a negative role model.

In the case of Mr. Two's mother, the Moon in the tenth house along with Virgo did point to a working mother, but the Pisces Moon was apparently a victim of the father rather than having the power which is sometimes found with a tenth-house mother. I have been resisting the temptation to bring in some of the newer asteroids since this book may be read by people interested in our other "paths to knowledge" who have minimal familiarity with astrology, so I have not wanted to make any of our models too complicated. But I have been impressed to note that Ms. One had Psyche in her first house of personal identity and action while Mr. Two has it in his tenth house of the mother, as well as in Pisces. I have frequently found Psyche a key to a sense of helplessness though, of course, it can indicate the opposite, someone who enjoys helping others. Ms. One swung between the two extremes in her relationship with her brutal husband. Mr. Two's mother lived in fear of her husband. Both women eventually had to leave the relationship to regain their strength.

I was also interested to hear that Mr. Two went in and out of school, rebelling against the conventional approach to learning. That reaction is so common with Aquarius in the ninth house. Such people are often underachievers despite high intelligence. I am very glad to know that Mr. Two plans to continue his education. He has the ability to work with his mind in any area of people and communication, though the tenth-house Moon does fit feeding people. It is interesting that our waitress and waiter both have that tenth-house Moon, but there are many types of work that involve providing emotional or material security needs to the public.

Although it is a tough field, Mr. Two could be effective in some kind of work with the media. In view of the depression which I think is coming for the U.S., I hate to encourage anyone to leave a practical job that is depression-proof. But I do want to encourage Mr. Two to continue to develop his mind and his artistic potentials. Work with modern technology is also possible with Aquarius in the tenth house, though this may simply indicate periodic changes in profession, to escape boredom. If Mr. Two does consider high tech, he would need to be working with people rather than just machines. For example, he could demonstrate computers to prospective customers rather than write programs for them or repair them. The most practical action may involve keeping a job that offers financial security and keeping the restless mind fed with hobbies. All of our models support a picture of a person who needs space for movement and change; the air-fire emphasis in the horoscope, the wide spaces between the words, lines, and even the letters in the handwriting, the wide space between life and head lines on the palms, and the psychological profile which pictures Mr. Two as self-reliant and self-sufficient (and a little self-indulgent) though also sensitive and trusting of others.

Ms. Three Revisited

It was fun to hear about Ms. Three's grandmother, her positive role model who did eventually manage to stay married and still keep her own identity with her painting, one potential for the artistic side of Neptune, Venus and Vesta in the maternal fourth house. Ms. Three's mother, in contrast, was a negative example of the fourth-house Neptune and Vesta, a victim with chronic illness. Then her stepmother brought in still another variation on the same principles, the critical side of Vesta, with its danger of alienation in human relationships when Vesta is associated with the "people" parts of a horoscope. I have often seen really poisonous relationships when Vesta is a key to a parent-figure, yet it can also simply mean a hardworking person who tries to do the right thing. Ms. Three's life offers a good illustration of the variety of details which are possible, all fitting the basic principles in the horoscope. The Moon and its sign and house may symbolize the mother or other "mother-figure" in the life, and several of the possible details may actually be manifested in the course of the life, all stemming from the same basic principles.

A person expressing the Vesta principle can simply "do a good job," or he or she can be too focused on flaws and therefore too critical, or there can be so much attention to the job that human emotional needs are sacrificed, or there can be a failure to function efficiently including troubles with work or health. When we see Vesta in relationships signs or houses in a chart, we know the person needs to achieve an integration between work and/or the work attitude versus the need for emotional close ties to other people. We don't know which of many varied details might have been manifested in the life, but we can assist the subject to understand the issue and, hopefully, to handle it effectively. Cases such as Ms. Three are highly helpful to show a range of choices, to aid us in making the compromises necessary if we are to satisfy all of these different sides to our natures.

Vesta also is centrally involved in the issue of Ms. Three's own potential for having children. It is actually just on the cusp of the fifth house in the Placidus system, uniting the fourth and fifth houses in a common issue. I have seen many cases with Vesta in either the fourth house of "home and family and parent" or in the fifth house of "procreation, among many other potentials," where the person either delayed or did not have children or where children were their main "job" until the kids were grown. The principle is still the same. Vesta wants to do it right, and would rather not do it at all than do it "halfway." I hope that Ms. Three can now have her children, since the "mother" identification is really strong in her nature, but I hope she will also continue to include other activities in her life. It is actually not healthy for the kids if we are totally absorbed in them.

I was also interested to learn that Ms. Three had two "father figures": the brother who was a nurturing person but who also did some of the intellectual overdrive for Ms. Three, and the father who was unable to express emotion (not uncommon with a Gemini-Virgo mixture; Saturn in Virgo in the Gemini house) and was gone a lot (Pisces and Aries in the tenth house with Mars in Sagittarius). The patterns showed the potentials, as listed in the original analysis for Ms. Three, but some were manifested by the brother and some by the father. Still another alternative of the third-house Saturn in Virgo is a possible lesson in efficient functioning in the physical world, which may indicate a challenge involving health. The sister who was ill and died young provided the negative example in this case.

In spite of her strength, Ms. Three went through a first marriage in which she "gave her power" to her husband and had to take it back: a common lesson with Capricorn on the seventh-house cusp. Such 7/10 combinations may manifest as using a father or grandfather as role model for the mate, that is, unconsciously picking someone like or the opposite of the father figure. Or, we may pick someone to be "father" to us, only to find we have acquired a boss. Or we may pick a weak person who lets us play father. Ms. Three did the worst of both: picked a person who was actually weak and tried to keep control through physical strength and violence. This case is a good example of the potential of projection of personal power. Astrologers have begun to realize this potential with Libra, but most still assume that Sun in Scorpio is so powerful that it must be expressed personally. But I have seen numerous similar examples of planets in Scorpio being projected into other people. In my experience, women are more likely to do this, encouraged by cultural pressures, but it is possible for both sexes.

Ms. Three's first husband actually manifested the critical potential of the Saturn in Virgo, in contrast to the father and brother who were more accepting. Again, we see the details varying in the different people we attract to help us to learn to handle our central issues. The principle remains the same: learning to be an equal in peer relationships, learning to accept people as they are, seeing both flaws and assets but not trying to change them, and learning to make room in the life for both work and relationships.

Ms. Three remarried with her progressed Jupiter on the seventh-house cusp, so it is not surprising that religious beliefs are a major issue in the relationship. We hope that she and her husband can work out the compromise between Catholicism and Christian Science. That is quite a dichotomy. But if Ms. Three believes, as I do, that all religions have some of the Truth while no one has it all, that our minds are not really capable of comprehending Final Truth at this stage of life, she may be able to accept the mystical core of Catholicism as a great glimpse of the Absolute. Her tendency is to want to "discover the Truth for herself," with Mars in Sagittarius conjunct Jupiter and with Moon, ruling the Ascendant, just inside the twelfth house. However, with Jupiter now in her seventh house, it is crucially important for her to develop a shared faith with her partner, and sharing means compromise.

From the interview material, it sounds as if Ms. Three is well on her way to handling her challenges for this lifetime: the mastery of the appetites, (her first husband gave her a negative role model for that lesson); working out the freedom-closeness and/or independence-dependence dilemma; making room for both work and relationships; keeping her expectations reasonable; and developing her talents, including awareness of her psychic potential but not letting it run her life. The fire planets and signs in earth houses have manifested in job changes and in choosing jobs which included variety. The best solution for such combinations is a job with variety, independence and intellectual stimulation. Readers will have to ignore my comments on her local house cusps in California. I did not have any information on the subjects in writing the original analyses, so simply assumed that they were all in the Los Angeles area.

HANDS

It amused me that Ms. Three with her totally connected letters in her handwriting is the one of our seven subjects who has actually been a professional psychic on occasion. So much for that theory. As I said in my discussion of handwriting principles, I was dubious of the theory. Not only was it too specific, but one can be both intuitive and logical or one may be neither one. Ms. Three's horoscope clearly showed her psychic potential, and it may be that there is no way to see it in handwriting. In palmistry, the lines on the Mount of the Moon and the Head Line sloping down toward the mount are both associated with intuition and openness to the subconscious mind. Ms. Three qualifies on both counts.

I had expected Ms. Three to make home and family the center of her life, and did not anticipate the early independence at age 17, though power struggles with parents or partners are certainly possible. We have to give that Mars in Sagittarius conjunct Jupiter with both of them opposite Uranus a little extra weight in her horoscope. Interestingly, her palm with the Head and Life Lines joined at their beginning also supports a preference for "togetherness" rather than isolation or self-reliance. Both hand and chart show a strong person but one who needs other people in the life. We hope that the new marriage and the new family that came with it continue to fulfill that need.

Mr. Four Revisited

Astrology is a never-ending fascination. You look at a chart and wonder how the individual is manifesting two grand trines in earth and water which suggest total security and success in handling the material world, but contrasted with Mars opposite Saturn suggesting some type of chronic challenge involving personal will versus the limits of personal will, with faith in a Higher Power as a major part of the issue (Saturn in Sagittarius and Mars progressed into the Sagittarius house). Then you get the life story and there it is.

One of the problems in the format of this book turned out to be the subjects' lack of familiarity with the technical language of astrology as well as a lack of understanding of my particular approach to the field. Since the book was planned as a guide to applying astrological principles to individual charts, inclusion of the technical details was essential, and several subjects found it difficult to sort out the psychological interpretations from the jargon. Of course, when doing a chart interpretation in person, the client can ask questions to clarify and expand the material. Also, I talk a lot more in a personal session than I wrote in the preliminary interpretations which were presented to our seven subjects.

The second problem is particularly an issue in this case. As most readers have gathered by now, my approach to astrology includes the theory that the horoscope shows psychological principles which may be manifested in the life in many different details depending on the degree of self-awareness and self-mastery of the individual. When interpreting a chart, I try to explain the principle and then illustrate it with a range of possible details. I may not include the right detail in some cases, but the illustrations should help people to understand the principle so that if they have had problems in handling that principle in their lives, they can see other ways of expressing it. In many cases, several of the options have been tried at different times in the life, but we don't know the details until we look at the life, unless we are using psychic ability and happen to be right. When I see a client in person, my initial statements emphasize these points. Mr. Four's estimate of the accuracy of the initial analysis seems to be based on an assumption that all the details which were listed as possibilities to illustrate the issues were to be taken as actual facts in his life.

The description of Mr. Four's parents is the one area in which a real discrepancy with the principles of astrology seems possible. Normally, the oppositions across the fourth and tenth houses show tensions or separations between the parents which did not occur, according to Mr. Four. But the Mars in Gemini is appropriate for the mother who was a former schoolteacher and very good in sports, while the fourth-house Capricorn Sun fits a father who was good at coping with the material world, enjoying fixing things and producing things. Mr. Four acknowledges being identified with his father and, in his case, the Sagittarius Saturn manifested as idealization of the father. He was a very positive role model. One of the possible details when we have the fourth house as a key to the father, especially with Virgo or Capricorn there, is a parent who is home more than most, such as farmers, men who work in the home or who have a home workshop.

From what Mr. Four says, his father did not play the critic, one of the common possibilities of the Capricorn parent, but Mr. Four does it with his own family. His "too high expectations" seem mostly directed at his family while the two grand trines have manifested as reasonable satisfaction with himself rather than the self-criticism which seemed such a danger in the chart. We can still wonder whether the mother was really so contented in the role of housekeeper for a dominant husband, but it was the normal woman's place in her time and she may have been able to satisfy her Mars in her competitive sports. That is always one of the outlets I advise when there is a possible conflict between self-will and realistic limits, or when the patterns suggest the danger of power struggles in the personal relationships. Competition in sports or business is a fine outlet for a dominant Mars. In a family of "all chiefs and no Indians," it is a little miraculous if there were really no power struggles between different family members, but we have to take Mr. Four's word for it. Probably the fact that the siblings were both girls in an age before the women's liberation movement contributed to the calm home, and we do have to remember the grand trine into the fourth house.

I found Mr. Four's discussion of his beliefs especially interesting. Father was connected to the faith issue with Saturn in Sagittarius and the same sign on the fourth house which we have assigned to father. Father did not need church and did not go, but mother took the children. Ceres (mother) is in Pisces in the Virgo house, so mother may have also had an issue in the area of faith, pulled between a traditional belief system (Pisces), a conventional upbringing which says one should go to church (Cancer in the tenth house of mother), and potential skepticism (the Virgo house placement of Ceres). But the Moon is also conjunct Jupiter and (more widely) Chiron, again connecting mother to faith, so it was an important issue to her. I suspect that the suggestion of tension between the parents (fourth house/tenth house opposition) operated in this area of faith. Remember that another possibility with the association of faith and parents is the idealization of the parents. Mr. Four seems to have put his major faith in his parents rather than in an abstract and unprovable Higher Power. Individuals with a strong earth identification are often turned off by the intangible. Agnosticism during at least part of the life is common with mixtures of letters six or ten connected to letters nine or twelve. Mr. Four has Saturn in Sagittarius (and the south node can sometimes be similar to Saturn), Pisces in the sixth house, Neptune in Virgo, Virgo in the twelfth house, and Mercury as a ruler of part of the ninth and twelfth houses placed in Capricorn.

Though he would not agree, the lesson of faith seems still

unresolved. But isn't the combination fascinating? Neptune, Jupiter, and Chiron (all keys to faith) are in a grand trine in water houses showing strong unconscious faith, while the six-ten nine-twelve mixtures fit the conscious skepticism. Fortunately, the unconscious wins, so Mr. Four is likely to come through successfully. His mother "did his faith for him" in his early life, and his wife seems to be carrying the projection now. The initial analysis pointed out all the astrological features connecting the partner with ideals-beliefs-values, etc. In addition to the options of freedom versus closeness and the search for a perfect partner (manifested in the late marriage), we can pick a partner who expresses faith for us.

A possible consequence of maintaining a "scientific," skeptical belief system which sees the world as physical-energy charges operating according to the laws of probability (chance) is a feeling of helplessness and vulnerability. If we believe that our character creates our destiny and that we can change our character, we can also have some power over our destiny. If we believe that everything operates by chance, there is no way to predict or to control our lives. We see a company's failure or move to another state as just "bad luck," rather than a possible consequence of our desire for variety or for more independence in conflict with our desire for stability-security. Compromise is the name of the game, but without self-awareness of the issues, and awareness that our inner conflicts influence our outer lives, we go on experiencing the consequences of the conflict as outer circumstances beyond our control. Such experiences are typical of the Mars-Saturn conflict which is so prominent in this chart. Traditional astrology says "Saturn did it." Traditional science says "chance did it." Occultism says "our character put us where we fit and if we change our character (beliefs and attitudes and actions), we can change our future fate."

In spite of the long-term Mars-Saturn opposition, Mr. Four's horoscope shows fine talent to handle the material world. The placement of Venus, a ruler of the first-house Libra, in the fifth house in addition to the Pisces and Taurus in the chart, including Juno in the Taurus house, have manifested in another detail which I did not anticipate: artistic talent expressed in singing in public. I had expected talent in craftsmanship. The Virgo-Pisces mixtures are typically skilled at making things that are both beautiful and useful. But the earth-water emphasis was so strong, I had not expected him to actually manifest the fifth-house potential for "onstage" performance. I should have paid more attention to Icarus just inside the fifth house. Icarus seems to be another "Sun" potential, so placement in the fifth house can encourage the capacity for and pleasure from showmanship. But I did emphasize that the fire and mutables in the chart would want to do many different things. Part of a Saturn conflict is typically against the constraints of time.

The issue of power is clearly present in the life. Employees and family should only need to be told once and they should do as they were told. Mother kept the home clean and wife (Moon in the eighth house) should do the same. Kids should idealize and obey him as he did Father, but he attracted part of the Aquarius and Aries sides of his nature in his wife and children, including possible rebellion against conventions and rules. The combinations suggest an unconscious attraction to family members who want equality and who challenge Mr. Four to learn that side of the lesson of Saturn and south node of the Moon in an air house. Air lessons can include learning how to take things lightly, including material possessions; learning how to be an equal with other people; learning how to accept people as they are and not try to change them; learning to trust and effectively use the abstract intellect and personal power to communicate. In light of the interview and personal material, Mr. Four may still be working on those issues. I sympathize with his frustration when the possessions he has earned or created are treated carelessly by the kids. Possessions can be very important to earthwater people, and Virgo especially hates waste. But I'm afraid that "Atlas" people invite irresponsible people into their lives. "Let Dad do it," as I said in the initial interpretation. And people who combine the potential for dictator and rebel will often manifest one end of the seesaw while others in the life express the other end.

So, on the whole, I have to conclude that Mr. Four's chart fits his life, though I was less effective in guessing the details than in some of the other cases. That result, too, is a fascinating confirmation of the power of the mind. I have to give Mr. Four's skepticism a little of the credit. Disbelief is a form of belief, and just as effective in producing results in our lives. Whether we are convinced that something is real or unreal, we attract and notice the experiences which reinforce and confirm our beliefs. This is also an appropriate place to comment on the inevitable projection which we all do, even when we are fairly self-aware. We tend to meet ourselves, everywhere we go, and we tend to assume that this will always be the case. So we assume that other people whose horoscopes show a similar dilemma to our own will be manifesting it in similar ways. Such will not always be the case. Even though I try to always present a lot of different possibilities in describing any principle, I do tend to emphasize the ones which have been personally experienced and they may not be the right details.

I am still curious about what happened in Mr. Four's life when he was about three to five years old. Perhaps it was only a change of residence or father changing jobs or just finding out that the parents were in control. The birthtime should be close to accurate since progressed Mars was conjunct the MC and square the Ascendant for the initial surgery around age eleven, with the progressed Ascendant still in or just past the opposition to Uranus. By the second surgery eleven years ago, progressed Ascendant was quincunx Uranus while progressed Saturn had just reached the opposition to natal Mars. The aspects show the conflict between personal will and power and the limits of our power, whether the limits are imposed by the general situation (including the economy, work challenges, etc.) or by the rights of peer relationships (the seventh-house Uranus). When inner conflict remains inside, it can hit the physical body. If we can acknowledge the frustrations and be satisfied with a compromise, we can remain healthy. The strong aspects between all three fire planets (Mars-Jupiter-Sun) in Mr. Four's chart show immense potential vitality and recuperative power so long as the desires they symbolize are not at war with each other. Of course, they also contribute to the danger of overdrive, wanting more than is possible, which seemed so likely to me in my initial interpretation, and since a heart problem (a "murmur" according to Mr. Four) is theoretically connected to threatened or thwarted ambitions or love-needs, we are pulled between astrology theories which fit the life and a personal statement that they are not accurate. Also, theoretically, it is the repressed conflicts which hit the physical body: those buried in the unconscious, of which the conscious side of the mind remains unaware. In addition, some of the discrepancies may simply be semantic problems. Different words might clear up the issues. I think my coauthor, Bill Wrobel, did a super job of interviewing our subjects and bringing out their experiences and feelings, but I would love to know many more things, including information on whether the heart condition was congenital, present from birth, or at what stage of the life it was discovered so that I could check the current patterns of the horoscope at that time.

PSYCHOLOGY AND NUMBERS

Since I did the astrology, numerology, palmistry, and handwriting for all of our subjects in that order, it was only when I read the contents of the handwriting sample that I realized there was a problem in the original interpretation. I was especially eager to see the results of the psychological questionnaire to see whether it threw additional light on the discrepancies. The psychological profile indicated that Mr. Four was the most aloof and reserved of our seven subjects. He and Mr. Two were both high in self-sufficiency and dominance. Mr. Four was also more realistic, possibly even cynical, than the rest of the subjects. Ms. One was the only other who came close to his score on that part of the profile. These results seemed accurate as he described himself. They left me with some doubts about his numerology. The five "1's" and another in the subtotals seemed quite accurate, but what do we do with two "3's" in the Birth Path for a person who says he is not wordy and often just keeps quiet? We could credit the three with another Gemini potential, hand dexterity in place of verbal fluency. The problem is clearly not lack of intelligence, since Mr. Four's score on that psychological scale was higher than several of our subjects. The third-house Saturn and south node of the Moon certainly fit a combination of ability but self-doubt about the ability until the individual has proved it to himself.

The emphasis on "nine" in the numerology is especially fascinating since I see that as a quest for the Absolute. The horoscope reinforces the importance of the issue, with Saturn and south node again pinpointing it as a lesson area in the life. Clearly, we cannot assume that the presence of many letters for a given number are a guarantee of that part of life being easily handled. As with Ms. One, an overload on one number may be a clue to a problem in that part of life. I know from massive personal experience that an overload on one sign or house in astrology is often a clue to a difficult part of the life. I speak of it as a danger of "blowing the fuse." This case, along with the "1's" in Ms. One's name, supports the same principle in numerology.

PALMISTRY

Mr. Four's personal independence showed in his separate Life and Head lines in the palms. If spiritual issues in the palm are symbolized by the Jupiter principle as they are in astrology, we would look to the index finger and its mount. Traditional palmistry like traditional astrology connects Jupiter to ambition and sensual excesses. As already mentioned, these areas of study grew up from observations of life. Many people do turn a part of life into an Absolute and consequently they overdo in that area. The lengths of the index and ring fingers are fairly similar for most people, but it is considered significant in palmistry if one is distinctly longer than the other. In

Mr. Four's case, the index finger is clearly shorter than the ring finger. Should we read this difference as support for his statement that he is not consciously overambitious, that he has no goals that are unachievable? If the finger length indicates the relative dominance of its principle in the life, and if the index finger is pro- totypically fire, and the ring finger is a blend of earth and air, the latter is clearly stronger for Mr. Four. Certainly, the conscious iden- tification in his horoscope is with the practical earth, including the Virgo Ascendant and its ruler, Mercury, in Capricorn. The "earth" lines running up his palms from the center area to the Mercury (lit- tle) finger are probably the clearest and strongest of any of our subjects.

With stronger conscious ambition, he might have pursued the singing career for which he apparently had the talent. Does the heart murmur which remains but has not gotten worse tell us that he chose wisely to remain content with reasonable security and not to become overextended? He seems to have achieved an integration of the Mars- Saturn opposition in his work. It sounds as if he is in a totally ap- propriate job and is doing it very well. Travel is another positive outlet for the fire restlessness and need to escape the humdrum, pro- saic earth. Sports provide another good outlet. Traditional palmistry reads the box-like marking on the Jupiter Mount of the right hand as a sign of good judgment in goals and aspirations. We do not see a similar mark on the left hand, so, unless the omission is due to lack of detail in the Xerox, the judgment is conscious and has been developed in the course of the life rather than being unconscious and brought from the past.

I still feel that astrology gives us much more information than is available from the rest of our models, but that may be due to in- adequate experience in the others. All of the approaches to under- standing humans can contribute to the final synthesis.

I do want to express my sincere appreciation for Mr. Four's will- ingness to describe himself and his life in spite of his skepticism about astrology. I'm sure his courage, drive, determination and competence will win in the end.

Ms. Five Revisited

After all the times I have written that Vesta in the fifth house is com- monly found with individuals who choose work rather than children, I still did not expect it to be expressed in that way in this chart because of the strong fourth house and the Cancer and Leo in the partnership houses. But Ms. Five chose to remain attached to her "family of orientation," the family into which she was born, rather than to shift to a "family of procreation" as an adult. The need for a rooted, secure nest is strongly present in the chart, as noted in the initial analysis, with the water-earth emphasis, and Ms. Five is very aware of this, including its common manifestation as a collector. Earth keeps things because they might be useful some day. Water keeps them out of sentimental, emotional attachment and because they give a sense of security. The strong Chiron and Jupiter, flanking the Sun in Ms. Five's chart could have indicated love of travel, but the water-earth emphasis has led this to manifest in reading and dreaming about it more than in doing it.

The danger of projecting the personal power remains an issue in Ms. Five's life in the relationship with her sister. Aries, her own power, is in the third house of siblings. The sibling rivalry that often is seen with one-three combinations was partly connected to the mother's favoritism when Ms. Five was young. Such overprotection by a parent may contribute to children being delayed in discovering their own strength. When the children do being to assert their personal power, often in the teens if it has not occurred earlier, the parent may be freaked out by the challenge as in this case.

Ms. Five is apparently still working on the issue of projection with her current male relationship, having chosen a person to express one side of her Mars (an intense need for freedom) and one side of her Neptune (unreachable standards). But since Ms. Five is also conscious that these desires are part of her own nature, the potential is there to work out a compromise. When we most want to clutch, we have to remember our need for space to live our own life, and when we most want to run, we have to remember our need for closeness. We also need to keep our search for the Absolute focused on God, and accept our own and others's humanness. It is OK to be human, on the way to perfection and to enjoy the journey. With her Ascendant ruler in Capricorn (by progression in Pisces), and in the Pisces house, Ms. Five is still struggling with the feeling that no matter what she does, it is not good enough; comparing the ideal with the possible.

Though I expected a strong mother, involved in the material world, with high standards, I must admit I was shocked to hear about the episode with the junvenile authorities. It is a little incredible that a mother with any real feeling for a child could do such a thing instead of just talking to the "other mother" to see first what was happening. The action expressed one of the most negative potentials of Taurus in a relationship area: the feeling that her children were her own possessions, to be totally controlled for her own gratification. We legitimately do that with our material possessions, but not with people. Ms. Five showed her core strength by not speaking to her mother for two years, and her genuine spirituality by eventually forgiving her parents. With both parents connected to letters nine and/or twelve (as described in the initial analysis of Ms. Five's horoscope), accepting their humanness, including faults and failings, was part of Ms. Five's growth for this lifetime. And she did eventually manifest her maternal potential by becoming parent to her parents. As mentioned in the original analysis, mixtures of parent and mate can indicate a lifetime, adult relationship with the parents, parents replacing a mate. But we hope that Ms. Five will be able to work out her freedom-closeness dilemma and her search for an ideal (both currently still somewhat projected) so that she can eventually establish a committed, close relationship. The south node in Scorpio conjunct Juno clearly shows a lesson in maintaining such a relationship. Father gave the power to Mother. Ms. Five was identified with father and consciously or unconsciously aware of her danger of doing the same thing with a mate, so has avoided the risk of marriage up to the present.

Unfortunately, Ms. Five's sister died of cancer before a resolution of the competitive relationship could be worked through to permit Ms. Five to recover the strength that had been given to the older sister. I recommend a place for healthy, game-playing competition precisely for this reason, as a way to recover our own power. I have seen so many people, mostly women, with Mars or a first-house ruler in the seventh or eighth house along with Cancer and Pisces in the chart being expressed as self-blocking, avoidance of testing personal power against others, whether due to fear of hurting others or fear of being hurt. If we can develop the "game-playing" attitude, we can stand up to others and defend ourselves without feeling crushed or unspiritual. Aries in the third house, or any one-three mixture, can have a sharp mind and tongue with the potential for great arguments with siblings, but if this capacity is projected and the personal power is inhibited, we end up with personal insecurity. With one-seven or one-eight mixtures in a chart, we need to have a place in our lives for competition as well as for cooperation and for helping people. Since Ms. Five's progressed Sun was crossing her seventh-house cusp as this book was being written, this period of her life offers an opportunity to work on the issue of shared power and closeness. No wonder she has marriage on her mind.

Since Ms. Five is both capable and self-aware, she has an excellent potential for growth, for working through the issues suggested in the horoscope. Intelligence, desire to do what is right, and willingness to work should facilitate her goals. She has the strength, and should have begun to realize it when she left the " baby" role in her relationship with her parents to be the "parent" to them. Now she needs to accept her strength as an equal to a potential mate. Compromise is the name of the game, but not surrender and retreat!

OTHER MODELS

I hope that Ms. Five will also develop her own artistic ability in addition to admiring it in others such as Emily Dickinson. The general sensitivity and softness in her nature is shown in both the handwriting and in the palms which look much more water than earth. We have to remember that at the start of life, we express the Moon, Mars and the rulers of their natural houses more than some others of the astrological factors. Ms. Five has both Moon and Mars in water signs while Saturn, ruling the Ascendant, is in a water house. A first-house Psyche might also be a clue to possible feelings of inadequacy.

With her projection of her power into mother, sister and potential mates, Ms. Five's earth has manifested primarily through her financial independence, through supporting herself by her jobs rather than becoming dependent on a husband. Taurus is the sign of personal resources, our ability to earn them and handle them, and I think Ms. Five was probably wise to maintain control over them. She is far more likely to be able to establish an equalitarian relationship if she continues supporting herself and continues to expand her self-confidence by being actively involved in the world. It is interesting that the highest score on Ms. Five's psychological profile involved self-sufficiency, being able to and preferring to make her own decisions. That score is surely her fire and earth side speaking.

We are all complex beings. The most we can hope to get from our varying mirrors, from these different models of human nature, is some insight into that complexity so that we can make inner peace between these different sides of ourselves. With her high score on intelligence, I'm sure that Ms. Five can increase her "air," her ability to take life more lightly, and can fully actualize the Taurus capacity to enjoy it along the way.

Ms. Six Revisited

After reading the personal statement and interview material from Ms. Six, I'm still puzzled by that missing 4 in her numbers. She has certainly done all the things I associate with number 4, including both home-family and productive work. For all her creativity and warmth, she is also highly practical, demonstrating her ability to cope with the material world as I had expected with the strong fire and earth in her horoscope. Perhaps the "dull details" associated with number 4 are the missing interest. As Ms. Six says, she would rather phone than write a letter, is not interested in "business things" or "figures." The rising Jupiter can be incredibly creative and dramatic, and Ms. Six was able to develop this potential very early in life.

Ms. Six is also a good example of the danger of alienation in relationships when Vesta is connected to them, in this case in the conjunction to Saturn which is a key to father and also a ruler of the house of marriage. As I suspected in my original analysis, Mother with her air (as seen in Ms. Six's chart) became a good role model, a sister (Ceres in the third house) and a friend; but Father was a driven man who was never happy and expressed the fire-earth conflict shown for him in Ms. Six's chart in violent anger and criticism. Ms. Six indeed married a father figure who acted as boss until she was able to reclaim her own fire and earth and to leave the nest. In this case, the third-house Mars marked the only child, and the south node lesson connected to mother was the chance to see the consequences of giving up equality to let a husband rule the roost. Though Ms. Six describes her present relationship as truly satisfying, her rejection of the women's liberation movement and continuing identification with female subordination to the males in their lives sounds as if she might still be working a little on that south node lesson. Since she is an extremely strong and competent person, her life may actually be manifesting equality while her romantic ideals talk about the man coming first. Still, she did tie with Mr. Seven for the lowest scores of our seven subjects on desire to dominate. It is fascinating that these low scores were present for our two subjects who have Jupiter on the Ascendant; one natally and one by progression. The Gauquelin research has found the rising Jupiter with actors, politicians and Nazi leaders: all people who usually seek power. But, as I had suggested, spiritual individuals could show the other side of the coin: identification with perfection and doing God's Will.

I was delighted to learn that Ms. Six was able to both have her own family and then continue in a counseling role in her profession. She is certainly in her right place, healing and helping, as an independent professional, including exploring nontraditional healing modalities such as hypnosis and past-life regression. It is great that she is able to use the innate psychic ability with discretion, and that she has accepted the inevitability of mistakes as long as we are here and human. She seems to be handling life very well, enjoying herself and contributing to the well-being of the world, once that major challenge of an equalitarian marriage was faced and handled. One of these days, I hope to meet our seven subjects. Since I share a belief in reincarnation along with scientific caution with Ms. Six, I would enjoy hearing about some of her cases. I'm always looking for cases with sufficient data to permit the calculation of horoscopes for two successive lives, to see how the continuity and growth show in astrology. If any readers know of such cases with reasonably good evidence, I would appreciate receiving the data: the astrological birth data, the evidence for the second person being a reincarnation of the first, and how the evidence was obtained.

OTHER MODELS
Returning to Ms. Six, our varied models all seem to fit a versatile person who is coping with life. The connected Head and Life lines might be a major clue to the long marriage despite the chronic frustration. Of course, with her seventh-house ruler, Saturn, in its own sign conjunct Vesta (super Virgo) in the Virgo house, and Uranus, another ruler of the seventh and eighth houses in the Capricorn house, with the Moon in the eighth house and a Cancer stellium, there could be incredible traditional conservatism and sense of responsibility. Adding that to the idealism, we can understand the devotion to duty. Yet, she had that example from her father (Saturn and Uranus are both father and husband in her chart) and even pushed her mother into a divorce. So often we are offered parents as a mirror of our own challenges, but it is not easy to see the parallels. If growth is the name of the game, as I believe, Ms. Six took a giant leap when she left the nest and found her role of professional mother in a nontraditional way. We hope the peer relationship continues to flow. Venus trine the eighth-house Moon in air signs shows she can be an equal if her value code allows it. My values are showing when I applaud it.

Mr. Seven Revisited

He is there, in front of the crowd, but has also found he does not have to be there. Mr. Seven has certainly fulfilled his potential as a teacher and preacher, with a life of service to God and humans. I was delighted to learn that he is in spiritual work with promotion, writing, and traveling all part of his earlier expression. He seems to have developed almost all of the potentials mentioned in the chart as possibilities, with true fire enthusiasm.

The description of Mr. Seven's parents and early life was quite fascinating. The unanimity of the parents (with Saturn and Moon in the same sign) in spite of major differences; their emphasis on discipline and work and service, so appropriate for the Virgo though financially they might have remained idle. Yet we are also told of real emotional detachment so common with Virgo and Vesta. At least, the relationship with the parents was not destructive as I have sometimes seen when Vesta is a key to a parent. Of course the need to do things "right" (the Virgo-Vesta motif) is added to the "freedom" needs shown in Mr. Seven's chart with Jupiter, Sagittarius, Aquarius and Aries all present, so we could anticipate some sort of space whether physical (removal to boarding school) or emotional. The detachment apparently has continued through two marriages and one son (a single son is common with a fifth-house placement of the Sun). After the first abortive marriage, Mr. Seven has managed a good compromise of the freedom-closeness dilemma by choosing a mate and having a son, both of whom valued personal independence and could accept it in each other.

In his strong identification with the spiritual quest, Mr. Seven has also attracted a wife and a son who to some extent do the "materialistic" side of life for him. As suspected, he is totally competent to do it himself, but is so strongly identified with the spiritual side of life that perhaps it is simply more convenient to let others emphasize the material side. But since his own material needs are simple and easily met through his preferred work, the earth lessons of Saturn and the south node of the Moon would seem to have been handled well, integrated with the Neptune-Jupiter-Sagittarius aspirations for "higher" things than the ordinary earth world, and with their accompanying reluctance to be tied down by the responsibilities associated with possessions. Too often, we end up possessed by our possessions, and Scorpio in the fourth house can present an acute form of this danger. The early lifestyle which may have included an overdose of the Puritan concept of "possessions as duties rather than as pleasures," along with the fire instinct to escape any confinement, may have assisted in the integration of that natural conflict between the fire and the water-earth part of the nature. The "duty-pleasure" mix is partly symbolized in the horoscope by the Virgo Saturn in the Taurus house.

The Scorpio in the fourth house can also symbolize the "psychological control" exerted by the parents, especially the mother "teaching patience." It also fits the roots from the past — a 900-year lineage of family and property. Mr. Seven has chosen the freedom of the fire in contrast to the attachment of the water.

Mr. Seven seems to also be handling the Scorpio challenge of being able to both receive and give. He has escaped or retired from the role of Atlas and God. As mentioned in the final discussion of Ms. Six, she and Mr. Seven had the lowest scores on dominance of our seven subjects. Both individuals also scored high on the capacity to be accommodating in their relationships with others. Yet Mr. Seven is at the top of the scale on self-sufficiency, preferring to make his own decision. The willingness to flow with life and others fits the rising Neptune; the independent decisions fit the rising Jupiter. Of course, Neptune can also imply independence of other humans if the individual has complete faith in the Absolute. Another "top of the scale" score shared by Ms. Six and Mr. Seven involved inner security including freedom from guilt and a sense of self-satisfaction. This result fits the strong Jupiter **if** the person feels he or she has arrived at the goal of union with the Absolute. So long as there is a feeling of wishing we could do better than we are doing, or of lingering guilt for past mistakes, we are not likely to score at the top of this scale. When we can truly forgive ourselves and others for being human, can do our best and then turn it all over to God, we can live at this untroubled level.

From Mr. Seven's comments, he seems to have faced and handled all the challenges listed in the initial analysis, including one I did not mention, maintaining efficient body functioning. Health in his case became an issue as a result of an accident. The fire prominence in the chart shows enormous recuperative powers connected to faith, vitality, energy, etc., but a Virgo emphasis in a horoscope can also indicate a challenge in body functioning sometime in the life. The fire side of the nature asserts our right and power to do what we please. The earth reminds us that there are physical limits to our power. Integration involves living voluntarily within the limits and gradually expanding the scope of our power while enjoying the journey.

As I conclude the discovery of the actual lives of the last of our seven subjects, I am still fascinated by the variety in life and human nature and the way that astrology can point to the issues while leaving us free to determine and to change the details. I would like to thank our seven brave souls who opened their lives and feelings to our inspection, and to hope that all of them are finding the joy described by Mr. Seven as his present state and as the inherent potential in all of us.

Postscript

The gestation period of a book is often longer than one for a baby. The birth process for this book began in 1983, and it will finally achieve printed form in 1986. In the meantime, its subjects have experienced a wide range of events which will be of interest to students learning to match horoscopes, palms, numbers, etc., with the actions of their owners. Coauthor, Bill Wrobel, has managed to get ink palm prints of most of our subjects which will offer palmistry students better information than was available to Zip in her initial interpretations. Astrology students can try their favorite techniques, and numerology students can check out the various systems of matching numbers with lives.

Ms. One regards her health as still "guarded," to use her word, but she remains active. She stays busy with her garden, family activities and volunteering at First Baptist Church. She has been blocked from starting her antique business by some businesses in the small town. She feels that the denial of her permit for a commercial business is due to her being a "stranger" in a small community, and she plans to fight it legally. She is also still involved in a medical lawsuit. Her former husband remains friendly, visits her several times a year and has proposed remarriage. Ms. One says she has forgiven him for her personal hurts and enjoys his present courtesy and helpfulness. When asked whether she might consider remarriage, she says, "I really don't know."

Mr. Two remains somewhat reticent about his personal life, though very friendly and talkative at social gatherings. The most serious event in his life was his mother's death from cancer in December 1985. He had been very close to her from his mid-teens, and feels her loss very much. He is also concerned about a sister. His father is still living.

Ms. Three is our tragedy. She is a good example of the danger of "faking good" on psychological questionnaires since she appeared so psychologically healthy on paper, yet people who knew her could see the problems, and her horoscope clearly showed the emotional vulnerability. Readers will remember that she had progressed Jupiter on her seventh- house cusp and had gone into a second marriage hoping that it would give her "heaven on earth." But though her new husband adored her, and his family was warm and accepting, something she had wanted all her life, Ms. Three felt torn between her own religious faith and her husband's differing, more orthodox faith — yet she wanted to please her husband and his family. Among other issues, she also ended up unhappy in her new home in the country, feeling trapped and isolated, in contrast perhaps to Southern California where most of her friends lived.

Ms. Three used to comment on occasion, "You should bite your tongue." Ironically, on the evening of her return visit to Southern California, she actually bit her tongue while eating a carrot. Perhaps she bit her own impulse to risk speaking openly about what truly bothered her, or maybe her unconscious allowed that to happen to help prevent her planned walk along the beach. She nevertheless declined the concerned suggestion of friends to go to the emergency room of a local hospital, insisting on walking the bluff along the beach. An hour later on that evening of June 25, 1985, she walked out to cross a busy street along the beach and was fatally struck by a car.

Traditional astrology would have trouble understanding a seventh-cusp Jupiter paired with unhappiness and feeling trapped in marriage, plus sudden death. Knowing that Jupiter symbolizes our search for the Absolute, it makes psychological sense to have religion an issue in the marriage; to want it to be perfect and to want to do the perfect thing in the situation; to feel trapped when there is no perfect solution; and to escape (directed by the unconscious side of the mind) to the next level of life. I find Jupiter almost always centrally involved when people leave their bodies. Whether we think of death as going home to God, or as a trip to another sphere, Jupiter patterns are appropriate at such times.

Mr. Four is handling his Mars on the MC beautifully. He continues in his managerial job and is also conducting classes twice a week on the "basic seven tools of quality circles" to encourage increasing productivity. Though he says he was "coerced to volunteer for the classes," they have helped his dramatic and teaching abilities to evolve to the point that his classes may be put on videotape for distribution to other factories. He is also working in his garden, a good outlet for the strong fire need for physical activity. He and his wife took a trip to Europe in late April — early May 1985.

Ms. Five continues to see a male friend, a relationship that has lasted some seven to eight years, but neither is sure they want a more formal commitment. Astrologically, for an emotional support system, the goal involves integration of the Taurus self-sufficiency with the fourth-house (Cancer) need for emotional roots. After the death of Ms. Five's sister, the inheritance of the family home and a large insurance policy have permitted Ms. Five to stop work. She enjoys her studies, garden and home.

Ms. Six remarried on June 23, 1984, and temporarily put aside her professional practice, except for needy cases. Her husband has been an acquaintance since she was 15 years old. His birth date is: August 15, 1930. His numbers include: 6 Soul Urge (vowels); 9 Personality (consonants); 6 Destiny[1] (full name); with a missing number 8 in the individual letters of his name. His Birth Path (sum of birth data) is 9. Between "hers" and "his," Ms. Six now has ten grandchildren. But, despite her insistence that she wanted to center her life on a man, by the middle of 1985, Ms. Six was thinking about putting more attention into her neglected career.

Mr. Seven reversed the pattern of Ms. Six. After thirty years of marriage to a very strong wife, Mr. Seven left her in April 1985. Astrology students note that his progressed Sun was conjunct Uranus in the eighth house (part of the marriage picture) and quincunx the Moon. It is quite typical to leave the past and move in a new direction with a quincunx. The freedom-closeness issue mentioned in his original interpretation is currently in high focus, since Uranus wants to escape restrictions; while Mr. Seven's progressed Mars in Scorpio conjunct Venus in the fourth house shows a desire for a deep, committed relationship. He has moved four times since leaving his wife and is currently dating a younger woman.

The strong Uranus patterns also fit Mr. Seven's weekly, **(now cancelled)** metaphysical radio show, and he remains busy teaching various classes. Through 1985, he also worked on establishing his financial security. Astrological aspects included progressed Moon opposite Neptune-Ascendant and quincunx the second-house Saturn. The challenges of the separation, the risk-taking, and the life changes have released new creativity. When Uranus and fire are activated in the chart, our natures are ready to break out of the cocoon and move in new directions.

We are indeed grateful that our brave subjects permitted us to share a little of their lives.

Zip Dobyns and Bill Wrobel

---

1. In some numerological circles, the Destiny number is the sum of the Name and the Life Path numbers.

Appendix
Questionnaire Used

NAME _____

ADDRESS _____

OCCUPATIONAL STATUS/TITLE _____

SCHOOLING & DEGREES _____

_____

_____

_____

SINGLE/MARRIED/SEPARATED/DIVORCED? AND HOW LONG?

_____

(SEXUAL STATUS: HETEROSEXUAL, GAY, BISEXUAL)(OPTIONAL QUESTION) _____

CHILDREN? GIVE NUMBER AND GENDER _____

_____

WHERE LIVED BEFORE? MAJOR CHANGES _____

_____

LIST AVOCATION & OTHER INTERESTS _____

_____

_____

_____

SEPARATE PAPER: (OR, IF YOU PREFER, CASSETTE RECORD)

(1) DESCRIBE YOUR BACKGROUND: WHERE YOU GREW UP; HIGHLIGHTS FROM YOUR CHILDHOOD; DID BOTH PARENTS RAISE YOU? YOUR PRIMARY CONCEPTION OF THEM; WHAT THEY EXPECTED OF YOU. BROTHERS AND SISTERS? WHICH PARENT HAD, IF ANY, A "GREATER" IMPACT ON YOU, NEGATIVE OR POSITIVE? WERE GRANDPARENTS OR COLLATERAL RELATIVES INVOLVED ACTIVELY IN YOUR RAISING? ADD ANY INFO ADDITIONALLY.

(2) LIST & DESCRIBE THE MAJOR, IMPACTFUL EVENTS OF YOUR LIFE & WHY.

(3) LIST THE TYPE OF JOBS HELD & WHICH YOU PRE-FERRED & THOSE DISLIKED.

(4) DESCRIBE THE BASIC CHARACTERISTICS & QUALITIES OF YOURSELF — YOUR TEMPERAMENT. E.G., OUTGO-ING? LONER? AMBIVERT? ARTISTIC? MUSICAL? MECHANICALLY-ORIENTED? COMPETITIVE?

(5) WHAT REALLY MOTIVATES OR AFFECTS YOU (TURN-ONS & TURN-OFFS? LIST.

(6) ARE YOU HAPPY? IF YOU ARE, STATE WHY. IF NOT, GIVE REASONS.

(7) IF APPLICABLE TO YOUR WAY OF THINKING, DESCRIBE YOUR BASIC WEAKNESSES OR GROWTH NEEDS IN YOUR CHARACTER. CHALLENGE/PROBLEM AREAS.

(8) LIST THE THINGS OR CONDITIONS YOU MOST WANT OUT OF LIFE.

(9) WHAT ARE YOUR GOALS & IDEALS & PRIMARY VALUES & BELIEFS?

(10) DESCRIBE YOUR DEFINITION OF SUCCESS.

(11) WHAT WOULD YOU DO IF YOU WERE TOTALLY WITHOUT FEAR TO DO IT OR BE IT?

(12) DESCRIBE SIGNIFICANT HEALTH PROBLEMS/OPERA-TIONS OR DYSFUNCTIONS NOW OR IN THE PAST.

(13) ADD ANY ADDITIONAL INFORMATION SPONTANEOUS-LY. SAY WHAT YOU FEEL IS IMPORTANT TO COMMUNICATE.

THANK YOU!

Bibliography

Abraham, Sylvia. *The Wonder of Numbers*. Van Nuys, CA: Astro Analytics Publications, 1979.

Adams, Mary. *Count Your Numbers and Keep on Counting*. Chicago, Illinois: Aries Press, 1948.

Benham, William. *How to Choose Vocations from the Hands*. London: G. P. Putnam's Sons, 1932.

_____. *The Laws of Scientific Hand Reading*. London: G. P. Putnam's Sons, 1935.

Broekman, Marcel. *The Complete Enclyclopedia of Practical Palmistry*. Englewood Cliffs, NJ: Prentice-Hall, 1972.

Campbell, Florence. *Your Days are Numbered*. New York: Ray Long and Richard R. Smith, Inc., 1936.

Falcon, Hal. *How to Analyze Handwriting*. New York: Cornerstone Library, 1964.

Gettings, Fred. *The Hand and the Horoscope*. London: Triune Books, 1973.

_____. *Palmistry Made Easy*. North Hollywood, CA: Wilshire Book Co., 1966.

MacKenzie, Nancy. *Palmistry for Women*. New York: Warner Paperback Library, 1973.

Marcuse, Irene. *Applied Graphology*. New York: Macoy Publishing Co., 1946.

_____. *Guide to Personality through your Handwriting*. New York: ARC Books, 1967.

McKenzie, Lucia D. *Astrographology*. Scottsdale, AZ: Aquarian Productions, Inc., 1971.

Niles, Edith. *Palmistry*. New York: HC Publishers, 1969.

Olyanova, Nadia. *Handwriting Tells. . . .* North Hollywood, CA: Wilshire Book Co., 1972.

Raymond, Pearl L. *Palmistry Explained*. New York: Vista House Publishers, 1958.

Roman, Klara G. *Encyclopedia of the Written Word*. New York: Frederick Ungar Publishing Co., 1968.

Saint-Germain, Comte C. de. *The Practice of Palmistry*. Hollywood, CA: Newcastle Publishing Co., Inc., 1973.

Sara, Dorothy. *Handwriting Analysis for the Millions*. New York: Bell Publishing Co., Inc., 1967

Spier, Julius. *The Hands of Children*. London: Routledge & Kegan Paul, Ltd., 1944.

Squire, Elizabeth D. *The New Fortune in Your Hand*. New York: Fleet Press Corporation, 1960.

Steinback, Marten. *Medical Palmistry*. Secaucus, NJ: University Books, 1975.

Teltscher, Harry O. *Handwriting — Revelation of Self*. New York: Hawthorne Books, Inc., 1971.

Wolff, Werner. *Diagrams of the Unconscious*. New York: Grune & Stratton, 1948.

Index

A
Abraham, Sylvia viii, 185
Accomplishment Cycle (*See* Second Cycle)
Ageless Wisdom 305
Ahamkara 305
alphabet model 3
Antivertex 41, 46, 63, 82, 90
Apollo Line 110
Aquarius 216, 243, 260-261, 268, 277, 295
Arabic parts 3
arcades 147-148
Aries 190, 243, 260, 273, 277, 304-305
Ascendant 20, 33, 38, 41-43, 50, 59, 61, 65, 68, 71, 72, 80, 82, 85, 90, 91, 190, 214, 217, 220, 230, 242-243, 246, 261, 277, 306, 316, 322, 328, 330, 333, 334, 341
Aseka Adept 296-297
aspect patterns 41
aspects 3, 5, 12, 14, 20-22, 30, 41
asteroids 11-12, 14, 16, 30, 33-35, 37, 42-43, 50, 63, 68, 72, 76, 79, 81, 83, 319 (*See also* minor planets)
Astral 296
Astrologer's Casebook vii
astrology ix, x, 2, 4-5, 13, 18-21, 25, 29, 30, 38, 93-94, 99-105, 120, 139, 140, 160, 323, 328
Atma 296

B
baseline numbers 203, 217, 229, 244, 266, 280-281, 300
Benham 111
Birth Path number 28, 39, 48, 49, 57, 74, 82, 92, 329
Birthday number 203, 214, 280, 299
Brahmavidya 305
bright stars 2
Buddhi 296

C
Campbell, Florence 28
Cancer 198, 230, 242, 262-263, 273, 277, 281, 295, 340
Capricorn 214-215, 242-243, 246, 261, 264, 283, 288, 293, 299, 308
Ceres 12, 30-31, 33-35, 47, 50, 53, 61, 63, 68, 71, 78-79, 89, 325 (*See also* asteroids)
Challenge xii, xvi, xx, xxiv, xviii, xxxii, xxxvi, **28-29, 203-204**

Chiron 16, 32, 43, 48, 51, 56, 59, 62, 68, 71, 73, 81, 88, 94, 121, 230, 261, 325, 331 (*See also* asteroids)
conjunct(ion) 20, 30-32, 35, 38, 41, 43, 44, 51, 54, 55, 59, 69, 73, 81-83, 85, 91, 316, 318, 322, 325, 328, 332, 335
Conscious Union with God 306
creative numbers 244
critical/judgmental numbers 241-242, 279, 298-299
cusp 4, 32 46, 321-322

D
Destiny 183, 199, 341 (*See also* Name)
Destiny Line 101 (*See also* Saturn Line or Fate Line)
Diagrams of the Unconscious 142
dilemma 22, 36, 38, 43, 47, 54, 60, 78, 88, 91, 94, 122, 132, 318, 322, 327, 332
dilemma, cardinal 22, 62, 81
dilemma, fixed 22, 53, 54, 75
dilemma, mutable 23, 64, 65, 81, 129, 161
Dobyns, Zipporah ix
dwads 3

E
East Point 41, 46, 55-56, 63, 70-71, 82, 88
eight (8) 200, 242 (*See also* number 8)
   Life Path 242
   missing 202, 227-228, 265
   one 8 243, 244, 279
   three 8's 216
   four 8's 299
eleven (11) 217, 295-296 (*See also* number 11)
   Personality 199
   Soul Urge 295
Emotional Column 187, 203, 217, 228, 244, 265, 280, 299
Encyclopedia of the Written Word 141
environment (*See* Pinnacle)
Ewald, Helen viii
Expanding Astrology's Universe 2
Expression (*See* Name)

F
Falcon, Hal 144-147, 152
Family Row 187, 203, 217, 228, 244, 265, 280, 300

Fate Line 101, 109-110, 120, 124-125, 128 (*See also* Saturn Line or Destiny Line)
Final Cycle (see Third Cycle)
Final Truth viii, 1, 3
Fire Line 134
First Cycle **205**, 229, 245, 266
five (5) 227, 261, 279, **297**, 299 (*See also* number 5)
   esoteric meaning 296-297
   Name 225, 230, 261, 296
   Soul Urge 212
   one 5 215
   two 5's 201
   three 5's 205, 243
   four 5's 264, 279
   five 5's 298
   seven 5's 227-228
four (4) 217, 242, 261, 265, 278-279 (*See also* number 4)
   missing 83, 263-264, 278-279
   Personality 241, 260-261, 264
   one 4 215, 227, 298
   two 4's 243
   three 4's 201
freedom numbers 212-213, 243, 262, 298
freedom/closeness dilemma 219, 262, 307 (*See also* dilemma)

G
garlands 147, 148
Gemini 214, 262, 280
Girdle of Venus (See Heart Line) 112, 113, 121, 123, 127, 133
Gittings, Fred 95, 104-105, 115
gnosis 184
gnostic tools 184-185
God 185, 248, 258, 305-306
Goldsmith, Joel S. 306
grand cross 41
grand trine 41, 53, 63, 68, 90, 323, 326
graphology ix, 139-140, 142

H
handwriting viii, xi, 139, 320, 328
handwriting analysis vii, **139-163**
Head Line 110, 113-115, 121, 123-127, 129, 131, 133-127, 323, 335
Health Line (*See* Hypatica Line)
Heart Line 111-115, 118, 120-121, 123, 126-128, 133, 135, 137-138
Higher Self 305

Also by ACS Publications, Inc.

All About Astrology Series
The American Atlas: US Latitudes and Longitudes, Time Changes
 and Time Zones (Shanks)
The American Book of Nutrition & Medical Astrology (Nauman)
The American Book of Tables
The American Ephemeris Series 1901-2000
The American Ephemeris for the 20th Century [Midnight]
 1900 to 2000
The American Ephemeris for the 20th Century [Noon] 1900 to 2000
The American Ephemeris for the 21st Century 2001 to 2100
The American Heliocentric Ephemeris 1901-2000
The American Midpoint Ephemeris 1986-1990 (Michelsen)
The American Sidereal Ephemeris 1976-2000
The Asteroid Ephemeris: Dudu, Dembowska, Pittsburgh, & Frigga
 (Stark & Pottenger)
Astrological Insights into Personality (Lundsted)
Astrological Predictions: A Revolutionary New Technique (Whitney)
Astrology: Old Theme, New Thoughts (March & McEvers)
Basic Astrology: A Guide for Teachers & Students (Negus)
Basic Astrology: A Workbook for Students (Negus)
The Body Says Yes (Kapel)
Comet Halley Ephemeris 1901-1996 (Michelsen)
Complete Horoscope Interpretation: Putting Together
 Your Planetary Profile (Pottenger)
Cosmic Combinations: A Book of Astrological Exercises (Negus)
Expanding Astrology's Universe (Dobyns)
The Fortunes of Astrology: A New Complete Treatment of the
 Arabic Parts (Granite)
The Gold Mine in Your Files (King)
Hands That Heal (Burns)
Healing with the Horoscope: A Guide to Counseling (Pottenger)
The Horary Reference Book (Ungar & Huber)
Horoscopes of the Western Hemisphere (Penfield)
Instant Astrology (Orser & Brightfields)
The International Atlas: World Latitudes, Longitudes and
 Time Changes (Shanks)
Interpreting Solar Returns (Eshelman)
Interpreting the Eclipses (Jansky)
The Koch Book of Tables
The Mystery of Personal Identity (Mayer)
The Only Way to...Learn Astrology, Vol. I
 Basic Principles (March & McEvers)
The Only Way to...Learn Astrology, Vol. II
 Math & Interpretation Techniques (March & McEvers)
The Only Way to...Learn Astrology, Vol. III
 Horoscope Analysis (March & McEvers)
The Psychic and the Detective (Druffel with Marcotte)
Psychology of the Planets (F. Gauquelin)
Secrets of the Palm (Hansen)
Spirit Guides: We Are Not Alone (Belhayes)
Stalking the Wild Orgasm (Kilham)
Tomorrow Knocks (Brunton)
12 Times 12 (McEvers)